Software Architecture Knowledge Management

Muhammad Ali Babar • Torgeir Dingsøyr
Patricia Lago • Hans van Vliet
Editors

Software Architecture Knowledge Management

Theory and Practice

Springer

Editors
Muhammad Ali Babar
University of Limerick
Lero-The Irish Software Engineering
Research Center
Limerick
Ireland
malibaba@lero.ie

Torgeir Dingsøyr
Norwegian University of Science
& Technology (NTNU)
Department of Computer
and Information Science
NO-7491 Trondheim
Norway
dingsoyr@idi.ntnu.no

Patricia Lago
Department of Computer Science
VU University Amsterdam
De Boelelaan 1081a
1081 HV Amsterdam
The Netherlands
patricia@cs.vu.nl

Hans van Vliet
Department of Computer Science
VU University Amsterdam
De Boelelaan 1081a
1081 HV Amsterdam
The Netherlands
hans@cs.vu.nl

ISBN 978-3-642-42489-2 ISBN 978-3-642-02374-3 (eBook)
DOI 10.1007/978-3-642-02374-3
Springer Dordrecht Heidelberg London New York

ACM Computing Classification (1998): D.2, K.6

Cover design: KünkelLopka, Heidelberg

Printed on acid-free paper

Springer is part of Springer Science+Business Media (www.springer.com)

Foreword

Architectural knowledge is becoming increasingly important in the software industry, both in the embedded and IT sides. To illustrate this, let us explore three situations that I have personally observed in the last few years.

The first situation was concerned with a software architect working closely with a sizeable development team to build a first-of-a-kind system. Although the development team was experienced, the architect was encountering a problem: almost every engineer came to talk to the architect because the design of the system was available, but the rationale behind it and the decisions leading to the design were not. As a consequence, the engineers repeatedly asked the architect to explain the reasoning behind the design of the system as it is quite possible to destroy the conceptual integrity by implementing architecture different from the architect's intention. The reason for the poor architect being harassed by all the engineers was that during the design process a significant amount of architectural knowledge had vaporized and was no longer available.

The second situation occurred earlier in the design process of a platform-as-a-service (PaaS) architecture for a specific domain. The architects were balancing different quality attributes, using quantitative predictions of the number of customers, average usage time, etc. and they were trying to take an informed design decision concerning data services and analytics. It turned out that in the company as well as in the industry very little information was available about the consequences of the design decision that had to be made. As a consequence, the architects were forced to decide on the architectural alternative based on their beliefs of what would be the best solution over time for the system at hand. Although one can claim that this is what architects do, i.e. use their experience to take decisions in complex and conflicting situations, the fact is that the architects lacked architectural knowledge concerning their design decision that would have improved their confidence quite significantly. However, despite the research in the domain of design patterns, we lack effective mechanisms to capture architectural knowledge in ways that allow architects to apply domain-specific architectural knowledge to systems in that domain.

The third situation concerned the evolution of a mature and aging software system that had to be adjusted to a set of new requirements affecting functionality and quality requirements, as well the platform on which the system was running. The architecture of the system, having evolved in yearly releases for many years, had eroded quite significantly to the point that the development team tasked with extending the system had to spend a considerable amount of the project budget to recreate the necessary part of the architecture in order to be able to refactor and rearchitect the system in response to the new requirements. Again, the knowledge about the architecture of the system had vaporized over time and caused significant inefficiency in the evolution of the system.

The situations that I have described above are quite prototypical of the experiences of virtually every engineer or architect who has spent some time in industrial software development. However, as a software engineering community we have grown accustomed to these problems, accepted them as facts of life and research has mostly focused on dealing with the symptoms.

Soon it will be five years since I changed my position in academia for one in industry. The reason for my decision to spend time in industry was that I felt I was getting out of touch with reality; that the perception that I had about how large-scale software engineering took place was different from the day to day existence of software development teams, software architects and engineering managers. So, what have I learned over the last years? The key lessons for me are twofold. First, software development is a people process first and technological one second. The customers of software products, services and systems, the engineers building it, the business leaders and product managers envisioning it, are human beings with all the psychological and sociological phenomena associated with the processes these stakeholders use. It is very easy to underestimate the consequences of this when working in academia or research in general. Second, there still is an enormous gap between the state of research and the state of practice, despite the heroic efforts of people on both sides to decrease it. There is a continuous need for people who are able and willing to cross the boundary back and forth, not only through research projects in collaboration with industry, but especially through immersion, i.e. working, in both worlds. These lessons are not necessarily novel or terribly insightful, but in life some things can only be understood by experiencing them and I believe in this more than ever.

The research presented in this book is unique and different in the sense that it is the result of close collaboration between academia and industry. In addition, the book addresses the root causes of the problems surrounding architectural knowledge. The core of the problem in the situations described above is the vaporization of architectural knowledge and the lack of a conceptual framework as wells as mechanisms, approaches and tools to avoid at least part of the problem. The book that you are holding right now presents an important and valuable step forward in addressing these concerns. When preparing to write this preface, I asked the chief architects at Intuit, the company that I work for, what was their understanding of architectural knowledge. Their thoughts focused on two key elements of architecting systems, i.e. the criticality of combining theoretical knowledge with practical experience and the importance of translating customer and business requirements into a vision that teams can rally around and execute. What better way to capture the importance of architectural knowledge as described here - capturing practical experience and translating it into generalized architectural knowledge and using this knowledge in the communication of a vision of the system that is to be built.

Although we have talked about architectural knowledge in general, there is one area that needs to be addressed explicitly: architectural design decisions. The key responsibility of software architects, when forced to describe it in one sentence, is to take architectural design decisions. The activities of the architect include the work to collect sufficient information leading up to the decision and, after decisions have been made, to communicate these and explain them to the people affected by them. However, in the end these activities are in service to the key responsibility for architects: to take the most appropriate design decisions that optimally balance all the technical and non-technical as well as short-term versus long-term forces. The research presented in this book is focused on that understanding and the results are presented from that perspective.

In conclusion, this book on architectural knowledge presents a very important and extremely valuable contribution to the field of software engineering and architecture research and practice. The Griffin project that produced a significant set of its chapters has more than proved its value and I am honored to congratulate the authors and editors on their results. I hope that this book and the research projects that led to it will see equally admirable successors in the future.

Mountain View, CA *Jan Bosch*
March, 2009

Preface

A software architecture manifests the major early design decisions. These early decisions determine the system's development, deployment and evolution. Thus, making better architectural decisions is one of the large challenges in software engineering.

Recently, there has been much discussion about how this challenge can be met by better managing architectural knowledge. Inspired by the general field of knowledge management and knowledge management approaches in software engineering, much focus is being given to methods, techniques and approaches for managing architectural knowledge.

This book presents a concise and accessible description of the subject of knowledge management in the software architecture discipline. We explain the importance of sound knowledge management practices for improving software architecture processes and products, and make clear the role of knowledge management in software architecture and software development processes.

The major objectives of this book are to:

- Create a concise, timely and approachable reference describing the theoretical concepts and their practical applications for managing architectural knowledge
- Provide a body of knowledge of software architectural knowledge by describing relevant and useful results from software architecture research and practice. Such a body of knowledge should help promote best practices in software architecture knowledge management
- Show the opportunities for improving the software architecture process by designing, deploying, and institutionalizing various methods of and practices in managing software architectural knowledge

Why Manage Architectural Knowledge

Many have argued that the availability of architectural knowledge can greatly improve the software development process. If not managed, critical design knowledge remains implicitly embedded in the architecture, becoming tacit knowledge which is eroded as personnel change or leave. Hence, there is a growing demand for a body of knowledge to help design, develop, and deploy effective knowledge management structures to facilitate the capture and management of architectural knowledge used or generated during architecture processes.

What makes this type of knowledge special? Is there any need to focus specifically on this type of knowledge? We believe it is important to use knowledge management mechanisms that suit the type of knowledge in question. Selecting the right approach can depend on several factors, from the transferability of the knowledge, the size of the environment that needs this type of knowledge to the character of the established practices.

Scope of the Book

This book examines architecture knowledge management in a wide sense, describing many approaches that are in use in software companies today, approaches that have been used in other domains, and approaches under development in academia.

Who Should Read the Book?

This book is relevant for information technology and software engineering professionals, in particular software architects and software architecture researchers. For the industrial audience, the book gives a broad and concise understanding of the importance of knowledge management for improving software architecture process and building capabilities in designing and evaluating better architectures for their mission- and business-critical systems. For researchers, the book will help to understand the applications of various knowledge management approaches in an industrial setting and to identify research challenges and opportunities. This book will give university faculty a concise reference to incorporate a specialized but emerging topic of architecture knowledge management in their courses on software architecture.

Book Organization

The introductory chapter provides an overview of the main concepts software architecture and knowledge management. The rest of the book is organized in three parts:

Part I, “Architecture Knowledge Management”, explains what architecture knowledge management is, how it relates to software architecture and to knowledge management, and why it is important in modern software engineering. In particular, this part provides an overview of what the software architecture community can learn from the knowledge management community, and the other way round.

Part II, "Tools and Techniques for Managing Architectural knowledge", shows what type of support is offered to architecture knowledge management in the practice by means of software tools and technologies. The tools are presented according to the typical cases they support. The technologies are discussed for their ability to support on-line architecture knowledge management communities within and across organizations.

Part III, "Experience with Architecture Knowledge Management", focuses on how theory in architecture knowledge management has been put into practice. Reports from companies cover both technical, managerial, and organizational practices and lessons learned.

Acknowledgements

We are most thankful to the many authors we invited to contribute a chapter within the scope and contents prescribed by us. We are also thankful to Remco C. de Boer, who converted most of the figures to a format we could work with.

Limerick
Trondheim
Amsterdam
March 2009

Muhammad Ali-Babar
Torgeir Dingsøyr
Patricia Lago, Hans van Vliet

Contents

Contributors

Muhammad Ali Babar
Lero, the Irish Software Engineering Research Centre, University of Limerick, Castletroy, Limerick, Ireland, Muhammad.AliBabar@lero.ie

Torgeir Dingsøyr
Department of Computer and Information Science, Norwegian University of Science and Technology (NTNU), NO-7491 Trondheim, Norway, dingsoyr@idi.ntnu.no

Rik Farenhorst
Department of Computer Science, VU University Amsterdam, De Boelelaan 1081a, 1081 HV Amsterdam, The Netherlands, rik@cs.vu.nl

Philippe Kruchten
Electrical & Computer Engineering, University of British Columbia, Kaiser 4046, 2332 Main Mall Vancouver, BC, Canada V6T 1Z4, pbk@ece.ubc.ca

Patricia Lago
Department of Computer Science, VU University Amsterdam, De Boelelaan 1081a, 1081 HV Amsterdam, The Netherlands, patricia@cs.vu.nl

Peng Liang
Department of Mathematics and Computing Science, University of Groningen, P.O. Box 407, 9700 AK Groningen, The Netherlands, liangp@cs.rug.nl

Eltjo R. Poort
Logica, Prof. W.H. Keesomlaan 14, Postbus 159, 1180 AD Amstelveen, The Netherlands, eltjo.poort@logica.com

Kurt Schneider
Software Engineering Group, Leibniz Universität Hannover, Welfengarten 1, 30167 Hannover, Germany, Kurt.Schneider@Inf.Uni-Hannover.de

Ioannis Stamelos
Department of Informatics, Aristotle University of Thessaloniki, 54124 Thessaloniki, Greece, stamelos@csd.auth.gr

Antony Tang
Faculty of ICT (H39) Swinburne University of Technology, John Street, Hawthorn, VIC 3122, Australia, atang@swin.edu.au

Hans van Vliet
Department of Computer Science, VU University Amsterdam, De Boelelaan 1081a, 1081 HV Amsterdam, The Netherlands, hans@cs.vu.nl

Olaf Zimmermann
IBM Research GmbH, Zurich Research Laboratory, Säumerstrasse 4, 8803 Rüschlikon, Switzerland, olz@zurich.ibm.com

Chapter 1
Introduction to Software Architecture and Knowledge Management

Torgeir Dingsøyr and Hans van Vliet

Abstract Designing the global structure of a software intensive system – the software architecture – is a knowledge-intensive process. The knowledge produced and consumed during this process is broad and complex, and needs to be shared and reused among different stakeholders, and across different life-cycle phases. Managing architectural knowledge is the topic of this book. This introductory chapter discusses the two fields that form the underlying basis for the topic of this book: *software architecture*, and *knowledge management*.

1.1 Introduction

The descriptions of software architecture and knowledge management given here is of necessity very short. Readers interested in software architecture may consult for example [34] or [136]. For knowledge management, consult [293].

A good design is the key to a successful product. Almost 2000 years ago, the Roman architect Vitruvius recorded what makes a design good: durability (*firmitas*), utility (*utilitas*), and charm (*venustas*). These quality requirements still hold, for buildings as well as software systems. A well-designed system is easy to implement, is understandable and reliable, and allows for smooth evolution. Badly-designed systems may work at first, but they are hard to maintain, difficult to test, and unreliable.

During the software design phase, a system is decomposed into a number of interacting components. The top-level decomposition of a system into major components

Torgeir Dingsøyr (✉)
Department of Computer and Information Science, Norwegian University of Science and Technology (NTNU), NO-7491 Trondheim, Norway, e-mail: dingsoyr@idi.ntnu.no
Hans van Vliet
VU University Amsterdam, The Netherlands, e-mail: hans@cs.vu.nl

M. Ali Babar et al. (eds.), *Software Architecture Knowledge Management*,
DOI: 10.1007/978-3-642-02374-3_1, © Springer-Verlag Berlin Heidelberg 2009

together with a characterization of how these components interact, is called its *software architecture*.

Software architecture serves three main purposes:

- It is a vehicle for communication among stakeholders. A software architecture is a global, often graphic, description that can be communicated with the customers, end users, designers, and so on. By developing scenarios of anticipated use, relevant quality aspects can be analyzed and discussed with various stakeholders. The software architecture also supports communication during development.
- It captures early design decisions. In a software architecture, the global structure of the system has been decided upon, through the explicit assignment of functionality to components of the architecture. These early design decisions are important since their ramifications are felt in all subsequent phases.
- It is a transferable abstraction of a system, to be read and inspected by people (as opposed to machines). The architecture is a basis for reuse. Design decisions are often ordered, from essential to nice features. The essential decisions are captured in the architecture, while the nice features can be decided upon at a later stage.

So a software architecture embodies knowledge, and the usages of software architecture constitute a form of knowledge management.

Knowledge management is a large interdisciplinary field, and there is an ongoing debate as to what constitutes knowledge management. We will use Davenport's broad definition of knowledge management as:

> A method that simplifies the process of sharing, distributing, creating, capturing and understanding of a company's knowledge [89].

The motivation for knowledge management is then to make better decisions in shorter time, saving rework, and improving quality of products, and this can be manifested through a range of actions, from applying information technology to re-design of office space.

1.2 Software Architecture

The traditional view holds that the requirements fully determine the structure of a system. Traditional design methods work that way. Their aim is to systematically bridge the gap between the requirements and some blueprint of an operational system in which all of the requirements are met. It is increasingly being recognized that other forces influence the architecture (and, for that matter, the design) as well:

- Architecture is influenced by the development organisation. In shop automation systems, for example, the hardware and software for reading bar codes might be subcontracted to some organisation having special expertise in that area. There will then be one or more system components with externally-dictated functionality and interfaces to deal with this part of the problem.

- Architecture is influenced by the background and expertise of the architect. If an architect has positive experience with, say, a layered architecture, he is likely to use that same approach on his next project.
- Architecture is influenced by its technical and organisational environment. In financial applications, for instance, government rules may require a certain division of functionality between system components. In embedded systems, the functionality of hardware components may influence the functionality of and interaction between software components. Finally, the software engineering techniques prevalent in the development organisation will exert influence on the architecture.

This mutual influencing between an architecture and its environment is a cyclical process, known as the Architecture Business Cycle (ABC) [34]. For example, an architecture yields certain units of work, corresponding to the components distinguished in the architecture. If the same components occur over and over again, expertise will be organized according to the functionality embedded in these components. The development organisation may then become expert in certain areas. This expertise then becomes an asset which may affect the goals of the development organisation. The organisation may try to develop and market a series of similar products in which this expertise is exploited.

Traditional software design is inward-looking: given a set of requirements, how can we derive a system that meets those requirements. Software architecture has an outward focus as well: it takes into account how the system fits into its environment. Software architecting includes negotiating and balancing of functional and quality requirements on one hand, and possible solutions on the other hand. This is further elaborated in Sect. 1.2.1.

One of the early definitions of software architecture is [296]:

> The architecture of a software system defines that system in terms of computational components and interactions among those components.

A more recent definition is [34]:

> The software architecture of a program or computing system is the structure or structures of the system, which comprise software elements, the externally visible properties of those elements, and the relationships among them.

The latter definition reflects, among others, the insight that there may be more than one structure that is of interest. In house construction, we also use different drawings: one for the electrical wiring, one for the water supply, etc. These drawings reflect different structures which are all part of the same overall architecture. We generally observe the architecture through one of these more specific views. The same holds for the software architecture. This is further elaborated in Sect. 1.2.3.

In the software architecture, the global structure of the system has been decided upon. This global structure captures the early, major design decisions. Whether a design decision is major or not really can only be ascertained with hindsight, when we try to change the system. Only then will it show which decisions were really important. A priori, it is often not at all clear if and why one design decision is more important than another [127].

Viewed this way, the architectural design process is about making the important design decisions. Next, these important design decisions need to be documented. Both the process of making architectural decisions and their documentation for later use are discussed in Sect. 1.2.2.

Today's work in software architecture is broad in scope. Almost any topic in software engineering is being rethought in architectural terms. The discussion in this chapter is focused on how to design, name, and document software architectures, since this is where the relation to knowledge management is most relevant.

1.2.1 Software Architecture and the Software Life Cycle

If software architecture is just global design, we would be selling old wine in new bottles. The design phase then is simply split into two subphases: architectural, global design, and detailed design. The methods used in these two subphases might be different, but both essentially boil down to a decomposition process, taking a set of requirements as their starting point. Both design phases then are inward-looking: starting from a set of requirements, derive a system that meets those requirements.

A 'proper' software architecture phase however has an outward focus as well. It includes negotiating and balancing of functional and quality requirements on one hand, and possible solutions on the other hand. This means requirements engineering and software architecture are not subsequent phases that are more or less strictly separated, but instead they are heavily intertwined. An initial set of functional and quality requirements is the starting point for developing an initial architecture. This initial architecture results in a number of issues that require further discussion with stakeholders. For instance, the envisaged solution may be too costly, integration with already existing systems may be complex, maintenance may be an issue because of a lack of staff with certain expertise, or performance requirements cannot be met. These insights lead to further discussions with stakeholders, a revised set of requirements, and a revised architecture. This iterative process continues until an agreement is reached. Only then will detailed design and implementation proceed.

1.2.2 Architecture Design

Design is a problem-solving activity, and as such very much a matter of trial and error. In the presentation of a mathematical proof, subsequent steps dovetail well into each other and everything drops into place at the end. The actual discovery of the proof went probably quite different. The same holds for the design of software. We should not confuse the outcome of the design process with the process itself. The outcome of the design process is a 'rational reconstruction' of that process.

During design, the system is decomposed into parts that each have a lower complexity than the system as a whole, while the parts together solve the user's problem.

There really is no universal method for this. The design process is a creative one, and the quality and expertise of the designers is a critical determinant for its success. Yet, during the course of the years, a number of ideas and guidelines have emerged which may serve us in designing software. These have resulted in a large number of design methods.

In a similar vein, architectural design methods have been developed. A good example hereof is Attribute Driven Design (ADD), described in [34]. The input to the ADD process are the requirements, formulated as a set of prioritized quality attribute scenarios. A quality attribute scenario is a scenario as known from requirements engineering, but whose description explicitly captures quality information.

ADD is described as a topdown decomposition process. In each iteration, one or a few components are selected for further decomposition. In the first iteration, there is only one component, 'the system'. From the set of quality attribute scenarios, an important quality attribute is selected that will be handled in the current refinement step. For instance, we may decide on a first decomposition of the system into three layers: a presentation layer, a business logic layer, and a data layer. In a next ADD step, we may decide to decompose the presentation layer, and select usability as the quality attribute that drives this decomposition. A pattern is then selected that satisfies the quality attribute. For instance, a data validation pattern [123] may be applied to verify whether data items have been entered correctly. Finally, the set of quality attribute scenarios is verified and refined, to prepare for the next iteration.

ADD gives little guidance for the precise order and kind of refinement steps. This is very much a matter of the architect's expertise. The same rather global support is given by other architecture design methods, as discussed by [146]. The global workflow common to these methods is depicted in Fig. 1.1. At the centre, the *backlog* is depicted. The backlog contains a list of issues to be tackled, open problems, ideas that still have to be investigated, and so on. The name derives from Scrum, an agile method [292]. There, the backlog drives the project. In (architecture) design projects, the notion of a backlog is usually not represented explicitly. Yet, it is always there, if only in the head of the architect. There are three inputs to the

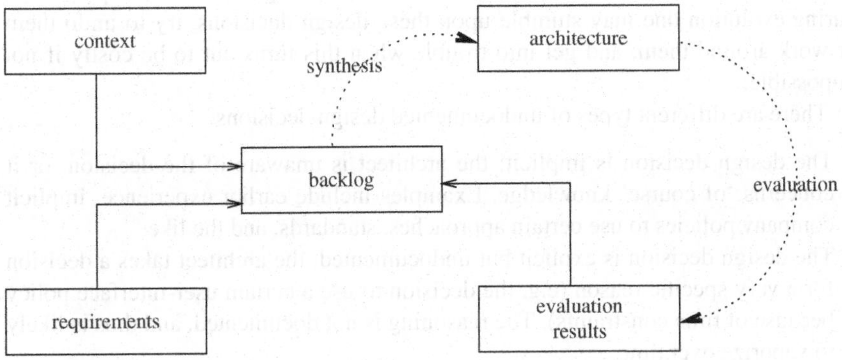

Fig. 1.1 Global workflow in architecture design

backlog: context, requirements, and evaluation results. The context refers to such things as upfront ideas the architect may have, available assets that can be used, constraints set, and the like. Obviously, the requirements constitute another important input. In each step of the architecting process, one or a few items from the backlog are taken and used to transform the architecture developed so far. The result of this transformation is evaluated (usually rather informally), and this evaluation may in turn change the contents of the backlog. New items may be added (for instance new problems), items may disappear or become obsolete, and the priorities of backlog items may change.

The architecture design process is very much driven by the architect's experience, much more so than by any of the so-called software design methods. An experienced architect *knows* how to handle a given issue, rather than that some method tells him how to perform a design iteration. Design methods that are applied at the more detailed levels of design usually give much more guidance than those for architecture design methods. But this guidance is used by inexperienced designers mostly. Since architecture design is usually done by experienced designers, the amount of guidance given, and needed, is less. Attention then shifts to techniques for documenting the *result* of the design process: the decisions, their rationale, and the resulting design.

1.2.2.1 Architecture as a Set of Design Decisions

If architecture is the set of design decisions, then documenting the architecture boils down to documenting the set of design decisions. This is usually not done, though. We can usually get at the *result* of the design decisions, the solutions chosen, but not at the reasoning behind them. Much of the *rationale* behind the solutions is usually lost forever, or resides only in the head of the few people associated with them, if they are still around.

So the reasoning behind a design decision is not explicitly captured. This is tacit knowledge, essential for the solution chosen, but not documented. At a later stage, it then becomes difficult to trace the reasons of certain design decisions. In particular, during evolution one may stumble upon these design decisions, try to undo them or work around them, and get into trouble when this turns out to be costly if not impossible.

There are different types of undocumented design decisions:

- The design decision is implicit: the architect is unaware of the decision, or it concerns 'of course' knowledge. Examples include earlier experience, implicit company policies to use certain approaches, standards, and the like.
- The design decision is explicit but undocumented: the architect takes a decision for a very specific reason (e.g. the decision to use a certain user-interface policy because of time constraints). The reasoning is not documented, and thus is likely to vaporize over time.

Table 1.1 Elements of a design decision

Element	Description
Issues	Design issues being addressed by this decision
Decision	The decision taken
Status	The status of the decision, e.g. pending, approved
Assumptions	The underlying assumptions about the environment in which the decision is taken
Alternatives	Alternatives considered for this decision
Rationale	An explanation of why the decision was chosen
Implications	Implications of this decision, such as the need for further decisions or requirements
Notes	Any additional information one might want to capture

- The design decision is explicit, and explicitly undocumented: the reasoning is hidden. There may be tactical company reasons to do so, or the architect may have personal reasons (e.g. to protect his position).

It is an illusion to want to document all design decisions. There are far too many of them, and not all of them are that important. And documenting design decisions takes time and effort from the architect, a very busy person. But we may try to document the really important ones.

A design decision addresses one or more issues that are relevant for the problem at hand. There may be more than one way to resolve these issues, so that the decision is a choice from amongst a number of alternatives. The particular alternative selected preferably is chosen because it has some favorable characteristics. That is, there is a rationale for our particular choice. Finally, the particular choice made may have implications for subsequent decision making. Table 1.1 gives a template for the type of information that is important to capture for each design decision. This template is based on [325].

Table 1.2 gives an example of a design decision. It concerns the choice for a three-tier architecture, consisting of a presentation layer, a business logic layer, and a data management layer.

Design decisions are often related. A given design decision may constrain further decisions, exclude or enable them, override them, be in conflict with them, and the like. And likewise, the notations and tools used to capture this information are very similar as well. A simple way to structure design decisions hierarchically is in the form of a decision tree. An example hereof is given in Fig. 1.2. The documentation of design decisions is further dealt with in Chap. 3.

1.2.3 Architectural Views

A software architecture serves as a vehicle for communication among stakeholders. Example stakeholders are: end users of the anticipated system, security experts, representatives from the maintenance department, owners of other systems that

Table 1.2 Example of a design decision

Element	Description
Issues	The system has to be structured such that it is maintainable, reusable, and robust
Decision	A three-tier architecture, consisting of a presentation layer, a business logic layer, and a data management layer
Status	Approved
Assumptions	The system has no hard real-time requirements
Alternatives	Alternatives are a service-oriented architecture (SOA), or a different type of X-tier architecture (e.g. one with a fat client including both presentation and business logic, and a data management tier)
Rationale	Maintenance is supported and extensions are easy to realize because of the loose coupling between layers. Both the presentation layer and the data management layer can be reused as is in other applications. Robustness is supported because the different layers can easily be split over different media, and well-defined layer interfaces allow for smoother testing
Implications	Performance is hampered since all layers have to be gone through for most user actions
Notes	None

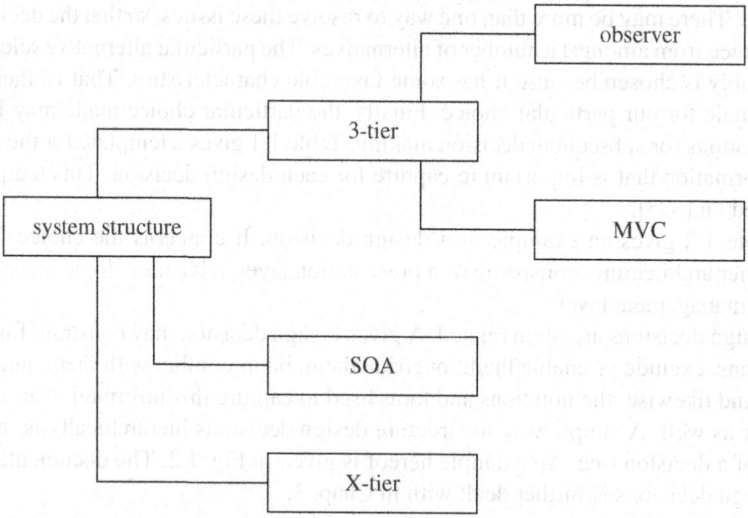

Fig. 1.2 Tree of design decisions

this system has to interface with, software developers, and of course the architect himself. These stakeholders all have a stake, but the stakes may differ. End users will be interested to see that the system will provide them with the functionality asked for. Software developers will be interested to know where to implement this functionality. Maintainers want to assure themselves that components are as independent as possible.

In some cases, it may be possible to devise one single architecture representation that serves all these stakeholders. In general, this will not work, though. A specific stakeholder is best served by a representation of the software architecture that highlights his concerns. Another stakeholder is likely to be better served by another representation. Just think of civil engineering, where one representation may highlight the outer appearance, while another highlights construction aspects.

IEEE standard 1471 [155] gives a general structure for software architecture representations. The main elements from this standard are:

- *Stakeholder*. An individual, team, or organisation (or classes hereof) with interests in, or concerns relative to, a system.
- *View*. A representation of a whole system from the perspective of a related set of concerns.
- *Viewpoint*. A viewpoint establishes the purposes and audience for a view and the techniques or methods employed in constructing a view.

So the stakeholder concerns determine which representations, called views, are appropriate for a specific software architecture. Each view has a corresponding viewpoint which gives the 'syntax' of the view, much like a construction drawing has an accompanying description telling what all the glyphs in the drawing mean.

IEEE 1471 does not tell you *which* viewpoints to use. In essence, it suggests we develop an appropriate set of viewpoints for each separate software architecture. It does have the notion of a library viewpoint, though, a viewpoint that might be useful across different software architectures. Bass et al.[34] give a collection of viewpoints that is useful across a wide variety of software architectures. These viewpoints fall into three classes:

- *Module viewpoints* give a *static* view of the system. They are usually depicted in the form of box and line diagrams where the boxes denote system components and the lines denote some relation between those components.
- *Component and connector viewpoints* give a *dynamic* view of the system, i.e. they describe the system in execution. Again, they are usually depicted as box and line diagrams.
- *Allocation viewpoints* give a relation the system and its environment, such as who is responsible for which part of the system.

Of course, one is not going to use all these viewpoints for a single software architecture. Usually, one from each category will suffice. One may for instance choose the decomposition, deployment, and work assignment viewpoints. It is also possible to combine viewpoints. In specific cases, additional architectural views may be helpful or needed. In systems for which the user interface is of critical importance, a separate user-interface view may be developed. In electronic commerce applications, a view highlighting security aspects may come in handy. And so on.

Many organisations have developed their own set of library viewpoints. A well-known set of library viewpoints is known as the '4 + 1 model' [188]. Viewpoints, and the capturing of design decisions in viewpoints, is further discussed in Chap. 3.

1.2.4 Architectural Knowledge

In the architecting process, a lot of knowledge is being used and produced. An important part of this architectural knowledge concerns the solution chosen, in terms of components and connectors, and as documented in views. From the previous discussion, it is clear that the decisions that lead to this solution, are an important ingredient of architectural knowledge as well. We thus arrive at the following definition: *Architectural Knowledge = Architectural Design + Architectural Design Decisions* [192]. This definition is used in most chapters of this book. From the literature survey on this topic discussed in Chap. 2, it is clear that other definitions of this notion exist. Chapter 5 takes an even broader perspective in that knowledge about the *architectural process* is included in the definition as well. The *documentation* of architectural knowledge (both the solution, in views, and the decisions) is discussed more extensively in Chap. 3.

1.3 Knowledge Management

To develop software requires deep technical knowledge in many specific domains, as well as other forms of knowledge related to human processes and to understanding how software applications will be used. Software development is therefore what we can call knowledge-intensive work, and we believe that knowledge-intensive work can be improved by learning how to managing knowledge better, which is the cornerstone argument for knowledge management in general.

To discuss knowledge management and learning, we begin with a brief discussion of the term knowledge and knowledge management, then proceed with an overview of theories related to knowledge and learning, and finally describe approaches to knowledge management within software engineering.

1.3.1 Knowledge and Knowledge Management

The Oxford Dictionary and Thesaurus [243] defines knowledge as: "awareness or familiarity gained by experience (of a person, fact, or thing)", "persons range of information", "specific information; facts or intelligence about something", or "a theoretical or practical understanding of a subject". In the philosophic literature, knowledge has been viewed as "justified true belief". Nonaka and Takeuchi [234] and many others refer to two main types of knowledge, tacit and explicit knowledge [255]. Definitions of these terms vary but many define tacit knowledge as knowledge that a human is not able to express explicitly, but is guiding the behaviour of the human. For example how to ride a bike is something that is difficult to express, which you have to learn by trial and error. Explicit knowledge is knowledge that we can represent, for example in reports, books, talks, or other formal or informal communication. So when we later discuss information systems for knowledge management, it is only the explicit knowledge that can be managed in these kinds of systems; the tacit knowledge remains in the people.

Knowledge management has gained much attention in many research fields, and has many origins. One origin is the book "The Corporate Memory" [334], which was published in 1974, and argued on the benefit of collecting information from different sources in a company and making it "searchable". At this time, the information was gathered on paper, and "search" would mean to submit a form to a department who would manually search through their files. The term corporate memory is still in use, but now meaning a computerised database for storing documents from many people in a company. The term "corporate brain" is also used to describe such a database. Another related term is "organisational memory", which does not really have a clear definition, but "intuitively, organisations should be able to retrieve traces of their past activities, but the form of this memory is unclear in research literature. Early efforts assume one could consider memory as though it were a single, monolithic repository of some sort for the entire organisation" [1]. Many see this term as meaning both a process of collecting and using information as well as a repository.

We have used Davenport's definition of knowledge management earlier in this chapter, which describes knowledge management as simplifying processes of sharing, distributing, creating, capturing and understanding the knowledge of a company [89]. In the introductory chapter for the handbook on knowledge management and organisational learning [108], Easterby-Smith and Lyles discuss the term knowledge management and related terms organisational learning, the learning organisation, and organisational knowledge. In the following, we will use knowledge management in a broad sense, which also incorporates the other related terms defined by Easterby-Smith and Lyles.

Knowledge management has received much attention in various fields, which is demonstrated by the publication of two "handbooks" [95, 108], one encyclopaedia [293], and numerous books.

One of the most cited books on knowledge management is "The Knowledge-Creating Company" by Nonaka and Takeuchi [234] seeks to explain the success of Japanese companies by their skills in "organisational knowledge creation", with more emphasis on tacit knowledge than in the west. They present a model of how knowledge is transformed and converted in an organisations, often referred to as the SECI-model after the four conversion mechanisms. We will present this model in further detail in Sect.1.3.2.

Another main influence on thinking on knowledge management has been the work on selecting a strategy on knowledge management Hansen et al. [143]. They refer to two main strategies for knowledge management:

- *Codification*. To systematise and store information that constitutes the knowledge of the company, and to make this available to the people in the company for reuse.
- *Personalisation*. To support the flow of information in a company by having a centralised store of information about knowledge sources, like a "yellow pages" of who knows what in a company.

Table 1.3 Earl's schools of knowledge management

School	Subschool	Focus	Aim	Unit
Technocratic	Systems	Technology	Knowledge bases	Domain
	Cartographic	Maps	Knowledge directories	Enterprise
	Engineering	Processes	Knowledge flows	Activity
Economic	Commercial	Income	Knowledge assets	Know-how
Behavioural	Organisational	Networks	Knowledge pooling	Communities
	Spatial	Space	Knowledge exchange	Place
	Strategic	Mindset	Knowledge capabilities	Business

Several have suggested a hybrid strategy, which provides a balance between the codified and personalized strategies [7, 92, 328]. For knowledge that is not subject to frequent changes, a codification strategy is useful, as it can be reused without too much effort to update it. On the other hand, much architectural knowledge is not stable. For such knowledge, a personalization strategy may be appropriate, enabling stakeholders to find "who knows what".

Earl [107] has further classified work in knowledge management into schools (see Table 1.3). The schools are broadly categorized as "technocratic", "economic" and "behavioural". The technocratic schools are (1) the systems school, which focuses on technology for knowledge sharing, using knowledge repositories; (2) the cartographic school, which focuses on knowledge maps and creating knowledge directories; and (3) the engineering school, which focuses on processes and knowledge flows in organisations. The economic school focuses on how knowledge assets relates to income in organisations. The behavioural school consists of three subschools (1) the organisational school, which focuses on networks for sharing knowledge; (2) the spatial school, which focuses on how office space can be designed to promote knowledge sharing; and (3) the strategic school, which focuses on how knowledge can be seen as the essence of a company's strategy.

Many have been critical to the concept of knowledge management, and in particular to the use of information technology in knowledge management. Hislop [145] questions the distinction between tacit and explicit knowledge. If explicit knowledge cannot be managed independently, this means that information technology will have a smaller part in knowledge management. This critique is also supported by McDermot [223], who argues that "if people working in a group don't already share knowledge, don't already have plenty of contact, don't already understand what insights and information will be useful to each other, information technology is not likely to create it". In addition, Swan et al. [309] criticize the knowledge management field for being too occupied with tools and techniques. They claim that researchers tend to overstate the codifiability of knowledge and to overemphasize the utility of IT to give organisational performance improvement. They also warn that "codification of tacit knowledge into formal systems may generate its own pathology: the informal and locally situated practices that allow the firm to cope with uncertainty may become rigidified by the system". The occupation with tools is further discussed in the works of Huysman and de Wit [150], who characterize knowledge management focusing on knowledge acquisition, exchange and creation as "first generation" knowledge management, and argue that the "second generation" must take more into respect the power of the people who hold the knowledge. Thus, the focus needs to move more to motivating people to share their knowledge. Huysman and Wulf [151], further argue that knowledge management tools needs to be embedded in the social networks of which they are part of in order to be used.

Schultze and Leidner [290] studied discourses of knowledge management in information systems research, and warn that knowledge can be a double-edged sword: too little can result in expensive mistakes, while too much can lead to unwanted accountability. In a study of research on information systems, they found that most existing research is optimistic on the role of knowledge management in organisations, and they urge researchers to give more attention to the critique of knowledge management.

1.3.2 Knowledge and Learning

In cognitive and organisation science, we find many models on how knowledge is transferred or learned at an individual and organisational level. We present four theories that are referred to widely: the double-loop learning theory of Argyris and Schön, Wenger's theory of communities of practice, and Nonaka and Takeuchi's theory of knowledge creation and Senge's model of the learning organisation.

Argyris and Schön distinguish between what they call single and double-loop learning [19] in organisations. In single-loop learning, one receives feedback in the form of observed effects and then acts on the basis solely of these observations to change and improve the process or causal chain of events that generated them. In double-loop learning, one not only observes the effects of a process or causal chain of events, but also understands the factors that influence the effects.

One traditional view of learning is that it is most effective when it takes place in a setting where you isolate and abstract knowledge and then "teach" it to "students" in rooms free of context. Wenger describes this as a view of learning as an individual process where, for example, collaboration is considered a kind of cheating [335]. In his book about communities of practice, he describes a completely different view: learning as a social phenomenon. A community of practice develops its own "practices, routines, rituals, artifacts, symbols, conventions, stories and histories". This is often different from what you find in work instructions, manuals and the like. Wenger defines learning in communities of practice as follows:

- *For individuals*. Learning takes place in the course of engaging in, and contributing to, a community.
- *For communities*. Learning is to refine the practice.
- *For organisations*. Learning is to sustain interconnected communities of practice.

Nonaka and Takeuchi [234] claim that knowledge is constantly converted from tacit to explicit and back again as it passes through an organisation. They say that knowledge can be converted from tacit to tacit, from tacit to explicit, or from explicit to either tacit or explicit knowledge through the following mechanisms:

- Socialisation means to transfer tacit knowledge to another person through observation, imitation and practice, what has been referred to as "on the job" training. Craftsmanship has usually been learned in this way, where oral communication is either not used or plays a minor part.
- Externalisation means to go from tacit knowledge to explicit. Explicit knowledge can "take the shapes of metaphors, analogies, concepts, hypotheses or models" [234].
- Combination is to go from explicit to explicit knowledge, that is, to combine and systematize knowledge from different sources such as documents, meetings, telephone conferences or bulletin boards. Systematizing this kind of explicit knowledge is to reconfigure it by sorting, adding, combining or categorizing the knowledge.
- Combination means to go from explicit to explicit knowledge, by taking knowledge from different sources such as documents, meetings, telephone conferences, or bulletin boards and aggregating and systematizing it.
- Internalisation means to take externalised knowledge and make it into individual tacit knowledge in the form of mental models or technical know-how. "Documents and manuals facilitate the transfer of explicit knowledge to other people, thereby helping them experience the experiences of others indirectly (i.e. 're-experience' them)" [234].

According to Nonaka and Takeuchi, knowledge passes through different modes of conversion, which makes the knowledge more refined and spreads it across different layers in an organisation.

In the much-cited book on learning organisations, The Fifth Discipline [294], we find further characteristics of learning organisations: the ability of "systems thinking" – to see more than just parts of a system. This often means to involve people in an organisation to develop a "shared vision", some common grounds that make the work meaningful, and also serve to explain aspects that you yourself do not have hands-on experience in. Another way of improving communication in an organisation is to work on "mental models" that support action, "personal mastery"; that people make use of their creativity and abilities. And finally "group learning" – to enhance dialogue and openness in the organisation.

1.3.3 Knowledge Management in Software Engineering

Companies developing information systems have failed to learn effective means for problem solving to such an extent that they have learned to fail, according to an article by Lyytinen and Robey [218]. One suggested mean to overcome this problem is an increased focus on knowledge management.

In software engineering, there has been much discussion about how to manage knowledge, or foster "learning software organisations" [22, 272]. In this context,

Feldmann and Althoff have defined a "learning software organisation" as an organisation that has to "create a culture that promotes continuous learning and fosters the exchange of experience" [118]. Dybå places more emphasis on action in his definition: "A software organisation that promotes improved actions through better knowledge and understanding" [105].

In software engineering, reusing life cycle experience, processes and products for software development is often referred to as having an "Experience Factory" [33]. In this framework, experience is collected from software development projects, and is packaged and stored in an experience base. By packing, we mean generalising, tailoring, and formalising experience so that it is easy to reuse.

A number of overviews of work on knowledge management in software engineering can be found in the literature. Bjørnson and Dingsøyr [41] give an overview of published empirical studies on knowledge management in software engineering in a systematic review. They categorized 29 empirical studies and 39 lessons learned reports according to the knowledge management schools of Earl, and found that most attention was given to the technocratic and behavioural schools. Rus et al. [272] present an overview of knowledge management in software engineering. The review focuses on motivations for knowledge management, approaches to knowledge management, and factors that are important when implementing knowledge management strategies in software companies. Lindvall et al. [211] describe types of software tools that are relevant for knowledge management, including tools for managing documents and content, tools for managing competence, and tools for collaboration. Dingsøyr and Conradi [96] surveyed the literature for studies of knowledge management initiatives in software engineering. They found eight reports on lessons learned, which are formulated with respect to what actions companies took, what the effects of the actions were, what benefits are reported, and what kinds of strategy for managing knowledge were used. Babar et al. [7] present studies on managing software architecture, and found that most published reports from research and practice focus on codification, while many companies the authors have worked with focus on a personalization strategy unintentionally. An overview of works on architecture knowledge management can be found in Chap. 2.

1.4 Summary

Software architecture is concerned with the description of elements from which systems are built, the interaction among those elements, patterns that guide their composition, and constraints on those patterns. The design of a software architecture is driven by quality concerns. The resulting software architecture is described in different views, each of which addresses specific concerns on behalf of specific stakeholders. This resembles the way different drawings of a building emphasize different aspects on behalf of its different stakeholders.

It is important to not only document the resulting solution, but also the decisions that led to that solution, its rationale, and other information that is helpful to guide its further evolution.

Software architecture is an important notion, for more than one reason:

- The comparison with traditional architecture reveals commonalities which help us to get a better grip on the software design process and its products. Software architecture is not only concerned with the blueprint that is the outcome of the design process. The notion of an architectural style has merits of its own and the relationship between style on the one hand and engineering and materials on the other hand provide additional insights into what software design entails [250].
- Phrasing a software design in software architectural terms promotes consistency during development and maintenance. Phrasing the global design in terms of an architecture forces us to think about its general flavor, in terms of types of component and connector, as well as a certain control structure. By making this intuition explicit, it both *describes* and *prescribes* how the system should look and how it may evolve over time.
- A software architecture captures early design decisions. The architecture can be used to evaluate those decisions. It also provides a way to discuss those decisions and their ramifications with the various stakeholders.

As software architecture constitutes the main decisions, this kind of knowledge is especially important when focusing on knowledge management in software companies. We have defined knowledge management broadly as a method that simplifies the process of sharing, distributing, creating, capturing and understanding a company's knowledge. The motivation for managing knowledge in the software engineering field, is that software development is knowledge-intensive work, and methods, techniques and tools for improving the way knowledge is managed is likely to improve the software products and the software development process. In this chapter we have observed that:

- There are many approaches to knowledge management, from focusing on codifying knowledge in different forms, like describing work processes and describing knowledge artifacts, such as the rationale for design decisions, to focusing on leveraging the knowledge of communities and designing office space in order to create arenas for knowledge sharing.
- Learning can be described in many ways. Double-loop learning describes learning that has a large potential for impact on products and processes. Others have given attention to learning as a social phenomenon, emphasizing that knowledge has to be put in a context to be useful. Learning can also be seen as a conversion process of knowledge from tacit to explicit through mechanisms such as socialization, externalization, combination and internalization. Finally, we have described the idea of the learning organisation as organisations that enable "systems thinking".
- Knowledge management has been given some attention for software engineering in general, mainly with a focus on codifying knowledge in different forms. Much of the previous work has been concerned with tools for knowledge management, such as tools for managing documents and content, tools for managing competence and collaboration tools.

Acknowledgements This research has been partially sponsored by the Dutch Joint Academic and Commercial Quality Research and Development (Jacquard) program on Software Engineering Research via contract 638.001.406 GRIFFIN: a GRId For inFormatIoN about architectural knowledge.

Part I
Architecture Knowledge Management

Knowledge management is a broad field, and this also applies for managing architectural knowledge. This part seeks to show the breadth of the field, and to provide a summary of central ideas that are used in subsequent chapters. Key questions discussed include: What is architectural knowledge? How can we represent architectural knowledge? What we can learn from other fields that focus on knowledge management? And how can the process of architectural design allow for effective knowledge management?

In answering these questions, the objectives of Part I are to explain what architecture knowledge management is, how that relates to software architecture and to knowledge management, and why it is that important in modern software engineering. This part provides an overview about what the software architecture community can learn from the knowledge management community, and the other way around.

Chapter 2 starts out by investigating definitions of architectural knowledge, and distinguishes between four views: The pattern-centric, the dynamism-centric, the requirements-centric and the decision-centric view. Rik Farenhorst and Remco C. de Boer studied published papers on architecture knowledge management, and found indications of a shift towards more overarching knowledge management approaches, combining the views.

How architectural knowledge is represented is characterised in Chap. 3. Representation has evolved from the intuitive and informal to the structured, abstract and formal. Focus has also moved from documenting architectural design to documenting architectural design decisions. Architectural knowledge should be made explicit, Philippe Kruchten argues, to ease the reasoning around architecture.

What approaches exist to knowledge management in general, and what we can learn from studies in software engineering, is the topic of Chap. 4. Relevant knowledge management schools are presented, with examples of how they are applied in software engineering. Some approaches are characterized as "technocratic", giving emphasis to information technology, while the "behavioural" schools emphasize more on the human aspects of knowledge management. The chapter ends with Torgeir Dingsøyr discussing the pros and cons of the schools with respect to managing architectural knowledge.

The software architecture process, and specifically how this process can be supported with knowledge management is discussed by Muhammad Ali Babar in Chap. 5. To develop a software architecture is a complex and highly knowledge-intensive activity, with many decisions to be taken and tradeoffs to be made. The activities, the roles, and the knowledge needs involved when designing the architecture are distilled into a model of architecture knowledge management.

These chapters define many of the concepts, which are subsequently used in Parts II and III of this book.

Chapter 2
Knowledge Management in Software Architecture: State of the Art

Rik Farenhorst and Remco C. de Boer

Abstract Architectural knowledge has played a role in discussions on design, reuse, and evolution for over a decade. Over the past few years, the term has significantly increased in popularity and attempts are being made to properly define what constitutes 'architectural knowledge'. In this chapter, we discuss the state-of-the-art in architectural knowledge management. We describe four main views on architectural knowledge based on the results of a systematic literature review. Based on software architecture and knowledge management theory we define four main categories of architectural knowledge, and discuss four distinct philosophies on managing architectural knowledge, which have their origin in the aforementioned views. Whereas traditionally tools, methods, and methodologies for architecture knowledge management were confined to a single philosophy, a trend can be observed that state-of-the-art approaches take a more holistic stance and integrate different philosophies in a single architecture knowledge management approach.

2.1 Introduction

Over the past few years, the concept of 'architectural knowledge' has become more prominent in literature and attempts are being made to arrive at a proper definition for this concept. In this chapter we present the state-of-the-art in architecture knowledge management. To this end, we look at what precisely entails architectural knowledge and what predominant philosophies exist for managing such knowledge.

In answer to the question 'what is architectural knowledge?', in Sect. 2.2 we describe four main views on architectural knowledge that emerged from a systematic

Rik Farenhorst (✉)
VU University Amsterdam, The Netherlands e-mail: rik@cs.vu.nl
Remco C. de Boer
VU University Amsterdam, The Netherlands e-mail: remco@cs.vu.nl

M. Ali Babar et al. (eds.), *Software Architecture Knowledge Management*,
DOI: 10.1007/978-3-642-02374-3_2, © Springer-Verlag Berlin Heidelberg 2009

literature review, and explore their commonalities and differences. Using two orthogonal architectural knowledge dimensions, we define four categories of architectural knowledge. The potential knowledge conversions between these categories, which we describe in Sect. 2.3, together form a descriptive framework with which different architecture knowledge management philosophies can be typified. This framework shows that the differences between the four views on architectural knowledge are very much related to the different philosophies they are based on.

Although there exist several single-philosophy approaches that have both their origin and scope on only one of the main philosophies, in recent years a shift towards more overarching approaches can be observed. Four of such trends for architecture knowledge management are discussed in Sect. 2.4.

2.2 What Is 'Architectural Knowledge'?

To be able to understand what architectural knowledge entails, we have conducted a systematic literature review in which we explored the *'roots'* architectural knowledge has in different software architecture communities. Details on the protocol followed in this systematic literature review can be found in Sect. 2.5. The review revealed four primary views on architectural knowledge. In Sect. 2.2.1 we elaborate upon these views, and in Sect. 2.2.2 we formulate a theory on architectural knowledge by looking at the commonalities and differences between these views.

2.2.1 Different Views on Architectural Knowledge

Architectural knowledge is related to such various topics as architecture evolution, service oriented architectures, product line engineering, enterprise architecture, and program understanding, to name but a few. In the literature, however, there are four main views on the use and importance of architectural knowledge. Those four views – pattern-centric, dynamism-centric, requirements-centric, and decision-centric – are introduced in this section.

2.2.1.1 Pattern-Centric View

In the mid-nineties, patterns became popular as a way to capture and reuse design knowledge. People were disappointed by the lack of ability of (object-oriented) frameworks to capture the knowledge necessary to know when and how to apply those frameworks. Inspired by the work of Christopher Alexander on cataloging patterns used in civil architecture, software engineers started to document proven solutions to recurring problems.

Initially, patterns focused mainly on object oriented design and reuse; the canonical work in this area is the book by the 'Gang of Four' [130]. The aim was to let those design patterns capture expert and design knowledge, necessary to know when and how to reuse design and code. Soon, however, the patterns community extended its horizon beyond object-oriented design. Nowadays, patterns exist in many areas, including patterns for analysis (e.g., [125]), architectural design (e.g., [128, 64]), and the development process (e.g., [82, 81]).

Patterns in software development serve two purposes. Patterns are reusable solutions that can be applied to recurring problems. They also form a vocabulary that provides a common frame of reference, which eases sharing architectural knowledge between developers. Although patterns are usually documented according to certain templates, there is not a standard template used for all patterns. The way in which patterns are codified make them very suitable for human consumption, but less so for automated tools.

2.2.1.2 Dynamism-Centric View

A more formal approach to architectural knowledge can be found in discussions on dynamic software architectures. Systems that exhibit such dynamism can dynamically adapt their architecture during runtime, and for example perform upgrades without the need for manual intervention or shutting down. Such systems must be able to self-reflect and 'reason over the space of architectural knowledge' [132], which invariably means that – unlike patterns – this architectural knowledge must be codified for consumption by non-human agents.

As the software itself must understand the architectural knowledge, architecture-based adaptation has to rely on rather formal ways of codification. A 2004 survey by Bradbury et al. [50] reveals that almost all formal specification approaches for dynamic software architectures are based on graph representations of the architectural structure. Purely graph-based approaches use explicit graph representations of components and connectors. In those approaches, architectural reconfiguration is expressed with graph rewriting rules. Other approaches, which use implicit graph representations, rely mainly on process algebra or logic to express dynamic reconfiguration of the architecture.

A particular family of formal languages for representing architectures is formed by so-called 'architecture description languages' (ADLs). Although not all ADLs are suitable for use in run-time dynamic systems, all ADLs are based on the same component-connector graph-like representation of architectures (cf. [224]).

2.2.1.3 Requirements-Centric View

The architecture is, ultimately, rooted in requirements. Therefore, architectural knowledge plays a role in enabling traceability in the transition from requirements to architecture. But there is an inverse relation too, namely the fact that 'stakeholders are quite often not able to specify innovative requirements in the required detail without having some knowledge about the intended solution' [254]. Hence, in order to specify sufficiently detailed requirements, one needs knowledge about about the (possible) solutions, which means that requirements and architecture need to be co-developed. This is a subtle, but important difference: the transition-view is a bit older and denotes the believe that problem is followed by solution, whereas the more recent co-development view emphasizes that both need to be considered concurrently.

The relation between requirements and architecture has been a popular subject of discourse since the early 2000s. Although the related STRAW workshop series is no longer organized, many researchers still focus on bridging the gap between requirements and architecture. A 2006 survey by Galster et al. [129] identified and classified the methodologies in this area, including Jackson's problem frames (later extended to 'architectural frames' [262]), goal-oriented requirements engineering, and the twin peaks model for weaving architecture and requirements [235].

2.2.1.4 Decision-Centric View

For many years, software architecture has mainly been regarded as the high-level structure of components and connectors. Many architectural description frameworks, such as the IEEE-1471 standard [155] therefore have a particular focus on documenting the end result of the architecting process.

Nowadays, the view on architecture seems to be shifting from the end result to the rationale behind that end result. More and more researchers agree that one should consider not only the resulting architecture itself, but also the design decisions and related knowledge that represent the reasoning behind this result. All such architectural knowledge needs to be managed to guide system evolution and prevent knowledge vaporization [48].

The treatment of design decisions as first-class entities enables the consideration of a wide range of concerns and issues, including pure technical issues, but also business, political and social ones. Architects need to balance all these concerns in their decision making. To justify the architectural design to other stakeholders, communication of the architectural design decisions plays a key role. In that sense, the decision-centric view is very much related to the (broader) field of design rationale.

2.2.2 *So, What Is Architectural Knowledge?*

If there's anything clear from the four views on architectural knowledge, it must be that there is not a single encompassing definition of what this knowledge entails. A 2008 survey of definitions of architectural knowledge revealed that most studies circumstantially define architectural knowledge. Those studies that do give a direct definition are of recent date, and all of them have roots in the decision-centric view [43].

The apparent importance of the decision-centric view in discussing and defining architectural knowledge may be explained when we look at the links between this view and the other views; decisions appear to be the linking pin between the different views.

The relation between patterns and decisions is discussed by Harrison et al. Their conclusion is that the two are complementary concepts, and that '[u]sing a pattern in system design is, in fact, selecting one of the alternative solutions and thus making the decisions associated with the pattern in the target systems specific context' [144]. Ran and Kuusela proposed a hierarchical ordering of design patterns in what they call a 'design decision tree' [261].

The relation between design decisions and requirements can be approached from two directions. Bosch conceptually divides an architectural design decision into a 'solution part' and a 'requirements part' [48]. The requirements part represents the subset of the system's requirements to which the solution part provides a solution. Van Lamsweerde, on the other hand, argues that for alternative goal refinements and assignments, 'decisions have to be made which in the end will produce different architectures' [199].

Formal graph-based architecture representations are especially suitable for automated reasoning. In other words, those representations enable automated agents either take design decisions themselves [50], or to inform human architects about potential problems and pending decisions [267].

Decisions may indeed be an umbrella concept that unify parts of those different views on architectural knowledge, because they closely relate to various manifestations of architectural knowledge concepts. Of course, there are differences between the views too: patterns are individual solution fragments, formal representations focus on the end result only, and requirements engineering is more occupied with problem analysis than solution exploration. If we want to better compare the different manifestations of architectural knowledge, it helps to distinguish between different types of architectural knowledge. Two distinctions are particularly useful: tacit vs. explicit knowledge, and application-generic vs. application-specific architectural knowledge.

Nonaka and Takeuchi draw the distinction between tacit and explicit knowledge [234] (see also Chap. 1). This distinction is applicable to knowledge in general, and its application to architectural knowledge allows us to distinguish between the (tacit) knowledge that an architect and other stakeholders built up from experience and expertise, and the (explicit) architectural knowledge that is produced and codified – for example in artifacts such as architecture descriptions.

The distinction between application-generic and application-specific architectural knowledge has been proposed by Lago and Avgeriou [195]. This distinction, which is not necessarily applicable to other knowledge than 'architectural' knowledge, allows us to distinguish between (application-generic) knowledge that is "a form of library knowledge" that "can be applied in several applications independently of the domain" and (application-specific) knowledge that involves "all the decisions that were taken during the architecting process of a particular system and the architectural solutions that implemented the decisions". In summary,

19.25

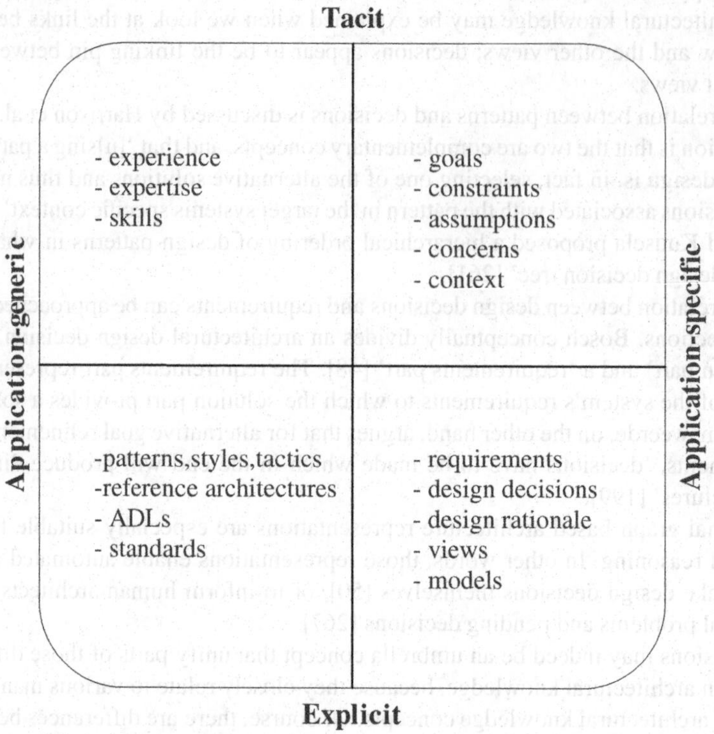

Fig. 2.1 Architectural knowledge categories

application-generic knowledge is all knowledge that is independent of the application domain, application-specific knowledge is all knowledge related to a particular system.

Since the two distinctions are orthogonal, a combination of the two results in four main categories of architectural knowledge, which are depicted in Fig. 2.1. That figure also provides examples of the type of architectural knowledge that fits each of the four categories.

- Application-generic tacit architectural knowledge includes the design knowledge an architect gained from experience, such as architectural concepts, methodologies, and internalized solutions.
- Application-specific tacit architectural knowledge concerns contextual domain knowledge regarding forces on the eventual architectural solution; it includes business goals, stakeholder concerns, and the application context in general.
- Application-generic explicit knowledge is design knowledge that has been made explicit in discussions, books, standards, and other types of communication. It includes reusable solutions such as patterns, styles and tactics, but also architecture description languages, reference architectures, and process models.

- Application-specific explicit architectural knowledge is probably the most tangible type of architectural knowledge. It includes all externalized knowledge of a particular system, such as architectural views and models, architecturally significant requirements, and codified design decisions and their rationale.

2.3 Philosophies of Architecture Knowledge Management

Knowledge from each of the four architectural knowledge categories can be converted to knowledge in another (or even in the same) category. This conversion lies at the basis of different architecture knowledge management philosophies. For some, architecture knowledge management may be mainly intended to support the transition from application-generic to application-specific knowledge. For others, the interplay between tacit and explicit knowledge may be the essence of architecture knowledge management.

Nonaka and Takeuchi defined four modes of conversion between tacit and explicit knowledge: socialization (tacit to tacit), externalisation (tacit to explicit), internalisation (explicit to tacit), and combination (explicit to explicit; cf. Chap. 1). Based on the distinction between application-generic and application-specific knowledge, we can define four additional modes of conversion:

- *Utilization* is the conversion from application-generic to application-specific knowledge. It is a common operation in the architecting process where background knowledge and experience are applied to the problem at hand.
- *Abstraction* is the conversion from application-specific to application-generic knowledge. In this conversion, architectural knowledge is brought to a higher level of abstraction so that it has value beyond the original application domain.
- *Refinement* is the conversion from application-specific to application-specific knowledge. Here, the architectural knowledge for a particular application is analyzed and further refined and related.
- *Maturement* is the conversion from application-generic to application-generic knowledge. It signifies the development of the individual architect as well as the architecture field as a whole; a kind of learning where new generic knowledge is derived and becomes available for application in subsequent design problems.

In total, there are 16 architectural knowledge conversions. Each conversion is formed by pairing one of the four conversions between tacit and explicit knowledge with one of the four conversions between application-generic and application-specific knowledge. Together, the 16 conversions form a descriptive framework with which different architecture knowledge management philosophies can be typified.

We saw earlier that the four views on architectural knowledge can all be related to decision making. At the same time, we saw that there are also obvious differences between those views. Those differences are very much related to the different architecture knowledge management philosophies they are based on.

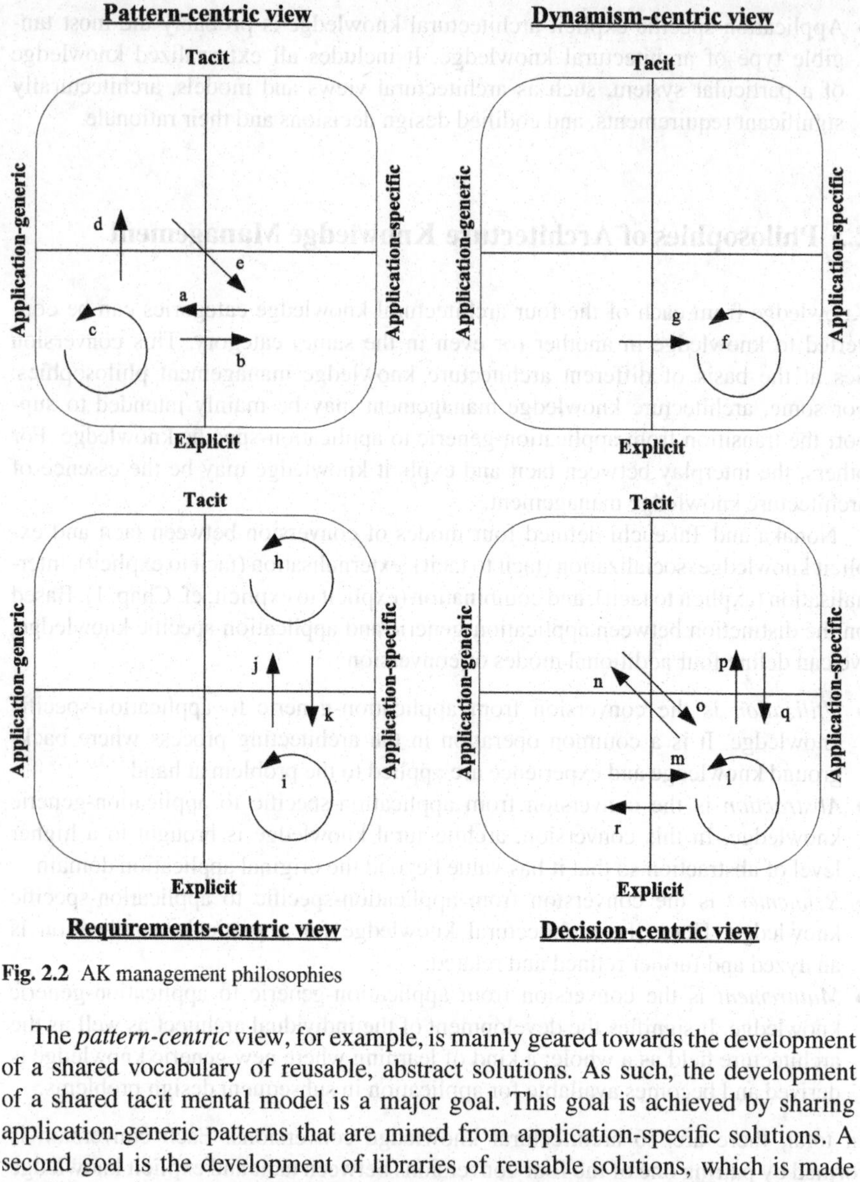

Fig. 2.2 AK management philosophies

The *pattern-centric* view, for example, is mainly geared towards the development of a shared vocabulary of reusable, abstract solutions. As such, the development of a shared tacit mental model is a major goal. This goal is achieved by sharing application-generic patterns that are mined from application-specific solutions. A second goal is the development of libraries of reusable solutions, which is made possible by maturement of documented patterns by cataloging them. The knowledge management philosophy in this view is primarily based on the following architectural knowledge conversions, which are also visualized in Fig. 2.2:

(a) *Abstraction and combination*. The most obvious example of this conversion is the process of pattern mining. Patterns are inherently abstractions. They are mined from existing architectural solutions and described in a clear and structured way to improve the reusability.

(b) *Utilization and combination.* One of the ways in which patterns can be reused in new designs is by looking them up in books, catalogs, or other repositories. Architects who wish to design a system comprised of several independent programs that work cooperatively on a common data structure could look up one of the many books available on architectural patterns (e.g., [64]) to find out that the 'blackboard' pattern is just what they need. Grady Booch works on the creation of a Handbook of software architecture, of which the primary goal is "to fill this void in software engineering by codifying the architecture of a large collection of interesting software-intensive systems, presenting them in a manner that exposes their essential patterns and that permits comparisons across domains and architectural styles" [47].

(c) *Maturement and combination.* Documented patterns may be organized in pattern catalogs. These catalogs present a collection of relatively independent solutions to common design problems. As more experience is gained using these patterns, developers and authors will increasingly integrate groups of related patterns to form so-called pattern languages [276]. Although each pattern has its merits in isolation, the strength of a pattern language is that it integrates solutions to particular problems in important technical areas. An example is provided by Schmidt and Buschmann in the context of development of concurrent networked applications [275]. Each design problem in this domain – including issues related to connection management, event handling, and service access – must be resolved coherently and consistently and this is where pattern languages are particularly helpful.

(d) *Maturement and internalisation.* Experienced architects know numerous patterns by heart. Such architects have no trouble discussing designs in terms of proxies, blackboard architectures, or three-tier CORBA-based client-server architectures. Their exposure to and experience with those patterns has led to internalised and matured pattern knowledge. The consequent shared, tacit vocabulary can be employed at will, without the need to look up individual patterns in order to understand what the other party means.

(e) *Utilization and externalisation.* When an architect has internalized several patterns, the use of those patterns as a means for communication or design is a combination of utilization (of the pattern) and externalisation (of the knowledge about the pattern and its existence).

While the pattern-centric view aims to support the development of tacitly shared application-generic architectural knowledge, the *dynamism-centric* view is much more focused on explicit application-specific architectural knowledge. Although some application-generic knowledge is utilized, the actual reasoning and reconfiguration uses application-specific knowledge. This architecture knowledge management philosophy is therefore primarily based on two conversions:

(f) *Refinement and combination.* Corresponds to the formal reasoning over codified architectural solutions in terms of models that are consumable by non-human agents. According to Bradbury et al., in a self-management system all dynamic architectural changes have four steps (initiation of change, selection of architectural transformation, implementation of reconfiguration, and assessment of architecture after reconfiguration) which should all occur within the automated process [50].

(g) *Utilization and combination.* Corresponds to formally specifying the application's components and connectors in generic languages such as ADLs or other graph representations. Medvidovic and Taylor propose a comparison and classification framework for ADLs, enabling the identification of key properties of ADLs and to show the strength and weaknesses of these languages [224]. In their comparison, Medvidovic and Taylor point out that at one end of the spectrum some ADLs specifically aim to aid architects in understanding a software system by offering a simple graphical syntax, some semantics and basic analyses of architectural descriptions. At the other end of the spectrum, however, ADLs provide formal syntax and semantics, powerful analysis tools, model checkers, parsers, compilers, code synthesis tools and so on.

For the *requirements-centric* view, the primary goal is tracing knowledge about the problem to knowledge about the solution. In co-development, an additional goal is to connect knowledge about problem and solution so that a stakeholder's image of the problem and solution domain is refined. In this view, the primary architectural knowledge conversions are:

(h) *Refinement and socialization.* Especially in co-development, architects and stakeholders will interact to align system goals and architectural solutions. Such interaction between 'customer' and 'product developer' is a prime example of a situation in which tacit knowledge is shared (cf. [234]). Pohl and Sikora discuss the need for co-development of requirements and architecture. They argue that such co-design is only possible is there is sufficient knowledge about the (course) solution when defining (detailed) system requirements: "instead of defining requirements based on implicit assumptions about the solution, requirements and architectural artifacts need to be developed concurrently" [235].

(i) *Refinement and combination.* Adding and maintaining traceability from requirements to architecture is a refinement step that combines explicit knowledge about elements from the problem and the solution space. Several techniques exist to guide the transition from requirements engineering to software architecture. In their 2006 survey, Galster et al. use architectural knowledge as knowledge about (previous) architectural solutions that can be reused when encountering similar requirements in a new project. They present patterns as a useful container for these reusable assets. Another approach for guiding the transition between requirements and architecture is that of feature-solution graphs [56]. De Bruin and Van Vliet use architectural knowledge as knowledge about quality concerns (represented as features) and solution fragments at the architectural level (represented as solutions). These are modeled together as Feature-Solution graphs in order to guide the explicit transition (or alignment) between the problem and solution world.

(j) *Refinement and externalisation.* Externalisation of application-specific tacit knowledge – such as concerns, goals, and the like – is an important part of the requirements process. Externalisation of tacit knowledge (problem-related as well as solution-related) is a precondition for maintaining traceability.

(k) *Refinement and internalisation.* The interaction between architects and stakeholders is not purely a matter of socialization. In co-development, for example, specifications and design artifacts play a major role as well and may be an aid to let the parties 're-experience' each other's experiences (cf. [234]). This internalization of explicit application-specific architectural knowledge may consequently lead to 'new ideas and insights concerning both the envisioned system usage and the architectural solution' [254].

Finally, the essential philosophy of the *decision-centric* view is externalizing the rationale behind architectural solutions (i.e. 'the why of the architecture') that can then be internalized and shape other people's mental models, so as to prevent knowledge vaporization. The architectural knowledge conversions central to this philosophy are:

(l) *Refinement and combination.* Corresponds to reasoning about codified architectural solutions, which need not be fully automated but may involve decision support. One such decision support approach is introduced by Robbins et al., who introduce the concept of 'critics' [267]. Critics are active agents that support decision-making by continuously and pessimistically analyzing partial architectures. Each critic checks for the presence of certain conditions in the partial architecture. Critics deliver knowledge to the architect about the implications of, or alternatives to, a design decision. Often, critics simply advise the architect of potential errors or areas needing improvement in the architecture. One could therefore see critics as an automated form of the backlog that architects use in the architecting process to acquire and maintain overview of the problem and solution space [146]. Another approach that fits this conversion is the Archium tool proposed by Jansen et al. which is aimed at establishing and maintaining traceability between design decision models and the software architecture design [163].

(m) *Utilization and combination.* This conversion amounts to the reuse of codified, generic knowledge (decision templates, architectural guidelines, patterns, etc.) 'to take decisions for a single application and thus construct application-specific knowledge' [195] (see Chap. 12).

(n) *Internalisation and abstraction.* Based on experience and expertise, an architect may quickly jump to a 'good' solution for a particular problem. Such a good solution can be a combination of several finer grained design decisions. This combination of design decisions may become so common for the architect that the solution is no longer seen as consisting of individual decisions. It may be hard for the architect to reconstruct why a certain solution fits a particular problem; the architect 'just knows'.

(o) *Utilization and externalisation.* When a solution has been internalized, and the architect 'just knows' when to apply it, it becomes difficult to see which other solutions are possible. Part of the decision-centric philosophy (e.g., in [56]) is therefore to reconstruct and document the constituting design decisions.

(p) *Refinement and internalisation.* This 'consumption' of architectural knowledge takes place when people want to 'learn from it or carry out some quality assessment' [195].

(q) *Refinement and externalisation.* The rationalization of taken architectural decisions, i.e. reconstruction and explanation of the 'why' behind them, is a crucial part of the decision-centric philosophy in which tacit knowledge is made explicit. In this respect, the software architecting can apply the best practices known from the 'older' and well-known field of design rationale. Regli et al. present a survey of design rationale systems, in which they distinguish between process-oriented and feature-oriented approaches [264]. Process-oriented design rationale systems emphasize the design rationale as a 'history' of the design process, which is descriptive and graph-based. A well-known example is the Issue-Based Information System (IBIS) framework for argumentation. A feature-oriented approach starts from the design space of an artifact, where the rules and knowledge in the specific domain must be considered in design decision making. Often these type of design rationale systems offer support for automated reasoning. A more recent survey on architecture design rationale by Tang et al. provides information about how practitioners think about, reason with, document and use design rationale [314]. It turns out that although practitioners recognize the importance of codifying design rationale, a lack of appropriate standards and tools to assist them in this process acts as barrier to documenting design rationale. Fortunately, the field of design rationale is working hard on developing more mature support. Recent developments have led to the creation of mature tooling such as Compendium and SEURAT [63], and models such as AREL [316] (see also Chap. 9).

(r) *Abstraction and combination.* The construction of high-level structures (templates, ontologies, models) to capture and store architecture design decisions. Various approaches to codify architectural design decisions in such as way have been reported. Tyree and Akerman present a template to codify architectural design decisions together with their rationale and several other properties relevant to that decision, such as the associated constraints, a timestamp, and a short description [325]. Kruchten proposes a more formal approach of codifying design decisions by using an ontology [190] (see Chap. 3. Ran and Kuusela present work on design decision trees [261].

2.4 State-of-the-Art in Architecture Knowledge Management

Based on the discussion of the four philosophies on architecture knowledge management and the primary architectural knowledge conversions of these philosophies, we can identify a few single-philosophy approaches to architecture knowledge management:

- *Rationale management systems.* In order to achieve refinement and externalisation of architectural knowledge, design rationale needs to be managed. Various tools and methods have been proposed over the last decade for doing exactly this.

- *Pattern languages and catalogs*. To allow for utilization and combination of architectural knowledge architectural knowledge needs to be categorized in pattern languages or catalogs. From these sources it can be quickly used in specific applications. In addition it enables learning and reasoning.
- *Architecture description languages*. ADLs enable utilization and combination of architectural knowledge in a formal way. Various types of ADLs exist, which range in level of formality and purpose, the latter ranging from aiding understanding of software systems to enabling powerful analyses.
- *Design decision codification*. To support refinement and combination of architectural knowledge much effort has been put in methods, tools, and techniques to codify architectural knowledge concepts. Design decisions are central to these methods and tools, but also related concepts such as rationale and alternative solutions are captured.

We saw earlier how the concept of 'decisions' seem to be an umbrella concept for all views on architectural knowledge. We can now explain this better: 'mature' architecture knowledge management unifies conversions from all architecture knowledge management philosophies, and is not merely limited to just one philosophy. This concept, which we call *'decision-in-the-large'*, is related more to the architecting process than to pure rationale management (which we could call *'decision-in-the-narrow'*), even though codifying rationale and preventing knowledge vaporization has been one of the prime drivers for the decision-centric philosophy. A focus on 'decision-in-the-large' seems driven more by architectural knowledge use cases than by anything else, often under the concept 'knowledge sharing'. A classification of such use cases is presented by Lago et al. [195], which distinguishes between architecting, sharing, assessing, and learning.

Obviously, some 'decision-in-the-large' approaches evolved from 'decision-in-the-narrow' approaches. But the former starts to play a more prominent role in the other philosophies, and hence the other views, too. In recent years, a shift towards more overarching state-of-the-art approaches can be observed. Four main trends for architecture knowledge management can be identified that mostly focus on specific use cases for architecture knowledge management. These trends will be elaborated upon in Sections. 2.4.1–2.4.4.

2.4.1 Sharing Architectural Knowledge

The trend of sharing architectural knowledge is focused on providing support for management of various types of architectural knowledge (both application-generic and application-specific). De Boer et al. propose a core model of architectural knowledge that provides further insight in what architecting entails (e.g. how design decisions are made) and which knowledge concepts are worth focusing on in support for architecture knowledge management [44]. This includes concepts that have their origin in the pattern-centric, requirements-centric and decision-centric view.

From knowledge management literature it is known that knowledge sharing can be achieved through codification or personalization [143]. Farenhorst et al. have come to the conclusion that a hybrid strategy might work best. They propose a platform for architectural knowledge sharing that combines codification techniques (design decision repositories, document management facilities) with personalization mechanisms (yellow pages, discussion forums) in order to enable Just-In-Time architectural knowledge: delivery of and access to the right architectural knowledge, to the right people, at the right time [113]; see also Chap. 8.

Another platform that allows managing different types of architectural knowledge concepts is the process-based architecture knowledge management environment (PAKME) proposed by Ali Babar et al. [8]. This environment allows storing application-generic architectural knowledge (such as general scenarios, patterns, and quality attributes), and application-specific architecture knowledge (such as concrete scenarios, contextualized patterns, and quality factors).

2.4.2 Aligning Architecting with Requirements Engineering

We observe a trend in architecture knowledge management literature towards aligning the architecting process with requirements engineering, since the two practices seem to have much in common. Pohl et al. propose COSMOD-RE, a method for co-designing requirements and architecture [253]. This methods supports the development of detailed requirements based on the specified architecture and the specified goals and scenarios. This co-design focus is fundamentally different from the focus on traceability from requirements to architecture, a predominant focus in the requirements-centric view.

With the transition from traceability to co-development/co-design the requirements engineering community appears to look beyond their own philosophy. In an attempt to better understand the relationship of requirements and architecture, De Boer and Van Vliet explore similarities between the two [46]. Based on their study they argue that there is no fundamental difference between architecturally significant requirements and architectural decisions, which also pleads for integrated methods and tools for architecture knowledge management that overarch requirements engineering and architecting.

2.4.3 Intelligent Support for Architecting

This trend focuses on specific architecting use cases related to intelligent and/or real-time support for architects. One of the state-of-the-art approaches focuses on providing architects or reviewers with a reading guide when looking for specific architectural knowledge [45]. To save time, architects use this intelligent discovery method to quickly get to the important knowledge while skipping less relevant documentation.

Other intelligent support approaches focus on modeling architectural knowledge concepts in such a way that learning and reasoning is stimulated. One example is provided by Kruchten, who proposes an ontology of architectural design decisions [190]. The templates he proposes allow acquiring insights in not only important properties of design decisions (e.g. the status), but also in the relationships between design decisions (e.g. 'enables' or 'conflicts with'). When proper visualization techniques are used this information is very useful for architects in the decision making process, for example to model the backlog [146].

2.4.4 Towards a Body of Architectural Knowledge

The last trend relates to establishing a body of architectural knowledge, to enable both learning and reuse. Recently, several approaches for setting up such a body of knowledge have been introduced. Lenin Babu et al. propose ArchVoc, an ontology for software architecture [24]. Based on knowledge from major textbooks on software architecture and by parsing parts of the web, they have constructed a software architecture vocabulary for reuse purposes. Their ontology of software architecture enables the architect in understanding the existing best practices and the relationships between them and also provide a means to apply them to the new systems to be developed.

The need for cataloging architectural knowledge is also expressed by Shaw and Clements, who argue that Booch' Handbook (cf. Sect. 2.3) "can provide important exemplars, but engineers also need reference material that organizes what we know about architecture into an accessible, operational body of knowledge" [295]. Chapter 12 gives a successful example hereof in the area of SOA infrastructure. This body of knowledge is thus not comprised of only patterns, but also other types of explicit application-generic architectural knowledge that can be utilized effectively. In an attempt to further define these types of architectural knowledge, Clements et al. have conducted empirical research to find out what set of duties, skills and knowledge is most important for an architect [73]. Codification of this architectural knowledge is perceived as "the beginnings of a road map for training and mentoring."

2.5 Justification

Our state-of-the-art overview on architecture knowledge management is the result of an extensive literature review conducted based on a predefined protocol. More details on this protocol can be found in [43]. The main phases executed are discussed in the remainder of this section.

In a systematic literature review of studies that define or discuss 'architectural knowledge', we identified 115 such studies [43]. These 115 studies form the basis for our discussion in this chapter. Consequently we will refer to these studies as the set of core studies (*C*).

Since we are interested in the community structures that underly the topic of architectural knowledge, we enriched our dataset with bibliographical links. We assume the community structure can be found, or approximated, by taking into account the bibliographical references that various authors make to each others work. Strong communities will display many intra-community references, and relatively few references to work outside the community. There are two types of bibliographical references: references *from* studies in *C* to other studies, and references *to* studies in *C* from other studies. We will use *B* (for 'bibliography') to denote studies that are referred to *from* studies in *C*, and *R* (for 'referring') to denote studies that refer *to* studies in *C*. Hence, the mapping $R \to C \to B$ summarizes the enriched data set used throughout this chapter.[1]

To determine *B*, we simply took all references listed in the 115 studies from *C*. To determine *R*, however, we had to do a 'reverse search' on the studies in *C*, since the information needed is not present in *C* itself. For construction of *R*, we used the Google Scholar search engine which provides such a reverse search facility through its 'cited by' feature. While constructing *R* and *B*, we also obtained results not necessarily found in sources from the sources list identified in our systematic review (cf. [43]). We do not see this as a limitation of our methodology. The goal of the dataset enrichment is different from the initial identification of primary studies in the systematic review; in the enrichment we are interested in community structures, and the different communities need not be limited to studies published through and indexed by the sources used for the review.

Together, *B*, *C*, and *R* comprise a 'social network' of scholarly publications and their interconnections. We analyzed this network using the Girvan–Newman algorithm [134]. The Girvan–Newman algorithm discovers communities in a graph, based on the 'betweenness' of edges, i.e., the number of shortest paths that run through an edge. The algorithm iteratively calculates the edge betweenness and removes the edge with the highest betweenness value, thereby eliminating edges that act as connections between different communities. Eventually, the algorithm results in a fully disconnected graph of 'communities' that consist of a single node.

Obviously, a disconnected graph is not the strongest community structure possible. Newman defines the modularity (Q) as a measure of strength of the community structure discovered in a network [233]. High values of Q ($0 \leq Q \leq 1$) indicate networks with a strong community structure. Newman's empirical evidence shows that local maxima of Q correspond to reasonable community divisions, hence it is good practice to stop the Girvan–Newman algorithm when a (local or global) maximum Q-value has been obtained. In our case, the first local maximum of Q occurred when the graph had been split up in 52 communities, while the global maximum occurred

[1] Note that *B*, *C*, and *R* are not completely disjoint; there are several occurrences of studies from *C* referring to other studies from *C*. Also, publications that are referred to from one study in *C* may themselves refer to other (earlier) studies from *C*.

at 59 communities ($Q \approx 0.7832$), which is extremely high (according to Newman, values above 0.7 are rare; typical values fall in the range $0.3 - 0.7$). Because of the data enrichment process we followed and the way the Girvan–Newman algorithm works, each of these 59 communities consists of at least one study from C, plus zero or more publications from either B or R.

In order to assign meaning to the 59 communities that came out of the algorithm we examined the set of papers for each of these communities in turn, and gave them a label that corresponded best to the papers in that community. Often, the non-core papers in the community did help in further characterizing the community and helped in phrasing a suitable label. When this was more difficult (for example when the non-core papers varied too much in subject), we looked more specifically at the core papers in that community since these actually talk about architectural knowledge and can therefore lead to more fitting for the community name. In the end we ended up with 59 labels for the communities, although some of those did overlap to a certain extent with each other.

In order to find out how exactly the communities had been discovered by the Girvan–Newman algorithm we examined the hierarchical structure of the identified communities. The hierarchical relations capture the order in which the communities have been identified. Based on the order of community-split-ups we could assign names to larger-order (i.e. parent) communities as well.

According to our definition a community should consist of at least two core papers (that talk about architectural knowledge) written by different authors. Based on this rule we further analyzed the data. We limited the number of main communities by removing the single-core-paper ones and the ones consisting of merely papers by the same author(s). In the end this refinement culminated into the four main communities discussed throughout this chapter: pattern-centric, dynamism-centric, requirements-centric, and decision-centric.

2.6 Summary

In this chapter we have analyzed the state-of-the-art in architecture knowledge management, and have shown that the concept of 'architectural knowledge' is becoming more prominent in literature. In Sect. 2.2.1 we have identified four main views on architectural knowledge: a pattern-centric view, a dynamism-centric view, a requirements-centric view, and a decision-centric view. The concept of 'decision' was found to be an umbrella concept that unifies parts of these views.

To better understand the concept of architectural knowledge in Sect. 2.2.2 we have defined four main categories (or types) of architectural knowledge based on a distinction between tacit and explicit knowledge on the one hand, and application-generic and application-specific architectural knowledge on the other hand. In total 16 knowledge conversions are possible between these four types of architectural knowledge. To articulate the commonalities and differences between the four views, in Sect. 2.3 we stated their main philosophies of architecture knowledge management and elaborated upon the architectural knowledge conversions that are central for these views. The conversions were further illustrated by examples of related work.

Based on the discussion of the main philosophies we identified four single-philosophy approaches for architecture knowledge management: rationale management systems, pattern languages and catalogs, architectural description languages, and design decision codification. All these approaches have both their origin in and scope on only one of the main philosophies. In recent years, however, a shift towards more overarching approaches can be observed. Four main trends for architecture knowledge management can be identified that mostly focus on specific use cases for architecture knowledge management (e.g. sharing, learning, traceability). This state of the art in architecture knowledge management indicates a shift from 'decision-in-the-narrow' to 'decision-in-the-large'.

We expect the interest in architectural knowledge to keep increasing over the coming years. Although it is unlikely that we will see a unified view on architectural knowledge anytime soon, the observed trends in architecture knowledge management indicate that future developments on managing architectural knowledge may further align the different views. We expect the trend towards 'decision-in-the-large' to continue, since both researchers and practitioners aim for a better understanding of what architects do, what their knowledge needs are, and how this architectural knowledge can best be managed in the architecting process.

Acknowledgements This research has been partially sponsored by the Dutch Joint Academic and Commercial Quality Research and Development (Jacquard) program on Software Engineering Research via contract 638.001.406 GRIFFIN: a GRId For inFormatIoN about architectural knowledge.

Chapter 3
Documentation of Software Architecture from a Knowledge Management Perspective – Design Representation

Philippe Kruchten

Abstract In this chapter we survey how architects have represented architectural knowledge and in particular architectural design. This has evolved over the last 3 decades, from very intuitive and informal, to very structured, abstract and formal, from simple diagrams and metaphors, design notations, and specific languages. As our understanding of architectural knowledge evolved, the importance of design rationale and the decision process became more and more prominent. There is however a constant through this evolution: the systematic use of metaphors.

3.1 Introduction

When we speak about the documentation of software architecture, we are clearly referring to the explicit aspect of architectural knowledge (see Sect. 1.2.2.1). "If it is not written, it does not exist," I used to tell members of an architecture team, prodding them to document, i.e., make very explicit, what we had discussed at length in a meeting, or the knowledge they had brought in from outside, their past experience in general, and especially the decisions we had just made.

Architectural knowledge consists of architectural design – the blueprints of the system under development – as well as the design decisions, assumptions, context, and other factors that together determine why a particular final solution is the way it is. Except for the architecture design part, most of the architectural knowledge usually remains hidden and tacit – in the heads of the architects. An explicit representation of architectural knowledge is helpful for building and evolving quality systems [192].

In this chapter, we will therefore focus on the lower right of the four quadrants of knowledge described in Fig. 2.1, the externalized part of architectural knowledge (as opposed to tacit knowledge): the *application-specific explicit knowledge*,

Philippe Kruchten
University of British Columbia, Vancouver, Canada, e-mail: pbk@ece.ubc.ca

M. Ali Babar et al. (eds.), *Software Architecture Knowledge Management*,
DOI: 10.1007/978-3-642-02374-3_3, © Springer-Verlag Berlin Heidelberg 2009

and, to a somewhat lesser extent, we will also focus on the lower left quadrant: the *application-generic explicit knowledge*.

Architecture representation implies the use of models, architectural models. But what is a model? M is a model of S if M can be used to answer questions about S, where S is the system under consideration.

3.2 Evolution of Architectural Representation

The first reference to the phrase "software architecture" occurred in 1969 at a conference on software engineering techniques organized by NATO [65]. Some of our field's most prestigious pioneers, including Tony Hoare, Edsger Dijkstra, Alan Perlis, Per Brinch Hansen, Friedrich Bauer, and Niklaus Wirth, attended this meeting. From then until the late 1980s, the word "architecture" was used mostly in the sense of system architecture (meaning a computer system's physical structure) or sometimes in the narrower sense of a given family of computers' instruction set. Key sources about a software system's organization came from Fred Brooks in 1975 [54], Butler Lampson in 1983 [198], David Parnas from 1972 to 1986 [244, 245, 246, 247], and John Mills whose 1985 article looked more into the process and pragmatics of architecting [227]. The concept of software architecture as a distinct discipline started to emerge in 1990 [297]. A 1991 article by Winston W. Royce and Walker Royce (father and son) was the first to position software architecture – in both title and perspective – between technology and process [269]. Eberhardt Rechtin dedicated a few sections to software in his 1991 book *Systems Architecting: Creating and Building Complex Systems* [263].

3.2.1 Boxes and Arrows

In the 1970s and through most of 1980s, because the concept of software architecture was not very well delineated from that of software design or "high-level design", there was very little agreement on how to document software architecture. Various mixes of "boxes and arrows" diagrams were used as models, far too often with not much precise semantics behind the boxes, and even less behind the arrows. Some of this remains today, and constitutes what I call the "PowerPoint" level of software architecture documentation. It is still very valuable in bridging the gaps between various groups of stakeholders (the various people the architect has to deal with), such as marketing, sponsors, quality, process, approval, certification, etc.

3.2.2 Views

Still today, modern software architecture practices rely on the principles that Perry and Wolf enounced in the late 1980s in their pretty and simple formula: Architecture = {Elements, Form, Rationale} [250]. The elements are the main constituents of any architectural description in terms of components and connectors, while the nonfunctional properties guide the final shape or form of the architecture. Different shapes with the same or similar functionality are possible, as they constitute valid design choices by which software architects make their design decisions. These decisions are precisely the soul of architectures, but they are often neglected during the architecting activity as they usually reside in the architect's mind in the form of tacit knowledge that is seldom captured and documented in a usable form. Software architecture started to take shape as an artifact of the design process that "encompasses significant decisions about:

1. The organization of a software system
2. The selection of the structural elements and their interfaces by which a system is composed with its behavior as specified by the collaboration among those elements
3. The composition of these elements into progressively larger subsystems" (from RUP [189, 152])

For years, the generalized practice and research efforts have focused solely on the architectural representation itself. These practices have long been exclusively aimed at representing and documenting the system's architecture from different perspectives called *architectural views*. These views, which represent the interests of different stakeholders, are offered as a set of harmonized descriptions in a coherent and logical manner and also used to communicate the architecture.

3.2.3 The Architecting Process

The period between 1996 and 2006 brought complementary techniques in the form of architectural methods, many of them derived from well established industry practices. Methods like RUP (at Rational, then IBM) [189, 152], BAPO/CAFR (at Philips) [237], S4V (at Siemens) [147, 300], ASC (at Nokia), ATAM, SAAM and ADD (at the SEI) [175], among others, are now mature design and evaluation practices to analyze, synthesize, and valuate modern software architectures. In some cases, the methods are backed by architectural description languages, assessment methods, and stakeholder-focused, decision-making procedures.

Since many of the design methods were developed independently [146], they exhibit certain similarities and differences motivated by the different nature, purpose, application domain, or the size of the organization for which they were developed. In essence, they cover essential phases of the architecting activity but are performed in different ways. Common to some of these methods is the use of design decisions that are evaluated during the construction of the architecture. These decisions are elicited by groups of stakeholders, under the guide of architects, but the ultimate decision makers are (a small group – often a single person) architects. Unfortunately, design decisions and their rationale were still not considered as first-class entities because they lack an explicit representation. As a result, software architects cannot revisit or communicate the decisions made, which in most cases vaporize forever.

3.2.4 Architectural Design Decisions

Rationale was present in the 1992 formula of Perry and Wolf, but in reality, it was rarely captured explicitly in a form that would allow it to be revisited. This remains a prevalent issue.

Rus and Lindvall wrote in 2002 that "the major problem with intellectual capital is that it has legs and walks home every day" [272]. Current software organizations suffer the loss of this intellectual capital when experts leave. The same happens in software architecture when the reasoning required for understating a particular system is unavailable and has not been explicitly documented. In 2004, Jan Bosch stated that "we do not view a software architecture as a set of components and connectors, but rather as the composition of a set of architectural design decisions" [48, 161]. The lack of first-class representation of design rationale in current architecture view models brought the need to include decisions as first-class citizens that should be embodied within the traditional architecture documentation.

There are several benefits of using design rationales in architecture as a mean to explain why a particular design choice is made or to know which design alternatives have been evaluated before the right or the optimal design choices are made. Benefits can be achieved in the medium and long term because documenting design rationale prevents the need for architecture recovery processes, which are mostly used to retrieve the decisions when design, documentation, or even the creators of the architecture are no longer available. In other cases, the natural evolution of a software system forces previous design decisions to be replaced by new ones. Hence, maintaining and managing this architectural knowledge requires a continuous attention to keep the changes in the code and the design aligned with the decisions, and to use these to bridge the software architecture gap.

3.2.5 Architectural Knowledge = Architectural Design + Architectural Design Decisions

It is in this new context that Perry and Wolf's old ideas [250] become relevant for upgrading the concept of software architecture by explicitly adding the design decisions that motivate the creation of software designs. Together with design patterns, reference architecture, frameworks, etc., design decisions are a subset of the overall architectural knowledge (AK) that is produced during the development of architecture. Most of the tacit knowledge that remains hidden in the mind of the architects should be made explicit and transferable into a useful form for later use, easing the execution of distributed and collective decision-making processes.

The formula, *Architectural Knowledge = Architectural Design + Architectural Design Decisions*, recently proposed by Kruchten, Lago and van Vliet [192], modernizes Perry and Wolf's [250] idea and considers design decisions as part of the architecture. We'll use this formula: AK = AD + ADD, to structure the rest of this chapter.

3.3 Architectural Design

For many years, architectural knowledge was represented in very ad hoc fashion: boxes and arrows of unspecified or fuzzy semantic value; the PowerPoint level of architectural description. The challenge was to describe in a truly multidimensional reality in a 2-dimensional space. Because the model, M, was poor, the set of questions that could be answered regarding the system it represented remained limited.

3.3.1 Viewpoints and Views

In the early 1990s, several groups around the world realized that the architecture of a large and complex software-intensive system was made of multiple entangled structures, and that the poor attempts of representing architecture using a single type of flat blueprint was inherently doomed to fail. Different parties (or stakeholders) are concerned by different aspects of an architecture. Each of these aspects is a viewpoint, and can be addressed by a certain kind of architecture representation, with a notation and language of its own. The views, however, do not correspond to a decomposition of the architecture in parts, but are different projections, abstractions or simplifications of a more complex reality.

Figure 3.1 is an example of a set of five views (from [152] and [188]). Very similar sets of views appeared at Siemens [300] and elsewhere.

This concept of multiple views is not new, and Paul Clements traced it to a 1994 paper by David Parnas: "On a buzzword: hierarchical structure" [245]. An architectural view is a partial representation of a system, from the perspective of a

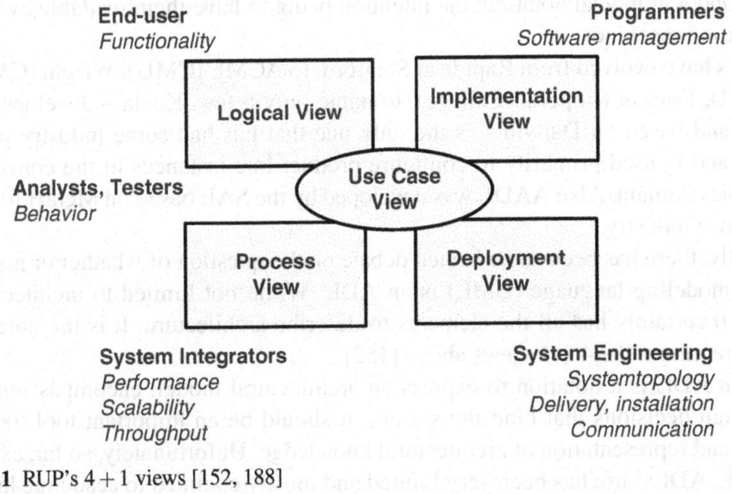

Fig. 3.1 RUP's 4 + 1 views [152, 188]

well-defined set of architectural concerns. A viewpoint is a set of conventions for the construction, interpretation, and use of a given architectural view. In a way, the viewpoint is to a view what the legend is to a map [158]. Of great importance are the view correspondences, that is, the relationships that exist between the elements in one view and the elements in another view.

Much has been written on the concept of views for architectural description, in particular by a group at the SEI led by Paul Clements [71] in their 2003 book *Documenting software architecture: views and beyond* and by Rozanski and Woods [270] who introduced the refinement of *perspective*. The IEEE standard 1471–2000 [155] provides a guide for describing the architecture of complex, software-intensive systems in terms of views and viewpoints, but it does not offer a detailed description of the rationale that guides the architecting process (see below).

3.3.2 Architecture Description Languages

Over the last 20 years computer scientists in academia around the world have tried to create architecture description languages (ADLs) to capture, represent, and reason about essential elements of the conceptual architecture of a software-intensive system. This follows the long tradition of programming languages: no computer scientist would be "complete" who has not created his or her own language, and the compiler that goes with it.

What ADLs have in common is that they are able to denote essential elements of an architecture – components, package, as well as the relationship between these components: connectors, interfaces, and to a certain extent some of the characteristics and behaviour of these components and connectors – so that some form of analysis, verification, and reasoning can occur, to derive or assess completeness, consistency, ambiguity, performance, and other qualities. ADLs often offer both a textual and a graphical notation, the intention being to have them readable by both humans and machines.

ADLs have evolved from Rapide at Stanford, to ACME (CMU), Wright (CMU), C2 (UCI), Darwin (Imperial College), to name only a few. Koala – developed by Philips and based on Darwin – is the only one that has had some industry penetration, and is used primarily to configure product-line instances in the consumer electronics domain. Also AADL was developed by the SAE based on MetaH for the automotive industry.

Finally, there has been some heated debate on the question of whether or not the unified modeling language (UML) is an ADL. While not limited to architecture, UML 2.0 certainly has all the elements to describe architecture. It is the notation used to represent the 4 + 1 views above [152].

As an ADL is a notation to express an architectural model, encompassing the key design decisions that bind the system, it should be an important tool for the capture and representation of architectural knowledge. Unfortunately, so far, except for UML, ADLs' use has been very limited and mostly confined to academic labs.

3.3.3 Application-Generic Knowledge: Patterns, Standards, Frameworks

When moving from application-specific to application-generic knowledge, across a domain or a technology or simply a community of architects, some application-generic architectural knowledge can be developed and captured, using pretty much the same tools and techniques we've seen above in Sect. 3.3.1 and 3.3.2.

Patterns and Frameworks
Tagging behind the work of the famous "Gang of Four", Buschmann and his gang of five captured architectural patterns [64] followed by a few others: SEI [74]. These patterns are technology neutral. But others can be technology and/or domain specific, such as the architectural patterns developed in Microsoft's practice and patterns group's handbook [225]. More ambitious, an architectural framework is a set of common practices for architectural description established within a specific domain or stakeholder community; it identifies generic concerns, and some predefined viewpoints which frame these concerns. Examples of frameworks are TOGAF (The Open Group Architectural Framework), MoDAF, the Zachman Framework, RM ODP and ISO 19439 (FDIS).

Standards
IEEE Std 1471 [155] was the first formal standard for architectural description, in active use since 2000. In 2007, IEEE 1471 became an international standard. Now ISO and IEEE are jointly revising the standard as ISO/IEC 42010, *Systems and Software Engineering – Architecture Description* [158].

There are new knowledge mechanisms in ISO/IEC 42010. In a sense, every standard is knowledge-based, embodying a community consensus by creating a filter on the world through its definitions, and establishing rules on what to do when those definitions apply. An important element of IEEE 1471:2000 was the explicit conceptual model (or ontology) upon which the standard was built. That model has been useful in codifying architectural practice, in education and in advancing the state of the practice. The most obvious knowledge mechanisms in ISO/IEC 42010 are those reflecting resources readily reusable by architects from one project to another: architecture-related concerns, stakeholder identification, and architectural viewpoints.

In the ongoing revision (working draft 3, Nov 8, 2008), ISO/IEC 42010 [158] is considering several new mechanisms:

- *Codifying architectural frameworks*: for large-scale reuse and knowledge sharing
- *View correspondences*: for linking between views
- *Architectural models and model types*: for finer-grain reuse
- *Enhanced architecture rationale and decision capture*

where IEEE 1471 codified a terminology base and best practices applicable to individual architecture descriptions, ISO/IEC 42010 introduces a further level of conformance in defining the notion of an architecture framework, which we define here as a set of best practices for a particular community or domain, characterized by a set of concerns, stakeholders, viewpoints, and the correspondences between those viewpoints.

From a knowledge perspective, the hope is that many of the practices currently called architecture frameworks in the community can now be defined in a uniform way, thereby raising the level of understandability and interoperability – some might say "reusability" – among architects working within different paradigms. One mechanism added to support architecture frameworks is view correspondence rules, a notion that was not ready for standardization in 2000 (R. Hilliard, personal communication).

Methods

Finally, methods pertaining to software architecture do also capture some architectural knowledge. This is the case for the Siemens method [147], IMB's RUP [152], the many SEI methods: ADD, ATAM, QAW [177, 34] or the *Software Architecture Review and Assessment* handbook [236], for example.

3.4 Architectural Design Decisions

3.4.1 What Is an Architectural Design Decision?

In his 2003 paper, Jan Bosch [48] stressed the importance of design decisions as "a first class citizen", but did not describe in detail what they consist of. Tyree and Ackerman describe the structure of an architectural design decision (see Table 1.1 in Chap. 1) [325]. Kruchten in [190], then with Lago and van Vliet in [192], introduce a more detailed template for documenting design decisions, particularly stressing relationships between design decisions and between design decisions and other artifacts. Tang [314], Dueñas and Capilla [66, 103] have variations, and the SHARK workshop in 2006 attempted to reconcile all these views.

Here is an example of attributes of an architectural design decision, from [190] and [192]:

- *Epitome (or the Decision itself).* This is a short textual statement of the design decision, a few words or a one liner. This text serves to summarize the decisions, to list them, to label them in diagrams, etc.
- *Rationale.* This is a textual explanation of the "why" of the decision, its justification. Care should be taken not to simply paraphrase or repeat information captured in other attributes, but to add value. If the rationale is expressed in a complete external document, for example, a tradeoff analysis, then the rationale points to this document.
- *Scope.* Some decisions may have limited scope, in time, in the organizations, or in the design and implementation (see the overrides relationship below). By default, (if not documented) the decision is universal. Scope might delimit the part of the system, a life cycle time frame, or a part of the organization to which the decision applies.

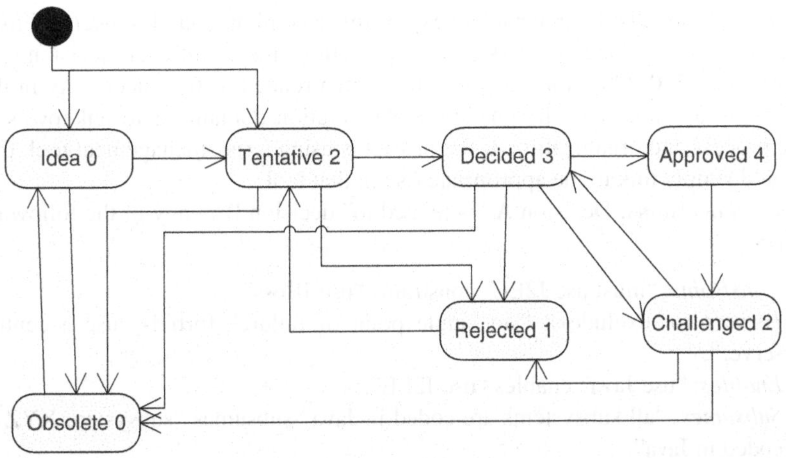

Fig. 3.2 Possible state machine for a decision, from [190]

- *State*. Like problem reports or code, design decisions evolve in a manner that may be described by a state machine (see Fig. 3.2):
  - *Idea*. Just an idea, captured so it is not lost, when brainstorming, looking at other systems etc.; it cannot constrain other decisions other than ideas.
  - *Tentative*. Allows running "what if" scenarios, when playing with ideas.
  - *Decided*. Current position of the architect or architecture team; must be consistent with other related decisions.
  - *Approved*. Approved by a review, or a board (for low-ceremony organizations, not significantly different than decided).
  - *Challenged*. A previously approved or decided decision that is now in jeopardy; it may go back to approved without ceremony, but can also be demoted to tentative or rejected status.
  - *Rejected*. A decision that does not hold in the current system; but we keep them around as part of the system rationale (see subsumes below).
  - *Obsolesced*. Similar to rejected, but the decision was not explicitly rejected (in favour of another one, for example), but simply became "moot," irrelevant, e.g., as a result of some higher-level restructuring.
- *Author, Time-stamp, History*. The person who made the decision and when. Ideally we collect the history of changes to a design decision. State changes are important, but so are changes in formulation and scope, especially with incremental architectural reviews.
- *Categories*. A design decision may belong to one or more categories. The list of categories is open ended. Categories are useful for queries and for creating and exploring sets of design decisions that are associated with specific concerns or quality attributes.
- *Cost*. Some design decisions have an associated cost, so it is useful to reason about alternatives.

- *Risk*. Traditionally documented by exposure – a combination of *impact* and *likelihood* factors – this is the risk associated with taking a particular decision (see IEEE Std 1540-2001, for example). It is often related to the uncertainty in the problem domain, or to the novelty of the solution domain, or to unknowns in the process and organization. If the project is using a risk management tool, this should simply link to the appropriate risk in that tool.
- *Related decisions*. Decision A "is related to" decision B in any of the following ways:

  - *Constrains*: "must use J2EE" constrains "use JBoss".
  - *Forbids* (or excludes): "sin single point of failure" forbids "use a central server".
  - *Enables*: "use Java" enables "use J2EE".
  - *Subsumes*: "all subsystems are coded in Java" subsumes "subsystem XYZ is coded in Java".
  - *Conflicts with*: "must use dotNet" conflicts with "must use J2EE".
  - *Overrides*: "the Comm subsystem will be coded in C++" overrides "the whole system is developed in Java".
  - *Comprises* (is made of, decomposes into): "design will use UNAS as middleware" decomposes into "rule: cannot use Ada tasking" and "message passing must use UNAS messaging services" and "error logging must use UNAS error logging services" and, etc.
  - *Is Bound to* (strong): A constrains B and B constrains A.
  - *Is an Alternative to*: A and B address the same issue, but propose different choices.
  - *Is Related to* (weak): There is a relation of some sort between the two design decisions, but it is not of any kind listed above and is kept mostly for documentation and illustration reasons.

  See Fig. 3.3 for an example.

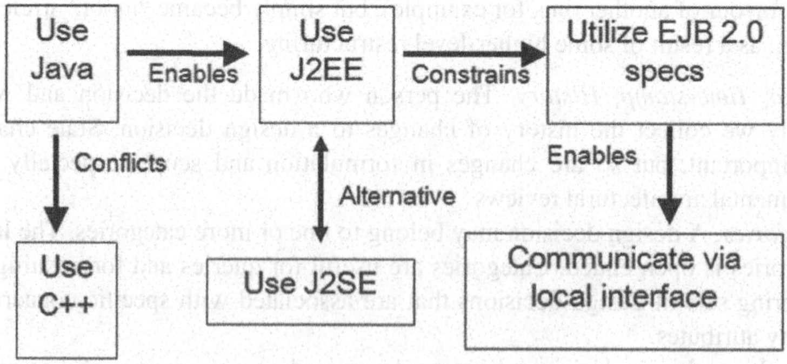

Fig. 3.3 Example of relationship between design decisions, from [203]

- *Relationship with External Artifacts.* Includes "traces from," "traces to," and "does not comply with." Design decisions trace to technical artifacts upstream: requirements and defects, and artifacts downstream: design and implementation elements. They also trace to management artifacts, such as risks and plans.

These relationships are almost as important as the decisions themselves. It is through these relationships that decisions can be put to practical use: understanding part of the rationale – the reason for certain decisions, for the choices made from among several alternatives, for the incompatibilities between choices – impacts the analysis of "what is affected if we were to change X, or Z?"

3.4.2 A Taxonomy of Architectural Design Decisions

Architectural design decisions do not all play the same role in the architecting process. Some are tightly coupled to the design itself, and can be traced directly to some element (e.g., a class, a process, a package or subsystem, an interface) in the system under development; other decisions are general properties or constraints that we impose to the system, that sets of elements must satisfy, and, finally, some are linked to the general political, sociological, and cultural environments of the development or deployment.

3.4.2.1 Existence Decisions ("ontocrises")

An existence decision states that some element/artifact will positively show up, i.e., will exist in the system's design or implementation.

There are structural decisions and behavioral decisions. Structural decisions lead to the creation of subsystems, layers, partitions, and components in some view of the architecture. Behavioral decisions are more related to how the elements interact together to provide functionality or to satisfy some nonfunctional requirement (quality attribute) or connector. Examples:

Dextrous Robot (DR) shall have a Laser Camera System.

DR shall use the Electromagnetic (EM) communication system to communicate with GroundControl.

In themselves, existence decisions are not that important to capture since they are the most visible element in the system's design or implementation, and the rationale can be easily captured in the documentation of the corresponding artifact or element. But we must capture them to be able to relate them to other, more subtle decisions, in particular to alternatives (see Fig. 2.1).

3.4.2.2 Bans or Nonexistence Decisions ("Anticrises")

This is the opposite of an existence decision, stating that some element will not appear in the design or implementation. In a way, they are a subclass of existential decisions.

It is important to document bans precisely because such decisions are lacking any "hooks" in traditional architecture documentation. They are not traceable to any existing artifact. Ban decisions are often made as possible alternatives are gradually eliminated.

3.4.2.3 Property Decisions ("Diacrises")

A property decision states an enduring, overarching trait or quality of the system. Property decisions can be design rules or guidelines (when expressed positively) or design constraints (when expressed negatively), of a trait that the system will not exhibit. Properties are harder to trace to specific elements of the design or implementation because they are often cross-cutting concerns, or they affect too many elements. Although they may be documented in some methodologies or process in design guidelines (see RUP, for example), in many cases they are implicit and rapidly forgotten, and further design decisions are made that are not traced to properties. Examples:

DR motion should be accurate to within +1 degree and +1 inch.

DR shall withstand all loads due to launch.

3.4.2.4 Executive Decisions ("Pericrises")

These are the decisions that do not relate directly to the design elements or their qualities, but are driven more by the business environment (financial), and affect the development process (methodological), the people (education and training), the organization, and, to a large extent, the choices of technologies and tools. Executive decisions usually frame or constrain existence and property decisions. Examples:

- Process decisions:
  All changes in subsystem exported interfaces (APIs) must be approved by the CCB (Change Control Board) and the architecture team.
- Technology decisions:
  The system is developed using J2EE.
  The system is developed in Java.
- Tool decisions:
  The system is developed using the System Architect Workbench.

Software/system architecture encompasses far more than just views and quality attributes à la IEEE std 1471-2000 [155]. There are all the political, personal, cultural, financial, and technological aspects that impose huge constraints, and all the associated decisions are often never captured or they only appear in documents not usually associated with software architecture.

3.4.3 Visualization of Set of Design Decisions

There are two delicate issues with sets of architectural decisions:

- How to capture them (and how much)?
- How to visualize them?

Capture is a process or method issue and will be covered in a subsequent chapter. How many decisions and how much information must be captured are hard questions that relate to the other, more fundamental, question: what is the scope of architecture? In Chap. 1 we stressed that architecture is a global, high-level, early process, aimed at making hard, long-lived, and hard-to-change choices. Still pertinent to the issue of knowledge representation is: how do we represent sets of interrelated decisions?

Assuming that we have captured a set of architectural design decisions, along the lines of Sect. 3.4.1 above, how would we want to visualize them? The tabular approach is not very exciting (see Fig. 3.4).

We can also represent architectural design decisions as graphs, stressing the relationships we have described in Sect. 3.4.1, but these graphs rapidly become very complex (see Fig. 3.5), and we need to introduce mechanisms for:

- *Eliding* (eliminating certain relationships), or zooming in and out (getting more or less information about decisions) (see Fig. 3.6).

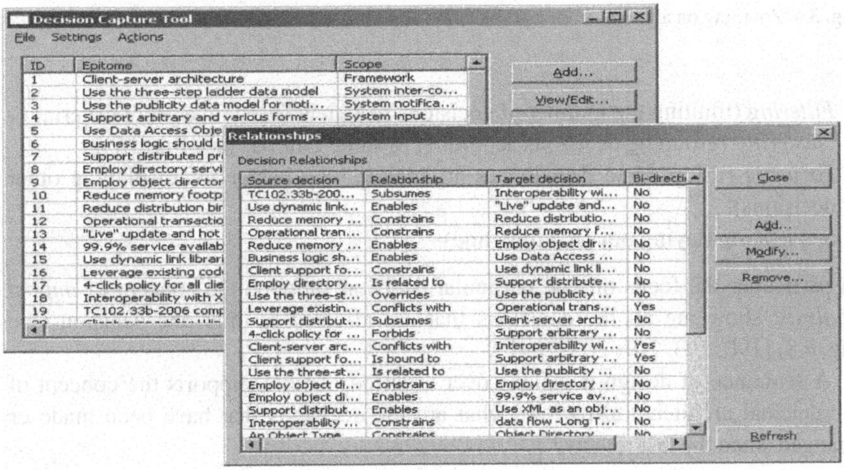

Fig. 3.4 The tabular representation (from [202])

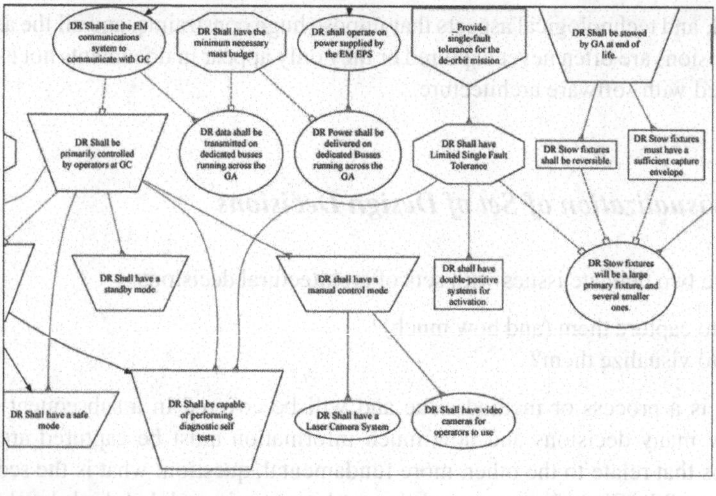

Fig. 3.5 Decision graph from Spar Aerospace Dexterous Robot (fragment) [190]

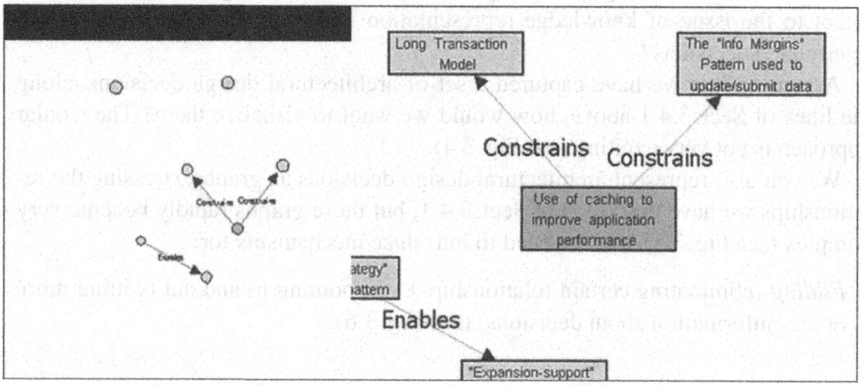

Fig. 3.6 Zooming on a graph (from [203])

- *Filtering* (limiting the number of decisions in a view based on a set of criteria) or *clustering* (grouping decisions according to some criteria) (see Fig. 3.7).
- *Focusing* (using some decision as an anchor, or a center for displaying other decisions).
- *Sequencing* (laying out on a time line).

In particular, the focus on one particular decision supports the concept of *impact analysis*: show me all the decisions that are affected by this one decision (see Fig. 3.8) [190, 193, 201, 203, 204].

A sequence of design decisions over a period of time supports the concept of incremental architectural review: what are the decisions that have been made or changed since the last review?

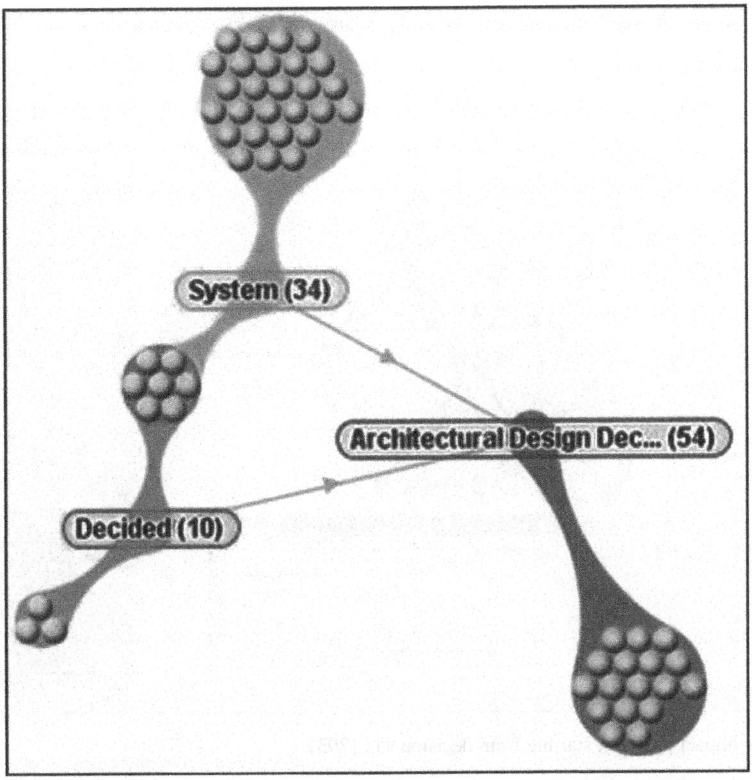

Fig. 3.7 Clustering decisions by classes (from [192])

3.4.4 A "Decisions View" of Architecture

If *views and viewpoints* are a good practice to document the design, and if a *set of design decisions* offers a good complement in capturing (externalizing) additional architectural knowledge, then there might be a way to combine the two approaches for more cohesiveness and homogeneity. This is what Dueñas and Capilla [103] have done in proposing a decision view of software architecture in which decisions are entangled with design for each architectural view.

This new perspective extends the traditional views that are described in the IEEE Std. 1471 [155] by superimposing the design rationale that underlies and motivates the selection of concrete design options. Figure 3.9 depicts a graphical sketch of the "decision view" [103, 191] in which design decisions are attached in the "4 + 1" view model [188].

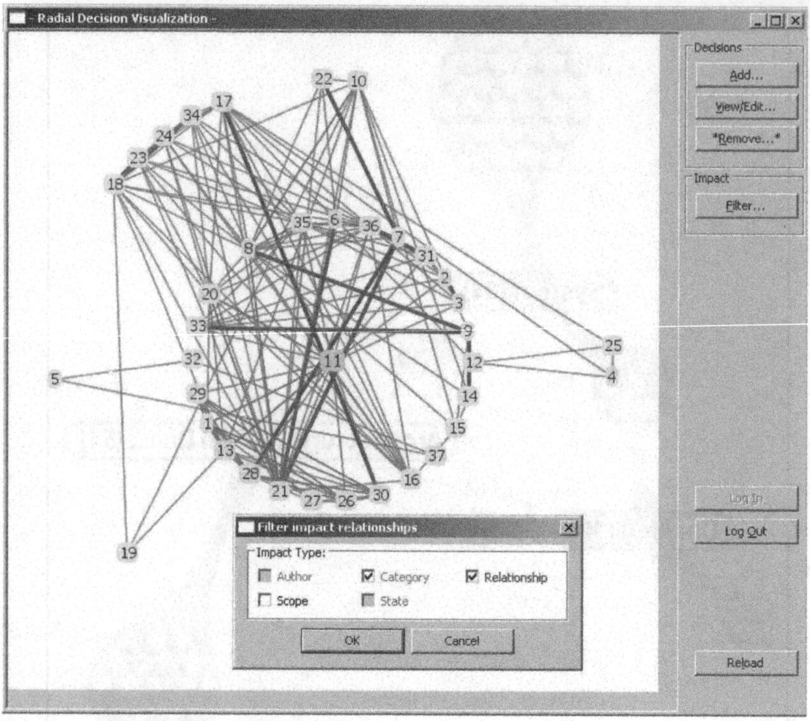

Fig. 3.8 Impact analysis, starting from decision #11 [203]

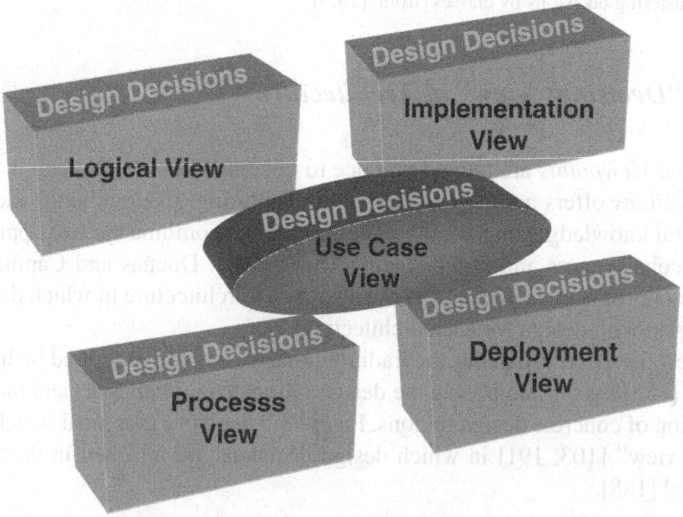

Fig. 3.9 A decision view embedded in the 4 + 1 views (from [191])

3.5 Rationale, or, the Missing Glue

Rationale, that is, an explicit articulation of the reasoning, the motivation of the choice implied by the decision, has been present in the mind of software architect all along; it was explicit in the formula of Perry and Wolf in 1992 [250]. The rationale can range from a simple pointer to a requirement to an elaborate trade-off analysis between alternative solutions. Often, it also has to show that various constraints or previous decisions are taken into account. But, in practice the effort to develop tools to capture and manage design rationale has not been very successful, as Jintae Lee eloquently described [200]. The primary reason is that capturing rationale, except for a handful of important decisions; it is too tedious and does not bring any immediate benefits to the person doing the capture. The benefit is largely down the line, weeks or months later and for stakeholders others than the decision maker.

We found that much of the rationale is actually captured by the relationship between design decisions (DDs) and other elements, in particular by tracing DDs to requirements (upstream), to other decisions (see above), and to elements in the design and its implementation (downstream).

3.6 Metaphors

There is one constant, though, throughout the whole (short) history of software architecture, and regardless of the formality of the approach: it is the systematic use of *metaphors* to describe architectural elements an architectures. Metaphors give meaning to *form* and help us ground our conceptual systems. A metaphor is a form of language that compares seemingly unrelated subjects: a rhetorical trope that describes a first subject as being equal or very similar to a second object in some way. A metaphor implies a *source domain*: the domain from which we draw metaphorical expressions, and a *target domain*, which is the conceptual domain we try to understand or to describe. The metaphor operates a cognitive transfer from the source to the target; it says in essence: "<the target> is <the source>."

In *Metaphors we live by* [197], Lakoff and Johnson describe metaphors as "a matter of imaginative rationality." They permit "an understanding of one kind of experience in terms of another, creating coherence by virtue of imposing gestalts that are structured by natural dimensions of experience. New metaphors are capable of creating new understanding and, therefore, new realities." (p. 235)

Metaphors are everywhere in software architecture. We use so-called *ontological metaphors* to name things: "clients and servers", "layers", "pipes and filters", "department stores and shopping cart," etc. We organize those using *structural metaphors* that are often visual and spatial: "on top of", "parallel to", "aligned with", "foreground, background", but include richer ones such as "network", "web", or "hierarchy" [245]. We use a wide variety of containers: "packages", "repositories", "libraries", "volumes", etc. In reality, in the target domain, i.e., in the memory of a computer, we would not find any up, down, aligned, packaged, etc. everything is pretty scattered around; just look at a "core dump" file.

A *mapping* is the systematic set of correspondence that exists between constituent elements of the source and the target domains. It allows some limited reasoning in the target domain by analogy and inference. In our case, the target domain – software architecture – is rather abstract, and we try to draw from source domains that are much more concrete. Then we use inference patterns from the source conceptual domain to reason about the target one. "Ay, there's the rub, for" we may abuse the inference or have a faulty inference. This leads to flawed metaphors, where the analogy "breaks" and the meaning in the target domain (in software) is confusing at best. It is also very common when we attempt to combine multiple metaphors, drawing form different source domains.

Metaphors have been used to describe general organization of software systems; they have played an important role in the object-oriented movement, and then were really put at the center of the pattern movement. No reasonable pattern can be successful that is not supported by an elegant metaphor [64, 130]. More recently Beck in *eXtreme Programming* (XP) described a practice he called "metaphor" to convey the concept of a simple summary of the architecture [38]. It is unfortunate that this practice has been the least successful of XP. Beck should have boldly called it *Allegory*: an extended metaphor in which a story is told to illustrate an important attribute of the subject, or even a *Parable*!

3.7 Summary

To return to our premises: Why do we want to represent architectural knowledge explicitly? We want to:

- Gain intellectual control over a sophisticated system's enormous complexity.
- Ensure the continuity, allowing these large systems to more effectively evolve and to be maintained.
- Transfer this knowledge to others.

More tactically, we want to be able to

- Analyze and evaluate architectures, implement them, evolve them, assess some of their qualities
- Support planning, budgeting, or acquisition activities

The more this architectural knowledge is left implicit, the more difficult or risky these activities will be. Moreover, we also want to be able to abstract some more generic architectural knowledge out of our collective knowledge in a given domain or with given technologies. This knowledge is a combination of the following.

1. Architectural design, generic, brought in by using expert architects, education, framework, methods, and standards. They are templates, exemplars of our models.

2. Architectural design, for the system under development, expressed using a combination of appropriate notations and tools, adapted to the concerns of the various parties involved (viewpoints). They are models of the system.
3. Architectural decisions, for the system under development, with their complex interdependencies, and tracing upstream to requirements, context, and constraints, and tracing downstream to the design, and even the implementation. They explain why the models are the way they are.

Chapter 4
Strategies and Approaches for Managing Architectural Knowledge

Torgeir Dingsøyr

Abstract Knowledge management is a large interdisciplinary field, and for companies focusing on knowledge management, there are different possible strategies and approaches. This chapter seeks to give an overview of the main approaches of knowledge management that has been studied in other research disciplines, with emphasis to research that has been done in software engineering. In particular, this chapter will identify the main pros and cons of approaches in relation to managing architectural knowledge.

4.1 Introduction

As described in the introduction to this book, knowledge management is a large interdisciplinary field. When a company wants to improve knowledge management practices, there are many possible options. The different options will focus on different types of knowledge. Some will require little resources, while other options might require heavy investments over time. Any knowledge management approach is dependent on humans, and the number and degree of involvement will vary between the options that are available. This chapter seeks to give an overview of the main approaches of knowledge management that has been studied in other research disciplines. I will give particular emphasis to research that has been done in software engineering, building on a recent systematic review on knowledge management in software engineering [41]. Further, I will use examples from studies to show aspects of the possible approaches. Finally, I will discuss what the main pros and cons of different approaches are in relation to managing architectural knowledge.

In the introduction, we distinguished between two main types of knowledge, namely the tacit knowledge that humans are not able to express explicitly, such

---

Torgeir Dingsøyr
Department of Computer and Information Science, Norwegian University of Science and Technology (NTNU), NO-7491 Trondheim, Norway, e-mail: dingsoyr@idi.ntnu.no

M. Ali Babar et al. (eds.), *Software Architecture Knowledge Management*,
DOI: 10.1007/978-3-642-02374-3_4, © Springer-Verlag Berlin Heidelberg 2009

as "how to ride a bike", and explicit knowledge, which is available in reports, books and informal or formal communication. Hansen et al. argued in an influential paper in Harvard Business Review published in 1999 [143], that companies should focus primarily on one of two strategies for knowledge management:

- Codification – to systematise and store information that constitutes the knowledge of the company, and to make this available to the people in the company.
- Personalisation – to support the flow of information in a company by having a centralised store of information about knowledge sources like a "yellow pages" of who knows what in a company.

Earl [107] has further classified work in knowledge management into schools (see Table 1.3). The schools are broadly categorised as "technocratic", "economic" and "behavioural". The technocratic schools focus on information technology or management in supporting employees in knowledge-work. The economic school focuses on how knowledge assets relates to income in organisations, and the behavioural schools focus on orchestrating knowledge sharing in organisations.

Choosing a knowledge management strategy means to take a high-level decision on either codification or personalisation, and then suggestions for actions can be taken from a relevant school. Some have argued that one should combine the schools, for example in settings such as global software development [92]. The main reasons for focusing on codification is in order to reuse knowledge (for an example hereof, see Chap. 12). Knowledge, which has been codified once can be reused many times. This is what many consulting companies do, and a strategy that requires heavy use of information technology. Critics of the codification strategy would argue that often, knowledge will be difficult to transfer across different contexts. Knowledge might become irrelevant or even misleading, and it will take much resources to maintain such knowledge. Personalisation is then a strategy that requires less information technology resources, but where it is crucial to make arenas where people who have knowledge to exchange can meet. In software engineering, the recent focus on agile software development [106] is a choice to mainly rely on tacit knowledge transfer, which is a personalisation strategy.

Earl's knowledge management schools will support different strategies. The codification strategy is supported either through the systems or engineering school. The personalisation strategy is supported either through the cartographic, organisational or spatial school. In the next sections, I will present approaches in the technocratic and behavioural schools, which I believe is relevant to managing architectural knowledge. I will not address the commercial and strategic schools, as they focus on issues more relevant for management in a company than the development department. Finally, I will discuss criteria for selecting an approach in Sect. 4.3.

4.2 Technocratic Approaches to Knowledge Management

The technocratic schools are the *systems school*, which focuses on technology for knowledge sharing, using knowledge bases or "repositories"; the *cartographic school*, which focuses on knowledge maps and creating knowledge directories;

and the *engineering school*, which focuses on processes and knowledge flows in organisations. I will now describe each of these schools more in detail.

4.2.1 Systems

The underlying principle of the systems school is that knowledge should be codified in knowledge bases. A knowledge base or knowledge repository stores knowledge, experience, and documentation, sometimes about one particular topic, for example "load testing of web applications". How the base is filled with information varies between repositories, some allow all employees to freely write down experience (such as in a wiki), while others have an editing process to make sure that experience is documented in a standard manner. Davenport and Prusak [89] divide between three types of knowledge repositories:

- External knowledge repositories such as competitive intelligence.
- Structured internal knowledge repositories, such as research reports, product-oriented market material.
- Informal internal knowledge repositories, such as reports of "lessons learned".

In software engineering, there are several studies of both structured internal repositories (a central concept in the Experience Factory [33]), and of informal internal repositories.

One of the studies of knowledge repositories in the software engineering literature describes a system, which is used extensively over time [99]. A screenshot is shown in Fig. 4.1. This example shows the simple structure of a note of experience; a title, describing text, keywords and the author of the experience note.

Examples of notes from this company were "how to remove garbage from an image in SmallTalk", "technical problems with cookies" and "an implementation of the soundex algorithm in Java".

The study reports that the repository worked as "a behavioural arena that people use in different ways, to create a culture of knowledge sharing, and [the tool] lets people experience that others make use of their knowledge". The tool was promoted by posters for example outside the staff canteen.

The study further shows that the knowledge repository was in heavy use in the company. Almost all of the developers interviewed in the study mentioned that they were using it, and had contributed with writing experience notes. However, the managers were not as active in using the notes as others. The study found five types of usage of the knowledge repository:

1. Solve a specific technical problem.
2. Get an overview of problem areas.
3. Avoid rework in having to explain the same solution to several people.
4. Improve individual work situation by adjusting technical tools.
5. Find who has a specific competence in the company.

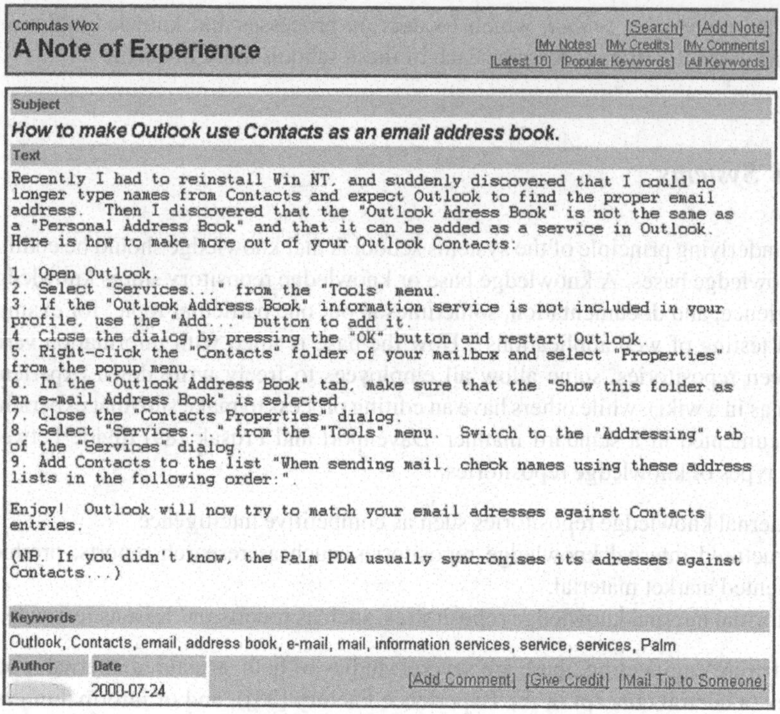

Fig. 4.1 A screenshot from a knowledge repository from a software consulting company

The combination of an easy to use tool and social incentives was identified in the study as reasons for the success of the knowledge repository.

A critique of this approach to knowledge management has been that such repositories are often not used in practice, creating what is referred to as "information junkyards". The systematic review of knowledge management research in software engineering [41] identified one more study in addition to the one described above, which shows that such tools are actually in use. The case studies show that it is possible to successfully implement knowledge repositories. Further the studies show that benefits can be realised quickly and a repository can be used for other purposes that support knowledge management than originally intended. However, it is important to note the importance of the context of the study, in particular the social incentives for knowledge management.

What kind of implications does these findings have on knowledge repositories aimed at architectural knowledge? First of all, a knowledge repository requires a certain number of users to make it cost-efficient. For small companies, it will probably make sense to make use of a personalisation strategy as much as possible. Some knowledge, however, will be of such a kind that is difficult to transfer orally, and some kind of codification is needed. A lesson learned from the studies in software engineering is to try to keep the structure of a repository as simple as possible.

4.2.2 The Cartographic School

The principal idea of the cartographic school is to make sure that knowledgeable people in an organisation are accessible to each other for advice, consultation, or knowledge exchange. This is often achieved through knowledge directories, skills management systems or so-called "yellow pages", which can be searched for information as required.

Skills can be broadly categorised in two groups – technical skills: Knowledge about technology issues, and soft skills: Competencies of a more personal and social flavour, like organising and handling complexities in project work, enabling people to contribute with their resources, and customer communication.

It is of major importance to get the right people with the right soft and technical skills to work on software development projects. Many companies have developed knowledge management tools to assist them in the tasks of managing technical skills, by surveying what kind of knowledge people have, and make an index of it. The process of surveying and indexing and making this type of information available, I will refer to as skills management, and I will focus on technical skills in the following.

A study from a software company reports on how tools for managing skills are used [100]. What purposes do such tools serve, and do they satisfy needs other than the expected use in resource allocation?

The tool in the study would indicate employee experience levels of 250 technical skills, such as "testing and testing techniques" in Fig. 4.2. Employees would rate themselves between "irrelevant" and "masters fully". In addition to the current level, people would indicate which level they wanted to be at in the future.

The tool was found to be in use for resource allocation and for short-term problem solving by identifying and asking experts on topics. Also, the problem solving had a long-term effect in letting employees know who to ask next time. Further, the skills management tool is used for identifying new project opportunities and to support skills upgrading. The tool was found to support learning practices and motivates use at both an individual and company (projects and processes) level. This double capability enabled integration and knowledge exchanges both vertically (between organisational levels) and horizontally (between individuals and projects).

Some employees were critical to how people evaluated their skills, others questioned the level of detail on the available skills, and yet others felt that information on soft skills was lacking.

But all in all, it seems that the usage of the tool was very much implanted in the daily work of the organisation, and the tool supports a multitude of functions.

An argument for this school is that although it requires a technical infrastructure, the investment is low because there is no need to codify knowledge.

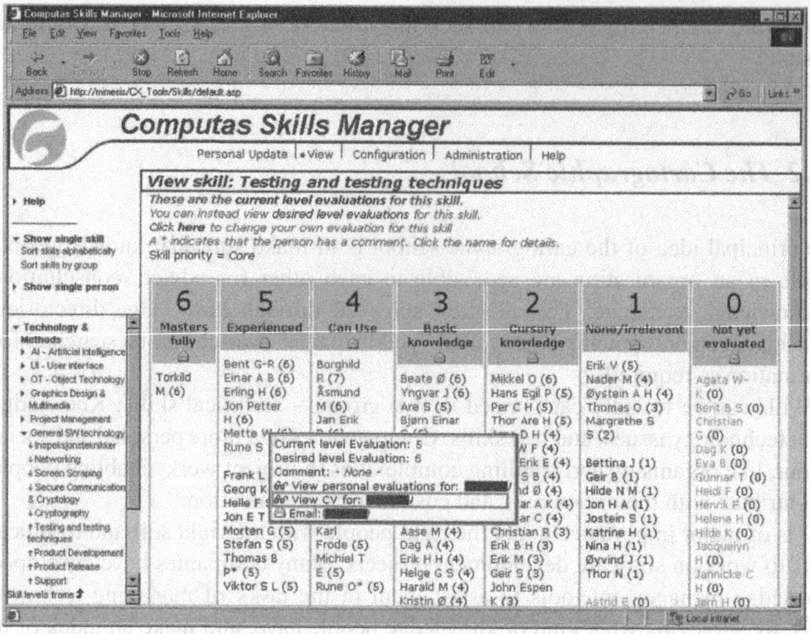

Fig. 4.2 A skills management system from a software consulting company

How might this school be relevant for managing architectural knowledge? It does not seem to be any studies of actual use of such systems for managing architectural knowledge in the software engineering research literature. However, for companies that employ a large number of people, knowledge of the particular skills of software architects would be valuable, in order to solve architectural problems that emerge, or for inviting people with particular skills to discussion or planning meetings.

4.2.3 The Engineering School

The engineering school of knowledge management has its roots in business process reengineering. Consequently it focuses on processes. The systematic review on knowledge management in software engineering found two major categories of engineering school approaches. The first contains work done by researchers who investigate the entire software process with respect to knowledge management. The second contains work done by researchers who focus on specific activities and how the process can be improved within this activity. The specific activities were formal routines, mapping of knowledge flows, project reviews, and social interaction.

In relation to development processes for software, the systems and engineering schools support sharing of explicit knowledge. Both of these schools require a technical infrastructure in order to facilitate knowledge sharing. However, a finding both

1. Discuss pros and cons of the software architecture in the initial design meeting. Document major design decisions as well as their rationale.
2. Organise discussions about the quality of the architecture during development; especially focus on the architecture's unforeseen consequences for the development.
3. Analyse the architecture after implementation through technical analysis of source code, CVS logs and other explicitly available information – look for suspicious effects. This step focuses on architectural knowledge derived from the evolution of the system.
4. Gather the responsible people for software architecture in a workshop - examine initial pros and cons of the architecture, suspicious effects, and ask:
   - Which major decisions were right?
   - Which major decisions were not right?
5. Challenge the architecture and enact the learning process through:
   - Analyse the impact of scenarios on architectural decisions;
   - Reason about the associated rationale, to identify whether/how it may change;
   - Modify the rationale and/or the architectural decisions to accommodate the scenarios;
   - Update the overall documentation of architectural knowledge.
6. Finally, analyse the cost and benefits of suggested architectural changes, and implement the most beneficial ones.

Fig. 4.3 Double-loop learning

from studies in other fields of the systems school [170] and studies of a specific engineering approach, electronic process guides, is that it is difficult to get such technology in actual use [98]. However, many companies have invested in such infrastructure, and this indicates that we need a better understanding of the factors that lead to effective knowledge sharing within these two schools.

Whether focusing on processes in general, or specific processes, the focus in this school is on making descriptions of processes so that work can be done more effectively or with higher quality than without such support. An example suggested process within management of architectural knowledge, is the described in Fig. 4.3, which aims at producing "thorough" learning, what some refer to as double-loop learning [97].

I have not found studies of how processes for managing architectural knowledge work in practice, but there are many frameworks for evaluating architecture, which has a learning component, for example ATAM [176]. However, findings from software engineering indicate that it is impossible to rely only on process descriptions when performing work tasks, access to human experts or discussion partners will be equally important. Also, studies from software engineering show that it is possible to define and implement software process in a beneficial and cost-efficient manner in small software organisations. However, special considerations must be given to their specific business goals, models, characteristics, and resource limitations.

4.3 Behavioural Approaches to Knowledge Management

The behavioural school consists of three subschools: 1) the organisational school, which focuses on networks for sharing knowledge; 2) the spatial school, which focuses on how office space can be designed to promote knowledge sharing; and 3) the strategic school, which focuses on how knowledge can be seen as the essence of a company's strategy. With respect to architectural issues, I believe the first two schools are relevant. The strategic school focuses of how knowledge management is used at a management level, and would not offer concrete guidance with respect to product development.

4.3.1 The Organisational School

The organisational school focuses on describing the use of organisational structures (networks) to share or pool knowledge. These structures are often referred to as "knowledge communities" or "communities of practice" [55]. A community of practice has been defined as "Groups of people who share a concern, a set of problems, or a passion about a topic, and who deepen their knowledge and expertise in this area by interacting on an ongoing basis" [336].

A central concept with communities of practice is what McDermott [222] calls the "double-knit" organisation. Double-knit refers to the fact that communities of practice are another form of cohesion in a company than the normal organisation in departments or projects. This gives employees larger networks for informal knowledge sharing, which can have positive effects.

A community of practice can be established or built on existing communication in a company. Typically, a group of people with common interests will meet regularly to discuss their topic of interest, and in addition to discussions develop tools or other artifacts, which are useful in their own work. For example, for larger software companies who organise their development work in projects, it would be natural to foster networks on topics that are relevant to most projects, like testing, project management and architecture. Table 4.1 shows possible benefits of a community of practice for the organization and for individuals.

Table 4.1 Possible benefits of communities of practice (from [336])

	Short-term value	Long-term value
Benefits to the organization	Arena for problem-solving Quick answers to questions Coordination	Use knowledge strategically Foresee technical developments
Benefits to the individual	Access to expertise Help with challenges	Forum for expanding skills Network in the organization

There are few studies of how such networks are applied in practice in software engineering. We find three studies of such networks, describing the role of networks and how they can be applied in improving software development processes. A finding in one study is that networks are likely to be successful if they are based on informal networks that may exist prior to the formal introduction.

With respect to software architecture, the organisational school is a low-cost opportunity for companies that have a sufficient number of employees working with or interested in architecture to establish a forum. General knowledge management studies advice that people-oriented approaches are used in addition to codification initiatives, and communities of practice is then a possible choice.

4.3.2 The Spatial School

How can office space be designed for knowledge sharing? This is the central question in the spatial school. The systematic review on knowledge management in software engineering did not identify works in this area, but this is something, which many companies use both to support creative processes and to give an image of themselves as "modern". Central arenas for knowledge sharing can be around the water cooler, coffee machine, printer or canteen, it can be meeting rooms for different purposes, like rooms especially designed for brainstorming. Whether employees use cubicles, open-plan offices or cell offices, are decisions that will impact knowledge sharing. In agile software development, some attention has been given to how the design of the office space allows informal communication, and especially on how status information is shown on "walls". Such walls are popular to make status information visible for team members and for colleagues, and typically display the information shown in Fig. 4.4.

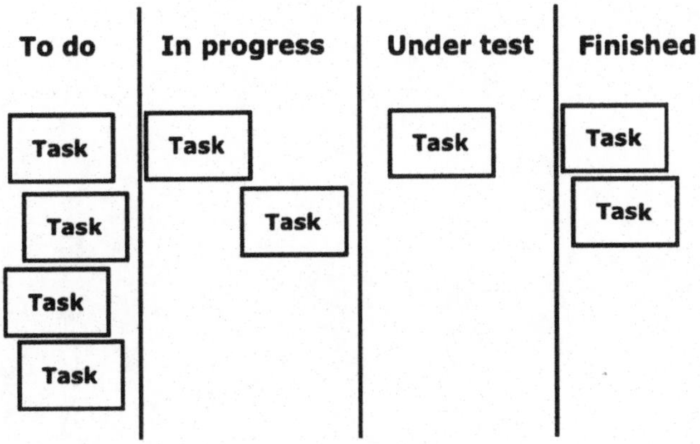

Fig. 4.4 A typical scrum wall, showing status of tasks

Could this school be relevant for managing architectural knowledge? Several elements could be relevant, both using the physical space available to show architectural design, status and discussions. Also, software architects could be placed in open-plan offices in order to stimulate learning, if they do not reside with development project teams.

4.4 Summary

As we have seen in the previous sections, there are many options when focusing on knowledge management, and many are relevant for knowledge related to software engineering and to architectural knowledge.

Software companies who want to establish better knowledge management practices need first of all to decide on which strategy is most important for them relating to the architectural knowledge. Is the knowledge that is important for the company of a kind, which can be shared between people, or is it of such a kind that some form of codification is needed. The size of the company and number of software architects and software development projects will be important when choosing a strategy. Larger volumes will in most cases require a greater need for codification. However, the nature of the knowledge to be shared is also important, architectural knowledge might be of a form, which makes codification more efficient than for example oral communication. Companies who have chosen agile development methods might benefit from managing architectural knowledge in the same way they manage other software engineering knowledge, through oral communication in frequent meetings and using visual assistance, like showing architectural information on a wall.

Chapter 5
Supporting the Software Architecture Process with Knowledge Management

Muhammad Ali Babar

Abstract The aim of this chapter is to describe how the software architecture process can benefit from providing knowledge management support to the software development professional in general and software architects in particular. This chapter focuses on the kinds of support that can be provided to capture and manage architectural knowledge consumed or generated during the software architecture process. The chapter briefly describes different activities of the software architecture process and identifies the kinds of actors involved and their respective knowledge needs. It shows how to organize different elements of architectural knowledge into a meta-model that can be initiated for tailoring organizational specific knowledge models and developing tool support. This chapter is based on the premise that managing knowledge is a management task rather than a technical problem of representing knowledge. Hence, this chapter finally discusses the management aspects by presenting a task model of managing architectural knowledge.

5.1 Introduction

Chapter 1 has provided an introduction and brief description of the important theoretical concepts related to the research and practice of software architecture and knowledge management disciplines. This chapter intends to identify the needs of knowledge management for different activities of the software architecture process and how various approaches, techniques, and tools can be used to capture and manage the knowledge that is required or generated during the software architecture process. By now, it has been mentioned many times that software architecting is one of the most important processes in developing and evolving large scale software-intensive systems. For the research in this chapter, software architecture is an artifact as well as the process used to develop and maintain that artifact, which is composed

Muhammad Ali Babar
Lero, Limerick, Ireland e-mail: malibaba@lero.ie

M. Ali Babar et al. (eds.), *Software Architecture Knowledge Management*,
DOI: 10.1007/978-3-642-02374-3_5, © Springer-Verlag Berlin Heidelberg 2009

of several large and small design decisions. Like any other process, the software architecture process also involves various activities, tasks, roles, and artifacts.

Software architecting is considered a complex and knowledge-intensive process [320, 268]. The complexity lies in the fact that software architecting involves a lot of decision making. Several dozens of tradeoffs need to be made to satisfy current and future requirements from a potentially large set of stakeholders, who may have competing vested interests in architectural decisions [3, 137]. The knowledge required to make suitable architectural design decisions and to rigorously evaluate those design decisions is usually broad, complex, and evolving. The requisite knowledge can be technical (such as patterns, tactics, and quality attribute analysis models) or contextual, also called Design Rationale (DR), (such as design options considered, tradeoffs made, assumptions, and design reasoning) [10]. The former type of knowledge is required to identify, assess, and select suitable design options for design decisions. The latter is required to provide the answers about a particular design option or the process followed to select that design option [104, 139]. We consider both kinds of knowledge as architectural knowledge, which is characterized by the information that is required or generated during the software architecture process consisting of several activities such as *architectural analysis*, *architectural synthesis*, *architectural evaluation*, *architectural implementation* and *architectural maintenance* [9, 146, 313]. All of these activities require and generate technical as well as contextual architectural knowledge. Hence, we assert that management of architectural knowledge is vital for improving an organization's architectural capabilities. Researchers and practitioners agree that if not appropriately managed, knowledge underpinning the key architectural decisions is lost, and hence is unavailable to support subsequent decisions to maintain and evolve the software architecture of a system [10, 23, 325].

Software architecture researchers and practitioners have developed several approaches to support the different activities of the software architecture process. However, until recently there has been little effort spent on providing appropriate guidance and/or effective infrastructure for capturing and managing the details on which design decisions are based, along with explanations of the use of certain types of design constructs (such as patterns, styles, tactics and so on). Chapter 12 provides one example hereof. It has been mentioned that such information may prove quite valuable throughout the software development lifecycle [48, 109]. The unavailability of suitable and systematic approaches to capturing and sharing architectural knowledge may preclude organizations from growing their architectural capabilities and reusing architectural assets. Moreover, the knowledge concerning the domain analysis, architectural patterns used, design alternatives considered and evaluated, and design decisions made is implicitly embedded in the architecture and/or becomes the tacit knowledge of architects [48, 320, 325].

Recently, there have been several efforts aimed at improving the quality of the software architecture process by developing effective knowledge management approaches, techniques, and tools (hereafter called architecture knowledge management (AKM) technologies) to facilitate the management of explicit and implicit architectural knowledge generated during the architecting process; see Chap. 6. This chapter is aimed to enumerate different activities and tasks involved in the software architecture process and to describe how those activities and tasks can be supported by knowledge management. It seems pertinent to mention that the major objective of knowledge management is to improve business processes and practices by utilizing individual and organizational knowledge resources. These include skills, capabilities, experiences, routines, cultural norms, and technologies [256]. It has already been mentioned in Chap. 1 that the software architecture process needs or generates both explicit and implicit knowledge. These are mutually complementary entities that interact with each other in various creative activities [234]. In the context of this chapter, we define architecture knowledge management as an approach to improving the software architecture process outcomes by introducing various processes and practices for identifying, capturing architectural knowledge and expertise and making it available for transfer and reuse across projects in an organization. More formally, we use the definition of knowledge management provided in [109] according to which knowledge management *"is the process that deals with systematically eliciting, structuring and facilitating the efficient retrieval and effective use of knowledge. It involves tacit knowledge of experts and explicit knowledge, codified in procedures, process and tools. Knowledge management stretches from know-how to know-what and know-why."*

5.2 Software Architecture Process

The software architecting process can be considered a macro level process, which may involve several micro-level processes composed of many activities and tasks for designing, documenting, evaluating and maintaining software architectures for systems. The software architecture community (i.e., researchers and practitioners) has proposed several design methods and models such as Attribute-Driven Design (ADD) method [34], Business Architecture Process and Organization (BAPO) [15], the rationale unified process, and Siemens' 4 Views (S4V) [147]. Others have focused on providing architecture evaluation frameworks and process models such as architecture tradeoff analysis method (ATAM), architectural level modifiability analysis (ALMA), and quality-driven architecture design and quality analysis method [220]. Recently, some researchers have proposed a general model of architecture design based on five previous design models [146] (see also Chap. 1). However, this model covers only three activities of the software architecture process:

1. Architectural analysis aims to define the problems to be solved. An architect examines architectural concerns and context in order to come up with a set of architecturally significant requirements.
2. Architectural synthesis aims to design architectural solutions for a set of architecturally significant requirements. An architect may consider several available design options before selecting the ones that appear to be the most appropriate and optimal.

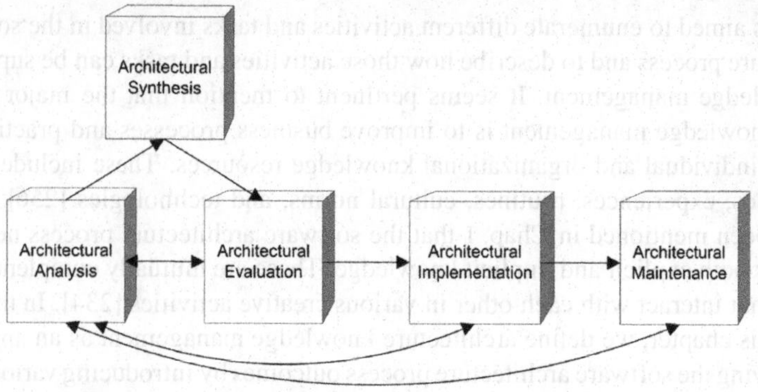

Fig. 5.1 A model of the architecture life cycle (reproduced from [313])

3. Architectural evaluation intends to ensure that the architectural solutions chosen during the previous activity are the right ones. Hence, the proposed architectural solutions are evaluated against the architecturally significant requirements.

There are two important points to be noted about the activities involved in this general model of architecture design. First, the abovementioned activities do not follow a sequential process as the waterfall model. Rather, these activities are undertaken in a quite iterative/evolutionary manner and tasks related to one particular activity can be performed and/or revisited while performing any other activity. Second, it is asserted that these are only three stages of the lifecycle of a software architecture that also needs to be implemented and maintained. Since one of the main goals of capturing architectural knowledge is to support architecturally related activities such as implementation and maintenance of a system and its software, we have extended the Hofmeister et al. model [146] to include the later stages of the lifecycle of a software architecture (see Fig. 5.1):

4. Implementing architecture involves designers and developers making several decisions for detailed design and implementation. Hence, they need to ensure that their decisions are in conformance with the architecture designed by an architect.
5. Maintenance of architecture involves making architectural changes as it evolves because of enhancement and maintenance requirements, which places several new demands on the architecture underpinning a system. From the knowledge management perspective, prior design decisions are reassessed for the potential impact of the required changes and new decisions are made to accommodate the required changes without having damaging effects on the architectural integrity.

We will limit our focus on the knowledge management support for the main stages of the lifecycle of software architecture: architectural analysis, architectural synthesis, and architectural evaluation.

5.3 Knowledge Management Problems

It has been mentioned that the software architecture process aims to solve a mix of ill- and well-defined problems, which involve processing a significant amount of knowledge. Architects require topic knowledge (learned from text books and courses) and episodic knowledge (experience with the knowledge) [268]. One of the main problems in the software architecture process is that the knowledge underpinning the design decisions and the processes and activities leading to those decisions [10, 48] is usually not sufficiently captured and managed. Hence, such knowledge is not available or not easily accessible if needed later on. This type of knowledge involves things like the rationale for selecting and the impact of certain middleware choices on communication mechanisms between different tiers, why an API is used instead of a wrapper, and who to contact to discuss the performance of different architectural choices.

Much of this knowledge is episodic and usually not documented [320]. The absence of a disciplined approach to capturing and managing architectural knowledge has many downstream consequences. These include:

- The evolution of the system becomes complex and cumbersome; resulting in violation of the fundamental design decisions
- Inability to identify design errors and
- Inadequate clarification of arguments and lack of information sharing about the design artifacts and process.

All these cause loss of substantial knowledge generated during the software architecture process, thus depriving organizations of a valuable resource, loss of key personnel may mean loss of knowledge [139, 165, 320].

Software architecture researchers and practitioners have developed several methods (such as a general design model [146], APTIA [173], ATAM[72], PAS [338]) to support the different activities and tasks of the software architecture process in a disciplined manner. Some of these do emphasize the need and importance of managing architectural knowledge to improve reusability and grow organizational capabilities in the architecture domain. Except for [71], there is no approach that explicitly states what type of knowledge needs to be managed and how, when, where, or by whom. Also, none of the current approaches provides any conceptual framework for identifying the required knowledge and tasks to be performed in order to provide the required knowledge. Our previous research has concluded that the lack of suitable techniques, guidance, tools, and resources is one of the main reasons that practitioners and organizations are not able to design and deploy appropriate knowledge management strategies to support the software architecture process [10, 12].

To address the issues caused by the general lack of knowledge management support throughout the lifecycle of the software architecture, researchers have recently been quite active in developing appropriate approaches and suitable tools for introducing the knowledge management in the software architecture process. One of the most focused topics among architecture knowledge management researchers has been the identification and modeling of knowledge claimed to be needed during the software architecture process. Researchers have also identified the architectural knowledge needed by software development teams, and have proposed the kinds of incentives required to encourage people sharing architectural knowledge. Other researchers have identified Use Case Models for managing architectural knowledge [193]. These Use Case Models identify the actors who either consume and/or generate architectural knowledge, and the Use Cases describing different ways in which the identified actors can capture or use the architectural knowledge using an appropriate knowledge repository. In order to provide suitable tooling support for the identified knowledge needs and actors, software architecture researchers have used either existing knowledge management tools [2, 193] or have developed new ones (see Chapter 6).

The main objective of the architecture knowledge management technologies (e.g., methods, techniques, tools) being developed is to help organizations as well as individuals to capture and manage the different kinds of architectural knowledge needed to support the software architecture process. Once the architectural knowledge needed to support the software architecture activities have been identified, it can be organized to provide some guidance for assessing and appropriately using the existing architecture knowledge management techniques and tools or developing the new ones where required.

5.4 Knowledge Needed

In this section, we describe the architectural knowledge needed to support the different activities of the software architecture process in more detail. The activities that are specifically addressed from the knowledge management perspective are shown in Fig. 5.2, which also identifies some of the elements of architectural knowledge either used or generated during the software architecture process.

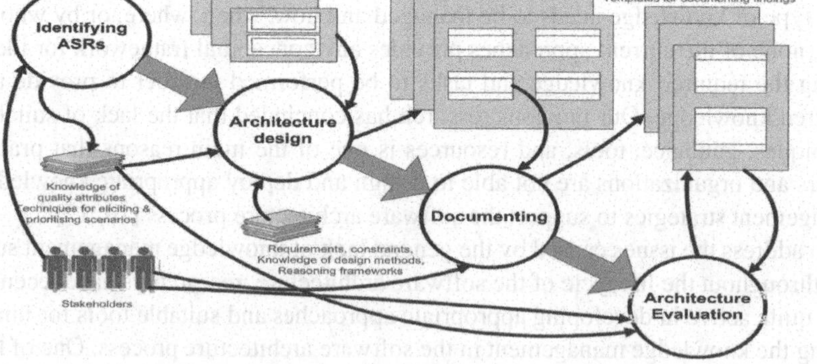

Fig. 5.2 A model of software architecture process (Adapted from [146])

Before we can discuss the knowledge needed or generated during different activities of the software architecture process, it is appropriate to also describe who are the potential consumers or producers of architectural knowledge. As previously mentioned, several researchers have presented architecture knowledge Use Case Models, which identify the actors who are expected to use, produce, and exploit architectural knowledge. Some of these actors are software architects, project manager, developers, researchers, maintainers, analysts, reviewers, and students. The descriptions of these actors can be found in [193]. It has been mentioned that in this chapter we would limit our discussion about those actors' knowledge needs that are usually involved in the activities shown in Fig. 5.2.

Figure 5.2 shows some of the key activities of the software architecture process, which usually starts with the identification of , also called quality attributes. The ASRs are usually derived from business goals in Quality Attribute Workshop (QAW [29]) kinds of sessions in which all major stakeholders participate. During this activity the stakeholders' need to have access to quality attributes' knowledge, general scenarios, and domain knowledge. The stakeholders are expected to bring with them the knowledge about the business drivers, organizational expectations of the system being developed and contextual and technical constraints. Such knowledge is explicated during the QAW sessions. Such knowledge is considered architectural knowledge as it usually guides the architectural decisions. Such knowledge needs to be captured for future reference, only scenarios may not be enough. The facilitator of the QAW workshop should have access to knowledge about the process to be followed, artifacts to be consulted or created, and pre- and post-conditions of each of each of activity in this process. It should also be known if there are some templates to be used in order to capture the knowledge and how to customize those templates based on the project or organizational requirements.

A software architect makes design decisions to satisfy the architectural requirements. Such decisions are made in an iterative process in which an architect or design team identify the available options, evaluate them for tradeoff analysis and select the most appropriate ones considering the technical, business, and organizational constraints. This process can be either ad-hoc or systematic by following the steps recommended by a design method such as Attribute Driven Design (ADD), which exploits the knowledge of architectural styles and design tactics. As shown in Fig. 5.2, the architecture design decisions are mainly motivated by ASRs, which provide the criteria used to reason about and justify the architectural choices [35]. The ADD method follows a recursive decomposition process in which each stage of decomposition results in certain decisions by choosing suitable architectural tactics and patterns to satisfy a set of ASRs. Architects usually enlist several design options, which are based on architectural patterns or tactics, that are expected to have the potential of satisfying different architecturally significant requirements characterizing the required quality attributes. The process of selecting suitable design options has implicit or explicit analysis of each available design option or tradeoff analysis between different design options [3]. Hence, the knowledge about different design methods, requirements constraints, quality attribute models, architectural styles and patterns and their potential impact on different quality attributes is usually needed to support the design decision making process. The architecture design activity produces knowledge about the assumptions underpinning the design decisions, tradeoffs performed, constraints considered, weaknesses, and strengths of the chosen design decisions and the rejected ones.

Once made, architectural design decisions need to be documented to support the subsequent design, analysis and development decisions. Software architecture community emphasizes the importance of documenting architecture design in terms of views (see Chap. 3), each view presents a different perspective of the architecture. During this activity, software architects need the knowledge about different approaches to describing software architectures (such as IEEE 1471 [155], V&B [71], and 4 + 1 [188]), guidelines on tailoring such approaches for specific situations, policies and procedures for documenting architectural decisions, and the kinds of contextual knowledge that should be captured. Moreover, they also need to know if there are generic or company specific templates to be used for describing key architectural decisions and rationale underpinning those design decisions. Additionally, it is also important to know which views are important to cater the needs of stakeholders.

Architecture design, documentation, and evaluation are iterative steps in the process [35]. Architecture evaluation attempts to ensure that the architectural decisions are the right ones. The main tasks of the software architecture evaluation activity are: generating utility tree for characterizing quality attributes with scenarios, identifying suitable reasoning frameworks to be used, determining and understanding architectural approaches (e.g., styles, patterns, and tactics) used, evaluating the proposed architectural approaches with respect to quality attributes and tradeoffs required, prototyping or simulating parts of the architectures that appear problematic, appropriately and sufficiently recording evaluation findings along with the rationale and justifications, and visualizing the risks and risk themes with an appropriate mechanism such as a results tree.

In order to perform these and other knowledge-intensive and complex tasks, software architects and reviewers need to have knowledge about the available architecture evaluation methods (such as reported in [39, 72]), and techniques and how to tailor them based on the contextual constraints. Several researchers have reported comparative and evaluation studies of software architecture evaluation methods in [13, 101, 174] that can be a good source of knowledge about the architecture evaluation methods and techniques. Based on more than ten years of research in software design and analysis methods and techniques, researchers from the Software Engineering Institute (SEI) have also proposed ten principles of architecture design and analysis [173]. A good knowledge of these principles and how to apply them is expected to improve the software architecture process and artifacts. Moreover, the evaluation team also needs to know the rationale and contextual constraints underpinning the proposed architectural choices. Such knowledge is expected to be sufficiently captured during the architecture design and documentation and made available to evaluators through a knowledge repository or suitable tool.

Having been evaluated an architecture is implemented. The architecture is also maintained in the face of changes and evolution. A modification request with architectural implications may results in the beginning of the whole cycle of the architecting process starting with identifying ASRs [35]. There are several kinds of knowledge required to support these two activities, however, a discussion about these activities is not within the scope of this chapter. Table 5.1 presents the main points of this chapter.

5.5 Architectural Knowledge Organization

Having identified the key kinds of architectural knowledge required or consumed during the software architecture process, the identified knowledge needs to be organized in a conceptual model. We assert that a conceptual model for organizing architectural knowledge can help organizations to define and obtain data on various aspects of their architectural assets and design rationale during the software architecture process. A model of architectural knowledge is also one of the earliest artifacts needed for the development of an automated system for storing and accessing the data that underpins the architecture design knowledge [182]. An appropriate conceptual model is a prerequisite for developing an integrated support environment to assist in the improvement of a certain software development process [166] such as the software architecture process for which knowledge management support needs to be provided. Recently, the software architecture community has proposed several models of organizing architectural knowledge such as reported in [2, 10, 44, 155].

These approaches model the process and artifacts related to architectural knowledge either using data modeling or Ontological approaches. Each of these approaches conceptualizes architectural knowledge based on the literature, field studies, and the experiences of the model's developers. These approaches describe the architectural knowledge consisting of entities and their properties, relationships among those entities and constraints enforced on them. These approaches identify the knowledge about the process, techniques, and artifacts used or generated by stakeholders when dealing with software architectural aspects of a system. However, these approaches model the architectural knowledge at different levels of abstractions, which are either too fine-grained or too coarse-grained; some of them also combine the models of elements that make up architectural knowledge as well as the activities to be performed on that knowledge.

We argue that a meta-model is needed in order to represent the architectural knowledge organizations that can provide a framework for building tailored models for representing architectural knowledge and building appropriate tooling support. Hence, we have developed a meta-model to represent a high level organization of architectural knowledge that has been identified as required by the different activities of the software architecture process presented in Sect. 5.4. Figure 5.3 shows the meta-model that consists of primitives or semantic elements, which characterize the

Table 5.1 Summary of the activities, tasks, participants and needed AK for the software architecture process

Activity name	Main tasks	Major participants	AK needed
Architectural analysis	The main tasks are: examine architectural concerns and context in order to come up with ASRs. Identify main quality attributes. Develop quality sensitive scenarios. Prioritize the scenarios. Facilitate a workshop as QAW.	Evaluation manager/project manager/evaluation team/architect and whoever required	Business goals, organizational processes and procedures, general scenarios, concrete scenarios, guidelines for running a QAW workshop, similar systems developed.
Architectural synthesis	The main tasks during this stage are: clarifying and understanding ASRs, identifying suitable design options, evaluating the design options with respect to desired level of different quality attributes, performing tradeoffs, selecting suitable design decisions.	Architect and senior software designers	Generic design options, architectural styles and design patterns, tactics. Rationale underpinning previous design decisions and quality attributes. Knowledge about the existing or future systems to be integrated.
Architectural evaluation	The main tasks are: generating utility tree, selecting suitable reasoning frameworks, assessing the suitability of design decisions and used patterns, recording findings and justifications for them, and building a results tree to visualize risks and non-risks.	Evaluation team, architect and all major stakeholders.	Rationale for design decisions. Reasoning framework, styles, patterns, and tactics. Checklists of tasks to be performed during evaluation, information about different architecture evaluation process models and methods. Standards and procedures to be followed and templates for recording evaluation findings.
Architectural implementation	The main tasks are: making detailed design and implementation decisions, implementing design, ensure implementation complies with architectural decisions and other constraints.	Designers and developers	Reasoning Knowledge to understand the architecture design, implementation standards, strengths and weaknesses of implementation frameworks.
Architectural maintenance	Many of the tasks performed during the previous stages. Impact analysis is performed to assess potential effects.	Developer, designer, and architect.	Apart from the knowledge required during the previous stages, justification for changes, and impact analysis techniques.

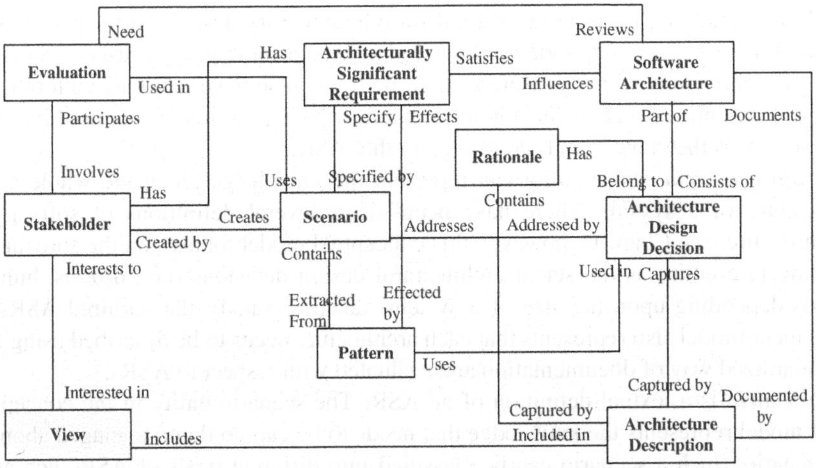

Fig. 5.3 A model of organizing architectural knowledge for supporting the software architecture process

constructs and terminology used when describing the software architecture process and its artifacts.

The model has been built by abstracting entities and their relationships from several available models such as DAMSAK [10], IEEE 1471 [155], and the SARA report [236]. The process of constructing this model was guided by the principles of the Entity Relationship (ER), a formal modeling methodology [36], and by using the Unified Modeling Language (UML) for database design [230]. Since the models upon which the meta-model is based have been taken from the literature or have been assessed with reference to the literature on software architecture such as reported in [155, 236], we do not consider the need of evaluating this meta-model. Following paragraphs provide a brief description of each entity and the type of architectural knowledge that is captured by each of them.

The *Stakeholder* entity characterizes those people who have any kind of interest in the architecture process or product [236] such as developers, testers, managers, evaluators, maintainers and many more [72]. This entity aims to manage the knowledge required to keep track of the people who contribute to or consult a knowledge base. Such information can be used to design a recognition program for motivating people to contribute or use an architectural knowledge repository. This entity also helps manage the knowledge about how a stakeholder is related to architectural significant requirements, scenarios, architectural views, and evaluation performed on a proposed software architecture.

Architecturally significant requirements (ASRs) are those requirements that have broad cross-functional implications. Such requirements are often called non-functional requirements (NFRs), also called quality attributes (QAs) [34, 236], but can also include functional aspects such as security functionality. This entity is used to describe and explain the various aspects of an ASR. Such as the relation of an

ASR with patterns to be used in a software architecture designed to satisfy that ASR. An ASR can be supported or hindered by one or more patterns used in a particular architecture decision. Moreover, an ASR can also have relations with other knowledge entities such as Stakeholders that may have proposed or opposed it and the scenarios that have been used to specify that ASR.

Software architecture entity can represent the knowledge about the whole architecture of a system. There have been given several definitions of software architecture (see Chap. 1), however, this conceptual model focuses on the software architecture entity as the set of architectural design decisions (i.e., dozens, hundreds depending upon the size of a system) taken to satisfy the required ASRs. The meta-model also represents that each architecture needs to be described using a standardized way of documentation and evaluated with respect to ASRs.

Scenario is a textual definition of an ASR. The scenario entity in the conceptual model represents the knowledge that needs to be captured and managed about a scenario. Such a scenario can be classified into different types of ASR such as availability, reliability, and modifiability [34]; a scenario can be either elicited from a stakeholder or distilled from a pattern. Moreover, a scenario also has a history of changes made to it. An abstract scenario can help identify one or more analysis models to analyze design decisions. The knowledge about a scenario also includes how it is related to other architectural knowledge entities such as stakeholders, patterns, and architecturally significant requirements.

Pattern characterizes known solutions to recurring problems in a particular context [130]. The pattern entity represents the pattern-specific knowledge. In the conceptual model, the term pattern denotes design pattern, architecture patterns, or architectural styles. A pattern provides a mechanism for documenting and reusing design knowledge accumulated in terms of problem, solution, forces, and usage examples by experienced practitioners. According to our organization of architectural knowledge, each pattern can be related to the architectural design decisions in which it is being used; scenarios that may have been extracted from that pattern; and ASRs that may be positively or negatively impacted by that pattern.

Architecture design decision entity represents the knowledge that needs to be captured and managed about the design decisions that make up a software architecture. An architectural design decision is a high level design decision taken to satisfy a set of ASRs. If we conceptualize the architecture design process as a decision making activity, an architecture decision is a choice among design options based on certain criteria [139]. A decision may have a history of the changes made to it along with any consequences of the changes on the other decisions. There may be interdependency between various decisions. For example, an earlier decision may limit the options available or impose some constraints on subsequent decisions. Any changes in a decision should consider the consequences for the dependency relationships. Apart from the knowledge about the technical decisions taken to design an architecture, this entity also represents the knowledge about the process followed to make the design decisions.

Rationale entity represents the knowledge about the contextual information and reasons for making an architectural decision as well as design options considered and evaluated. The rationale entity also characterizes all the background information that may be used or generated during the process of making architectural design decision. Such information is valuable to people who deal with the product of the decision making process [48]. Each architectural design decision is supposed to have a rationale attached to it and that rationale is captured along with the architecture description. Hence, the Rationale entity is associated with both the architecture design decision and the architecture description entities.

Architecture Description entity characterizes the data required to document an architecture according to certain standards or approaches (see Chap. 3). The V&B [71] approach also emphasizes the need to capture information that cuts across several views as well as rationale for architectural design decisions. This entity is related to architecture description, software architecture, and view entities.

A *View* or an architectural view is a model of an architectural structure or other elements of software architecture from the perspective of a related set of concerns that interest to a particular group of stakeholders [155]. Views are used to describe a software architecture throughout its lifecycle for the specific purpose of understanding and analyzing the different aspects of system development and performance. This entity represents the contemporary practice in this discipline where views are a necessary part of any architectural description; and views provides stakeholders with necessary knowledge to design architectural structures and to understand different aspects of a system's design.

The *Evaluation* entity characterizes the architectural knowledge required and generated during architecture evaluation. It also captures and managed the knowledge about the activities undertaken to determine the quality of an architectural design decisions and to predict the quality of a system whose architecture comprises of the evaluated architectural design decisions. Moreover, it also represents the knowledge that is captured about the findings from evaluating a given architecture. This entity is related with stakeholders, who participate in evaluation, scenarios, which are used in evaluation, and the software architecture being evaluated.

5.6 A Model of Architecture Knowledge Management

Having identified the architectural knowledge consumed or produced in different activities of the software architecture process and presenting a meta-model to represent a high level organization of the key elements of the architectural knowledge, we are going to discuss the tasks required to manage architectural knowledge. The proponents of knowledge management discipline claim to help organizations to improve their technical capabilities and processes [89, 322]. Like many other disciplines, the methods, techniques and tools developed by the knowledge management community have raised great expectations in the software engineering community as well. The software engineering community has been investing significant amount of resources to leverage the knowledge management technologies to support different activities and tasks involved in developing software [41, 272]. The results from deploying knowledge management approaches in software engineering have been quite mixed because of several technical and non-technical factors [93, 121]. One important message that has emerged from all the successful and failed attempts of knowledge management in software engineering is that knowledge management as a discipline does not intend to ignore the value or need to address the key software development aspects, such as process and technology, nor does it seek to replace them. Instead, the knowledge management technologies (i.e., methods, techniques, and tools) work towards software process improvement by explicitly and systematically addressing the needs of managing knowledge. This includes acquiring, structuring, storing and maintaining knowledge [272].

Though, each of the knowledge management approaches mentioned in Chap. 1 (codification, personalization, hybrid) are being explored for supporting the architecture knowledge management, a vast majority of knowledge management initiatives in software architecture discipline have mainly adopted the codification approach backed by centralized repositories to store and disseminate architectural knowledge [7, 8]. While the codification supported by appropriate knowledge-based systems has proved useful in various areas of software engineering, it also suffers from serious limitations, which may turn the organizational knowledge repositories into knowledge graveyards [7]. To address the limitations of these approaches, organizations have recently started applying codification and personalization approaches in terms of a hybrid strategy: one of them in a primary and the other in a secondary role [139]. A hybrid approach to managing knowledge is considered an effective and efficient mechanism of maximizing the benefits of codification and personalization strategies for globally distributed software development teams [94].

We have already mentioned that this chapter is concerned with describing architecture knowledge management from the perspective of management tasks involved. To this objective, we have adopted a knowledge management task model to describe different aspects of architecture knowledge management support for the software architecture process. Like the work of other software engineering researchers reported in [104, 185], our approach to managing architectural knowledge can also be described using a knowledge management task model shown in Fig. 5.4. This model has been modified for architecture knowledge management based on the original model described in [256]. This model consists of two strategic and six operational tasks. These tasks are called the architecture knowledge management building blocks, which represent the activities directly related to managing architectural knowledge. The model presents an integrated approach to managing architectural knowledge. This means ignoring one or more of the building blocks can interrupt the cycle of managing architectural knowledge as described in [256]. For example, if contextual information about designing an artifact in a certain way is not preserved, it disappears from organizational or individual memory, making reusability of that artifact difficult. When a certain piece of knowledge about an architectural artifact disappears, it is called vaporization of architectural knowledge [48] and the tasks of the knowledge management models are intended to stem and/or minimize the architectural knowledge vaporization.

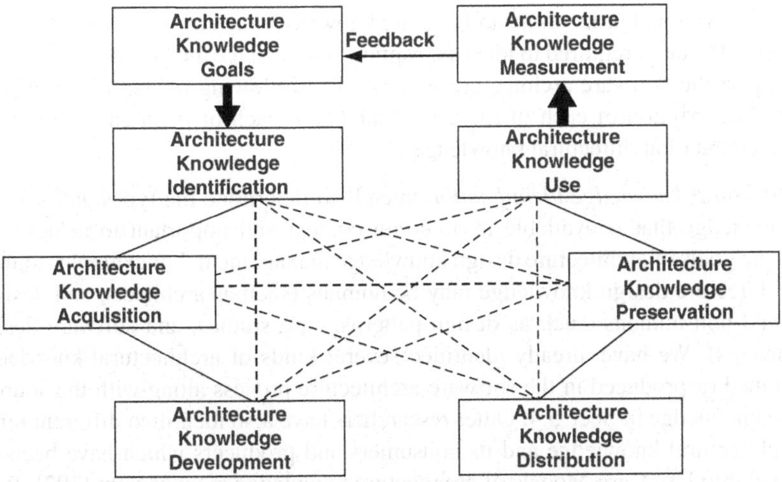

Fig. 5.4 A task model of architecture knowledge management

Setting and monitoring *architectural knowledge goals*, a strategic task, describes the objectives of managing knowledge and the expected benefits. For instance, some of the strategic goals for managing architectural knowledge can be to improve the software architecture process, provide a better support for architectural decision making, reusability of architectural artifacts, and effective and efficient architecture maintenance and evolution. Architectural knowledge measurement is another strategic level task aimed at ensuring the quality of the knowledge management process by comparing the results with the expected benefits. This task needs to define and assess several metrics for that purpose. For example, the number of concrete scenarios instantiated from general scenarios, the number of design options transformed into architecture decisions applied in different projects, and the number and positions of employees who accessed or contributed to organizational knowledge repository, and others.

The feedback from the *architectural knowledge measurement* results in modifications in the architectural knowledge goals. It is expected that the design and performance of these two strategic level tasks in any system of architecture knowledge management can be guided by the Quality Improvement Paradigm [32] and goal/question/metric (GQM) approach [33]. For example, the goal (G) of an architecture knowledge management initiative can be to improve the reusability of design decisions for architecting systems in the same domain such as online share trading applications. That specific goal can be decomposed into specific questions (Q) such as how many design decisions about a database connection management for scalability have been reused in similar applications. Each question can have associated concrete measures to be collected in order to answer the question and assess the achievement of the goal specified for improving the reusability of design decisions.

The operational tasks of the architecture knowledge management task model are related to the tasks required to identify, capture, and manage the knowledge required to support the software architecture process. The following paragraphs provide a general description of each of these tasks and how each of them can support the management of architectural knowledge:

Architectural knowledge identification intends to determine the types and sources of knowledge that is available in a certain context and important to achieve the strategic goals of architecture design knowledge management. For example, sources of architecture design knowledge may be humans (such as architects, and designers) and non-humans (such as design patterns, case studies, and software design documents). We have already identified several kinds of architectural knowledge consumed or produced in the software architecture process along with the sources of the knowledge in Sect. 5.4. Other researchers have also identified different kinds of architectural knowledge and its consumers and producers which have been organized into Use Case Models of architecture knowledge management [192]. Both of these sources have identified main kinds of architectural knowledge that needs to be acquired and managed for supporting the software architecture process as we describe in the following paragraphs.

Architectural knowledge acquisition is required to elicit the architectural knowledge from the sources of the knowledge determined as part of the previously described task. This is particularly important for implicit architectural knowledge. If the source of the implicit knowledge is humans then the performance of this task should take into account the socio-psychological aspects of gathering knowledge from humans, as human sources may not necessarily be motivated to give away their knowledge. There are several kinds of approaches, developed in the sociological and psychological disciplines, which can be exploited to acquire knowledge from human sources. We have enlisted several of such knowledge acquisitions techniques (such as interviews, brainstorming, repertory grid, protocol analysis, and Delphi technique) along with their respective advantages and disadvantages in [10]. For acquiring knowledge from literature and case studies, we have developed an architectural knowledge acquisition approach, call pattern mining [11]. We have demonstrated that this is very promising approach that can help organizations to distill great amount of knowledge from literature with relatively less amount of effort and time.

Architectural knowledge development purports to package, consolidate, and enhance the available architectural knowledge. This task is usually achieved through communicating the knowledge, integrating knowledge from different sources, and representing it in a certain format. For example, software architecture community has proposed several templates to organize and present architectural knowledge in a format that is considered succinct and able to represent the captured knowledge at a suitable abstraction level [2, 9]. The architectural knowledge development task can also exploit the concepts provided by the Experience Factory approach to improving software quality [32]. According to this approach, a separate business unit is responsible for identifying, acquiring, and repackaging reusable knowledge for improving the software quality by reusing knowledge and experience. We have also proposed similar approach to reusing architectural knowledge [9]. However, we do not recommend a separate business unit responsible for this task. Rather, we embed such task in the process of acquiring, managing, and reusing architectural knowledge.

Architectural knowledge distribution supports the distribution of knowledge to the relevant consumers in a relevant context. Acquired and developed knowledge needs to be distributed to those who need it. There can be several ways of distributing knowledge. Organizations need to identify, develop, and deploy the most effective and efficient mechanisms of distributing the knowledge. Researchers have developed approaches and tools for delivering context-aware knowledge to the developers [341], however, there is hardly any approach developed for delivering context-aware architectural knowledge to people working at the higher (i.e., architectural level) or lower (i.e., code level) levels of abstraction. Currently, this task is usually supported by knowledge management technologies, such as data repositories, various search mechanisms and web-based delivery channels. For example, we have developed a Web-based tool, PAKME (Sect. 6.4.2), to distribute architectural knowledge to collocated and distributed teams of software developers. EAGLE (Sect. 6.4.1) is another architecture knowledge management portal for improving architectural knowledge sharing. EAGLE supports the distribution of architectural knowledge by enabling stakeholders to connect to their colleagues or other involved stakeholders by retrieving "who is doing what" and "who knows what".

Architectural knowledge use aims at improving the return on investment made in the knowledge management initiatives. It is commonly known that even if knowledge is effectively acquired and efficiently distributed, there is no guarantee that the knowledge would also be used optimally. A successful performance of this task may require several incentives to increase the use of the knowledge, so organizational resources can be optimized by improving the use/reuse of the available knowledge. Moreover, people need to be trained in using/reusing available knowledge instead of inventing the wheel. Organizations need to define and deploy new processes in order to improve the reuse of the currently available knowledge. However, these processes need to be seamlessly integrated in the existing software development processes and activities, otherwise, people would reject new processes. We argue that software architects and designers are usually quite eager to reuse available knowledge in designing new systems as it is evident from the popularity of using design patterns, which are reusable knowledge of potential solutions to recurring problems. However, there should be sufficient training at the individual level as well at the team level to improve the reuse of architectural knowledge in an organization.

Architectural knowledge preservation intends to prevent uncontrolled loss of architectural knowledge. This task includes selection and storage of new knowledge as well as adaptation of existing knowledge (including controlled deletion). This supports one of the key factors to motivate the use, namely that the knowledge is kept updated. If knowledge is not kept updated or preserved, it tends to either loose its value for the potential users or disappears as people forget or move on other projects or jobs. Hence, there is a vital need to have appropriate processes and techniques to support this task of preserving architectural knowledge and keeping it updated.

Many of the current approaches to managing architectural knowledge recently proposed have been developed with the motivation of stemming the vaporization of architectural knowledge and preserving it along with other architectural artifacts in order to support the maintenance and evolution of software architecture.

5.7 Summary

This chapter aims to explain how the software architecture process can be supported by knowledge management. We have discussed different challenges caused by the lack of appropriate knowledge management support in the software architecture process. We have also identified the activities and tasks that need to be undertaken in order to manage the knowledge that is either consumed or produced during the software architecture process. To help provide appropriate mechanism of managing architectural knowledge, this chapter first identifies the knowledge that is relevant to the different phases of an architecture lifecycle. We have identified the knowledge needs of different stakeholders involved in the activities of the software architecture process. A meta-model has been presented that can help organize the architectural knowledge consumed or produced. This meta-model can be tailored to provide appropriate tooling support for managing architectural knowledge. Then, we have presented a task model of managing architectural knowledge. This task model identifies two strategic level and six operational level tasks that need to be performed in order to provide an integrated support mechanism for managing architectural knowledge. We have also explained the different approaches and measures that are required to perform each of the tasks of the architecture knowledge management task model.

We assert that the architecture knowledge management task model shown in Fig. 5.4 coupled with the theoretical concepts and practical approaches provided by different knowledge management school of thoughts as described in Chap. 1 and available tooling support as described in Chap. 6 can provide sufficient guidance, a framework and tools to provide knowledge management support throughout the lifecycle of a software architecture as shown in Fig. 5.1 following the software architecture process shown in Fig. 5.2. Moreover, the presented meta-model of Fig. 5.3 shows how to organize the knowledge needed by different stakeholders in order to benefit from or perform different tasks of the architecture knowledge management task model presented in this chapter.

Acknowledgement This work is partially supported by Science Foundation Ireland under grant number 03/CE2/I303-1. I am also thankful to my colleague Nour Ali for proofreading this chapter.

Part II
Tools and Techniques for Managing Architectural Knowledge

Architecture knowledge management is crucial in modern organizations acting in increasingly complex, dynamic and distributed IT markets. To remain competitive and create new opportunities, software professionals must be able to effectively manage the knowledge created during software architecting. As the size, scope and complexity of systems increase, more stakeholders need to be efficiently involved, both within the same organization and across different enterprises linked by various types of business relationships. Efficient involvement requires appropriate tools and techniques.

This part gives an overview of the tools and technological approaches that either explicitly or implicitly offer solutions for managing architectural knowledge. It addresses the problem of supporting architecture knowledge management from a technological and organizational perspective. Key questions discussed in this Part include: Who should use an architecture knowledge management tool? For what purposes? To what extent do current tools and technological approaches support architecture knowledge management? How can we support on-line architectural communities in modern organizations?

In answering these questions, the objectives of Part II are to explain what are the typical use cases characterizing architecture knowledge management, which use cases are supported by existing tools, and how the existing technologies can support the establishment and the management of on-line social networks and communities aimed at knowledge sharing in business contexts. This Part provides material for reflection to both researchers and practitioners about what already exists, and the related opportunities and future challenges.

Chapter 6 describes a number of use cases for architecture knowledge management tooling extracted and elaborated from both academic and industrial work. These support actors to consume, produce and maintain architecture knowledge, as well as to provide intelligent support for automating architecture knowledge management tasks. Peng Liang and Paris Avgeriou discuss nine tools on their support for knowledge types and management strategies, and emphasize their special focus with respect to more general architecture knowledge management features. A number of loose technologies and mechanisms are also discussed by indicating their possible contributions to the use cases.

While Chap. 6 looks at the tools and technologies offered to individuals for their everyday work, Chap. 7 provides a broader perspective on the technologies that can organize such individuals (and their preferred tools) into social networks and on-line communities aimed at knowledge sharing. This Chapter focuses on the distributed nature of managing architectural knowledge and the need for organizations to offer the best fitting networking platforms to support their employees in collaborating on-line and acting as social, knowledge communities. Patricia Lago explains peer-to-peer network models, Business Grids and Semantic Web as technological approaches for sharing architectural knowledge within and across organizations; Web 2.0 as new paradigm bringing innovation and openness in the way knowledge is shared on the Web, and Wiki's as a promising technology thereof. A reference framework of relevant architecture knowledge management aspects is used to compare and contrast the various approaches. In doing so, their potentials and combinations are highlighted and exemplified.

These chapters use many of the concepts defined in Part I and discuss the technological and organizational contexts exploited in various industrial practices reported in Part III.

Chapter 6
Tools and Technologies for Architecture Knowledge Management

Peng Liang and Paris Avgeriou

Abstract As management of architectural knowledge becomes vital for improving an organization's architectural capabilities, support for (semi-) automating this management is required. There exist already several tools that specialize in architecture knowledge management, as well as generic technologies that can potentially be used for this purpose. Both tools and technologies cover a wide number of potential use cases for architecture knowledge management. In this chapter, we survey the existing tool support and related technologies for different architecture knowledge management strategies, and present them according to the use cases they offer.

6.1 Introduction

Architecting is a multifaceted technical process, involving complex knowledge-intensive tasks [195]. The knowledge that is both produced and consumed during the architecting activities is voluminous, broad, complex, and evolving and thus cannot be manually managed by the architect. Furthermore, such architectural knowledge (AK) [193] needs to be shared and reused among a number of different stakeholders, and across a number of the lifecycle phases. Especially as the size and complexity of systems increase, more stakeholders need to get efficiently involved in the architecting process and the knowledge management issues become quite challenging. The problem is exacerbated in the context of multi-site or global software development [75]. Finally the industry has also come to realize the need for efficient inter-organization AK sharing [76].

Therefore, the management of AK needs to be automated or semi-automated by appropriate tool support. This can be achieved similarly to traditional knowledge management tool support, by emphasizing the characteristics of software architecting. For example, tool support for architecture knowledge management (AKM) may

Peng Liang (✉) and Paris Avgeriou
University of Groningen, The Netherlands, e-mail: liangp@cs.rug.nl,paris@cs.rug.nl

M. Ali Babar et al. (eds.), *Software Architecture Knowledge Management*,
DOI: 10.1007/978-3-642-02374-3_6, © Springer-Verlag Berlin Heidelberg 2009

concern enforcing an architecting process, reusing architecting best practices, documenting architecture decisions, providing traceability between design artifacts, and recalling past decisions and their rationale. AKM tools can support a wide number of use cases, thus reducing the complexity of knowledge management in the architecting process and facilitating the knowledge-based collaboration of the involved stakeholders.

In knowledge management, a distinction is often made between two types of knowledge: implicit and explicit knowledge [234]; see also Chap. 4. Implicit (or tacit) knowledge is knowledge residing in people's heads, whereas explicit knowledge is knowledge which has been codified in some form (e.g. a document, or a model). Two forms of explicit knowledge can be discerned: documented and formal knowledge. Documented knowledge is explicit knowledge which is expressed in natural language or images in documents. Typical examples of documented AK are Word and Excel documents that contain architecture description and analysis models. Formal knowledge is explicit knowledge codified using a formal language or model of which the exact semantics are defined. Typical examples of formal AK models include AK ontologies [190] or AK domain models [10, 44, 325] that formally define concepts and relations, and aim at providing a common language for unambiguous interpretation by stakeholders. Organizations can employ three distinct strategies for managing their knowledge: *codification*, *personalization* [7, 143], and the *hybrid* strategy which combines the previous two [92]; see also Chap. 1. Figure 6.1 presents these different knowledge types in the vertical dimension combined with two knowledge management strategies in the horizontal dimension.

In this chapter, we first present a set of possible use cases that can be supported by AKM tooling. The set is not meant to be exhaustive; however it is well-grounded as it comprises a superset of the use cases either implemented or being in the wish-list of the existing AKM tools. In Sects. 6.2 and 6.3, we present existing tool support for the codification and hybrid knowledge management strategies, respectively. To the best of our knowledge there are no tools that support purely the

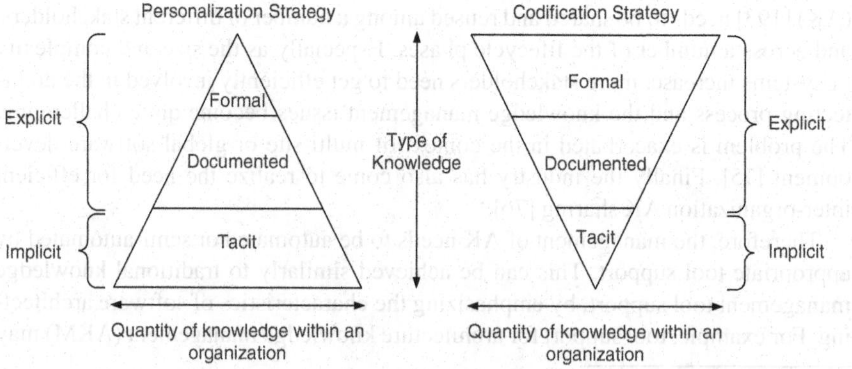

Fig. 6.1 Pyramid of knowledge types and the associated knowledge management strategies [159]

personalization strategy without any codification. However we will present some technologies for personalization in Sect. 6.5. Some of the technologies are mature and can be used off-the-shelf while others are still applied in an experimental setting and are presented here as a future research challenge.

6.2 Use Cases of AK Management

In this section, we describe use cases for AKM tooling to present the potential set of tool features in this domain and also set the stage for presenting existing tools and technologies (discussed in Sects. 6.3–6.5). The use cases define the requirements for developing an AKM tool, i.e. who would use it (actors), to do what (use cases)? We came up with this use case model by surveying a series of papers [10, 113, 192, 326], which provide at least some kind of usage of AK (requirements, services, functions, use cases, etc.). We formed a superset of use cases by selecting, merging, and generalizing from the use cases of the individual approaches. Some of them came from interviews with practicing architects, while others originate from researchers' experience. Furthermore some use cases have been implemented in tools, while others remained in the "wish-list" of researchers.

6.2.1 Actors

Who would use the AKM tool?

- *Architects* designing a system (or a subsystem of a large system) by making decisions. They keep the tacit AK in mind or transform it from tacit to documented or formalized knowledge [326].
- *Reviewers* involved in judging the quality or progress of an architecture [192].
- *Requirements engineers* who view AK from the problem space [192]. *Developers* involved in the implementation of the architecture design and decisions [326].
- *Maintainers* who evolve or maintain the system and need to understand the correlation between the decisions they take and existing, relevant AK [326].
- *Users* of the AKM tool are the entire set of system stakeholders [192]. All the actors mentioned above are specialized actors of *User*.

6.2.2 Use Cases

We present the use cases (UC) by grouping them into four distinct categories, as illustrated in Fig. 6.2: Actors either *consume* AK by using it for specific purposes, or *produce* AK by creating new or modifying existing AK [195]; *knowledge management* concerns general low-level functionality to manage AK data; and *intelligent*

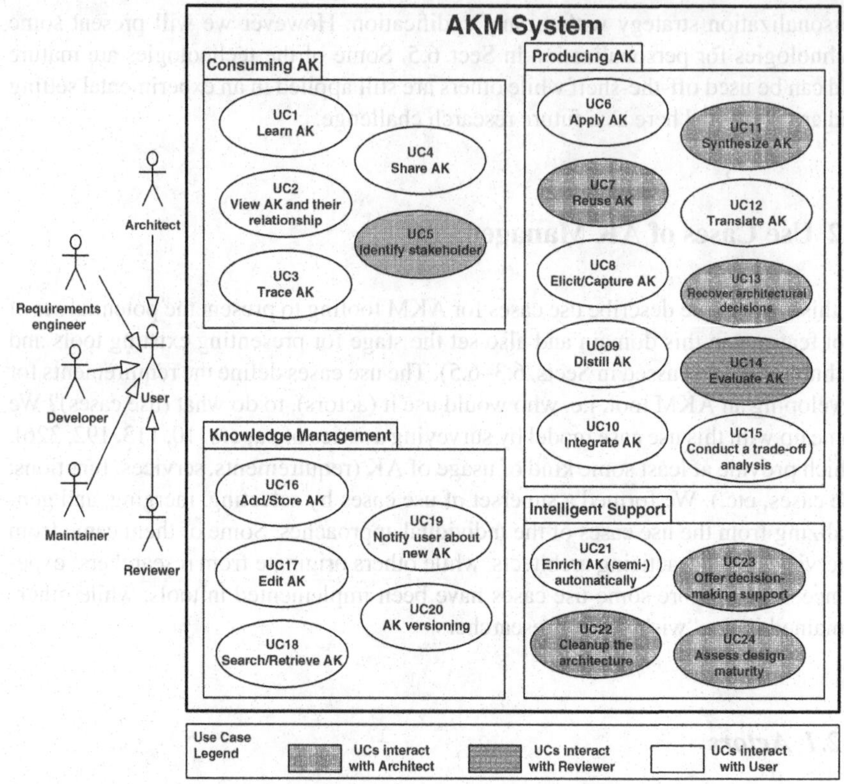

Fig. 6.2 Panorama of the AKM use case model

support concerns automating AKM tasks within the architecting process that require either rigor or intelligence.

We do not claim that the list of use cases is exhaustive, but they do capture all use cases in the surveyed literature. Some use cases are kept unchanged from the original source (e.g. *Assess design maturity* [326]) while others have been merged (e.g. *Reuse AK* [326] includes *Clone AK* [192] and *Stimulate reuse of best practices* [113]), or generalized (e.g. *Identify stakeholders* is generalized from *Identify the subversive stakeholder* [192] and *Identify affected stakeholders on change* [326]). These use cases, together with their included and specialized use cases, are discussed within the presentation of the AKM tools in Sects. 6.3 and 6.4. In this section, we very briefly discuss each use case, and refer to the original sources for more information. It is noted that the actors are explicitly specified only for the use cases whose actor is the *Architect* or the *Reviewer* and not the generic *User*. Also we consider the generalization relationship between use cases as in [40].

Consuming AK

- UC1, *Learn AK* [313]: learn and comprehend the AK, e.g. understand the rationale of a design decision.
- UC2, *View AK and their relationships* [196]: view both AK elements and relationships e.g. the architectural decisions made and the relationships between these decisions.
- UC3, *Trace AK* [12]: trace between various AK elements, e.g. design decisions, rationale, and design.
- UC4, *Share AK* [313]: share knowledge with one or more actors of the system.
- UC5, *Identify stakeholder* [192, 326]: the architect identifies a stakeholder according to certain criteria, e.g. who has the most "weight" on the architectural decisions.

Producing AK

- UC6, *Apply general AK* [313]: use application-independent AK, e.g. apply architecture patterns to solve the problems at hand.
- UC7, *Reuse AK* [326]: the architect reuses AK in another project context, e.g. reusing architectural design decisions from an old to a new project.
- UC8, *Elicit/Capture AK* [10, 196]: elicit and capture AK from various resources, e.g. individuals, teams, or documents.
- UC9, *Distill AK* [313]: distill specific knowledge from a system into general knowledge (e.g. architecture pattern) that can be reused in future systems.
- UC10, *Integrate AK* [313]: integrate different types of information into concrete AK, e.g. integrate stakeholder requirements, system context, and technology constraints into system requirements.
- UC11, *Synthesize AK* [313]: the architect applies the design decisions and produces the system design (e.g. components and connectors).
- UC12, *Translate AK* [208]: translate the formal AK based on a given AK domain model into another domain model to facilitate reuse.
- UC13, *Recover architectural decisions* [326]: the architect reconstructs decisions with their associated rationale from an existing or 3rd party system.
- UC14, *Evaluate AK* [313, 326]: the reviewer performs a critical evaluation of the AK, e.g. to make sure that requirements have been satisfied in the architecture design.
- UC15, *Conduct a trade-off analysis* [326]: analyze the architecture by trading off different quality attributes.

Knowledge Management

- UC16, *Add/Store AK* [192]: add and store elements of AK into the knowledge repository.
- UC17, *Edit AK* [10]: modify or delete AK elements in the repository.
- UC18, *Search/Retrieve AK* [196, 313]: search through the existing AK using certain criteria (e.g. keywords and categories, etc.).

- UC19, *Notify user about AK changes* [113]: subscribe to specific AK elements, and subsequently get notified about changes to them.
- UC20, *AK versioning* [192]: create and manage different versions of the AK.

Intelligent Support

- UC21, *Enrich AK (semi-) automatically* [196]: generate AK content proactively, e.g. automatically distilling and interpreting AK from text without the users' intervention.
- UC22, *Cleanup the architecture* [326]: the architect makes sure that all the dependencies of removed AK (e.g. the consequences of an architectural decision) have been removed as well.
- UC23, *Offer decision-making support* [113, 196]: provide automated support for the Architect in the process of making decisions, e.g. through well-founded advices and guidelines.
- UC24, *Assess design maturity* [326]: the architect evaluates when the architecture can be considered as finished, complete, and consistent, e.g. verify whether a system conforming to the architecture can be made or bought.

6.3 Tool Support for Codification

In this section, we present the AKM tools that support the codification strategy by discussing for each one: a brief introduction, how they support the use cases listed in Sect. 6.2.2 (full or partial support) and their special focus (e.g. architecture design support, evaluation support, etc.). The order of presenting the tools is organized according to the type of knowledge they support: the SEI-ADWiki supports documented AKM; ADkwik and ADDSS support both documented and formal AKM; and the rest support formal AKM.

6.3.1 SEI-ADWiki

This tool is a wiki-based collaborative environment for creating architecture documentation and is used by students in the Carnegie Mellon University Master of Software Engineering program [26]. The tool is not named, so we call it SEI-ADWiki for ease of reference within this chapter.

Supported Use Cases

6.3.1.1 *View AK and their relationships* (UC2): users can view the content of architecture documents and relationships within that content (e.g. mapping between architecture views) through a navigation bar.

6.3.1.2 *Trace AK* (UC3): users can create traceability between architectural artifacts (documented AK represented in wiki pages) through hyperlinks.

6.3.1.3 *Share AK* (UC4): users can share the content of architecture documents with other users after saving the content in wiki pages.
6.3.1.4 *Add/Store AK* (UC16): users can add and save architectural artifacts in wiki pages.
6.3.1.5 *Edit AK* (UC17): users can change and remove the content of architecture document in wiki pages.
6.3.1.6 *Search/Retrieve AK* (UC18): users can use the search box on every wiki page to search the entire wiki by keywords.
6.3.1.7 *Notify user about the AK changes* (UC19): users can opt to receive notification (e.g. by email) when a monitored wiki page (documented AK) is modified by other users or when a new wiki page is created.
6.3.1.8 *AK versioning* (UC20): users can create different versions for the architecture artifacts represented in wiki pages through the versioning function of wiki.
6.3.1.9 *View the change history of AK* (includes UC20): users can view the change history based on the versioned AK. The change history documents which part of the architecture has been added or modified since the last review. AK versioning produces versioned AK for viewing the AK change history, therefore this UC includes UC20.

Special Focus
SEI-ADWiki is able to create and maintain architecture documentation in a dynamic and collaborative way. The basic form of knowledge in SEI-ADWiki is the wiki page (documented AK), which provides a combination of editing and version management tools with the advantage of open access.

6.3.2 ADkwik

ADkwik[1] (Architectural Decision Knowledge Wiki) is a Web 2.0 system which supports the collaborative decision-making work of software architects [291]. Similarly to other wikis, the users (team members) only need a Web browser to work with the system. But still ADkwik is different from a plain standard wiki which is explained in details below. An elaborate application of ADkwik is discussed in Chap. 12.

Supported Use Cases

6.3.2.1 *View AK* (UC2): users can use the navigation bar to view the AK in a dynamic wiki page (e.g. all dependencies to an architectural decision) using Web 2.0 context-aware mashup techniques [17].
6.3.2.2 *Trace AK* (UC3): users can create and manage dependency relationships based on the SOAD architectural decision model [346].

[1] www.alphaworks.ibm.com/tech/adkwik.

6.3.2.3 *Share AK* (UC4): users can share AK across project boundaries with other users. Special attention is given to architecture decisions, which are codified in formal AK and shared according to the SOAD model.
6.3.2.4 *Reuse AK* (UC7): users can reuse the AK about enterprise application architectures contained in the architectural decision repository.
6.3.2.5 *Harvest AK* (*generalized* UC from UC8 and UC9): users can update the AK with new decisions, experiences, patterns and rationale gathered by both successful and failed projects. This UC concerns eliciting/capturing AK (e.g. decisions) and distilling AK (e.g. patterns) and, therefore it is a generalized UC from UC8 and UC9.
6.3.2.6 *Search/Retrieve AK* (UC18): users can search/retrieve the AK from the tagged wiki pages.
6.3.2.7 *AK versioning* (UC20): users can manage different versions of the AK by tracing the wiki changes at the page level.
6.3.2.8 *Offer decision-making support* (UC23): users can find and reuse appropriate decisions in the architectural decision repository.

Special Focus
The main difference of ADkwik from other wikis is that ADkwik is an application wiki as opposed to a plain standard wiki. It is supported by relational database underneath whose tables are structured based on the SOAD domain model [346], while standard wikis also have databases, but the tables are wiki pages. The AK in ADkwik is also structured according to SOAD model to enable formal AK sharing between stakeholders and projects. Consequently ADkwik combines the open access of wikis and formal knowledge based on the underneath domain model to provide efficient AK sharing and management.

6.3.3 ADDSS

ADDSS[2] (architecture design decision support system) is a Web-based tool for storing, managing and documenting architectural design decisions taken during the architecting process and providing traceability between requirements and architectures through the decisions [67].

Supported Use Cases

6.3.3.1 *Learn AK* (UC1): users can understand the architectural decisions by viewing and replaying the evolution of decisions over time.
6.3.3.2 *View AK and their relationships* (UC2): users can easily view the AK and their relationships presented in Web pages and structured according to specific templates.

[2] http://triana.escet.urjc.es/ADDSS.

6.3.3.3 *Trace AK* (UC3): users can trace architectural decisions to other elements (e.g. Architecture, Stakeholder) based on the ADDSS architectural decision domain model.

6.3.3.4 *Share AK* (UC4): users can interact and share AK through groupware support in order to check and solve their conflicts. Another solution to share AK in ADDSS is to generate standard documents (e.g. PDF) with all the architectural information, and send it to related stakeholders.

6.3.3.5 *Elicit/Capture AK* (UC8): users can capture the architectural design decisions using a template that consists of mandatory and optional attributes.

6.3.3.6 *Chronological view of AK* (*included* in UC2): users can view the architectural decisions in a chronological order, to better understand the decision making process. This is a special case of viewing AK and their relationships and, therefore it is an included UC of UC2.

6.3.3.7 *Add/Store AK* (UC16): users can add/store architectural design decisions or design patterns and architectural styles. Decisions can be described using free text, and patterns/styles can be described using graphical and textual description.

6.3.3.8 *Search/Retrieve AK* (UC18): users can query the system about related requirements, decisions and architectures.

6.3.3.9 *Offer decision-making support* (UC23): users can make design decisions by selecting well-known design patterns and architectural styles.

Special Focus

ADDSS uses a flexible approach based on a set of mandatory and optional attributes for characterizing architectural design decisions. Hence, ADDSS provides a customizable codification strategy that makes capturing AK more flexible. ADDSS focuses on the evolution of AK by capturing both architecture designs and architectural design decisions following an iterative process, and visualizing this evolution over time. ADDSS also stresses on applying general knowledge (e.g. architectural patterns).

6.3.4 Archium

The Archium[3] [161, 163] aims at providing traceability among a wide range of AK concepts such as requirements, decisions, architecture descriptions, and implementation. The tool facilitates the maintenance of this AK (e.g. resolve conflicts and synchronize various parts) during the life cycle of a system. All these AK concepts can be expressed in a single language: the Archium language.

Supported Use Cases

6.3.4.1 *Trace AK* (UC3): users can trace architectural decisions to requirements, architectural models and implementation in the Archium language.

[3] www.archium.net.

6.3.4.2 *Distill patterns of architectural decision dependencies* (*specialized* of UC9): users can discover general patterns of dependencies between architectural decisions by viewing their functional dependencies. The patterns of architectural decision dependencies are a type of AK, so this is a specialized UC of UC9.

6.3.4.3 *Add/Store AK* (UC16): users can add/store architectural decisions specified in the Archium language into the repository.

6.3.4.4 *Retrieve AK* (*included* in UC18): users can manually select any component or connector and retrieve the relevant architectural decisions.

6.3.4.5 *Check superfluous architectural decisions* (*included* in UC22): users can identify one class of superfluous decisions in Archium: the unnecessary decisions that have no effect on the architecture. Checking superfluous architectural decisions is a prerequisite for cleaning up the architecture and, therefore this UC is included in UC22. The same reason applies for the next UC.

6.3.4.6 *Get consequences of an architectural decision* (*included* in UC22): users can get the consequence of a decision by viewing the dependency graph of architectural decisions.

6.3.4.7 *Check for consistency of architectural decisions* (*included* in UC24): users can employ the Archium compiler and run-time environment supporting the Archium language to check different types of consistency between architectural decisions, design and implementation. For example, they can check whether dependencies such as *refines* or *dependsOn* of an architectural decision are satisfied with other decisions. Checking consistency of architectural decisions is part of accessing design maturity and therefore this is an included UC of UC24. The same reason applies for the UCs 6.3.4.8–6.3.4.10.

6.3.4.8 *Validate architectural decisions against requirements* (*included* in UC24): users can check whether all requirements are addressed in one or more architectural decisions based on the Archium language.

6.3.4.9 *Check implementation against architectural decisions* (*included* in UC24): the Archium compiler generates code by transforming the architectural elements (e.g. components, connectors) into Java classes. During the process, the compiler also analyzes and verifies whether the transformed Java classes comply with the architectural decisions.

6.3.4.10 *Check for completeness* (*included* in UC24): users can check whether any elements (e.g. motivations, causes, and problems) of an architectural decision are missing.

Special Focus

Visualization and traceability of architectural decisions are the core features of Archium, which are essential for better understanding the architecture design. Archium provides a pragmatic approach to using architectural decisions in architecting: the decisions are bidirectionally linked with the system implementation through transformations, which are transparent to user.

6.3.5 AREL

AREL[4] (Architecture Rationale and Elements Linkage) is a UML-based tool that aims in creating and documenting architectural design with a focus on architectural decisions and design rationale [316]. Three types of AK are captured in AREL: *design concerns, design decisions* and *design outcomes*, which are all represented in UML. An extensive example of the use of AREL in design reasoning is provided in Chap. 9.

Supported Use Cases

6.3.5.1 *Learn AK* (UC1): users can understand the design outcome with its associated *design rationale* (*concern* and *decision*) based on the AREL causal model.

6.3.5.2 *View AK* (UC2): users can view the AK elements and relationships in UML diagrams.

6.3.5.3 *Trace AK* (UC3): users can trace *design concerns* and *design outcomes* to *design decisions* using the UML dependency relationship.

6.3.5.4 *Identify AK change impacts* (*included* in UC14): users can identify all the *design decisions* and other AK elements, that are directly or indirectly impacted when AK is modified, based on the AREL causal model. This UC provides information for evaluating AK, e.g. evaluate the impact of AK change, so this is an included UC of UC14.

6.3.5.5 *Elicit/Capture AK* (UC8): users can capture AK during the architecting process using a UML modeling tool. They can also elicit AK from text-based requirement specifications using UML models.

6.3.5.6 *Synthesize AK* (UC11): users can implement design decisions into the system design in UML diagrams, based on the AREL domain model.

6.3.5.7 *Conduct a trade-off analysis* (UC15): cross-cutting concerns often require trade-off analysis at multiple decision points, and users can conduct such an analysis by tracing between *design concerns* and *design outcomes* that implement the cross-cutting concerns (especially the non-functional requirements).

6.3.5.8 *Add/Store AK* (UC16): users can save the elicited/captured AK in UML models.

6.3.5.9 *Edit AK* (UC17): users can edit the AK through the corresponding UML models.

6.3.5.10 *Search/Retrieve AK* (UC18): users can use the search and retrieval functions provided by the UML modeling to find AK elements within the UML models.

6.3.5.11 *Detect architecture design conflicts* (*included* in UC24): users can detect the design conflicts by looking at the missing links (design gaps) between *design concerns* and *design outcomes* using the AREL causal model. This

[4] www.ict.swin.edu.au/personal/atang/AREL-Tool.zip.

UC can be used for accessing design maturity and, therefore it is included in UC24.

Special Focus
AREL represents various AK elements using UML profiles, thus integrate AKM into a UML modeling tool (e.g. Enterprise Architect). This enables the architect to record the design decisions as part of the architecture design. AREL focuses on linking the problem space (*design concerns*) to the solution space (*design outcomes*) through design decisions in a uniform way.

6.3.6 Knowledge Architect

The Knowledge Architect (KA) is a tool suite for capturing, using, translating, sharing and managing AK. It is based on a common AK repository accessed by different clients (Document Knowledge Client, Excel and Python Plug-in, Knowledge Explorer and Knowledge Translator) [208]. The tool suite makes extensive use of technologies developed for the Semantic Web to allow for formal AK management. The Knowledge Architect is one outcome of the GRIFFIN project, discussed in Chap. 8.

Supported Use Cases

6.3.6.1 *View AK and their relationship* (UC2): users can view the AK entities and their relationships in the Knowledge Explorer.
6.3.6.2 *Trace AK* (UC3): users can create traceability between AK entities using the different client tools.
6.3.6.3 *Share AK* (UC4): users can share AK entities with other users by storing it centrally in the Knowledge Repository and accessing it using the various client tools.
6.3.6.1 *Elicit/Capture AK* (UC8): users can elicit/capture AK by annotating architecture documents and models using the KA client tools.
6.3.6.5 *Integrate AK* (UC10): users can integrate various types of AK (from requirements to design artifacts) into the Knowledge Repository based on a common domain model.
6.3.6.6 *Translate AK* (UC12): users can perform automatic translation based on different AK domain models through the Knowledge Translator [207].
6.3.6.7 *Add/Store AK* (UC16): users can save the captured (annotated) AK entities into the Knowledge Repository through the client tools.
6.3.6.8 *Edit AK* (UC17): users can edit the AK entities through the client tools.
6.3.6.9 *Search/Retrieve AK* (UC18): users can query the AK entities and their relationships in the Knowledge Repository through its Query Engine, using the RDF query language.
6.3.6.10 *Check completeness of AK* (*included* in UC24): users can check the completeness of AK in a document (e.g. whether a *Decision Topic* has been addressed by at least one *Alternative*) through the Document Knowledge

Client. Checking completeness of AK is part of accessing design maturity, so this is an included UC of UC24.

Special Focus
The Knowledge Architect focuses on capturing AK through annotating information in different sources (e.g. Word, Excel documents), and sharing it in a central repository. The tools suite also focuses on traceability management and intelligent support, as AK entities and relationships are semantically specified in OWL [37].

6.3.7 SEURAT

SEURAT[5] (Software Engineering Using RATionale system) is an Eclipse plug-in that is targeted to rationale knowledge management in an integrated development environment (IDE), from requirements to design and finally to source code [60][62]. The concept of rationale knowledge in SEURAT is composed of design decisions, alternative solutions considered, and the reasons (arguments for each solution) behind the final decisions.

Supported Use Cases

6.3.7.1 *Learn AK* (UC1): users can understand rationale knowledge and all its parts. It is represented with a formal argument ontology (for details on the argument ontology see [59]), which semantically assists the understanding of the rationale knowledge.

6.3.7.2 *View AK* (UC2): users can view rationale knowledge within the Eclipse environment in a hierarchical view – from list of decisions to alternative solutions and finally to the "arguments" for or against each solution. Users can also view rationale knowledge through the rationale hierarchy report (in the same layout as in the hierarchical view) and the rationale traceability matrix report generated by the tool.

6.3.7.3 *Trace AK* (UC3): users can trace the rationale knowledge (e.g. "*how do we compare dates?*") to source code (e.g. function *compareDates()*) directly in the Eclipse environment using bookmarks. Users can also trace requirements to the decisions made and captured in the rationale.

6.3.7.4 *Elicit/Capture AK* (UC8): users can capture rationale knowledge during source code development. They can also import rationale knowledge from Word documents where text has been annotated as rationale.

6.3.7.5 *Decision evaluation and impact assessment* (*included* in UC14): users can evaluate decisions by calculating the "support score" for each alternative solution based on the arguments for and against it. Users can also disable some requirements when stakeholders change their mind about them, and see which decisions may require re-examination due to the impact

[5] www.users.muohio.edu/burgeje/SEURAT/Downloads.html.

assessment of requirements. This UC aims at evaluating design decisions, a type of AK, so this is an included UC of UC14.

6.3.7.6 *Conduct a trade-off analysis* (UC15): users can conduct trade-off analysis of a decision based on the "background knowledge" (e.g. "*A more flexible solution costs more to develop*") of this decision which is explicitly recorded in the rationale.

6.3.7.7 *Add/Store AK (UC16)*: users can add rationale knowledge using an editing interface integrated in Eclipse and store it in a relational database.

6.3.7.8 *Edit AK* (UC17): users can edit the text of rationale knowledge using the editing interface.

6.3.7.9 *Search/Retrieve AK* (UC18): users can search/retrieve rationale knowledge elements through keyword-based search, including requirements, decisions, alternatives and arguments.

6.3.7.10 *Offer decision-making support* (UC23): users can get decision-making support using the "support scores" for each alternative solution.

6.3.7.11 *Check for completeness and consistency of rationale knowledge (included in UC24)*: users can detect the incompleteness and inconsistency of the rationale knowledge through inferencing based on the argument ontology, e.g. for completeness, checks are made to ensure that there are alternatives proposed for each decision. This UC can be used for accessing design maturity and, therefore it is included in UC24.

Special Focus

SEURAT is not specifically used for the management of AK but for rationale knowledge. However, in a broad sense, rationale knowledge about architecture design (e.g. arguments linked from requirements to alternative design solutions) is an important part of AK. In addition, SEURAT mainly focuses on the application of rationale knowledge supporting software maintenance [61].

6.4 Tool Support for the Hybrid Strategy

In this section, we present the AKM tools that support the hybrid strategy in the same structure as in Sect. 6.3.

6.4.1 EAGLE

EAGLE [114, 113] is an AK sharing portal that implements best practices from knowledge management for improving AK sharing. The main features of EAGLE include integrated support for both codified and personalized AK, support for stakeholder-specific content, and AK subscription and notification. EAGLE is a result of the GRIFFIN project, discussed in Chap. 8.

Supported Use Cases

6.4.1.1 *Share AK* (UC4): users can share AK in both personalized (e.g. news, events and experience with colleagues) and codified (e.g. best practices, documents) formats.

6.4.1.2 *Find a colleague based on expertise or competence* (*included* in UC4): users can find the right person, whose personal knowledge may match a specific AK request. This UC provides information for personalized AK sharing, so it is an included UC of UC4.

6.4.1.3 *Overview of personal information of colleagues* (*included* in UC4): users can get an overview of "who knows what" and "who is doing what" among their colleagues. This UC also provides information for personalized AK sharing, so it is an included UC of UC4.

6.4.1.4 *Add/Store best practices* (*specialized* of UC16): users can add best practices to a repository (codified AK) for reuse and decision making support. Best practices are a special type of AK, so this is a specialized UC of UC16.

6.4.1.5 *Add/Store architecture document* (*specialized* of UC16): users can add architecture documents to a repository according to various AK categories. Similarly to the UC in 5.1.4, this is also a specialized UC of UC16.

6.4.1.6 *Search/Retrieve AK* (UC18): users can access generic documentation (different types of company documents) by document title, keywords or categories, and also search for project-specific AK documentation.

6.4.1.7 *Search/Retrieve related AK* (*included* in UC18): users can access external information sources to find related AK, such as white papers (codified AK), seminars and trainings (personalized AK) or other corporate communication, e.g. discussion board (personalized AK). Related AK is a special kind of AK, so this is a specialized UC of UC18.

6.4.1.8 *Notify user about new AK* (*specialized* of UC19): user can stay up-to-date about new AK through subscription and notification mechanisms. New AK is a kind of AK change and, therefore this is a specialized UC of UC19.

6.4.1.9 *Offer decision-making support* (UC23): Users can get intelligent support by answering a questionnaire during the decision-making process, and automatically receiving a number of architectural guidelines that match their answers.

6.4.1.10 *Overview of project stakeholders* (*included* in UC24): users can have an overview about project stakeholders, e.g. contact information and expertise area. They can subsequently request all the involved stakeholders to access the design maturity and, therefore this is an included UC of UC24.

Special Focus

EAGLE focuses on stakeholder collaboration during the architecting process, by enabling them to connect to colleagues or other involved stakeholders by retrieving "who is doing what" and "who knows what". In addition, codified AK in a document repository or best practice repository can also be easily accessed using advanced search mechanisms.

6.4.2 PAKME

PAKME[6] (Process-based Architecture Knowledge Management Environment) is a Web-based tool aimed at providing knowledge management support for the software architecture process. PAKME supports both codification and personalization as it not only provides access to AK but also identifies the knowledge source [8, 12].

Supported Use Cases

6.4.2.1 *View AK and their relationships* (UC2): users can view AK elements (e.g. architectural patterns) in template-driven Web pages, and their relationships through hyperlinks.
6.4.2.2 *Trace AK* (UC3): users can trace AK using hyperlinks and relationship types (e.g. *constrain* or *conflictWith* relationships between architectural design decisions) defined in PAKME.
6.4.2.3 *Share AK* (UC4): users can share the AK stored in the PAKME repository through the Web user interface.
6.4.2.4 *Apply general AK* (UC6): users can apply general AK (e.g. patterns, general scenarios) to design a suitable architecture for a new application.
6.4.2.5 *Reuse AK* (UC7): users can reuse alternative design solutions in 4 steps (searching, retrieving, reviewing and integrating).
6.4.2.6 *Elicit/Capture AK* (UC8): users can use various Web forms based on templates (e.g. architectural decision and pattern templates) to elicit, structure and capture AK before storing it into the repository.
6.4.2.7 *Add/Store AK* (UC16): users can use various Web forms to enter generic or project-specific AK into the repository, including the knowledge producer information.
6.4.2.8 *Edit AK* (UC17): users can modify and delete the AK stored in the repository through the Web user interface.
6.4.2.9 *Search/Retrieve AK* (UC18): users can search/retrieve AK elements through keyword-based search, advanced search and navigation-based search. For personalization purposes the source of AK (e.g. knowledge producer) can also be retrieved.

Special Focus

PAKME focuses on various collaborative AK management features for geographically distributed stakeholders involved in the architecture process by managing and sharing codified AK (pattern, decision, etc.) and personalized AK (contact management, online collaboration, etc).

6.5 Technologies

Some of the AKM tools described in the previous sections were not built from scratch but made use of various technologies. Such technologies are generic and can be employed to support the AKM use cases presented in Sect. 6.2. In this section, we

[6] http://193.1.97.13:8080/.

present a number of these technologies to demonstrate their value for AKM tools, and to assist tool vendors in selecting the appropriate ones for their own needs. The order of presenting the technologies is organized according to the type of knowledge they support: Web portal, blog and wiki support the hybrid strategy, voting and ranking support the personalization strategy, and the rest support the codification strategy.

6.5.1 Web Portal

A Web portal [131, 319] is a Web site that provides integrated modules, like hosted databases, yellow pages, discussion boards, news push, document management, email and more. Web portals automatically personalize the content generated from these modules to provide a personalized experience to users. The yellow pages module can record the expertise area, involved projects and contact information of all the architects in an organization, thus providing support for personalized *AK sharing* (UC4). Emails, news push and discussion boards provide communication support for *AK sharing* (UC4) through a collaboration space among users. News push also supports *AK changes notification* (UC19) when personalized information is changed (e.g. personnel movement).

This technology is also useful for codified AK management. The hosted central databases and client/server architecture can facilitate *AK sharing* (UC4), and Web forms can be used for *tracing* (UC3), *eliciting/capturing* (UC8), *adding/storing* (UC16), and *editing* (UC17) *AK*.

6.5.2 Blog and Wiki

Different from yellow pages, blogs and wikis are both editable Web pages by individual users who are distributed over the network. Blogs are for single users, and wikis are designed to enable anyone to contribute or modify content, so they both support personalized *AK sharing* (UC4). For example individual users can provide up-to-date and more reliable personal information, such as their expertise area and personal knowledge.

As a collaborative Web editing system, wikis also support codified AK management for both documented and formal AK. We classify the wikis as general wikis for documented AKM (e.g. SEI-ADWiki) and semantic wikis for formal AKM (e.g. ADkwik). Both types of wikis can support the following AKM use cases: *AK viewing* (UC2) and *AK traceability* (UC3), *adding/storing AK* (UC16), *editing AK* (UC17), *searching/retrieving AK* (UC18), *user notification about AK changes* (UC19), and *AK sharing* (UC4). Some practical experience of applying wikis to support AK sharing can also be found in [116].

Generic wikis simply document AK in the wiki pages. On the other hand, semantic wikis provide semantic support through formal models (e.g. semantic annotation and semantic query of AK). In addition, wikis have also been used in requirements engineering to support requirements knowledge management in a codification strategy, e.g. for documented requirements [91] and formal requirements knowledge [212].

6.5.3 Voting and Ranking

Voting and ranking is a method to evaluate and rank the characteristics (e.g. credibility and reliability, etc.) of objects or people by different users in an online community. It has been widely applied in many social networking systems (e.g. LinkedIn) and C2C business platforms (e.g. eBay) for the evaluation and ranking of personal information.

The personal information recorded in Web portals, wikis and yellow pages has unavoidably personal and subjective bias (e.g. the expertise of an architect). Using the voting and ranking mechanism can partially mitigate this problem, and provide more credible personal information. For example ranking the expertise of different stakeholders on a technology platform by other members of an organization helps to create reliable "who knows what" information, and thus efficient personalized *AK sharing* (UC4).

6.5.4 Natural Language Processing

Natural language processing (NLP) is concerned with the understanding of human natural languages by computers. Since documentation in natural language is dominant in AK resources (most documented AK is in natural language), it is beneficial to introduce NLP techniques in AKM tools.

Several AKM use cases have been supported by NLP techniques. The LSA (Latent Semantic Analysis) technique has been used to *elicit/capture AK* (UC8) semi-automatically [45]. Text mining techniques have been used to *enrich AK* (UC21) [114], and *offer decision-making support* (UC23) [196].

6.5.5 Ontologies

Ontologies are formal structures supporting knowledge representation, management, sharing and reusing [120], and have been widely used in various fields, such as the Semantic Web. They represent explicitly the semantics of structured and semi-structured information and so enable sophisticated automatic support for acquiring, maintaining and accessing information [90]. Formal AK, as a kind of formal knowledge, can be represented by ontology models (see for example [190]). Various ontology techniques have been explored in AKM tools, including ontology modeling, ontology database, ontology mapping, and ontology-based inferencing. These techniques will be elaborated in the following paragraphs.

Ontology modeling can be used to describe domain concepts and their relationships. In this respect, AK ontology models are composed of AK domain concepts (e.g. *Design Decision*, *Alternative*, and *Risk*) and relationships (e.g. *addressedBy* and *containedIn*). Related standards on ontology specification to specify the ontology modeling results have been defined by the W3C, e.g. RDF [184] and OWL [37], with ontology modeling tools support, e.g. Protégé[7]. Combined with ontology models, an AKM tool can support the following use cases of formal AK management: UC1 (*Learn AK*) - the ontology concepts and relationships can help users understand the meaning of AK; UC2 (*View AK and their relationships*), UC3 (*Trace AK*) and UC22 (*Clean up architecture*) - these use cases are supported by using the semantic relationships defined between AK concepts.

Ontology databases store data in ontological data models. For example the RDF store Sesame [53] stores data in the RDF triple format. Ontology databases provide semantic querying using their specific query language, e.g. SPARQL [258] of the W3C, SeRQL for Sesame. For example, one can query the ontology database by posing question like "*Tell me all the alternative solutions addressed to decision topic 'the control method over the data processing pipelines' which are not in conflict with each other*". The following use cases can be supported by ontology databases in formal AK management tools: *Add/Store AK* (UC16) in ontological data models, *Search/Retrieve AK* (UC18) by query languages, and *Share AK* (UC4) after getting the query results.

Ontology mapping is an activity to semantically relate two ontologies [112]. It provides a semantic translation between heterogeneous ontologies and therefore enables knowledge sharing in a semantically sound manner [169]. This is essential for sharing AK that originates from different organizations and is based on different AK ontologies. UC4 (*Share AK*) and UC12 (*Translate AK*) can be supported by ontology mapping techniques (see e.g. the Knowledge Translator [208]).

Ontology-based inferencing concerns retrieving knowledge and creating deductive knowledge based on ontology models with logic-based reasoning [333]. In AKM tools, the inferencer can be mostly used to automatically infer the relationships that exist between the formal AK entities, e.g. an inverse relationship between AK elements (for traceability) or a mapping relationship between elements from different AK domain models (for translation). The inferencer can support the following use cases: *Search/Retrieve AK* (UC18) e.g. by the SeRQL query language of OWLIM inference engine [181], *Check for completeness* (included in UC24) e.g. by the KA client tools [208], and *Translate AK* (UC12) e.g. by the Knowledge Translator [208].

[7] http://protege.stanford.edu/.

6.5.6 Plug-in

A plug-in consists of a program that connects and interacts with a host system (e.g. a Web browser or an email client) to provide a specific function on demand. This technology is quite beneficial for promoting AK usage through tools that architects have being working and are familiar with. Typical tools that architects use through the architecting process include word processors for architecture documentation, spreadsheets for quantitative architecture evaluation and UML modelers for architecture design.

Examples of the tool plug-in technology include the KA Document Knowledge Client (Word plug-in) and AREL (UML modeling tool plug-in). Both plug-ins support the following AKM use cases: *Learn AK* (UC1), *View AK* (UC2), *Trace AK* (UC3), *Elicit/Capture AK* (UC8), *Synthesize AK* (UC11), *Add/Store AK* (UC16) and *Edit AK* (UC17).

6.5.7 Version Management

This technology concerns the management of multiple revisions of the same unit of information. The versioning function of wikis, SVN (Subversion) and CVS (Concurrent Versions System) are typical examples of this technology. Wikis can track the version changes at the page level. For every page, it is easy to look up earlier versions, display the differences between two versions, and revert to an older version. SVN and CVS provide similar functions for the version management of files which can be used to record documented AK (e.g. Word documents) and also formal AK (e.g. RDF files). AK evolves rapidly during the architecting process, and effective version management of AK can support directly *AK versioning* (UC20) and indirectly *viewing the change history of AK* (includes UC20).

6.5.8 Web 2.0

Web 2.0 aims to enhance creativity, information sharing, collaboration and functionality of the Web. Interesting techniques in Web 2.0 for codified AKM include push and pull mechanisms, tags and context-aware mashups. Push and pull mechanisms (e.g. RSS – Rich Site Summary) can be used to *notify user about AK changes* (UC19) for subscribed users [114]. Tags can be used to *search/retrieve AK* (UC18) for Web pages that have been tagged. Context-aware mashups can be used to *view AK and their relationships* (UC2) e.g. all the inter-dependent elements of an architectural decision can be shown in a dynamic mashup Web page, which combines the AK elements from more than one source into a single integrated Web page [17].

6.6 Summary

For the effective usage of AK in the architecting activities, the AKM tools have been recognized as a great contribution [7]. In this chapter, we provide a survey of current tools and technologies with respect to the AKM strategies they adopt and the use cases they support. We hope to help AKM tool developers in understanding the state-of-the art and practice and get inspired in building their own tools. We expect that depending on their specific needs and organizational context, they will mix and match the appropriate technologies and ideas from existing tools, in order to build customized AKM tools. We are confident that, as more AKM tools are built, more AK will be used in practice and shared among organizations and thus contribute to establishing AKM in the daily organizational practices.

It is noted that the following use cases, identified in Sect. 6.2, have not been fully supported (implemented) by existing AKM tools: UC5 (*Identify stakeholder*), UC11 (*Synthesize AK*), UC13 (*Recover architectural decisions*), UC14 (*Evaluate AK*), UC21 (*Enrich AK (semi-) automatically*), and UC24 (*Assess design maturity*). We regard these use cases as the future challenges, which AKM tool developers can work on to provide more added value to existing AKM. We also believe that some promising technologies can be the key for implementing these use cases, such as NLP for intelligent support (advices and guidelines for making decisions) [196], context-aware text mining for the elicitation of user interests about AK, and ontology inferencing for the enrichment of AK.

Acknowledgements This research has been partially sponsored by the Dutch Joint Academic and Commercial Quality Research & Development (Jacquard) program on Software Engineering Research via contract 638.001.406 GRIFFIN: a GRId For inFormatIoN about architectural knowledge.

Chapter 7
Establishing and Managing Knowledge Sharing Networks

Patricia Lago

Abstract This chapter gives an overview of the approaches supporting the establishment and the management of social networks aimed at knowledge sharing. We identify two approaches. The first approach is made of networks driven by technologies and potentially providing support for architecture knowledge management, like grid computing and peer-to-peer technologies. These were initially meant for implementing very specific and low level services; nowadays they cover broader spectra like knowledge management in a distributed setting and knowledge grids. The second approach is made of networks autonomously created from already existing social communities. These are further enabled by Web 2.0 technologies and services.

The chapter describes the approaches and their inter-relations, and it highlights the needs for architecture knowledge management they can potentially support. An overview of some widely known approaches in the current practice further emphasizes which potential architecture knowledge management needs have been actually fulfilled. In this way, we illustrate what has been already experimented with, and what are the architecture knowledge management needs requiring further investigation.

7.1 Introduction

Software developers are knowledge workers. They take decisions on design issues, apply patterns, negotiate solutions, and so on. These software developers usually do not operate in a vacuum, but are part of one or more *social networks*, communities of people they interact with. Such a social network may consist of just the members of the current project, a circle of experts in a specific area, the members of a standardization body, etc.

Patricia Lago
VU University Amsterdam, The Netherlands, e-mail: patricia@cs.vu.nl

M. Ali Babar et al. (eds.), *Software Architecture Knowledge Management*,
DOI: 10.1007/978-3-642-02374-3_7,

Social networks can be supported by tools that facilitate communication, sharing, and exchange of information. For instance, a software architect searching for information on security on the company's intranet may be pointed to colleagues having experience in that area. The focus of this chapter is the characterization of solutions supporting the establishment of such social networks of professionals.

We recognize two main approaches behind such networking platforms. The first approach focuses on the creation of platform technologies to inter-connect sites that are geographically distributed. Such platforms initially supported very basic applications, like CPU optimization, distributed data processing, database duplication/distribution. In a second stage they evolved to support broader, more user-centric applications for specific domains, like enterprise virtual workspaces/offices, e-shopping, entertainment and gaming, collaborative software development, and tele-teaching. Examples of this first type of approach include peer-to-peer networks and grids. This approach is bottom-up, in that it started with implementing the lower-level technology, and thereafter evolved to support broader, higher-level applications.

The second approach started with pre-existing communities of people and organizations, autonomously created to share common interests and problems, and to deepen their knowledge and expertise in some areas. In a second stage, such communities discovered that the Web, and the recent Web 2.0 technologies, could serve very well in facilitating community interaction and knowledge sharing. Examples of this second type of approach include social networks (addressing both leisure and professional networking) and wiki's (addressing mainly knowledge communities within organizations). This second approach is top-down, in that it started with existing communities and their needs, and thereafter evolved to make use of the right technologies to support them.

Both approaches do not have a specific application objective in mind and can be used for a potentially wide range of applications, including architecture knowledge management on networks of software architects, or more generally communities of practice in the field of software architecting. Therefore, after describing the approaches as is, we analyze their suitability for use in architecture knowledge management (AKM). We use both characteristics of AKM (type of architectural knowledge to be shared and AKM strategies) as well as characteristics of the networking approaches (dynamism, support for knowledge description, support for knowledge discovery), and discuss the extent to which they can support AKM. This can be a starting point to decide on the selection of the right platforms for setting up an AKM network in a given context.

7.2 From Networking Platforms to Knowledge Communities

7.2.1 Networking Platforms

Architecture Knowledge Management is distributed in nature. Independent from the type and location of the participating sites, people and resources, AKM generally requires the contribution of multiple persons to a common body of knowledge.

People can always use architectural knowledge in isolation. For instance, share their own expertise, but also consume knowledge from a shared knowledge pool. However, when looking at the big picture, a body of knowledge is always the result of multiple contributors; it evolves thanks to active consuming and incremental refinement; it implies motivation and shared interests; it should represent a real added value to individuals and/or organizations.

To achieve the characteristics mentioned above, AKM needs the support of some kind of *networking platform*, i.e. a framework enabling and supporting people and systems to carry out activities on a network (typically the Internet). A network is often identified with *physical computer network*, i.e. a group of computers interconnected via a physical network. In modern times, however, platforms also (and especially) support the creation and management of *virtual social networks*, i.e. social structures of nodes (typically individuals or enterprises) hiding the details of the underlying physical network and tied together by higher level relations, such as values, friendship, vision; but also business, profession and expertise.

With this differentiation in mind, we can decouple a physical computer network from a virtual social network. As an example, Fig. 7.1 shows an enterprise organized in two branches (Branch A and Branch B): in each branch there is a virtual group made of three member nodes. This example can be visualized as a virtual social network (upper part of the figure), which hides the details of the underlying physical computer network (in the lower part of the figure). In this chapter we specifically focus on the upper part, the virtual social network. We discuss how peer-to-peer networks, Grids and the Semantic Web can support social networking in the specific context of AKM. To this end, we first explain the AKM characteristics we use for discussion.

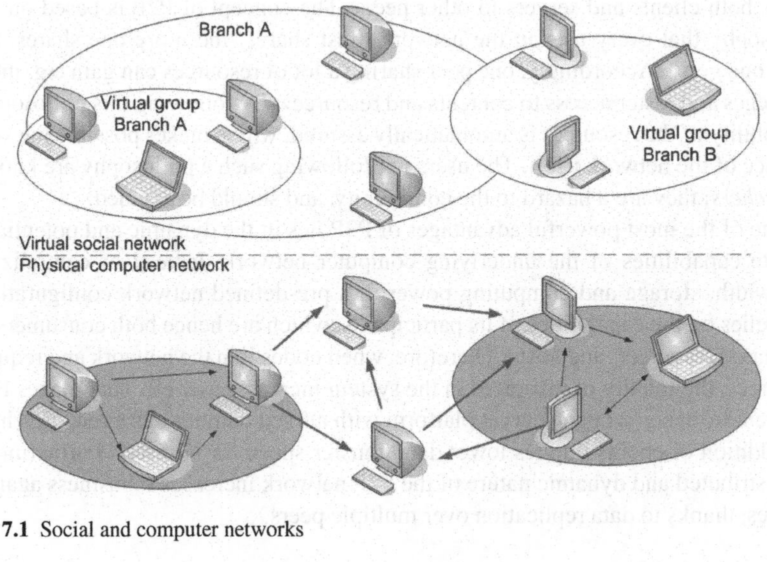

Fig. 7.1 Social and computer networks

Table 7.1 AKM aspects

AKM aspect	Examples	Further info
AK type	Tacit, explicit	Chap. 1
AKM strategy	Personalization, codification, hybrid	Chap. 1
KM school	Technocratic, behavioral, ...	Chap. 4

7.2.1.1 AKM Characteristics

To discuss the suitability of the different networking platforms for AKM we use the AKM aspects summarized in Table 7.1.

By supporting the flow (and not necessarily the storage) of information on a network, a *personalization strategy* aims at sharing *tacit knowledge* among participants. A *codification strategy*, instead, helps in systematizing, storing and making available *explicit knowledge*. A *hybrid strategy* looks for the right balance between personalization and codification, and therefore the right mix of tacit and explicit AK.

Moreover, as we focus on networking platforms, two of the three knowledge management schools discussed in Chap. 4 can be applied: the *technocratic school* focusing on systems for knowledge codification and personalization, and the *organizational school* focusing on models for orchestrating knowledge sharing in communities and enterprises.

AK types, AKM strategies and KM schools will be used to discuss the AKM support provided by the different types of networking platforms.

7.2.1.2 Peer-to-Peer Networks

A peer-to-peer (P2P) network is a social network of participating nodes (peers) acting as both clients and servers to other peers. The concept of P2P is based on the philosophy that every user in the network must share: "the more one shares, the more one gets". Accordingly, one peer sharing a lot of resources can gain e.g. more privileges and faster access to contents and resources. By following this philosophy, availability of the resources is automatically assured, which makes possible the subsistence of the network itself. The users not following such a philosophy are known as *leechers*; they are a hazard to the community, and should be avoided.

One of the most powerful advantages of P2P lies in the dynamic and potentially infinite capabilities of the underlying computer network. Instead of centralizing bandwidth, storage and computing power in a pre-defined network configuration, P2P relies on the capabilities of its participants, which are hence both consumers of the shared resources, and hosts. Therefore, when nodes join the network and request resources, the totality of resources in the system increases as well. That makes P2P different from e.g. a client–server platform with a fixed number of servers, in which the addition of clients implies lower data transfer speed for all users. Furthermore, the distributed and dynamic nature of the P2P network increases robustness against failures, thanks to data replication over multiple peers.

P2P networks have three main characteristics: self-organization, symmetric communication and distributed control [265]. They are *self-organizing* in the sense that they automatically adapt to the arrival, departure and failure of nodes. P2P networks go beyond services offered by typical client–server systems since communication is *symmetric*, where all peers act as both clients and servers. Lastly, P2P networks are *distributed* systems in nature, without any hierarchical organization or centralized control.

These main characteristics of P2P technologies make them well suited for architectural knowledge sharing among different stakeholders. By supporting an AKM community with a P2P network, the participants (organizations, departments or individuals) can dynamically join the community, maintain their own architectural knowledge while exchanging information [110]. A P2P network can further facilitate scalable composition of knowledge scattered across multiple and potentially heterogeneous sources (peers) and integrated opportunistically when needed [6]. In more detail, P2P network technologies can differ in how the peers are organized to build a network topology, and in how they can share information. P2P networks have been further classified into two main models, structured and unstructured (summarized in Table 7.2).

The *structured P2P networks* organize peers in a tightly controlled topology, where content is placed at pre-defined locations. This ensures higher performance of data discovery than in unstructured P2P networks. Still, some freedom is maintained by allowing each peer to be responsible for its content shared in the network. Structured P2P networks can efficiently locate rare items. In contrast, when queries concern popular contents, they encounter higher overhead. Due to its static architecture, this model resembles traditional client–server distributed architectures, and complies much less with the general P2P philosophy. It can fit very well in enterprises with a hierarchical organization and a static culture. There, AKM communities are typically planned in advanced and are less likely to change very quickly, or to cross the boundaries of the company. AK is typically explicit, following a codification strategy and reflecting a more technocratic KM school, where the knowledge is typically stored in knowledge bases and the AKM processes are documented.

According to the general model of **unstructured P2P networks**, the placement of the data is completely unrelated to the network topology: the peers are directly connected to each other, and they do not share any information about the data they contain. On the one hand, unstructured P2P networks are easier to implement than the structured ones, and require little maintenance. On the other hand, they are less scalable, which makes them not suitable for large-scale communities.

To solve some of the limitations mentioned above, unstructured P2P networks have been further specialized into hybrid centralized, purely decentralized and partially decentralized [16]. *Hybrid centralized networks* (in Fig. 7.2.a) became popular with Napster [231]. They use some managed infrastructure (the directory server), which maintains a global index of the files currently shared on the network. This introduces some scalability issues due to the limited size of the directory server and its capacity to respond to queries [214]. When searching for some content, a peer

Table 7.2 AKM aspects of different P2P network models

	STRUCTURED	UNSTRUCTURED		
		Hybrid centralized	Purely decentralized	Partially centralized
Summary	Pre-defined topology of both peers and contents	Central directory server in a star topology of peers	Dynamic, flat topology of random peers	Dynamic topology of super-peer network and attached groups of peers
Dynamism	(−) Static structure and pre-defined location of contents	(−) Static structure and location of contents	(+) Dynamic structure configuration	(+) Dynamic structure configuration
Semantic description of knowledge	(−) Keywords	(+) Keywords, but the presence of a directory server enables the use of more advanced semantic descriptions shared in the network	(−) Keywords	(+) Keywords, but the presence of the super-peers enables the use of more advanced semantic descriptions, eventually different for the different peer groups
Knowledge discovery	(+) Efficient	(+) Efficient	(−) Inefficient discovery of rare contents	(+) Efficient
AK type	Explicit	Explicit	Tacit	Explicit, tacit
AKM strategy	Codification	Codification	Personalization	Hybrid
KM school	Technocratic	Technocratic	Technocratic, organizational	Technocratic, organizational

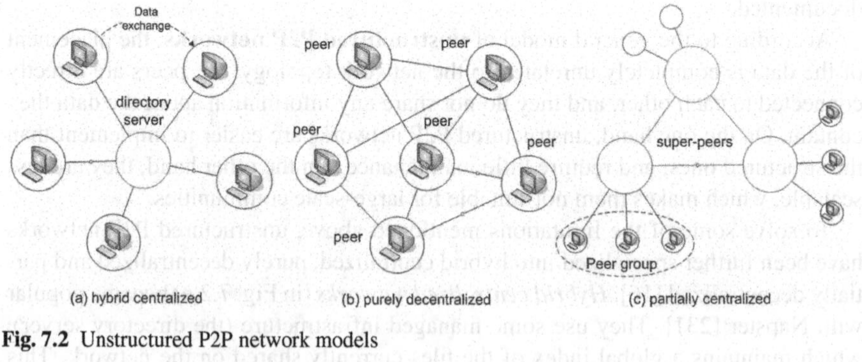

Fig. 7.2 Unstructured P2P network models

first contacts the central peers to receive the list of who shares it. Thereafter, the peer can directly connect to the peers in the list. Discovery information is quick and efficient. Nonetheless, hybrid centralized networks have a single point of failure which makes them vulnerable to attacks. If the central server (the "center of the star") is down, the network collapses completely. This has been demonstrated by the nowadays known "Napster case", where the Records Industry forced Napster to shut down, proving the vulnerability of the hybrid centralized network model.

In this type of network AK can be naturally managed at the central server. Both codification and personalization strategies could be supported, in that the participating peers could share either content or the information about their skills and expertise. Nonetheless, in both cases the failure of the central server would make the whole network unavailable, which makes this type of network quite unsuitable for AKM. A kind of hybrid approach could be to use this network for codification purposes only, and rely on an alternative more reliable technology for personalization, which demands higher availability to build trust among the participants.

Purely decentralized networks (in Fig. 7.2b, also called *pure* P2P networks) are distributed systems without any centralized control. All nodes are equivalent in functionality. They are organized in a random graph and use floods to discover contents stored by peers. Each node visited during a flood (each node chooses a neighbor at random) evaluates the query locally on the data items that it stores. This model does not impose any constraint on the topology or on the placement of the shared contents. It is suitable for very dynamic communities, sharing contents with similar characteristics and existing in multiple duplicated copies, like mass-market data sharing applications. It cannot efficiently locate rare data items, for which a large fraction of the network must be visited.

Extreme dynamism and freedom makes purely decentralized networks very suitable for implementing personalization strategies in dynamic enterprises with an open organization culture: AK sharing mechanisms like yellow pages and experience profiles can be easily exchanged, and the drawback of temporarily disconnected peers has less importance than in codification strategies (who is not available cannot help either). Still, peers can share their codified knowledge with the (maybe positive?) effect of "taking the knowledge with them when they are not connected". This can create important incentives in favor of AK sharing, e.g. authorship is automatically recognized as the shared knowledge is identified with the peer itself. Following the technocratic KM school, purely decentralized networks (like all P2P networks) have been created to share contents, in this case creating distributed knowledge bases that dynamically change in terms of both structure and available contents. Such P2P networks also follow the organizational KM school by supporting dynamism, i.e. informal networks and autonomous creation of communities of practice. Without any type of central point of control, though, poor support can be given to important AKM aspects like architecture compliance or alignment to shared terminology.

Partially centralized networks (in Fig. 7.2c) combine the efficiency and resilience of centralized networks, with the dynamics of decentralized ones. They yield a hierarchical topology made by two types of peers: the *super-peers* establish a backbone network of (centralized) index servers; they maintain the central indices for the information shared by the peers connected to them, called *leaf nodes*, or simply peers. When a new peer joins the network, it connects to a single super-peer, which gathers and stores the information about the peer and its shared contents. Super-peers are assigned based on certain criteria (typically bandwidth and processing capacity). In spite of their central role, super-peers are not single points of failure: if one of them fails, another peer will be promoted to super-peer and replace it. By forwarding queries only to those peers that potentially provide matching contents, super-peers significantly reduce discovery time, and overall network traffic.

Thanks to the balance between dynamism (of the peers) and centralization (supported by the super-peers), partially centralized networks can support hybrid AKM strategies: central information about expertise and skills, codified architectural knowledge, its classification and location can be managed by the super-peers, whereas personalization strategies can be implemented by dynamically available peers. Moreover, super-peers can represent (sub-)communities that remain available also when peer members are disconnected.

Looking back to Table 7.2, the majority of the P2P network models here discussed exhibit the following properties:

Dynamism. Once assigned, peer's neighbors cannot be dynamically re-organized to mirror the relativity of the current knowledge shared on the different nodes. In this way, peer groups cannot mime *too dynamic* situations like teams of professionals assigned to certain projects for a limited duration. Knowledge communities need the dynamic reconfiguration of the peer groups driven by the evolution of the shared knowledge.

Semantic knowledge description. Knowledge sharing is too coarse grained: contents are typically shared at the "file level", hence limiting the scope of the searches to an external, pre-defined classification scheme. In this way, successful sharing depends very much on having a common terminology shared among all network members, and classification keywords that fit all their needs and well represent the knowledge they want to share. Both preconditions are not feasible in communities spanning heterogeneous expertise, geographical boundaries, multiple departments, or different enterprises [44].

Heterogeneity. Heterogeneity in knowledge and/or expertise is not well supported. Apart from the fact that a basic P2P principle is in the peers being all the same, the actual contents (i.e. the semantics) of the shared knowledge is not well described. In AKM communities architectural knowledge is typically very variable and of diverse granularity. Hence, semantic support for knowledge description is absolutely necessary.

To overcome these limitations, P2P networks can be combined with other approaches. Both Grids and the Semantic Web provide interesting solutions to the shortcomings just mentioned.

7.2.1.3 Grids

Grids can be defined as groups of interconnected nodes. A grid is a form of distributed computing whereby a cluster of networked, loosely-coupled computers act in concert to perform very large tasks. A key characteristic of grid technologies is that the resources of different companies are grouped to enable and facilitate the collaboration of a group of people or organizations [312]. As such, grids present a great level of *heterogeneity* (no assumption is made on the hardware, network technologies, operating systems, administrative domains or security policies involved). This is the main difference with computational grids, where groups of twin nodes are connected via a high-speed network and coordinated by a master node to execute a single application in parallel on multiple machines.

The paradigm of the grid has been originally adopted from industries for delivering IT resources as a utility. Accordingly, grids have been addressed for a long time as infrastructures clustering low level resources such as computing-, network- and storage services. The last years, though, witnessed phenomena like globalization and the ever increasing use of the Internet as backbone for big organizations. This led to the definition of a variety of grid models under the umbrella of *business grids*, i.e. the assembly of resources according to organizational principles and their related management policies, to support overall business applications. Communities of practice in the software architecture field are one example of business grids.

The applications supported by business grids are inherently interactive, requiring requests and responses to be executed in a timely fashion. Typically, business applications have a number of requirements currently not addressed by grid technologies, resulting in a gap between the future business grids and traditional grid technologies. Types of business grids (extracted from [232]) are visualized in Fig. 7.3:

Enterprise grid is a grid within an organization. They naturally include grids across different departments and within a wider organization. Accordingly, they

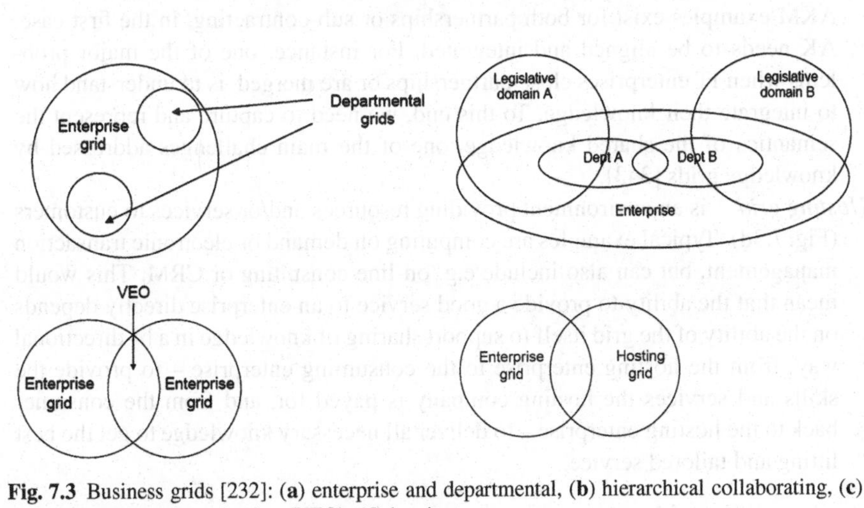

Fig. 7.3 Business grids [232]: (**a**) enterprise and departmental, (**b**) hierarchical collaborating, (**c**) Virtual Enterprise Organization (VEO), (**d**) hosting

can be seen as "grids of grids" including smaller (or departmental) grids. Depending on the level of integration, enterprise grids can be organized as loose collections of departmental grids (shown in Fig. 7.3a) or as integrated, hierarchical networks of collaborating grids (in Fig. 7.3b): the more integration, the higher the synergistic value delivered to the whole enterprise. A clear advantage of the latter type of integration is that departments can exchange and share their knowledge still remaining within the enterprise boundaries. In the case of departmental grids, instead, only computational resources can be shared, hence leading to a collection of islands with no transfer of knowledge.

Communities of practice in the software architecture field can be mapped on enterprise grids in a quite straightforward way: they reflect departments (or project and teams within them); the more integrated the grids, the better the AKM strategies. Nonetheless, success of AK sharing depends very much on the culture of the organization, and on the policies in place [77].

Enterprises spanning multiple countries (thus crossing multiple administrative domains as illustrated in Fig. 7.3b) may differ in legal requirements each department should comply with. This can have a non-negligible impact on the type and ways knowledge can be shared, as typically occurs in large organizations carrying out global software development with off-shored departments.

Virtual Enterprise Organizations (VEOs) occur when different organizations (falling under different administrative domains) collaborate. In this case, the VEO (in Fig. 7.3c) regards only a subset of the whole enterprise grid. This type of grid can be adopted in case of partnership- or sub-contractor relationship between companies. In a partnership, VEOs have a "peer" relationship, which is typically regulated by a combination of the policies of the partners. In a sub-contractor relationship, the one administrative domain (the main contractor) has priority over the other, hence imposing its policies on the VEO. This typically means that knowledge is transferred from the supplier (fulfilling the contract) towards the main contractor, and less in the other direction.

AKM examples exist for both partnerships or sub-contracting. In the first case, AK needs to be aligned and integrated. For instance, one of the major problems when IT enterprises close partnerships or are merged, is to understand how to integrate their knowledge. To this end, we need to capture and represent the semantics of the shared knowledge, one of the main challenges addressed by knowledge grids [343].

Hosting grid is an environment providing resources and/or services to customers (Fig. 7.3d). Typical examples are computing on demand or electronic transaction management, but can also include e.g. on-line consulting or CRM. This would mean that the ability to provide a good service to an enterprise directly depends on the ability of the grid itself to support sharing of knowledge in a bi-directional way: from the hosting enterprise to the consuming enterprise – to provide the skills and services the hosting company is payed for, and from the consumer back to the hosting enterprise – to deliver all necessary knowledge to get the best fitting and tailored service.

To our knowledge, hosting has not been discussed in the literature, at least not from a technological point of view. In our opinion, grid technologies could offer new business opportunities, for instance to transform AK as a business asset and offer on-line knowledge-based expertise and support through a hosting grid connection.

Ian Foster [124], the "father" of Grid, proposed a checklist for three main Grid characteristics: (1) coordination of resources/contents that are not subject to centralized control, (2) use of standard, open, general-purpose protocols and interfaces, and (3) delivery of non-trivial qualities of service.

The business grids discussed so far denote the specific adaptation of the grid paradigm to the context of business applications. Business applications (like AKM in the context of enterprises) have not been explicitly excluded from traditional Grid environments; however, their specific nature has been most often ignored. Business grids in general, and their use for AKM in particular, clearly feature characteristics (2) and (3) of the Foster definition: an open standards-based approach (characteristic (2)) is key for realizing a shared infrastructure spanning different administrative domains; business applications certainly require nontrivial qualities of service (characteristic (3)) due to their highly networked nature, i.e. their coexistence with other applications and services. For instance, the knowledge grid of a global enterprise, unifying the AK communities of practice at all sites, must ensure qualities like security, availability, performance, just to mention some.

Coordination of resources/contents (characteristic (1)) is fulfilled in most of the cases, even if we should distinguish between centralized control and organizational policies. For example, whilst different IT systems even within a single enterprise may well be controlled (managed) by the various groups that use them, there is likely to be some central policy set upon each of these by the enterprise. In more advanced scenarios (such as, again, communities of practice that cross organizational boundaries) even a central policy may not exist. To support this situation, decentralized solutions become more attractive, like those featured by the unstructured P2P network models discussed in Sect. 7.2.1.2.

The grid models discussed in this section are independent from the type of knowledge they share, and how they do it. Moreover, the notion of grid does not prescribe if AK is tacit or explicit, or if the applications implemented by a certain grid support codification or personalization strategies. Rather, grids aim at supporting *heterogeneous* knowledge and *hybrid* strategies, and unify them in a networked matrix of participants. Thus, P2P networks and grids mainly differ (and complement each other) in heterogeneity: grids support heterogeneous contents and participants, P2P networks support heterogeneous structures of similar contents and twin participants.

7.2.1.4 Semantic Web

The Semantic Web [329] is intended to make the Web more intelligent by improving the value of, and interactivity with, the vast amount of data on the Web. It is based on three building blocks [117]: the *Resource Description Framework* (RDF) is the basic format to describe information on the Web. On top of that, *ontology languages* define the terms used to describe and represent an area of knowledge [330]. The Web Ontology Language (OWL) can define ontologies in a standard way for them to be compatible and hence comparable. Thirdly, *inference engines* analyze ontologies to find new relations among terms and data.

The wide and fast spreading of the Semantic Web is tangible in daily life: by inserting a sentence in a Web browser we can be easily connected to that one-matching web site, or suggested with amazingly fitting hits. But this is just the top of the iceberg: companies crowd-source their most innovative products by analyzing opinions expressed in social networks, whereas medical research counts enormous advances by connecting knowledge bases once isolated and nowadays merged into a richer, global body of knowledge.

Thanks to standard ontologies and inference engines able to scan the "Web of data", the Semantic Web can offer advanced approaches for data integration, knowledge management and decision support. This is a powerful framework usable in any type of context, including networks of professionals and data in the field of architecture knowledge [117]. Still, the integration of knowledge born in different contexts remains a very difficult and still insufficiently addressed problem. The Semantic Web recognizes two main approaches to translate, or *match*, different ontologies [5]:

Direct matching defines the relations between pairs of ontologies using solely the information contained in those two ontologies. The resulting information depends on the actual contents of the used ontologies. It is very expensive and inefficient, as each time a new ontology is created, new ad hoc matchings must be added. This approach seems to be applicable only in very specific contexts where different ontologies share a large enough number of common data items.

Indirect matching uses external background knowledge to derive the matching. The relations between two (or more) ontologies is defined in terms of a core, shared vocabulary that acts as standard reference. This approach assumes that the knowledge context yields some level of maturity where a core vocabulary can be defined.

We can find back these approaches in AKM, where enterprises use different, often similar terms to mean same concepts. For instance, Liang et al. [207] compare direct and indirect matching in AK management to measure their cost-effectiveness. The GRIFFIN Grid (discussed in Chap. 8) exploits an indirect ontology matching approach to loosely integrate collaborating organizations in a virtual and distributed knowledge sharing community. Much work has been done in mining existing AK bases or bodies of knowledge to generalize and codify AK instances in formalized ontologies.

The Semantic Web provides the technology to define ontologies (thus supporting a codification strategy) so that the represented knowledge can be shared by and become interoperable for any type of knowledge communities, including AKM communities. For this to become true, the knowledge users need to discover new ontologies, which are not known to them before, and use them to annotate the content and formulate their information requests. This demands for environments that support creating and maintaining ontologies, and sharing them in a controlled manner.

It must be noticed that the main focus in Semantic Web is on codification of knowledge, even if the very same mechanisms are applicable to realize personalization strategies, for instance, to semantically relate the information shared by people in social networks and put them into contact [248]. This is already being done in many social networking applications like Facebook or LinkedIn.

7.2.2 Supported Knowledge Communities

Table 7.3 summarizes the properties of Business Grids and the Semantic Web separately, and highlights their respective pros and cons w.r.t. the AKM aspects. In various application domains and research communities, the literature reports on attempts to combine these approaches to support (either implicitly or explicitly) knowledge communities. Here we report on some examples, with the aim to illustrate how they can support AKM.

As discussed in Sect. 7.2.1.2, P2P networks do not account for semantic relationships amongst resources. Many surveys have been carried out to solve these shortcomings (e.g. [6, 110, 16]), with almost equivalent solutions: the combination of P2P and the Semantic Web technology in an attempt to overcome such limitations.

Table 7.3 AKM aspects of Business Grids and the Semantic Web

	BUSINESS GRIDS	SEMANTIC WEB
Summary	Groups of nodes with hybrid characteristics. Types of business grids are: (hierarchical) enterprise and departmental, VEOs, hosting grids	Web of semantically annotated information and services, and related enabling technologies. Seen as one, global platform, no specific organization is assumed
Dynamism	(−) Possible but not explicitly addressed	(−) Possible but not explicitly addressed
Semantic description of knowledge	(−) Possible but not explicitly addressed. AK sharing is supported if the right business grid models are chosen (e.g. VEOs enable AK sharing, departmental grids don't)	(+) Semantic Web technologies are especially conceived to describe and retrieve knowledge and associated semantics
Heterogeneity	(+) Support both heterogeneous resources and services, and heterogeneous knowledge. The latter can be used to support hybrid AKM strategies	(+) Supports integration of any type of knowledge, for both codification and personalization AKM strategies
AK type	Any	Any
AKM strategy	Any	Codification (to enable any AKM strategy on top)
KM school	Organizational	Technocratic

For instance, Siebes et al. [299, 140] aim at supporting personalization strategies in knowledge sharing. They introduced a model to semantically describe the expertise of peers and how peers promote it as advertisement messages in a network, in which a shared ontology is used. This model assumes that one ontology is shared among all community members. This makes is very suitable for AKM communities within the same domain or practice, but less attractive for e.g. VEOs where sub-communities need their own ontology. In the latter case, the ontology matching problem must be solved to translate the knowledge from one ontology to another.

Works like [21, 6] realized environments that support the dynamic reconfiguration of group memberships depending on the evolution in e.g. the knowledge shared or the interests of the individuals. By sharing expertise descriptions and sending around advertisements, AKM communities can grow and change dynamically.

An emerging trend in virtualization is Cloud Computing. Both Grid Computing and Cloud Computing implement the more general model of Utility Computing [183]. However, while the first evolved in a scientific community as a means to solve computationally challenging tasks, the latter focuses on Web-scale applications and services, and introduces innovative business models. By building services on a Cloud Computing infrastructure, enterprises are suddenly granted with potentially unlimited resources in terms of both storage, execution, services and application logics. This way they can solve increasingly pressing issues like scalability, availability, performance, flexibility, time to market; and they can realize the promise of the Internet to offer same opportunities to e.g. large organizations and startups. As summarized in BusinessWeek [179], "The term 'cloud computing' encompasses many areas of tech, including software as a service, a software distribution method pioneered by Salesforce.com about a decade ago. It also includes newer avenues such as hardware as a service, a way to order storage and server capacity on demand from Amazon and others. What all these cloud computing services have in common, though, is that they are all delivered over the Internet, on demand, from massive data centers.". As such, Cloud Computing encompasses many areas of technologies from software-as-a-service, to hardware-as-a-service, to social networks or Web 2.0, further discussed in Sect. 7.3.

7.3 From Knowledge Communities to Social Networks

In contrast to the networking platforms discussed in Sect. 7.2, some communities first emerged from the practice and organized themselves as *networks* de-facto, and only later considered how emerging technologies could act as enablers.

McDermott [222] gives some advice on the establishment of communities of practice. He describes the complementarity of cross-functional teams and communities of practice within an enterprise. *Cross-functional teams* link together people from different professions, who work in close proximity to deliver well defined, shared outputs (typically products). They are driven by clear tasks and have clear boundaries determined by a pre-defined selection of team members. *Communities of practice (COPs)* are groups of people sharing common interests and expertise, who arise naturally as organic networks with permeable boundaries, where people join and leave depending on how interests evolve, or 'hot topics' shift, over time. Such communities are driven by the value (information, interests or practices) provided to the members of the community. The focus is on learning.

Because communities of practice are voluntary, what makes them successful over time is their ability to generate enough excitement, relevance, and value to attract and engage members [336]. While teams are very efficient in producing a final product resulting from cross-functional expertise, they may hinder cross-team interaction, hence leading to isolation. COPs, in turn, can bridge this isolation gap by cross-connecting knowledge.

This self-organization of COPs does not preclude the possibility for enterprises to start them intentionally, and provide the right mechanisms for them to grow. Gongla and Rizzuto [135] indicate three forces that are influential in COPs evolution, namely people, processes and technology. Among the lessons learned, the authors highlight that successful communities always grow around people who share a common interest or expertise, and fail if, for instance, too much attention is given to process and technology. While technologies are fundamental to support the sharing of tacit and later of explicit knowledge, they should always be flexible to fit the needs of the people, and adapt to their specific habits and preferences. A similar observation has been reported by Thomas et al. [321] for virtual teams working in global settings. While technology results absolutely crucial to effectively support collaboration, its successful use should be regularly monitored and timely changed if not fitting well in people's work.

Various studies report on technologies supporting knowledge communities. Thomas et al. [321] report on the top 20 technologies used in more than 20 organizations. Next to what they call "comfort technologies" common to all organizations (audio conferencing, email and phone) the mostly used tools are related to project- and task management, version management and people-to-people communication (all used in between 73% and 80%). More complicated tools like knowledge portals and wiki's score relatively low (55% and 7%, respectively). Technologies explicitly mentioned in [135] include on-line directories, search engines, and yellow pages to identify individuals and groups according to their knowledge and expertise. These aim at supporting personalization strategies – for COPs to grow, build community identity and trust, and to quickly link individuals on cross-functional teams with their peers. Technologies mentioned to support codification strategies include on-line repositories, classification and categorization schema tools, portals, and tools for collaboration and decision-making.

7.3.1 Social Communities

By looking at existing communities, we can distinguish between knowledge communities and social networks. Knowledge communities focus on the human and motivation aspects of groups of people to come together. Social networks focus on the creation of technology-supported networks that link them together on a distributed network like the Web.

Nowadays there is little difference between knowledge communities and social networks. Rather, they are two sides of the same entity, i.e. social communities. Examples of social communities in the software architecture field span from professional bodies (like the International Association of Software Architects, The Worldwide Institute of Software Architects and the IFIP Working Group 2.10 on Software Architecture) to enterprise communities (like www.bredemeyer.com or the Architecture blogs of professionals and companies like Microsoft and IBM).

7.3.2 Support for Social Communities

Two main technologies play an increasingly important role in supporting social communities, Web 2.0 and wiki systems. Chapter 6 addressed them from a technological perspective, by describing which AKM use cases they can support. Here we further describe their ability to support social interaction in Web-based communities.

7.3.2.1 Web 2.0

The term Web 2.0 became prominent after the O'Reilly Media Web 2.0 conference in 2004. According to O'Reilly [242], "Web 2.0 is the business revolution in the computer industry caused by the move to the Internet as a platform, and an attempt to understand the rules for success on that new platform." As such, Web 2.0 represents a paradigm shift in how people use the Web [209], introducing social more than just technological innovation. For instance, Web 2.0 introduces open contribution of knowledge, and its global (if not free) access. This has been a major revolution in what enterprises always considered as industrial secret and their differentiating factor.

Lin [209] defined this social innovation in terms of three principles that Web 2.0 technologies should support: *simplicity* to attract and involve common people, *scalability* to ensure global access, and *sensibility* to report about and influence popularity.

Though recognizing that the definition of Web 2.0 remains elusive, Clarke [70] identifies four key aspects of Web 2.0 from a marketing perspective: syndication of (1) content, (2) advertising, (3) storage and (4) effort. There, *syndication* refers to the loose, unincorporated affiliation of people or companies, and the loose distribution of media material. In its essence, the central aspect of Web 2.0 can be identified in the transformation of the Web into a global platform for information sharing (corresponding to content syndication) coupled with the ability of both individuals and organizations to contribute new information and modify existing one. This led to cascading effects, like open access to any type of resources, new business models, and new privacy and ethical concerns.

In Clarke's classification, effort syndication is especially relevant for AKM communities. He observes that individuals perceive themselves as participating to a community, whereas their efforts and behaviour are part of an economy being used (either officially or unofficially) for profit. The communitarian perspective implies a fifth key aspect of Web 2.0 termed *social syndication*, this embracing "cross-leveraging and collaboration of content, effort and infrastructure".

Yakovlev [340] gives an overview of widely known Web 2.0 mechanisms that enable the autonomous creation of virtual communities of peers. Among them we find wiki's (used by enterprises to aggregate input from members of various focused groups), RSS feeds (allowing community members to remain up-to-date on selected subjects), social networking (supporting autonomous community building) and folksonomies (supporting users of a social environment in collaboratively creating and managing tags to annotate and categorize content).

As observed by Passant et al. [248], the emergence of social networks allow to build apparently unrelated islands of information. Semantic Web capabilities and Web 2.0 technologies together can support detecting complex networks of relations among these islands, hence inferring new knowledge.

7.3.2.2 Wiki's

First created in 1994 (WikiWikiWeb), wiki systems' initial goal was to give people the ability to quickly put content on the Web. While very much used in private communities within enterprises, wiki's were meant for the general public – to gather content bottom-up, delegate control on content to its contributors and reach consensus.

O'Leary [240] describes the pros and cons of wiki systems in making tacit knowledge explicit. By making available information about contributors, wiki's can link people with common interests. They are very suitable to describe best practices, and gather and structure information like vocabularies and taxonomies. On the other hand, wiki's typically lack referees or peer reviews, fact that can lead to inaccurate information. Nonetheless, some limitations are mitigated by more advanced features, like the ability to control changes by alerting the original contributors or people interested in a particular subject, and by categorizing contributors by reliability or level of expertise.

Semantic wiki's combine wiki's properties, such as ease of use, collaboration, and linking, with Semantic Web technologies, such as structured content, knowledge models in the form of ontologies, and reasoning. They offer simple ways to semantically annotating information, seamless semantic search, and extraction of metadata from contents like articles and documents.

Recently, wiki's are being increasingly used as knowledge management tools. As reported in [274], a weakness of *normal* wiki's is that knowledge is easy to create but increasingly difficult to retrieve. Semantic wiki's provide a solution to this problem, by allowing its uses to easily enrich the captured knowledge, and further instantly benefit from the unavoidable additional effort. Several European Union projects investigated knowledge management in semantic wiki's [www.kiwi-project.eu, nepomuk.semanticdesktop.org].

AKM demands for a mix of generic and domain specific features. Farenhorst and van Vliet [116] observed that wiki's can be very supportive to the architecting process. Nonetheless, in their list of do's and dont's, very little turns to be specific to architectural knowledge, and the main strengths of using wiki's resulted to be their support for a central storage place for any type of information and its use for connecting people. In comparing the existing AKM tools, they further identify a main advantage shared by all of them, namely their use of a tailored database and underlying knowledge model that support well knowledge retrieval. Wiki's are weak in this respect: simplicity is indeed at the cost of efficiency. Nonetheless, semantic wiki's might have been solved this issue.

A different though successful approach based on wiki's is discussed in Chap. 12 where the focus is purely on supporting AK codification and sharing.

7.4 Summary

As we have seen in the previous sections, we recognize two overall approaches supporting the establishment and the management of social networks aimed at knowledge sharing. Section 7.2 presented and compared peer-to-peer networks, Grids and the Semantic Web, and how they can support knowledge communities from a main technological perspective. AKM communities can be mapped on the various types of business grids, and depending on their characteristics and their AK sharing objectives the best fitting P2P model and/or Semantic Web technologies can be adopted.

Section 7.3 presented the concept of social communities and how they can be supported by Web 2.0 and Wiki's. Here we considered Web 2.0 as *the loose affiliation of people and companies, and the loose distribution of content, resources and effort*. As such, it includes an overarching umbrella of technologies that can support any type of AKM community, for instance combining the approaches discussed in Sect. 7.2. Wiki's are one example of such technologies gaining in popularity and maturity in the AKM industrial practice. Wiki's take a codification approach, but to potentially support any type of AKM strategy.

From a holistic perspective, the approaches we discussed complement each other in realizing AK sharing social networks. Peer-to-peer networks and Grids use the Internet to inter-connect sites, thus building a *Web of people (and organizations)*. The Semantic Web uses the Internet to inter-connect knowledge, thus building the *Web of data* (i.e. the AK to be shared by people). Finally, Web 2.0 uses the Web of people and data to inter-connect services, thus offering the mechanisms for AK sharing (i.e. the *Web of services*). While paradigms and technologies for knowledge sharing social networks seem mature enough for use in the practice, we feel that they are still largely unexplored in their combination, and full potential.

Acknowledgements We would like to thank Frank van Harmelen and Maarten van Steen for their helpful comments.

This research has been partially sponsored by the Dutch Joint Academic and Commercial Quality Research and Development (Jacquard) program on Software Engineering Research via contract 638.001.406 GRIFFIN: a GRId For inFormatIoN about architectural knowledge; and by the European Community FP7 grant agreement 215483 Software Services and Systems (S-Cube) Network of Excellence.

Part III
Experience with Architecture Knowledge Management

Irrespective of the sophistication and theoretical soundness of a software development technology, it is hard to predict with any level of confidence how it would perform in real-world scenarios, how well it would be accepted by the intended users, or how easy or hard it would be to integrate it in the current development processes. Methods, techniques, and tools for managing architectural knowledge are no exception to the rule. Rather, any technology related to a multidisciplinary area such as knowledge management can pose more technical and non-technical challenges than a pure technical solution. Only practical experiences from real-world settings can show whether and how a particular architecture knowledge management technology works and what challenges can be expected. In this Part, the focus is on exactly these aspects of architecture knowledge management solutions.

The lessons learned and experiences gained from developing and implementing technologies for managing architectural knowledge will provide useful insights to readers interested in gaining knowledge about the industrial use of the methods and tools presented in this book. The chapters in this part are focused on showing the practical applications of the theoretical approaches, tools, and technologies for supporting the architecture knowledge management. Having described the theoretical approaches, techniques, and tools in the first two parts of this book, this part reveals how to put them into practice to support the activities and processes for managing architectural knowledge. Moreover, practitioners can also be interested in knowing the potential implications of and the required resources for introducing architecture knowledge management initiatives in their respective organizations.

To answer these questions, this part of the book presents several case studies, experience reports, and empirical studies of the architecture knowledge management technologies. It also provides insights into the human and organizational aspects of capturing and sharing architectural knowledge based on empirical studies carried out in large organizations.

This part starts with a chapter on lessons learned from a Dutch research project, GRIFFIN, which aims to develop notations, tools, and methods to extract, represent and manage architectural knowledge to support the architecting processes. The project team, Hans van Vliet, Paris Avgeriou, Remco de Boer, Viktor Clerc, Rik Farenhorst, Anton Jansen, and Patricia Lago, reflects upon their experiences of developing and deploying various methods and tools for managing architectural knowledge. They highlight the key achievements of this four year long project and summarize the lessons learned from the case studies they carried out during the project. The reported experiences also provide useful insights into the mechanics and pre-requisites of successful research and industry collaboration for developing and empirically assessing architecture knowledge management solutions.

Reasoning is an integral part of a decision making activity like designing architectures. Most of the time, the reasoning is not performed systematically and explicitly. That means the reasons underpinning design decisions remain implicit and undocumented. In chap. 9, Antony Tang and Hans van Vliet propose a method for supporting systematic reasoning during the architecture design process. This chapter provides an overview of the limitations of existing design rationale approaches and details different aspects of the proposed method. The authors also report an industrial case study carried out to assess the proposed method. The findings from the case study provides the evidential support for the practical benefits of the presented method and associated graphical representation for explicitly modeling design decisions and reasoning.

Feedback loops and experience-based learning are necessary for improving an organization's abilities of sharing architectural knowledge. However, many organizations may not be able to design and deploy effective and efficient feedback and experience flows for sharing architectural knowledge. In Chap. 10, Kurt Schneider and Daniel Lübke describe an approach to modeling information flows as a means of sharing architectural knowledge in an organization. He demonstrates the use of the information flows for sharing knowledge about Service-Oriented Architecture (SOA) in a project.

Open Source Software (OSS) has become a major force behind the reuse of platforms, components and code between organizations. However, there is hardly any reliable information about the practices of sharing knowledge about architectural decisions in OSS projects. It is assumed that knowledge sharing is mainly implicit with the project owners or package owners being the sources of architectural knowledge. Ioannis Stamelos and George Kakarontzas tackle this issue in Chap. 11 by providing a detailed account of the different mechanisms used to share knowledge about architectural decisions in OSS communities. They also identify some of the most commonly used ways of storing architectural knowledge, which is easily accessible to the developers and users of OSS projects.

IBM is well known for having effective and efficient processes and technologies to support knowledge management within its business units. In Chap. 12, Olaf Zimmermann, Petra Kopp, and Stefan Pappe describe the practices and technologies they have introduced in one of the business units of IBM for capturing and sharing architectural knowledge. The authors provide a detailed account of their approach to building and using a Service-Oriented Architecture (SOA) infrastructure reference as a mechanism of managing architectural knowledge. Their case study also provides useful information about various ways of identifying, distilling, and distributing architectural knowledge from industrial projects.

It is a common observation that there is quite less information available about the industrial practices of managing and sharing architectural knowledge. Even lesser is known about the socio-psychological factors that need to be taken into account for designing and deploying architectural knowledge sharing strategies. Chapter 13 provides important information on this vital topic. In this chapter, Eltjo Poort, Agung Pramono, Michiel Perdeck, Viktor Clerc, and Hans van Vliet report the findings from a survey study that aimed to explore the opinions and experiences of software architects about various aspects of architectural knowledge sharing in a major Dutch IT services company. Their analysis of the gathered data provides interesting insights into the challenges involved in sharing architectural knowledge and the relationships between knowledge sharing and successful projects. The results reported in this chapter can help practitioners to understand the different factors that can motivate software architects for sharing architectural knowledge. This chapter also appears in the Proceedings of the 2009 Conference on the Quality of Software Architectures (QoSA).

Chapter 8
The GRIFFIN Project: Lessons Learned

Hans van Vliet, Paris Avgeriou, Remco C. de Boer, Viktor Clerc, Rik Farenhorst, Anton Jansen, and Patricia Lago

Abstract GRIFFIN is a joint research project of the VU University Amsterdam and the University of Groningen. The GRIFFIN project develops notations, tools and associated methods to extract, represent and use architectural knowledge that currently is not documented or represented in the system. The research is carried out in a consortium with various industries, both large and small, that provide case studies and give regular feedback. Paraphrasing [327], the goal of the GRIFFIN project can be summarized as "What architects know, and how they know it". In this chapter, we give an overview of the results of the GRIFFIN project, and lessons learned with respect to software architecture knowledge management.

8.1 Introduction

GRIFFIN is a joint research project of the VU University Amsterdam and the University of Groningen, both in the Netherlands. GRIFFIN stands for "GRId For inFormatIoN about architectural knowledge". The project is supported by the Dutch Joint Academic and Commercial Quality Research and Development (Jacquard) program on Software Engineering Research, and runs from 2005–2009. The research is carried out in a consortium with various industrial partners, both large and small. These partners provide us with case studies and give regular feedback. The domains of these case studies range from a family of consumer electronics products to a highly distributed system that collects scientific data from around 15,000 sources to a service-oriented system in a business domain.

Hans van Vliet (✉), Remco C. de Boer, Viktor Clerc, Rik Farenhorst, and Patricia Lago
VU University Amsterdam, The Netherlands, e-mail: [hans,remco,viktor,rik,patricia]@cs.vu.nl

Paris Avgeriou and Anton Jansen
University of Groningen, The Netherlands, e-mail: paris@cs.rug.nl,gradius@fmf.nl

M. Ali Babar et al. (eds.), *Software Architecture Knowledge Management*,
DOI: 10.1007/978-3-642-02374-3_8, © Springer-Verlag Berlin Heidelberg 2009

The GRIFFIN project develops notations, tools and associated methods to extract, represent and use architectural knowledge that currently is not documented or represented in the system. In GRIFFIN, Architectural Knowledge is defined as the integrated representation of the software architecture of a software-intensive system) or a family of systems), the architectural design decisions, and the external context/environment.

GRIFFIN was partly inspired by earlier research we carried out in design space analysis. In [57], we analyzed the complete design space of an electronic commerce system. In the end, three feasible solutions remained. For each of these feasible solutions, trade-offs had to be made, and certain requirements had to be relaxed on the way to the final solutions. After the exercise, we confronted an experienced architect in the domain of electronic commerce with our analysis. He told us he knew these three solutions existed. But he also told us he did not (anymore) know of the trade-offs made on the way to these solutions. This architectural knowledge had apparently vaporized. This is typical for many a software development processes. Architectural knowledge is like material floating in a pond. When not touched for a while, it sinks and disappears from sight. The original goal of the GRIFFIN project was to make this architectural knowledge explicit as much as possible, to prevent it from getting out of sight. Paraphrasing [327], this can be summarized as "What architects know, and how they know it". In the next sections, we give an overview of the case studies carried out and the results obtained, and conclude with lessons learned w.r.t.software architecture knowledge management. In terms of the classification given in Chap. 2, our research fits the *decision-centric* view on software architectural knowledge, with specific attention to three of the four trends mentioned in Sect. 2.4: *Sharing architectural knowledge*, *Aligning architecting with requirements engineering*, and *Intelligent support for architecting*.

8.2 The Beginning

In the first year of the project, we tried to characterize the use of architectural knowledge in the Netherlands at that time. We devised a model of architectural knowledge, an abstract conceptualization of the architectural knowledge domain, and applied this model to various participating organizations. We also constructed a series of use cases for architectural knowledge, and performed survey-based research to get insight in the way practitioners view and use architectural knowledge.

8.2.1 Core Model of Architectural Knowledge

Our initial model of architectural knowledge was based on existing literature and our own insights and ideas. We next tried to map actual usage of architectural knowledge in four participating organizations onto this model. These four organization can be described as follows:

- *RFA*, a large software development organization, responsible for development and maintenance of systems for among others the public sector.
- *VCL*, a large, multi-site consumer electronics organization where embedded software is developed in a distributed setting.
- *RDB*, an SME performing independent software product audits for third parties.
- *PAV*, a large scientific organization that has to deal with software development projects spanning a long time frame (up to a period of more than ten years).

The initial model exhibited a number of mismatches between our theory and industrial practice. The initial model highly conformed to the IEEE-1471 standard for architectural description [155]. IEEE-1471 prescribes the use of so-called 'Viewpoints to describe the architecture from the perspective of different stakeholders. The resulting 'Views (partial descriptions of the architecture) are aggregated in a single architecture description. Although stakeholders and their concerns play a key role in any software architecting process, the tight coupling of the model to IEEE-1471's Views and Viewpoints turned out to be a mismatch with most organizations practice. In hindsight this need not come as a big surprise, since organizations can (and do) use other approaches for documenting their architectures, which need not coincide with the IEEE-1471 way.

From a closer inspection of the mismatching concepts we learned that those concepts could either be expressed in terms of other concepts already present in the model, or as more generic concepts that are used by the organizations. We therefore constructed a new model of architectural knowledge that is both minimalistic and complete. We regard a model as complete if there are no concepts from other approaches that have no counterpart in the model. With 'minimalistic we signify the feature that it should not be possible to express some concepts from the model in any other concepts from the model. Based on these insights we modified the initial model to obtain a model that is both complete and minimalistic. Because of this latter feature, we refer to our model as a core model of architectural knowledge; elements that can be modeled in terms of core elements do not belong to the core.

Our core model of architectural knowledge is depicted in Fig. 8.1. As a result of the minimalistic aspect of this model, the core model leaves room for the use of different architecture description methods, including IEEE-1471. In our core model of architectural knowledge, the concepts of Stakeholder and Concern coincide with the, widely accepted, definitions of these terms in IEEE-1471: a stakeholder is "an individual, team, or organization (or classes thereof) with interests in, or concerns relative to, a system" [155]. Both IEEE-1471 concepts of Architectural Model and View are subsumed in our notion of Artifact, i.e. an inanimate information bearer such as a document, source code, or a chapter in a book. Storing or describing the Architectural Design in either of these artifacts can be abstracted to a single action to reflect. The Architectural Design can be reflected using different Languages, including models, figures, programming languages, and plain English.

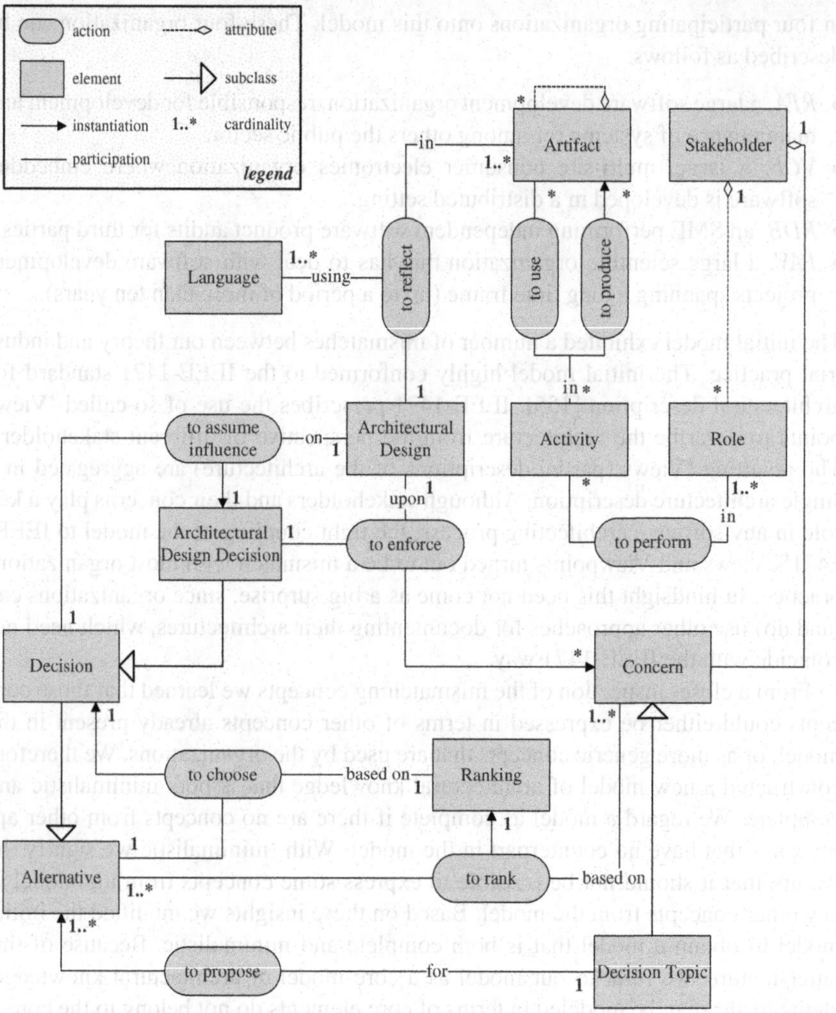

Fig. 8.1 Core model of architectural knowledge

Constructing an architectural design is essentially a decision making process. In our core model, decision making is viewed as proposing and ranking Alternatives, and selecting the alternative that has the highest rank, i.e. the alternative that, after careful consideration based on multiple criteria (i.e. Concerns), is deemed to be the best option available with respect to the other alternatives proposed. It is especially this process of proposing, ranking, and selecting which is hard to articulate and distinguishes the good architects from the weaker. The chosen alternative becomes the Decision. The alternatives that are proposed must address the Decision Topic, and can be ranked according to how well they satisfy this and other concerns.

Architectural Design Decisions are defined as those Decisions that are assumed to influence the Architectural Design and can be enforced upon this Architectural Design, possibly leading to new Concerns that result in a need for taking subsequent decisions. This decision loop captures the relations between subsequent Architectural Design Decisions. This loop also corresponds to the divide and conquer technique of decision making, in which broadly scoped decisions are taken which may result in finer grained concerns related to the broader concern. It also mimics the feedback loop identified in [146].

Although the original model did not entirely fit all organizations, diagnosis of the use of architectural knowledge in those organizations at least showed that each of the organizations has its own perspective on architecture knowledge management, resulting in different issues at each of the organizations. The central issue within RFA was how to share architectural knowledge between stakeholders of a project. The main question within VCL was how compliance with architectural rules can be enforced in this multi-site environment. RDB was mainly concerned with how auditors can discover the architectural knowledge they need to do a proper audit. The main challenge for PAV was how to improve traceability of its architectural knowledge. While the mismatches between theory and practice still prevented us from pinpointing the exact areas of improvement, at least we had an idea where to search for those areas in a next research iteration. These insights provided the basis for the subsequent research in each of these areas, as discussed in Sects. 8.3–8.6. More details about the core model as well as the mapping of architectural knowledge use of the four participating organizations onto this model can be found in [44].

Another use of the core model of architectural knowledge is as a common vocabulary for different organizations. The architectural knowledge of each organization remains expressed in its own terminology, and the core model is used as a shared, reference standard defining the mapping between different knowledge concepts. In our vision, organizations can collaborate on the Web in a grid-like configuration of connected sites, forming a virtual community. In this scenario, the AK mapping via the core model can be used to integrate the services shared on the grid, and therefore facilitate further AK sharing, and collaboration.

8.2.2 The Architect's Mindset

In a next step, we devised a series of typical usages (use cases) of architectural knowledge, and conducted a survey-based study to get insight into the importance practitioners attach to these use cases. These use cases are listed in Table 8.1.

We cluster the use cases based on the purpose of the individual use cases. Some use cases clearly deal with stakeholders only. Consequently, we grouped these use cases into a single cluster. The use case cluster *Architectural decision set* presupposes that a set of knowledge entities (i.e. architectural decisions) and relations between these knowledge are aimed at managing that set. Several other use cases have to do with assessing or reviewing an architecture. Within this *Assessment*

Table 8.1 Use cases for architectural knowledge

Use case cluster	Use cases
Architectural decision set	11. View the change of the architectural decisions over time
	15. Recover architectural decisions
	20. Identify incompleteness
	22. Detect patterns of architectural decision dependencies
	23. Check for superfluous architectural decisions
	24. Cleanup the architecture
Assessment – reqs.→arch.→impl.	1. Check implementation against architectural decisions
	5. Check correctness (i.e. architecture versus requirements)
	18. Evaluate the impact of an architectural decision
	19. Evaluate consistency
	27. Get consequences of an architectural decision
Assessment – risk, tradeoff analysis	4. Perform a review for a specific concern
	16. Perform incremental architectural review
	17. Assess design maturity
	21. Conduct a risk analysis
	25. Conduct a trade-off analysis
Stakeholder-centric	2. Identify the subversive stakeholder
	3. Identify key arch. decisions for a specific stakeholder
	6. Identify affected stakeholders on change
	7. Identify unresolved concerns for a specific stakeholder
	8. Keep up-to-date
	9. Inform affected stakeholders
	26. Identify important architectural drivers
Forward Architecting	10. Retrieve an architectural decision
	12. Add an architectural decision
	13. Remove consequences of a cancelled decision
	14. Reuse architectural decisions

cluster, we distinguish between use cases that imply a forward-engineering approach to architecture (i.e. from requirements, to architecture, to implementation), and use cases that target at performing different kinds of analyses and reviews. The first set aims at verification of the architecting activities (are we still on the right track?) whereas the second set aims at validation. Seven use cases form the cluster *Stakeholder-centric*. These use cases concern identification of stakeholders and communication of the architecture to specific stakeholders. The cluster *Forward Architecting*, finally, consists of use cases that create, request, reuse or remove architectural decisions. A summary of the survey results is given in Table 8.2.

The use cases for architectural knowledge within the cluster *Architectural decision set* assume that a set of architectural decisions is at the practitioners disposal. In terms of the use cases, architecting thus boils down to managing and manipulating that set of architectural decisions. Our survey shows that viewing the architecture as a set of architectural decisions and managing that set has not yet transferred to practice, nor is it of particular value to the practitioners.

Table 8.2 Survey results for architectural knowledge use cases

Stakeholder-centric	+
Forward architecting	+
Assessment - reqs.→arch.→impl.	+
Architectural decision set	−
Assessment - risk, trade-off analysis	−

The cluster labeled *Assessment - reqs.→arch.→impl.* covers traceability of architectural decisions to the actual implementation, the relation between decisions themselves, and from architectural decisions back to the requirements that have been set for the information system. Especially respondents in 'construction' roles with respect to architecture (such as architects, designers, developers) regard these use cases as important. This confirms our idea that practitioners involved in the construction of architectures have a need for traceability of architecture. The use cases in the cluster *Assessment - risk, trade-off analysis* are mostly not regarded as important.

A difference that exists between the two subclusters within *Assessment* could lie in the architects mindset. The results of the cluster *Assessment - reqs.→arch.→impl.* reveal a mindset with a linear (i.e. non-iterative) approach to designing an architecture that satisfies the posed requirements and subsequently have the implementation satisfy the architecture. Use cases that offer traceability in this approach are regarded as important. The use cases in the cluster *Assessment - risk, trade-off analysis*, on the other hand, all are aimed at having an intermediate period of reflection to verify what risks apply, or what quality attributes could be affected by certain architectural decisions. These use cases are not directly related to either requirements or implementation. In summary, in contrast to the literature stating that architecture offers a good means to assess the correctness and suitability of the desired solution (e.g. [34, 147]), our results reveal architects regard the use cases for architectural knowledge in the *Assessment - risk, trade-off analysis* cluster as not particularly important. Literature points out that an architecture enables us to assess the design maturity, perform incremental, iterative design reviews, and periodically identify the largest risks pertaining to the architecture. Apparently, these benefits of architecture are not valued by our respondents, which is surprising. Moreover, the use cases in the cluster *Assessment - risk, trade-off analysis* aim at finding possible problems in a certain architecture. Since practitioners do not regard these use cases as important, we might infer that practitioners do not favour a period of reflection in which the current state of the architecture is explicitly tested. Yet, this is one of the main reasons stated in the literature for developing an architecture. Apparently, these intended benefits of architecture have not yet been firmly established in the mindset of architects. The lack of value contributed to the intended benefits reveals a mindset of positiveness ("architects always take the right decisions"), which supports the findings of [314]. Respondents do not like to use architectural knowledge to identify potential weaknesses of their design.

A number of use cases for architectural knowledge are *Stakeholder-centric*. These use cases involve identifying stakeholders and communicating the architecture towards these stakeholders. Five out of the seven use cases in this cluster are regarded as important by the respondents. The remaining use cases identify affected stakeholders on change and identify key architectural decisions for a specific stakeholder are deemed neutral. Furthermore, stakeholder-centric use cases are regarded as more important at the business oriented architecture levels, confirming the general idea that at these levels, communicating architecture to non-IT stakeholders is an important issue. The other way around, practitioners engaged in technical architecture fields do not regard communication of the architecture to stakeholders as important. Apparently, at these levels, practitioners mainly capture architectural decisions for themselves and not for communication to other stakeholders. This in itself is not bad, but reveals that different communication needs exist for different architecture levels.

Four use cases for architectural knowledge fall into the cluster *Forward Architecting*. When we regard the use cases in this cluster we see that adding an architectural decision is deemed important at all architecture levels and by most architectural roles. The use case remove consequences of a cancelled decision is not deemed very important. We can identify two reasons for this. Firstly, this use case requires that a practitioner is able to cancel an architectural decision. Consequently, the practitioner should determine the decision that needs to be cancelled. This requires the practitioner to make a review iteration. Secondly, this use case does not directly contribute to the forward-engineering paradigm we identified when we analysed the *Assessment* use cases. Other use cases in this cluster, such as reuse architectural decisions and retrieve an architectural decision are deemed important by all architectural roles and at all architecture levels. These results show that the practitioners regard architectural decisions as an important asset to be reused in developing a specific architecture.

In summary, the mindset of architects in the Netherlands (as of 2006) reveals an approach which is focused on to create and communicate rather than to review and maintain. This reflects a general pattern as e.g. highlighted in [314]. A more elaborate discussion of our findings is given in [78].

8.3 Sharing Architectural Knowledge

Our research into sharing architectural knowledge took place in a large software development organization, responsible for the development and maintenance of systems for among others the public sector, termed *RFA* in Sect. 8.2.1. We started from the premise that architectural knowledge sharing is best supported by codifying this knowledge in terms of our core model. In our first case study in *RFA*, we found that stakeholders will only share knowledge if the necessary incentives are created [115]. We continued this line of reasoning in a second case study, resulting in a hybrid codification/personalization knowledge management strategy [114], allowing for a

Just-In-Time architectural knowledge sharing portal [113]. In our current work, we are implementing these ideas using Web2.0 technologies such as wikis [116]. This is in line with the trend identified in Sect. 2.4.1 of Chap. 2.

We started our research in **RFA** with a diagnosis of how architectural knowledge was perceived in the organization. We used three main sources for this diagnosis: a questionnaire containing several use cases for architectural knowledge, a documentation study of standards, best practices and architectural descriptions, and finally a set of open interviews with various stakeholders of the architecting process.

As a result, we have distilled four issues related to sharing architectural knowledge in *RFA*:

- *No consistency between architecture and design documents.* There is no alignment between the architecture descriptions and the functional design and technical design documents used by developers and maintainers.
- *Communication overhead between stakeholders.* Developers occasionally have to explain the architects technical decisions more than once. The reason for this is that decisions made in earlier meetings, including the rationale for these decisions, are not adequately stored in the architecture description.
- *No explicit collaboration with maintenance teams.* Although maintainers are targeted in the architectural documentation, they are not involved as a stakeholder in the architecting process.
- *No feedback from developers to architects.* Developers sometimes wear the hat of the architect and also make design decisions. However, architects are not informed on the decisions made by the developers unless explicit meetings take place.

From these observations, we concluded that architectural knowledge sharing was still immature. We next suggested an improved process, essentially centered around better means to codify architectural knowledge [115]. One of our recommendations for example was to establish a central architectural knowledge repository.

Literature though presents warnings that not all knowledge sharing implementations are automatically successful. In [133] several factors that make knowledge sharing difficult are listed, such as the fact that knowledge sharing is time consuming, and that people might not trust the knowledge management system. Another warning is that striving for completeness is infeasible. In addition, we should be aware of the fact that a lot of the available knowledge cannot be made explicit at all, but instead remains tacit in the minds of people [234]. Sharing such tacit knowledge is very hard.

In order to design successful tools for knowledge sharing, a strategy needs to be chosen. In Chap. 1, we distinguished two main knowledge management strategies: codification and personalization. In the architecting process, some architectural knowledge might benefit from a codification strategy, whereas other types of knowledge could be better shared using personalization approaches. A hybrid approach, first coined in [92], is therefore worth considering. Such a hybrid approach could provide a balance between formalized and unstructured knowledge. According to [141], such a balance is an important prerequisite to stimulate the usage of tools.

To define in more detail how a hybrid architectural knowledge sharing approach should look like we can draw on a study about knowledge sharing by Van den Brink [52]. Van den Brink describes four steps need to be executed in order to create "an interconnected environment supporting communication, collaboration, and information sharing within and among office and non-office work activities; with office systems, groupware, and intranets providing the bonding glue. Firstly, information and explicit knowledge components must be stored online, indexed and mapped, so people can see what is available and can find it (e.g. using digitally stored documents or yellow pages). Secondly, communication among people needs to be supported, by assisting in the use of best practices to guide future behavior and enable sharing of ideas (e.g. emails, bulletin boards, or discussion databases). Thirdly, tacit knowledge needs to be captured using for instance communities of practice, interest groups, or competency centers (e.g. groupware and electronic whiteboards). Lastly, methods are required that offer a virtual space in which a team can collaborate interactively, irrespective of geographic distribution of the team members or time.

We designed and implemented a web-based knowledge sharing portal along these lines: EAGLE – an Environment for Architects to Gain and Leverage Expertise [114]. A second implementation of EAGLE used an Enterprise wiki environment for storing and managing both architectural knowledge and non-architectural knowledge [116]. A screenshot of this wiki is depicted in Fig. 8.2.

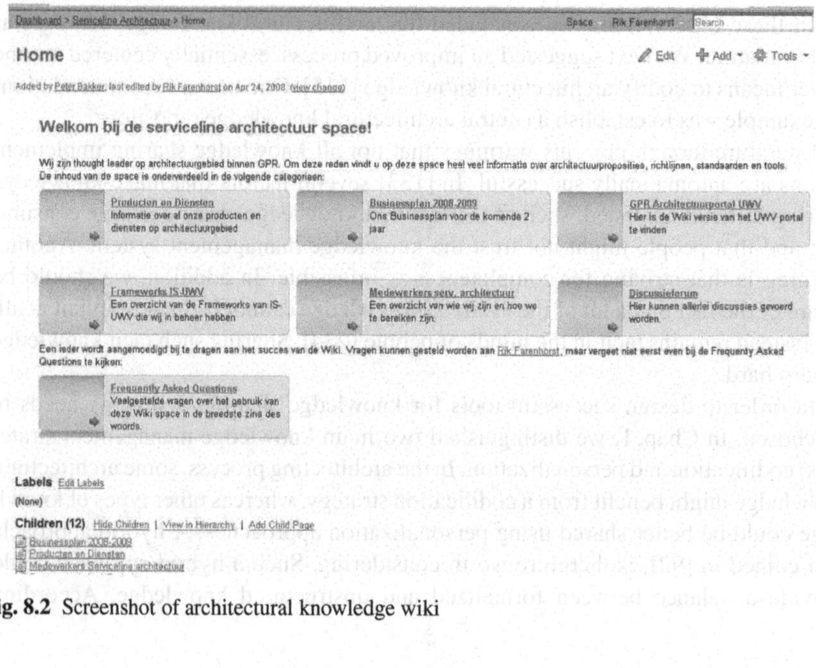

Fig. 8.2 Screenshot of architectural knowledge wiki

To support architectural knowledge codification, parts of the wiki were filled with reusable architectural principles and rules (one per wiki page), after which an overview page was generated using a table of contents plugin. The same approach has been used for codifying architectural knowledge concerned with architectural technologies and patterns. To support architectural knowledge personalization, the wiki offers discussion facilities, the ability to send notifications to subscribed knowledge, and personal pages for all wiki users to mimic a 'yellow pages' system.

By working closely together with **RFA**, over the past few years we have acquired substantial insight in what architects really do, what kind of architectural knowledge needs they have, and how they can be motivated and supported in sharing this knowledge. The tooling discussed above is a first step in making the life of architects a bit easier, but should not be regarded as a silver bullet. In order to further improve the state-of-the-practice, we plan to conduct more empirical research on how architects can best be supported in managing and sharing architectural knowledge.

8.4 Discovering Architectural Knowledge

The research within *RDB*, an SME performing independent software product audits for third parties, started from a very real problem: how to find and comprehend the architectural knowledge that resides in software product documentation [45]. This in turn led to investigating further "ontological" problems: how is architectural knowledge, in particular design decisions, related to evaluation criteria that auditors use when searching for relevant information. We noted a remarkable similarity between architectural decisions and requirements [46].

Auditors have three major questions regarding software product documentation and the architectural knowledge contained in it. These three questions are:

1. Where should I start reading?
2. Which documents should I consult for more information on a particular architectural topic?
3. How should I progress reading? In other words, what is a useful 'route' through the documentation to gain a sufficient level of architectural knowledge?

Auditors who perform a software product audit would greatly benefit from tools and techniques that can direct them to relevant architectural knowledge. We refer to the goal of such tools and techniques as 'Architectural Knowledge Discovery'. A core capability of Architectural Knowledge Discovery is the ability to grasp the semantic structure, or meaning, of the software product documentation. Employing this structure transforms the set of individual texts into a collection that contains architectural knowledge elements and the intrinsic relations between them. A technique we deployed to support the discovery of directions to relevant architectural knowledge is Latent Semantic Analysis (LSA) [205].

In [45], we describe the application of LSA to an example audit case involving 80 documents. The case concerns the reconstruction of the early phase of the software product audit, in which the auditors need to attain a global understanding of the software product in order to further assess its quality.

In general, when auditors commence a software product audit they want to gain an initial, high-level understanding of the software product. This global understanding is necessary to successfully perform the audit, since it is a prerequisite for subsequent audit activities. For instance, in scenario analyses the supplier of the software product is asked how the product reacts to certain change scenarios or failure scenarios. In order to judge the answer the supplier provides, an auditor needs to have a thorough understanding of the software product. Otherwise, the supplier might provide an answer that is incomplete or inconsistent with the real state of the product, without this being noticed.

Auditors who want to attain overall comprehension of the software product can be guided through the documentation using the semantic structure discovered by LSA. A route that is preferred by all auditors we interviewed is to start with high-level, global information and gradually descend to texts that contain more detailed and fine-grained information. A single term that can be expected to cover the high-level information about the software product well is the term 'architecture'. By using LSA in combination with 'architecture' as the term of interest, we were able to identify a 2-page fact sheet that contained a condensed architectural overview, without ever using the word 'architecture' itself.

Since we were investigating the use and findability of architectural knowledge in quality audits, it was almost inevitable that we ran into the question of the nature of architectural knowledge in this context. A quality audit is different from a 'normal' forward-engineering situation in that auditors will form an opinion about the actual state of the software product and compare that with their opinion on what this state should be. It became obvious to us that in this way auditors take 'virtual' architectural decisions which they compare with the actual architectural decisions taken for the software product.

Since the auditor's virtual architectural decisions form a baseline for comparison, they are often referred to as evaluation criteria. Given their status as things that should be present, one could alternatively refer to them as (architectural) requirements, albeit requirements with a different origin than the client. This, in turn, led to a more general investigation of the relation between requirements and architecture.

Although many would agree that there is some relation between architecture and requirements, the conventional view is that requirements and architecture belong to different domains. From our investigation, we believe that this view may be false. That, metaphorically speaking, architecturally significant requirements and architectural design decisions accumulate in some kind of a 'magic well'. Observers peering into the well see what they wish for. People wishing to find architecturally significant requirements will see architecturally significant requirements; people looking for architectural design decisions will find architectural design decisions.

Currently, the challenges in requirements management and architecture knowledge management are approached as if there are two separate 'information wells'. Both communities perform research on comparable challenges without paying too much attention to what the others are doing. A focus on architectural design decisions provides an opportunity to recognize and acknowledge that both communities are in fact looking at the same 'magic well' from different angles, we open the door for tighter collaboration between the fields as well as reuse of each other's research results. We see great potential value in further exploring and exploiting the commonalities between architecturally significant requirements and architectural design decisions to enhance support for requirements management and architecture knowledge management alike.

One of the areas in which architecture knowledge management and requirements management meet is in decision support for evaluation criteria selection. We codified *RDB*'s evaluation criteria in a structure derived from the ontology of design decisions of Philippe Kruchten [190], our own work [44], and a collection of informally defined quality criteria within *RDB*. The resulting *quality ontology* can be used to construct an "audit project memory". Such a memory supports reuse of those evaluation criteria in different quality audits. From these codified criteria, new knowledge can be discovered, e.g. through data mining techniques. We are currently implementing a prototype system of an audit project memory that aids authors in their decision making process of including or excluding certain quality criteria in a particular audit.

8.5 Compliance with Architectural Knowledge in Distributed Settings

Nowadays, software development occurs more often in geographically distributed locations. Our research at **VCL** showed that architectural knowledge may be deployed to overcome some of the challenges that are experienced in global software development. Different fragments of architectural knowledge can be shared across different development sites to effect this. A first case study showed that thorough verification of compliance with these fragments is necessary to allow the knowledge to sink in properly at the different development sites [77]. Next, we compared the results obtained at *VCL* with an organization that has adhered to an alternative strategy for communicating architectural knowledge to the development sites [77]. The differences experienced have led us to develop a set of practices to effectively introduce architecture knowledge management in distributed settings [75].

The *VCL* organization is a distributed software development organization for a series of consumer electronics products. The development organization is located at seven sites spread across the globe. Each site has a number of subsystem teams allocated to it that are in charge of developing the subsystem's functionality required for the end products. A central team of architects located at a single site maintains the software architecture and addresses subsystem-exceeding issues like configuration management, subsystem interdependencies, and naming conventions of the various software artifacts. Solutions to these subsystem-exceeding issues were addressed by a set of architectural rules that need to be complied with throughout the organization. The organization, however, found the rules to be formulated too abstract and did not always understand these rules. We studied the organization to identify reasons for these problems. Our research, described in [77], learned that root cause of these problems was not the description of the rules, but the process by which these rules were developed and subsequently communicated across the development sites. The major improvements included ongoing communication between the central team and the various development sites, implementing compliance verification and explicitly registering deviations from the architectural rules.

To further substantiate these results, we next researched the contribution of architectural knowledge (architectural rules in particular) to overcome the challenges experienced in global software development. We compared *VCL* with another organization (*ABC*) involved in global software development. Whereas *VCL* focuses on the formulation of rules pertaining to the architecture of the product, *ABC* focuses on rules and measures regarding the architecture process. Our research showed that some of the challenges of global software development cannot be addressed by product-based rules alone. In addition, measures in the process are necessary to overcome cultural and team-collaboration challenges experienced in global software development [77].

Reflecting on the research performed and the literature on global software development, we concluded that, based on the differences that exist, there is no one-size-fits-all software development process that addresses all challenges involved in global software development. Consequently, we shifted our focus towards the identification of a set of practices related to the management of architectural knowledge to overcome specific issues. These practices can be incorporated in existing software development methodologies.

We collected a set of practices [75], and characterized these practices by, among others, determining the strategy towards knowledge management supported by these practices (i.e., a personalization strategy or a codification strategy, following [143, 92]). Examples of practices include frequent traveling of key individuals, conducting a shared kick-off meeting in which principles of the software architecture are exchanged, and different forms of frequent communication across development sites. We performed a large-scale validation of these practices at an industrial partner that joined the GRIFFIN project (*VCL2*). This organization has a number of software development centers at different locations and focuses on improving its capabilities by using architecture knowledge management efficiently across these locations. For the validation, we conducted a large empirical study aimed at establishing a baseline of the current architecting practice. As a part of this case study we validated our set of practices for architecture knowledge management with the architects of *VCL2*. We learned, among others, that practices that focus on a personalization strategy for architecture knowledge management are preferred over practices that support a codification strategy.

In future research, we intend to augment these practices by delving architecture knowledge management practices from a series of global software development projects on which independent software products audits have been performed.

8.6 Tracing Architectural Knowledge

The research within **PAV** is concentrated on the traceability between different entities of AK. *PAV* designs and builds large scientific instruments that advance significantly beyond the state of the art. The unique characteristic of this domain, is that these sizeable and complicated systems are often designed during a whole decade before they are actually built. During this long design period, extensive design space exploration takes place where design problems lead to multiple design alternatives with particularly complex trade-offs involved. This exploration takes many different forms: the development and evaluation of (small scale) real world prototypes, quantitative prediction models, and coarse-grained qualitative evaluations. Hence, during this exploration a fairly large amount of AK is created.

In the beginning of the project, **PAV** posed two research questions that concerned the design exploration:

- How can architectural analysis become more transparent? In practice, architecture analysis remained to a large extent a "black art" within *PAV*, since the various analysts possessed very deep and specialized AK that was hardly shared and understood by the rest.
- How are architectural documents related? The sheer volume of documents produced during the design exploration phase rendered the relationships between the document contents practically impossible to locate.

At first glance, providing traceability addresses both these questions. Firstly, traceability should make architectural analysis more transparent by offering an explicit traceable reasoning path between the different analysis models. Secondly, providing traceability both within and between documents makes relationships between documents explicit. This is very much in line with the knowledge management perspective, which requires to make both the knowledge entities and their relationships explicit.

We have come up with an approach towards AK traceability that is based on codifying AK and particularly emphasizes the relationships. The approach, called the Knowledge Architect, consists of a method and a supporting tool suite. The method consists of the following six different activities:

1. *Identify knowledge management issues.* In this activity, we identify the deeper AK management issues an organization is facing. In the case of *PAV*, the need of making the architectural analysis more transparent is derived from the fact that current analysis results are not widely *understandable*. The need of knowing how architectural documents relate comes from the issue that *PAV* is uncertain with respect to the maturity of its design, i.e. is the design complete, consistent, and correct enough to be built and fulfill the requirements?
2. *Derive a domain model.* This activity aims at identifying the actual AK entities that can help in dealing with the issues mentioned in the aforementioned activity. We formalize this knowledge with the help of ontologies [18]. For **PAV**, this means that we identify what AK is important to know and to relate for making a

quantitative analysis transparent (see [164] for an in-depth description), and for inter-relating architecture documents (see [160]). In both cases emphasis is put on making this knowledge traceable.
3. *Capture AK*. Once the AK and its relationships are made explicit, we capture this AK using a codification approach, thereby creating the missing traceability. The supporting tool suite offers several tools that use the ontology of the derived model to assist a stakeholder with capturing relevant AK. To decrease the burden on the stakeholders, these tools are integrated in a non-intrusive way with the tools in which the AK is created and also provide some automated support. For quantitative analysis, we have developed two analysis model tools, one for Python, and one for Excel [164]. We have applied and validated these two tools during architecture analysis at *PAV* concerning performance and cost models. For relating documents, the suite incorporates the Document Knowledge Client, a plug-in for Microsoft Word [160]. Similarly, we have applied this plug-in on software architecture document and validated it within the purpose of architecture evaluation activities.
4. *Use AK*. Once the AK and its relationships have become explicit and therefore traceable, it may be used to address the identified knowledge management issues identified in the first activity. Typically, this involves specialized visualizations to highlight concrete issues. For example, the Document Knowledge Client can colour pieces of text in a document that require further elaboration, when the AK is incomplete, inconsistent, or incorrect. Another example are the dependency graphs rendered by the analysis model tools that allows system analysts in *PAV* to identify the inter-dependencies between the system parameters of their analysis models that influence the design space.
5. *Integrate AK*. Typically, AK is described in various forms and is captured by different tools. To have a complete perspective on the software architecture, the Knowledge Architect uses a central AK repository to integrate the AK of various knowledge sources, e.g. Word, Excel, Python, Excel, etc. Since AK might come from different organizations, each having their own specific domain model, this repository supports ontology mappings. Using these mappings, the AK of different sources can be integrated to form a single overall traceable picture of the architecture. We have developed various models to predict the quality and costs of such mappings (see [206, 207]).
6. *Evolve AK*. AK constantly evolves over the life-time of a system and this evolution also needs to be explicit. The Knowledge Architect tool suite supports the documentation of the AK evolution in two ways. Firstly, the central AK repository offers versioning of the AK in the central AK repository, thereby making the history of AK traceable. Secondly, the repository will be integrated with a SCM to have a traceable co-evolution with the artifacts the AK originates from.

In the future, we want to explore two activities in more depth: evolving and integrating AK. Firstly, we would like to investigate in real life cases *how* the AK evolves over time. Can we perhaps identify patterns in this evolution and strategies to deal with this evolution? Secondly, regarding AK integration, we would like to know to what extent and under which conditions our predictions of the cost and quality of AK integration hold.

8.7 The GRIFFIN Grid

The core model of architectural knowledge can be used as a common vocabulary for different organizations. Each organization typically develops its own terminology, defined through the years to reflect its business domain, background, know-how and organizational culture. In GRIFFIN, this *local* vocabulary is called *shell* [44].

When different organizations collaborate, it is especially difficult (and time consuming) to understand one another. Imagine to share artifacts and documents expressed according to different terminologies. At the same time, it would be unrealistic for companies to aim at reaching a consensus on one, common terminology, and translate the pre-existing documents accordingly. The GRIFFIN approach is to keep the architectural knowledge expressed in the own terminology of an organization (i.e. according to the shell vocabulary) and refer to a shared standard mapping similar concepts. The core model for architectural knowledge can act as "esperanto" to define the mapping between different shells.

Within GRIFFIN, we envision a virtual and distributed community of collaborating organizations and professionals willing to create and share architectural knowledge. Such a virtual community is meant to support a community of professionals (software architects) to effectively carry out their daily work and further contribute to (and learn from) the community with its own (architectural) knowledge. A combination of strategies for knowledge codification and personalization should provide each individual with the necessary flexibility, to fit in the own working practice and to provide sufficient incentives for successful AK management.

As illustrated in [196], organizations can share AK in a grid-like configuration of connected sites where employees carry out collaborative activities. Software architects can work in their *virtual space* where they can manage their own architectural knowledge and eventually share part of this knowledge with (remote) counterparts in a collaborative social network of professionals.

From a service integration perspective, the core model can be the means to integrate the services that a grid infrastructure may provide [44]. These services may "speak the same language" by exchanging data expressed in concepts from the core model. For instance, the AK codified in the EAGLE portal presented in Sect. 8.3 could be made accessible to other grid partners, and mapped (through the core models) on the AK terms according to their own shell terminology. In a similar way, any of the use cases illustrated in Sect. 8.2.2 can be implemented as a service, and share and exchange data integrated via the core model. In this way, the core model, being shared among multiple sites, realizes a more generic infrastructure.

8.8 Summary

In the GRIFFIN project, we have carried out a number of case studies within participating industries. The close collaboration between research and industry has given us a number of important insights in what works and what doesn't in software architecture knowledge management:

- Different industrial domains have different knowledge models, and we need an infrastructure that deals with that.
- Software architects are not likely to (extensively) codify their knowledge of and by themselves.
- Effective software architecture knowledge management follows a hybrid knowledge management strategy.
- Software architecture knowledge management needs support of lightweight, just-in-time, tools.

It is an illusion to try to coerce different organizations, or even different groups within the same organization, into adopting the same domain structure and terminology. Our core model, as discussed in Sect. 8.2.1 can act as an "esperanto" to allow for a mapping between different local vocabularies. This core model can then be used to share architectural knowledge in a grid-like configuration.

Software architects are busy people. It is their job to find, negotiate, and implement solutions. It is not their job to codify knowledge. At best, we may expect them to partially codify their knowledge. If we deem it important to support software architects in the management of their knowledge, such support of necessity has to be able to deal with incomplete information, such as a design decision without a rationale, or a decision topic with a very incomplete set of design alternatives. To stretch the idea even further, it would be advantageous to be able to mine architectural knowledge from "normal" artifacts produced by architects.

Many knowledge management initiatives start with the idea to codify knowledge. We did too, and learned that this is not the best way to go. Part of the knowledge of software architects will remain tacit, and in circumstances we must be able to find the right person, instead of the right document. Software architecture knowledge management therefore should follow a hybrid strategy, incorporating both codification *and* personalization.

Finally, software architecture knowledge management can successfully be supported by a wide variety of tools. In order to be used at all, these tools should be easy to learn, and fit the daily practice of the architects. If such tools have a steep learning curve, they are not likely to be used. Since architects are already overwhelmed with information, the tools should lead them to the right information at the right time.

Acknowledgements This research has been partially sponsored by the Dutch Joint Academic and Commercial Quality Research and Development (Jacquard) program on Software Engineering Research via contract 638.001.406 GRIFFIN: a GRId For inFormatIoN about architectural knowledge.

Chapter 9
Software Architecture Design Reasoning

Antony Tang and Hans van Vliet

Abstract Despite recent advancements in software architecture knowledge management and design rationale modeling, industrial practice is behind in adopting these methods. The lack of empirical proofs and the lack of a practical process that can be easily incorporated by practitioners are some of the hindrance for adoptions. In particular, the process to support systematic design reasoning is not available. To rectify this issue, we propose a design reasoning process to help architects cope with an architectural design environment where design concerns are cross-cutting and diversified. We use an industrial case study to validate that the design reasoning process can help improve the quality of software architecture design. The results have indicated that associating design concerns and identifying design options are important steps in design reasoning.

9.1 Introduction

Software architects make a series of design decisions when designing system architecture. Despite the need to make correct architectural design decisions, architects often omit to provide design rationale or justifications for their design decisions. Software architects instead focus on creating design outcomes. Presently there are no commonly accepted practices in the industry to carry out systematic design reasoning, architects often rely on their experience and intuition when making design decisions. Such an unstructured decision making approach has certain implications on design quality, experienced architects are more likely to make better design decisions. On the other hand, inexperienced designers may not design as well. This case

Antony Tang (✉)
Swinburne University of Technology, Melbourne, Australia, e-mail: atang@swin.edu.au

Hans van Vliet
VU University Amsterdam, The Netherlands, e-mail: hans@cs.vu.nl

M. Ali Babar et al. (eds.), *Software Architecture Knowledge Management*,
DOI: 10.1007/978-3-642-02374-3_9, © Springer-Verlag Berlin Heidelberg 2009

study illustrates a methodology to overcome the ad hoc practice of architectural design decision making and to improve the quality of software architecture design.

In general, practitioners learn software architecture design principles through textbooks and formal training, exercising these design principles in practice often requires knowledge and experience that is mostly learned on the job. Software design knowledge and experience are difficult to teach and articulate. Recent studies have shown that such knowledge is design rationale related [48, 71]. Design rationale can be characterized in two ways (1) they are the reasons for making a decision and choosing a solution, and (2) explaining the relationships between a solution and the context of that solution. By externalizing design reasoning, it is aimed to improve decision making and to capture documented evidence for design verification and system maintenance.

In this chapter we explain the basic elements in architectural design reasoning. We demonstrate the modeling of these elements in a UML-based model called Architecture Rationale and Elements Linkage (AREL) in Sect. 9.3. In Sect. 9.4, we describe a design reasoning process to support software architectural design activities. In Sect. 9.5, we describe an industrial case that demonstrates how a reasoning process can improve the quality of an architectural design.

9.2 Software Architecture Design Reasoning

In software architecture design, architects apply cognitive reasoning even though they may not think about it consciously. An understanding of such a reasoning process can be quite helpful to delivering good design. Designers' judgment can be inadvertently biased due to personal preferences and past experiences. This situation is quite common and it may have an adverse effect on the quality of a design. However, many systems have been built quite successfully without the explicit employment of design reasoning methods, why? This may be due to the involvement of experienced people. Successful projects often rely on people with experience and good judgment. Some IT professionals seem to have an uncanny way of foreseeing problems, formulating solutions and making just the right decisions consistently. On the contrary, there are practitioners who design poorly, they over-engineer a solution, underestimate the effort, miss out key requirements, select the wrong technologies and deliver poor quality design. The challenge is how to systematically improve the reasoning abilities of designers to consistently deliver a satisfactory design, and to improve the quality-assurance process of architecture design.

In a study that examines if design reasoning techniques make any difference to design quality [318], test participants in the experiment were given a simple reasoning process, they were asked to use this process and verbally explain their design reasoning as they designed. As a result they generally produced a higher quality design, especially those who were less experienced could produce designs similar to those by experienced designers. The study shows that those who were required to externalize their design reasoning were probably more careful and methodical in designing their solutions. This contrasts with the participants of the control group who largely used intuition and knowledge to design. The control group's objective was to complete the design and satisfy the requirements without having to justify them. Other studies have also shown that design rationale documentation helps designers understand and reason about their design [51, 171].

A well-designed architecture should be justifiable through sound and logical design rationale. The design reasoning process ought to consider all relevant architecture requirements, address the design issues, consider trade-offs between the design options before deciding on the outcomes. The explicit representation of this tacit knowledge serves many purposes in the development life cycle such as review and maintenance. Table 9.1 summarizes the purposes for having such a rationale-based architectural design approach.

Back in 1958, it was suggested that argumentation could be used to induce conclusions from contextual data [323]. This approach explicitly represents the design deliberation process. One of the characteristics is that they model as links the relationships between design goals and design results. Examples include Issue-Based Information System (IBIS), Decision Representation Language (DRL), and Questions, Options and Criteria (QOC) [228]. Unfortunately, these methods have not been successful in practice because of their difficulties in capturing and communicating design rationale [298, 200].

Another approach is to use templates to aid design reasoning capture, including [71] and [325]. Such an approach is beginning to receive attention in the industry as practitioners recognize the importance of recording design reasoning. UML CASE tools such as Rational Rose and Enterprise Architect[1] provide some easy-to-use facilities to capture design rationale. Although template-based methods can capture design rationale, they provide limited support to relate the contexts of design decisions.

In order to make design reasoning easy to adopt by software development organizations without losing the design reasoning capabilities of argumentation-based methods, we have developed AREL as a hybrid approach that incorporates design rationale template and design reasoning relationships based on these previous works [71, 228, 325]. AREL has been designed to capture useful design reasoning information with minimal documentation overheads.

9.3 Modeling Architecture Design Reasoning

What exactly is design reasoning? Is it a reason for having a system or is it some justifications on how a system is designed? First of all, let us consider a simple reasoning model that comprises of three elements: *inputs–decisions–outputs*. The *inputs* are the requirements and goals that need to be met by a system; the *decisions* are the decisions made in designing the system; the *outputs* are the results of

[1] Design rationale support in Enterprise Architect is implemented using the AREL plug-in tools.

Table 9.1 Purposes for having a rationale-based architectural design approach

Support Software Architecture Design
Deliberating and Negotiating Design – design rationale allows designers to systematically clarify the issues and possible solutions, and to evaluate decisions against well-defined criteria. As such, it allows designers and stakeholders to deliberate and negotiate a solution
Justifying Design Decisions – design rationale can explicate tacit assumptions, clarify dependencies and constraints, and help justify why a particular choice is selected from amongst the alternatives
Applying Trade-off Analysis – a design decision often involves resolving conflicting requirements that cannot be fully satisfied simultaneously. When trade-off analysis method such as ATAM [34] is applied, the prioritized requirements and utility tree form the reasoning of the compromised decision
Structured Design Process – design rationale supports a structured and accountable design practice. It provides a pertinent understanding of the context, the stakeholders, the technologies and the situations in a project
Design Validation – design rationale explains why certain design decisions have been made, and provides the necessary information for independent architecture design validation and review
Communication and Knowledge Transfer – design rationale can help business analysts evaluate conflicting requirements and new designers learn the architecture design
Support Maintenance Activities
Retaining Knowledge – if system maintainers are not the same people who originally developed the system and the design rationale is not available, maintainers would have to second-guess the intangible rationale
Understanding Previous Design Alternatives – design alternatives can help maintainers appreciate what choices had been considered in a decision. They help maintainers to understand design options that were considered unviable or allow them to consider an alternative that was not viable at the time but can now be used
Understanding Design Dependency – design decisions can be interdependent and cut across a number of issues. Changing a decision may have ripple effects on other parts of a system. Recording design rationale and their interdependency helps alleviate the concern of overlooking related issues
Improving Maintenance Productivity – in an experiment, it was shown that a group of designers equipped with the design rationale can work faster and identify more changes that are required in a system maintenance exercise than a control group without the design rationale [51]
Predicting Change Impact – design rationale could assist maintainers to predict which part of the system is subject to consequential change [317]
Providing Traceability – maintainers would be able to trace how design artifacts satisfy requirements in a system with some explanation [259]

the design. Without the inputs, we would miss out on the contextual information that tells us why we need the design. Without the design decisions, we may not understand the justifications or reasons for choosing a design. Therefore, in modeling design reasoning, we need to depict the causal relationships between the design inputs, design decisions and design outputs. We suggest that this relationship is a simple causal relationship between the causes of a design and the effects of a design.

In this way, *design reasoning* is modeled by a description of the design context, the design justification, the design outcome and their causal relationships.

IEEE-1471-2000 specifies that architectural rationale should provide the evidence for the consideration of alternative architectural concepts and the rationale for the choices made. It is a general guideline that does not provide much detail to help implement a design reasoning model. In a discussion session on updating IEEE-1471, some refinements have been suggested to overcome this issue [23].

AREL captures both the design rationale and the design model, which is realized through a UML tool, Enterprise Architect (EA). The design model includes architecturally significant requirements and the actual architecture design. AREL supports the association between the design model and the design rationale of its design decisions. The AREL model is based on the reasoning model described earlier: (a) design concerns raise a design decision, (b) design decision captures design issues and design rationale; (c) the design outcomes are the results of a design decision.

Figure 9.1 shows the conceptual model of AREL. Design concerns such as requirements cause the need for design decisions to be made. When a design decision is made, it is justified by its design rationale. To make a design decision, different design options may be considered, these alternative designs can help architects consider their relative pros and cons. When a design decision is finally made, there would be a chosen design and may be some alternative designs. Alternative designs are those design options that have been considered but discarded. Alternative designs are important because they are evidence to show that the designers have considered more than one design options before making a design decision, they also show the reasons why these alternatives are not as appropriate as the chosen design.

A chosen design element is a UML entity to model the design, e.g. class, component or database table. Each design element can influence other parts of a system due to its behavior or constraints. These design elements will in turn become design concerns that influence other parts of a design. For instance, using AJAX to construct web pages creates a consequential issue of having to handle the web browser's BACK button. AJAX being part of the solution space therefore becomes a part of the problem space, i.e. a new design concern. Such design consequences could trigger a chain of interdependent designs and design decisions.

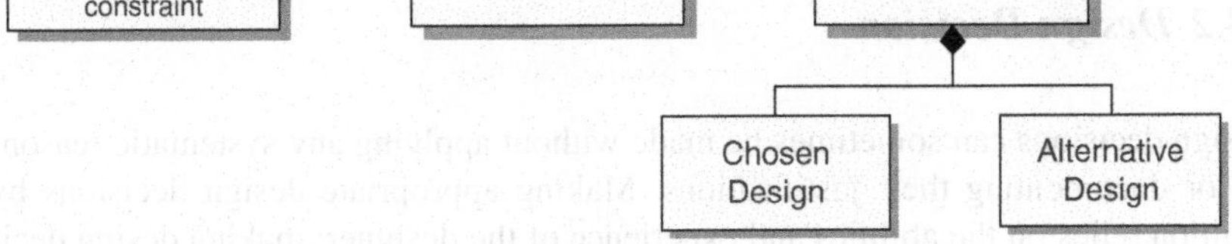

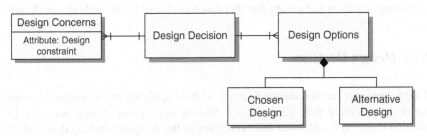

Fig. 9.1 A conceptual model of design reasoning in AREL

Table 9.2 Types of design concern

Purposes and goals – the business goals of a system
Functional Requirements – functional goals of a system
Non-Functional Requirements – quality attributes that a system must fulfill, e.g. performance and usability
Business Environment – organization and business environmental factors that influence architecture design, e.g. long-term or strategic organization goals
Information System (IS) Environment – environmental factors that influence the construction and implementation of the system, e.g. budget, schedule and expertise
Technology (IT) Environment – technological factors that influence the architecture, e.g. current organizational technologies and policies
Design – a chosen design (outcome) has some influence on the rest of the architecture, e.g. the selection of an operating system constrains the choice of the development tools

9.3.1 Design Concern

Capturing the causes of a design decision is vital to comprehending the reasons of a design. The inputs that are the causes or motivations of a decision are *design concerns*. Design concerns represent the context of a design. They can be anything that influences the design decision. Functional and non-functional requirements are examples of design concerns. There are, however, many design concerns that are often omitted even though they play a significant role in software architecture.

There are different types of design concerns (see Table 9.2) and they influence decisions in different ways. *Requirements* drive and motivate the creation of designs. *Purposes and goals* provide a context to guide the design. *Environmental* factors constrain the available choices of an architecture design. In a case where an architect designs a B2B website, examples of the environmental design concerns could be (a) business environment – outsourcing of a system has implications on the maintainability and support requirements; (b) IS environment – time to market is 3 months; (c) IT environment – organisation standards to use ASP.Net and Oracle.

These design concerns exert constraints or influence on design decisions and the eventual architectural design. A design constraint is a limiting factor which specifies the conditions that a viable design solution must fulfill, e.g. the performance of a database engine. As design constraints are important to design decisions, architects must recognise them and ensure that they can be satisfied by the architecture design.

9.3.2 Design Decision

Design decisions can sometimes be made without applying any systematic reasoning or documenting their justifications. Making appropriate design decisions by intuition relies on the abilities and experience of the designer; making design decisions through systematic reasoning, on the other hand, requires explicit justification using design rationale. Documenting design rationale for the entire system can be

Table 9.3 Architecture design rationale

Qualitative design rationale
Design Issue – the issue to be dealt with in a decision
Design Assumptions – document the assumptions that are made in a decision
Design Constraints – document the constraints on a decision that can be of a technical or contextual nature
Strengths and Weaknesses – state the strengths or weaknesses of a design option
Trade-offs – document a balanced analysis of what is an appropriate option after prioritizing and weighing different design options
Risks and Non-risks – document the considerations about the uncertainties or certainties of a design option
Quantitative design rationale
Cost – quantifies the relative cost in areas such as development efforts, platform support, maintenance cost and other intangible costs such as potential legal liabilities
Benefit – quantifies how well a design option may satisfy the requirements and the quality attributes
Implementation Risk – represents the risk that a development team may not implement the design successfully due to reasons such as the lack of capability or experience
Outcome Certainty Risk – represents the risk that a design may not satisfy the requirements because they are technically unachievable or not well-defined

very costly and probably unnecessary, and so we focus on architectural issues that are often complex, intertwining and require much investigation.

Design rationale is the reasons for choosing a particular design from a range of alternatives at a decision point. To do so, we must first articulate the design issues to resolve. An issue may simply be designing to satisfy some design concerns. For instance, what data do I need to show in the user interface? More often than not in architectural design, issues are more complicated because of conflicting and competing influences from different design concerns such as quality requirements. For instance, how do I retrieve the data securely and maintain system performance? There may be more than one possible solution. Design rationale therefore helps the reasoning process and captures the justifications for selecting a solution. It explains why a design is better than the other alternatives. AREL uses qualitative and quantitative design rationale to capture such justifications (see Table 9.3).

Qualitative design rationale supports design reasoning by way of arguments. Architects may document the justifications of a decision by arguing the relative advantages and disadvantages of different design options, or using a trade-off analysis method such as ATAM [34]. Quantitative design rationale records the relative costs, benefits and risks of a design option using ordinal numbers, between 1 (the lowest) and 10 (the highest). The main reasons for capturing quantitative rationale are to allow a quantifiable comparison between alternative design options, and enable architects to highlight risky or costly decisions that need to be investigated further. For example, if the implementation risk is high, architects may continue to decompose the architecture through a series of decisions until the risk becomes manageable [315].

9.3.3 Design Outcome

The result of a design decision would be some chosen designs that are a part of the total solution. This chosen design either realizes the requirements of a system, or it provides some design structures that are used in realizing the requirements. The design outcomes can be any design artifacts, example are architectural model, database models, design components and classes.

A chosen design outcome may influence another part of a solution and as such it becomes a design concern to a new decision, as we have seen in the AJAX example earlier. Since a design outcome can associate with other decisions through the causal relationship, it is possible to have a graph that consists of a chain of relationships that connect design concerns, decisions and design outcomes.

9.4 An Architectural Design Reasoning Process

AREL is a model which defines the information used in design reasoning, it underpins the software architecture design reasoning process described here. Design methods such as the waterfall method, iterative method or agile method focus on the organization of events and teams in software development; technology based methods such as object-oriented analysis and design focus on modeling techniques that produce specific design artifacts. A reasoning based design method, however, has a different perspective – the focus is on using reasoning to create and justify design decisions made for architectural design. The considerations used in a design reasoning approach are therefore broader and not just focusing to producing design artifacts. The design reasoning approach is not meant to replace other design methods, but rather it adds a new dimension to designing software architecture to complement existing design methods.

The architectural life-cycle described by [146] comprises three distinct activities: architectural analysis, architectural synthesis and architectural evaluation. Architectural synthesis is the design activity in this architectural life-cycle. The design reasoning process described in this chapter primarily addresses the architectural synthesis activity but it also covers architectural analysis and evaluation. The shaded area in Fig. 9.2a shows the scope of the design reasoning process with respect to the architectural activities described in [146]. The architectural design reasoning process spans across architectural synthesis and the other activities because design reasoning would involve analysis as well as evaluation.

Chapter 1 describes architectural design as a problem-solving activity, the design workflow consists of three activities: requirements gathering, backlog creation and design evaluation. Creating backlog is an important activity in which architects articulate what design problems are there to be solved. It requires design context and requirements as inputs for defining the design problems in the backlog. All three activities require design reasoning support (shaded area in Fig. 9.2b).

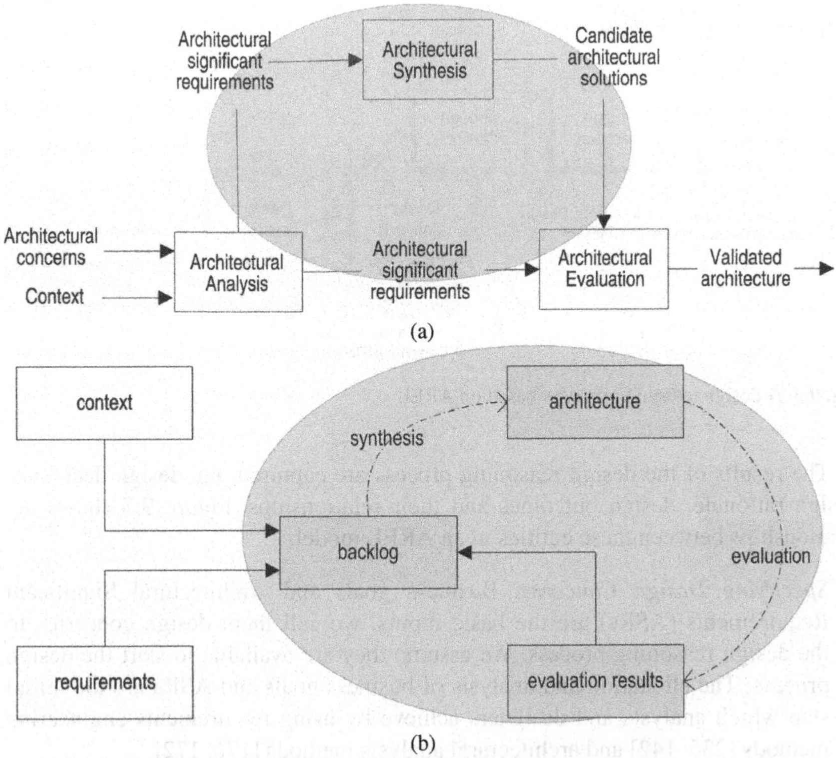

Fig. 9.2 **(a)** and **(b)** Design reasoning coverage at two levels of architectural design

Design is a cognitive activity that requires the architects to organize, induce and assimilate different kinds of information. Early work has indicated that this cognitive process can differ between architects where experienced architects generally use a better design approach, and therefore yielding better results [318]. As such, it would be advantageous to investigate into design reasoning strategies, making them explicit so that there is a systematic approach to considering design problems. A conceptual model for design decision has been suggested by [162] where they describe the architecting process, however key activities that are required to support this model have not been articulated.

In order to address the design reasoning gap in software architecture, our starting point is to make use of the causal relationships between design concerns, design decisions and design outcomes. We suggest to take five steps in the design reasoning process. The five steps (i.e. step 1–5) are depicted by the numbered arrows between the entities (Fig. 9.3). The arrows indicate the design reasoning steps, and they can be repeated for a design. By connecting AREL entities that are causally related, designers can trace the causes and effects of those design decisions. These 5 design reasoning steps are performed repeatedly to decompose the design and create design details, shown by the layers of decisions in Fig. 9.3.

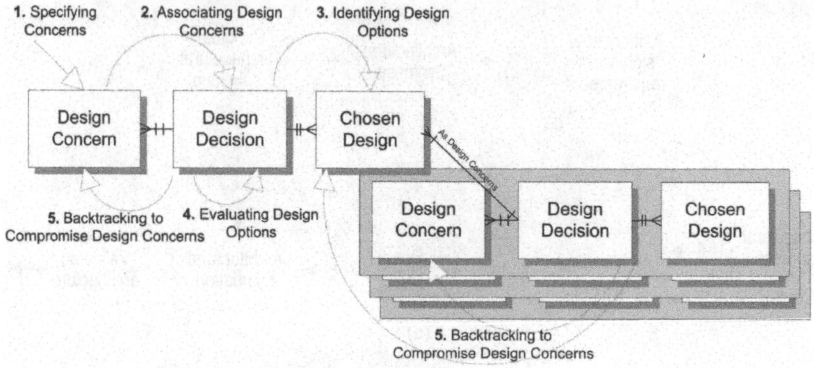

Fig. 9.3 A design reasoning process based on AREL

The results of the design reasoning process are captured, i.e. design decisions, design rationale, design outcomes and their relationships. Figure 9.3 shows the relationships between these entities in an AREL model.

1. *Specifying Design Concerns.* Business goals and Architectural Significant Requirements (ASRs) are the basic inputs, we call them design concerns, to the design reasoning process. We assume they are available to start the design process. The elicitation and analysis of business goals and ASRs are the initial step which analysts and designers achieve by using requirements engineering methods [235, 142] and architectural analysis methods [176, 172].
   Business goals and ASRs themselves reflect important architectural decisions that have been made and these decisions would influence subsequent architecture design [46], so should a design reasoning process be extended to deal with ASRs? A clear delineation between requirement analysis and design can be difficult to define because they influence each other mutually. At a broad level, specifying design concerns are different from synthesizing a design solution. However, as seen in some architecture analysis methods [176, 173], architectural design can compromise ASRs in order to create a workable solution. This process is described in step 5.
2. *Associating Design Concerns.* Design decisions are made because architects need to work out how to design for particular situations that arise from a combination of design concerns. The idea is to consider relevant design concerns in conjunction and finding a solution for them. This concept is similar to the ideas of creating design topics in [44] or populating the backlog (Chap. 1). For instance, to make a decision on how to design an authentication server, two design concerns, i.e. security requirement and performance level, must be considered. If performance as a design concern is not associated to this decision, one may end up having a design that addresses the security requirement with poor performance.
   This idea of grouping design concerns and relating them to a decision bears similarities to eliciting use case scenarios where multiple requirements are involved

[172], or eliciting architectural issues for design synthesis [85]. The graphical modeling of the causal relationships between design concerns and design decisions in AREL enables architects to visually relate them for inspection and traceability. Current practice in the industry requires an architect to have the knowledge and experience to associate related design concerns, and they often do that from a set of textual specifications. It is therefore easy to omit a design issue where interrelated design concerns should be considered in a design scenario.

How does one know that certain design concerns must be considered together to form a design topic? This is essentially asking how an architect knows what to design. There are two possibilities: Firstly, a software architect would have certain basic knowledge and understanding of the design principles for associating related design concerns; secondly, architectural design knowledge can assist architects by showing general design concern associations with design topics.

A design decision can trigger a chain of subsequent decisions, and typically it is for deciding how to further design the system. For instance, the layering of software components might be a high-level decision to group related components together, and follow-on decisions are required to define common interfaces between software layers.

So how deep should the design reasoning process go before an architect is satisfied? This is a question related to how much details is enough in an architectural design to enable detailed design and development. We address this issue by employing a risk mitigation strategy. Architects are required to estimate the risk of implementing a design. If the risk is low, it means that the architect is confident that the design contains sufficient details, otherwise the architect needs to further explore the design [315].

3. *Identifying Design Options*. An important aspect of design reasoning is to identify possible design options. This is a key step in synthesizing a design. It requires an architect to have sufficient knowledge of the problem and certain creativity in deriving potential solutions. This can come from understanding the relevant first principles of design, having some design experience and so on.

   In a study [318], it has been observed that architects and designers tend to bias towards the first impression of a design. For participants who were involved in a test procedure to use a design reasoning process, it has been observed that they would modify their initial design after they consider alternative design options. On the other hand, designers who do not use a design reasoning process, especially for the inexperienced designers, the first impression of a design usually becomes the final design. This observation implies that designers who can identify and consider alternative design options can improve the design quality.
4. *Evaluating Design Options*. At each decision point, an architect would need to choose which identified design options is best suited to meet all the related design concerns and fulfilling the design constraints exerted by these design concerns. There are a number of possible results from an evaluation: (a) there is no design solution that can meet the relevant design concerns; (b) there is a single possible solution; and (c) there are more than one possible design solutions. In case of (a), certain trade-offs may have to take place to relax the constraints of the decision,

different trade-off analysis methods could be employed [176, 3]. In case of (c), an architect has to evaluate the pros and cons of the available options to choose the best option.
In analyzing the pros and cons of different design options, a qualitative reasoning approach may work quite well. The approach proposed in [325] employs different types of design rationale as a guideline for architects to assess the weakness, benefits and other aspect of a design.
5. *Backtracking Decisions to Revise Design Concerns*. Design decisions are often interrelated, a software design decision often leads to a chain of subsequent design decisions. Subsequent design decisions have to be made because (a) the initial design decision lacks design details and thus requires further elaborations; (b) the initial design decision has created new design issues that need to be resolved. As interrelated design decisions are made, architects may find that the eventual solution is not viable. Therefore previous design decisions have to be revised and new decisions to be considered.
When no design solutions can be found at a decision point, the design concerns that dictate the decision must be re-examined because of their causal relationships. Each design concern constrains a design decision in some ways, when the constraints cannot be satisfied by any solutions, then the decision is not viable. A compromise can be reached if some of these constraints are relaxed. To do so, architects can backtrack design decisions to relax their constraints.
If a design constraint comes from a requirement, architects would have to negotiate with the relevant stakeholders in order to have them relaxed. If a design constraint to be relaxed is itself a design outcome, then changing the design outcome implies reconsidering all previous decisions that have led to this design outcome (see step 5 in Fig. 9.3). In this case, design reasoning backtracking involves revisiting previous decisions and design constraints to ensure that the design constraints of all related design concerns can be fulfilled.

The design reasoning process focuses on how to reason with a design. The key steps in the design reasoning process are associating design concerns to decision points, justifying each decision point, checking that all design constraints are met, and backtracking to revise decisions if no viable solution is found. These simple steps can be used in conjunction with other design methodologies.

9.5 Applying AREL to an Industrial Case Study

In an industrial case study, we apply the AREL model to a software development project to see if a design reasoning process can improve design quality in comparison with the conventional design process. A consulting and software development firm had a contract to supply a document management system to a large company in Australia. The system will provide document repository functionality, document classification, knowledge search, workflow, single-sign-on and ubiquitous access facilities to this engineering firm. The design and implementation is phased, and in this

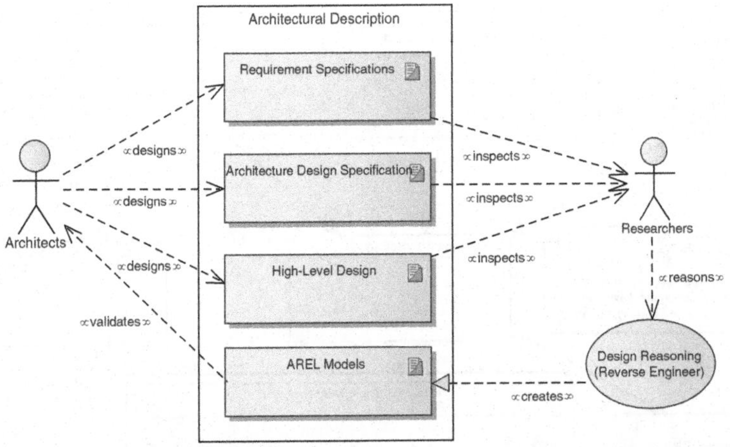

Fig. 9.4 Research approach used in the case study

case study the architectural design for the system infrastructure and two application systems are studied.

The consulting firm has a *design team* formed by architects and designers to carry out requirement elicitation, architectural and software design. There were four architects/designers in the design team. All of them have had many years of experience in the IT industry and at least 5 yrs. on document management applications. The firm uses an internal development and documentation standard, and they also have an internal and external review process. The development methodology can be typified as structured analysis and design. The design team does not use any design reasoning methods during design.

The *research team* consists of two researchers who work independently of the design team to analyze the information. The research team analyzes the specifications prepared by the design team, these specifications include functional requirement specification, architectural design specification, high-level design specification and traceability matrix between requirements and designs. With the supplied documentation, the research team constructed the AREL models using the design reasoning process to reverse engineer the design decisions made. The design team then validate the issues and questions raised by the design reasoning process with the design team.

9.5.1 Analyze the Design by Reasoning

The researchers first examine the specifications, it has been observed that there is very little documented design rationale. When they exist, they are buried within the text of the specifications. The researchers then apply the reasoning process to reverse engineer the design decisions. The researchers imported the summarized specifications into an AREL model. This was achieved by a custom developed software to

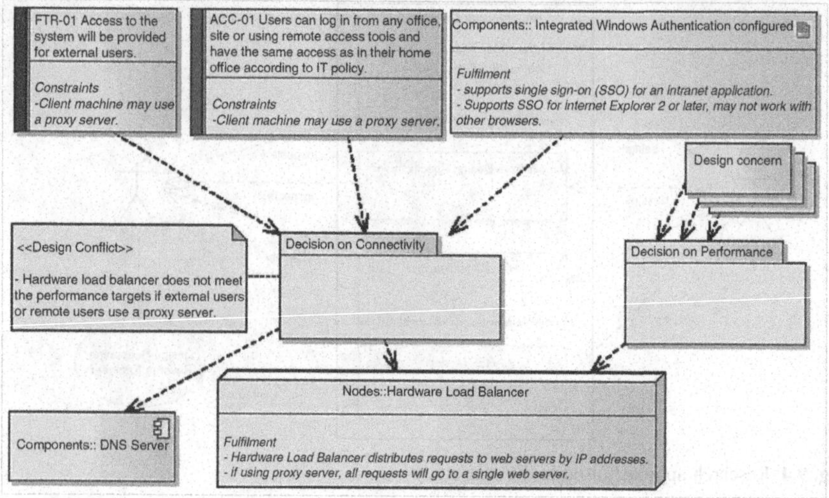

Fig. 9.5 An example AREL decision diagram

scan the specifications and retrieve the requirements. The import process created the *design concerns* and *chosen designs* as UML artifacts stereotyped by ≪architectural elements≫. The nodes in the model contain a unique identity and a brief description of a requirement or a design component. There are a total of 419 design concerns, consisting of 254 functional requirements, 77 non-functional requirements and 88 pieces of contextual information about the system. All of them were imported from the specifications into the model. There are also a total of 86 design components.

Using the AREL model, the researchers carried out a reverse engineering exercise to discover the design decisions. This is done by *associating* relevant design concerns to a design decision (using reasoning step 2), and then find all the possible design outcomes that are affected by this decision (using reasoning step 3). Using this process, the researchers hope to uncover the design reasoning and find any design issues. The result was a series of AREL decision diagrams, an example is shown in Fig. 9.5.

The example in Fig. 9.5 shows the requirements related to secured access to the document management system. The researchers have associated the relevant requirements to a design decision node (i.e. Decision on Connectivity). The design concerns are: (FTR-01) access to the system will be provided to external users; (ACC-01) users can log in from any office or from home using remote access tools; Component to support integrated Windows Authentication Server; and performance requirements. The decision to consider connectivity is to employ a hardware load balancer to realize the design and to use a DNS server.

It was indicated in the specification that the hardware load balancer cannot support external proxy server connections because web accesses cannot be routed to the right server if proxies are used. The design to use a load balancer is primarily for the performance requirement. The design outcome obviously contradicted with the requirements where external users most likely would access through a proxy server. This fundamental requirement cannot be satisfied by the existing hardware. Moreover, if the designers attempt to implement this unwittingly, the performance of the web site would be adversely affected.

By associating the relevant requirements to the design outcomes, we can identify the contradictions in the design because not all the design concerns can be fulfilled by the design. Furthermore, inter-related design may conflict each other. If the load balancer does not support connections through the proxy servers, then there is no way to support external and internal users who access the system from home. This design conflict was raised with the design team and the design team acknowledged this oversight because they had not associated the external access requirement to the load balancer design.

9.5.2 Applying Design Reasoning in the Case Study

The researchers analyzed the system by reverse engineering the design decisions made to create the software architecture. Many cases of ambiguous design rationale were identified. These cases were then presented to the design team to validate if they were real design issues, and all the findings were confirmed to be valid. Through this exercise, it was shown that a systematic design reasoning process would help architects to uncover design issues and achieve a better quality architectural design.

Using the design reasoning approach, researchers have identified 83 issues, of which 29 are ambiguous design concerns, eight issues related to designs that cannot be fully justified through reasoning with the design concerns, and 46 issues that are ambiguous description of design outcomes. With the identified design issues, we analyze the likely causes of why they occur so that we have some insights on how design reasoning may help to improve the situation. The following are cases where design reasoning has uncovered architectural design issues. These cases represent failures that could be avoided if design reasoning steps are taken.

1. *Missing cross-cutting design* Design concerns can cut-across different parts of the software architecture. In the case study, there are many examples of not considering cross-cutting design concerns. These cross-cutting design concerns need to be considered or associated together when designing because they affect each other. An example from the case study is the missing association between user authentication of internal and external users. Currently the company employs an Active Directory to authenticate intranet users, this mechanism supports single sign-on for software applications within the company. Single sign-on is a company policy. However, the architects have omitted to associate this mechanism to another future requirement (FUT-004-01), i.e. supporting external users' login. When these two requirements are associated together, a new significant architectural issue arises – "how to authenticate external users?".

When the architects were interviewed, they indicated that they had not really considered this particular aspect. When the researchers discussed the possible impacts of this omission, the architects then started to identify potential design issues that can arise from it. There are two new design issues concerning security policies, redefining user group privileges and access rights, and access control of external users. The architects agreed that these newly discovered design issues should be addressed. This example illustrates that missing associations of cross-cutting design concerns can cause architectural significant design decisions to be omitted. The likely reasons for such omission are because the system is inherently complex, and system analysis and design is based on textual specifications where minor details can be overlooked. Design reasoning step 2 (see Sect. 9.4) can circumvent this problem by encouraging architects to consciously associate related design concerns to identify new design issues.

2. *Conflicting design concerns*. When the researchers map the design concerns or requirements to the AREL model, it has been found that some design concerns cannot be realized by the current design because they conflict with each other. Architects did not realize that interrelated design concerns should be dealt with together, resulting in hidden requirement conflicts that are not detected by the architects.

   For instance, one requirement is to allow users to ubiquitously access the system and retrieve all types of documents using remote access tools (ACC-002-01); another requirement specifies that all files are to be converted to readable format for viewing when the user does not have the program installed (EDM-008-01); the system design specifies that remote tools such as Citrix and blackberries are to be used (AA-ASM-908). These requirements and design come from different areas of the specifications. When they are analyzed together, conflict arises: (a) requirement ACC-002-01 is by itself ambiguous, it is not specific as to what remote tools should be included in the supported list of tools. This is somewhat clarified by the design assumption AA-ASM-908; (b) when blackberries are required to render documents for viewing, a design conflict is detected. The blackberry device cannot render documents for viewing.

   In this example, the conflict was detected when relevant design outcomes and requirements are linked together. The design issue becomes visible and when it is realized that no design option can satisfy the combined requirements, a design conflict is thus detected.

3. *Ambiguous design concerns*. When the researchers map the design concerns, in terms of requirements, to the design components using the AREL model, the researchers found some inconsistencies between the design concerns and the design outcomes. Most notably, there were design components that could not be traced to the specific design concerns. For instance, the architectural design specified the use of the load balancer, the idea was to distribute web requests to multiple web servers. However, there were no specific non-functional requirements that outline what level of performance was required. There were, however, general requirements which state that the system must have "improved client performance" and "automated failover". The researchers verified

that these design concerns were the ones that had driven the design decision on performance.

The architects were asked about this decision, and the architects thought that it would be a good idea to have a load balancer. The architects might be right intuitively with regards to improving the general performance of a system. However, the decision from this ambiguous design concern had created two architectural issues: firstly, what level of performance should the system deliver? Secondly, the use of a load balancer has created new design issues relating to preserving stateful user sessions in the application design. Subsequent to this realization, the architects have backtrack the decision and revisited this design area (step 5 of the design reasoning process).

4. *No apparent reasons for a design decision*. Even though the requirement and design specifications of the system were organized and extensive, there was very little design rationale that was explicitly documented in these documents. After reconstructing the AREL design reasoning map, it was discovered that in some of the designs, the design reasoning could not be deduced by the researchers. For instance, requirements PRO-007-01 and PRO-007-02 specified that documents that are stored in the application system would be reviewed periodically. The architects chose to realize these requirements by using a standard reporting module that require the document reviewers to search for the documents available for review.

   When the researchers inquired what other design options had been considered, it was found that the first solution that came to mind (i.e. standard reporting module) was the final solution. There was no evaluation of alternative design solutions. One of the possible design solutions in this case was to create an event driven reporting mechanism where reviewers are notified automatically when documents are due for reviews. If a design reasoning approach was used, the architects might have considered this alternate solution. Another study [318] has shown that designers who do not employ design reasoning can fail to consider alternative design options.

In summary, it has been found that the design process undertaken by the architects were inadequate to address all the architectural design issues of the system. We suggest that this is due to the lack of a systematic design reasoning process. Architects' design analysis are functionality focused, and this approach seems to be ineffective when dealing with cross-cutting concerns in architectural design. A design reasoning approach offers a new perspective to systematic architectural design.

9.5.3 Other Findings

Interviews were conducted with the design team at the end of each review session. They were asked to comment on the research findings and the methodologies, the following comments were given by the architects and the designers:

1. *Graphical communication tool*. The AREL model can be a useful tool to communicate design reasoning with their clients because it is easy to trace the graphs. Architects want to use them to validate requirements and architectural design reasoning with their clients. They suggested to have the clients sign-off the design reasoning model, and use it to manage any potential changes to the design reasoning.
2. *Facilitate negotiation*. The AREL model can depict line of reasoning to the client, including the viable options and their pros and cons. It allows the software architects to argue the necessity to compromise certain requirements. Thus it becomes a reasoning tool to help discussions and deliberations of requirements and design.
3. *Traceability*. Supporting tools are available to import specifications to create AREL models, making it easier to build the AREL model. This facility enables the software architects to build models for visualization and better traceability. The requirement traceability matrix that is developed by the design team currently does not completely document the relationships between requirement and design, the AREL model has provided a better traceability in this case.
4. *Facilitate learning*. The information contained in the UML diagrams enables architects in other areas of design to quickly understand the design and its reasoning, making it easier to comprehend the overall design.

There are overheads in creating an additional model to support design reasoning. The question is if the costs justify the benefits. At this stage, we do not have empirical data to support the costs and benefits of this method. However, if the reasoning model is built during the design process, the time taken to create the reasoning models should be a lot less than reverse engineering because the designers already have the background of the system and the UML entities do not need to be reentered again. On the other hand, if design issues were not uncovered at the early stage, it would be a lot more costly to fix them.

9.5.4 Benefits of Design Reasoning

During the course of the architectural design, the software architects had created a traceability matrix between requirements and design components. The architects initially thought that such traceability matrix would allow them to thoroughly analyze and design the system, it turned out that it was only partially useful. In summary, the researchers are able to pinpoint architectural design reasoning gaps in the design. Through analyzing the gaps, we have noticed that ad hoc design decision making does not provide a systematic approach to architectural design. As a result, conflicts in requirements and design have occurred, certain requirements are ambiguous, and decisions have not been well-thought out. The results of this study have indicated that design reasoning can help to achieve the goals described in Table 9.1, a summary is shown in Table 9.4.

Table 9.4 How design reasoning process serve architectural design

Architectural activities	How design reasoning benefits architectural design
Deliberating design	*Associating* interrelated design concerns to identify a design issue, or a design topic, is an essential step in architectural design. It formulates what decision has to be made, from that architects need to *identify* the design options that can address the design issues.
Justifying design decisions	Having *identified* the design options, architects should justify why a certain option is chosen and how it satisfies the design concerns, using argumentation or trade-offs analysis method. If a design concern cannot be fully satisfied, then *backtracking* to change previously made decisions allow the architects to iteratively improve the design.
Structured design process	The design reasoning process supports a structured approach to software architecture design. It is an improvement that allows architects to synthesize a design by exploring and associating design concerns systematically.
Design validation	Design reasoning has allowed systematic analysis of the architectural design by the researchers, the method enables architects and reviewers to find hidden design issues, and serves to validate the architecture design.
Communication and knowledge transfer	The architects have noted that the AREL UML representation can be used to communicate and discuss design reasoning process and trade-offs with the stakeholders. The decision diagrams can also serve as documented agreements between stakeholders.
Support architectural maintenance	The architects have noted that capturing the design rationale can help new staff to understand the system and quickly becoming productive.

9.5.5 Limitations in the Case Study

A qualitative research method is used in this empirical case study. The researchers reverse engineered the design reasoning models of the system using its requirement and design specifications. The design reasoning model was used to assess if a design reasoning process could improve the design process. A direct application of the design reasoning method to the system would have been the preferred approach for testing this method. If another design team that does not use the method carries out the same design in parallel, the comparison between the two would yield directly comparable results. However for sizable real-life system development, this is almost impossible because of funding issues. As such, we have opted to use the reverse engineering method as a mean to obtain design data for comparisons.

One could argue that the researchers can benefit from the hindsight. However, the designers have more experience in the application domain than the researchers. Without a similar background, the researchers' only method is the design reasoning approach. The researchers were not aware of the possible issues that might appear in this type of applications. Therefore, the design issues that have been uncovered by the researchers to a large extent can be attributed to the design reasoning technique.

Although the design team has more experience in this domain, the researchers have similar years of general design experience, so it is possible that such experience may bias the findings. It is very difficult to distinguish to what extent design experience or design reasoning attribute to a high quality design. An empirical study has shown that design reasoning can help inexperienced designers to design better [318]. Using the results from both studies, we suggest that the need for experience and design reasoning is relative to the complexity of the architectural design. Although we cannot distinguish which one of the two factors (i.e. reasoning or experience) is more important, we think that highly complex problems would require design reasoning techniques to aid the thought process.

9.6 Summary

In this chapter, we have outlined a design reasoning method that comprises of five steps. This method is iterative in nature, and it is based on the causal relationships between *design concerns*, *design decisions* and *design outcomes*. Using the AREL model, we have applied this design method to a real-life system. In the empirical study, it has been found that design reasoning steps to *associate design concerns* and to *identify design options* are the two important reasoning steps in design.

The architects involved in this case study were interviewed at the end of the study. They have confirmed that by using design reasoning, it helps them to deliberate and negotiate design, determine trade-offs and review the architectural design. They have also noted that the graphical representation of AREL is simple, thereby making the design reasoning process intuitive and easy to use. From this observation, we suggest that such simplicity can overcome some of the issues faced by existing design rationale models where complex representations have hindered their implementation [79, 58, 206].

Acknowledgements This research has been partially sponsored by the Dutch Joint Academic and Commercial Quality Research and Development (Jacquard) program on Software Engineering Research via contract 638.001.406 GRIFFIN: a GRId For inFormatIoN about architectural knowledge.

Chapter 10
Modeling and Improving Information Flows in the Development of Large Business Applications

Kurt Schneider and Daniel Lübke

Abstract Designing a good architecture for an application is a wicked problem. Therefore, experience and knowledge are considered crucial for informing work in software architecture. However, many organizations do not pay sufficient attention to experience exploitation and architectural learning. Many users of information systems are not aware of the options and the needs to report problems and requirements. They often do not have time to describe a problem encountered in sufficient detail for developers to remove it. And there may be a lengthy process for providing feedback. Hence, the knowledge about problems and potential solutions is not shared effectively. Architectural knowledge needs to include evaluative feedback as well as decisions and their reasons (rationale).

In order to address this issue, this chapter proposes two concepts: (1) Integrating feedback and experience exchange mechanisms to facilitate architectural experience reuse and (2) an approach for modeling information flow in a project. Feedback and experience flows are designed to support effective learning. Each cycle produces a growing knowledge about the application. Service-oriented architectures (SOA) are used as an example to illustrate this general challenge in software architecture.

10.1 Introduction

Creating and using an effective architecture for a new application requires a wide variety of skills and knowledge. As the above questions illustrate, information and knowledge needs to come from the users of an application. Familiarity with the domain is indispensable in understanding business processes and requirements. At the same time, technical knowledge is a mandatory requirement for developing an

---

Kurt Schneider (✉) and Daniel Lübke
Leibniz Universität Hannover, FG Software Engineering, Hannover, Germany, e-mail: Kurt.Schneider,@inf.uni-hannover.de, Daniel.Luebke@inf.uni-hannover.de

M. Ali Babar et al. (eds.), *Software Architecture Knowledge Management*,
DOI: 10.1007/978-3-642-02374-3_10,

application. Maintaining and evolving existing components and services requires both technical and domain knowledge, and experience.

Finding the requirements and architecture for a new application is often a wicked problem [266]: by presenting a solution, the problem changes [260]. A new application changes the processes and dependencies in its domain. Even valid requirements may become invalid through the presence of new features. A requirements-centric view as described in Chap. 2 is not sufficient. For that reason, the development and operation of a long-lived application often resembles an ongoing evolution and learning process. Architectural decisions may need to be revised or extended under the influence of real-world feedback. Therefore, a better vision for designing large business applications is a co-evolution of requirements and architecture as described by Pohl and Sikora [253].

Giving and getting feedback may appear simple at a first glance. However, it faces many challenges well known in the field of Systematic Learning from Experiences [32, 283]. Obviously, handling feedback consumes time and effort. Knowledge management [88] and experience-based process improvement [279] have identified many additional challenges, including psychological and practical issues. For example, the workplace of a typical travel agent is not designed to encourage feedback on applications and their behavior. Giving feedback requires an agent to neglect value-added sales activities and write a note or report. It is, thus, not surprising that developers and users know little about each other – although they could collaborate to improve their applications.

Kruchten et al. characterizes architectural knowledge as:

architectural knowledge $=$ *architectural design* $+$ *architectural decisions* [192].

However, since neither design nor decisions are static, we claim that a term "+ feedback" should be added to the equation. Design rationale may be falsified as context and environment change. A decision based on an outdated rationale should be reconsidered. In this chapter, I address two related topics of exchanging information and knowledge in the area of designing application architecture. Service-oriented architectures will be used as an illustrated example: They serve to describe both the problem and concrete opportunities for solving it.

1. Information and experience flow modeling [287, 288] is proposed for analyzing communication between users, developers, and other stakeholders. By considering light-weight information transfer innovative links and shortcuts in the communication surrounding an application and its evolution are envisioned and designed.
2. Communication is supported by integrating concepts and mechanisms of experience exploitation [280] into an application.

The result is a map of communication. It contains the information flows around application development, and an overview of the mechanisms introduced for learning. An Experience Forum is proposed as an integral part of that application. The forum reduces the threshold for reporting feedback and experience. It also provides architects and developers with opportunities for eliciting and validating evolving users' needs.

This chapter describes the concept of using information and experience flow for improving the architectural knowledge sharing in software development process. It also demonstrates how to explicitly model the flow of information and experience. The rest of the chapter is structured as follows. Section 10.2 presents information flow modeling as a technique to visualize and discuss communication and flow of experience in a software project. It has been developed at Leibniz Universität Hannover. This technique is illustrated on a large business project, in Sect. 10.3, leading to an overview map. It contains a feedback capturing mechanism and an Experience Forum as architectural building blocks for effective learning and evolution. Section 10.4 discusses options for experience exploitation mechanisms as a special case for knowledge management. We have implemented those aspects for SOA projects, exploiting its flexible architecture and process-related building blocks (Sect. 10.5). Related work is addressed within each section.

10.2 Information Flow Modeling

In every software development project, requirements must flow from customers and users to the developers. Feedback must flow back to developers, as the effective flow of information and feedback is a prerequisite to the above-mentioned learning cycles. Modeling the flow of information in a project can, therefore, help to understand some dependencies and opportunities better. We use the term "information flow" as a generalization of the different types of information flowing, such as requirements, feedback, and context information.

10.2.1 Information Flow: Concept, Focus and Purpose

Kwan et al. propose to observe communication in software projects in order to derive models [194]. Since they suggest using automated mechanisms for collecting data, their main focus on documents and electronic sources, which are easier to trace and monitor. However, Damian concedes that it is not sufficient to observe written and documented information alone [87]. Although it may be interesting to monitor real communication in a specific project, we propose to determine and *design* communication channels.

Observing real communication can support tracing. Traces in requirements engineering are normally used for linking design decisions with requirements. The requirements-centric view described in Chap. 2 focuses on tracing requirements to architectural decisions. Winkler focuses on information flow from a tracing perspective [339]. Kwan et al. trace communication activities like emails. Winkler is interested in establishing relationships between artifacts based on the flow of information among them. Unlike Kwan et al. [194], Damian [86], and Winkler [339], our information flow models make informal communication explicit. It complements document-based communication with oral or informal information flows wherever appropriate.

I propose to discuss the integration of experience exploitation into development by visualizing, discussing and optimizing information flows. There is also an overview of the design that needs to be implemented later.

According to the iterative and learning aspects of software projects, we are interested in information flows from a specific perspective. We want to design information flow in order to support the construction of an SOA application. Feedback and experience need to flow in support of ongoing maintenance and evolution. Information flow models are supposed to visualize all those flows, and enable us to improve and support them.

Stachoviak's *model theory* [304] has a few basic concepts that are also stressed in our information flow models. Each model represents a part of reality with respect to:

1. Certain users of the model
2. For certain purposes
3. At a certain time

Relevant properties of the original system are mapped onto the model system. Most models have additional properties that are not mapped from the original system, but facilitate handling of the model. For example, a wind tunnel model of a car may consist of clay. The shape of the car is a property mapped onto the shape of the model. According to the *purpose* of wind tunnel experiments, shape is relevant. Clay as a material is a property of the model, but does *not* represent (i.e., map) any aspect of the car. Instead, clay was chosen since it is easy to shape. When a model is constructed, it is important to keep (1) users (2) purpose and (3) time of use in mind.

Depending on the intended users, purposes, and usage times, information flow modeling may be carried out in very different ways. Therefore, it is important to define purposes of modeling information flow for software projects (Table 10.1). We describe those purposes and reference publications to related application in industry.

Increasing Awareness and Overview is the basis for all other purposes. Existing processes and communication structures can be improved – or *new* flows can be *designed* using information flow models. Building on the new situation, selected information flows can be supported by providing dedicated support tools or technique.

Table 10.1 Overview of the purposes of information flow modeling in software projects

Supporting new flows through tools and techniques		
Improving requirements processes and practices	*or*	Designing use and Flow of experiences
Increasing awareness and overview		

Increasing awareness and overview. A model of information flows corresponds to a map of project communication. Stakeholders and participants can use it to find a relevant document or person. Not all stakeholders in a project may be aware of their role. Some may not know all sources and paths of information available. In particular, flows of feedback and experience may be unclear or difficult to follow. Knowledge of information flows and their properties is needed by architects. Architects should consider information flow when they design an application for long-term use and evolution. Discussing and modeling flows can increase the awareness and provide an overview for all participants.

We applied the information flow models for visualizing the original equipment manufacturer (OEM) vs. subcontractor relationship in requirements engineering for electronic control units at a car manufacturing company. Allmann [14] discussed different variants of that relationship.

Improving requirements processes and practices. Requirements engineering processes are often based on informal communication. Requirements in a SOA project are expected to flow along different paths. That is why choice of appropriate information flows are considered essential for improving those processes effectively. Therefore, visualizing communication and information flows is expected not only to increase awareness [288] but also to supports improving the processes and practices with respect to information flows. The criteria for "better" flows depend on the constraints and requirements. By identifying the constraints that are the characteristic of SOA application development, we identify the criteria for appropriate flows. We evaluated a large process model with respect to information flow in a financial institution [307]. A custom-made search tool helped us to identify over 100 findings. We found that some were simple modeling flaws, while others uncovered potential for improving information flow.

Designing use and flow of experience. Experience is often neglected in process models. Information flow models according to the style presented below are intended to include experience sources, sinks, and flows. Besides visualizing those aspects in the map, new processes can be designed to install flows that do not yet exist. We have developed a mechanism for SOA application. As a result, innovative feedback channels can be established. The above-mentioned learning cycles rely on rather specific patterns of experience flow. Identifying, designing, and supporting those patterns include designing the use and flow of experience. Other areas of architecture will require different solutions to implement.

We used information flow analysis in the automotive industry to plan for the introduction of a Wiki system [306]. It was supposed to improve the flow of requirements and information.

Supporting new flows through tools and techniques. Understanding existing flows is a prerequisite for improving them. With the purpose of improvement in mind, one will reroute some flows in business projects. However, implementing a redirected or novel flow will not work by simply "defining" it. As an incentive to participants, following the desired flows should be advantageous to using the old paths. This is a lesson learned in experience exploitation [280] and knowledge management alike [88]. A tool or technique can be offered to facilitate the work of stakeholder. This support can make the new flows more attractive and contribute to their acceptance. By design of the tool or technique, new flows are encouraged or enforced. For example, it is possible to build tools and techniques specifically for improving certain flow patterns. The *FastFeedback* tool provides feedback on use cases while they are elicited during stakeholder interviews. It was built for analyzing concrete information flow models in the requirements elicitation phase of a large administrative project [281].

Information flow models are usually created in an interactive process of interviews, consistency checks and workshops. A moderator uses a visualization to focus and document discussions. Information flow models can be considered a type of knowledge in their own right. Learning about communication in a project will be captured and expressed in information flow models in Sect. 10.5.

10.2.2 Key Concepts and Modeling Notation in FLOW

Information flow modeling needs to address the above purposes. A number of concepts were developed during the FLOW project at Leibniz Universität Hannover. These concepts enable model builders to focus on relevant properties of communication and information flow, while omitting most other aspects of an SOA project.

Fluid representations include meetings and oral communications, blogs, chats, informal Wikis, phone calls, and personal e-mails not accessible to others. Fluid information is commonly used in most development organizations, but many current process models are restricted to solid information.

Solid representation refers to documents and stores with certain characteristics:

1. Information can be retrieved by others
2. Without the help of the author or source
3. Even after some time has expired and
4. In a form that supports dissemination

All other representations are called *fluid*.

Not every act of fluid communication is relevant to a project (e.g., personal chat, random meetings at the coffee machine). However, ignoring fluid requirements leads to errors, misunderstandings, and parallel work. There are trade-offs: Creating solid representations and retrieving information is often more effort-consuming than fluid exchange via human interaction. In turn, fluid information can be forgotten, and it is limited in access. Combining advantages of both styles is the basis for designing individual networks of flows.

It is important to note that we do *not* assume each and every requirement or piece of information needs to be solidified in the end. For some purposes, fluid

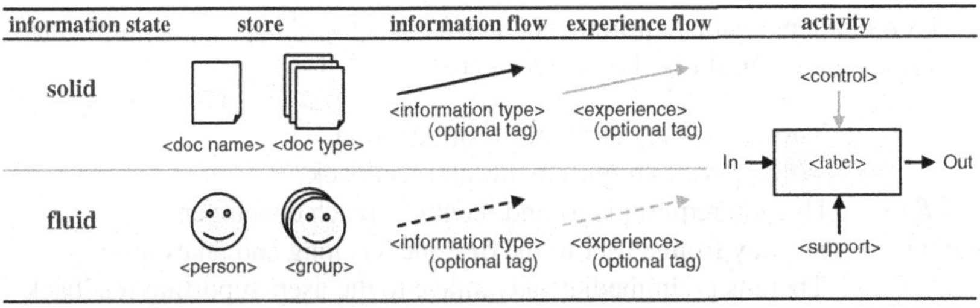

Fig. 10.1 FLOW Syntax

representations are more appropriate than solid. For example, many users will prefer giving oral or informal feedback over writing reports. FLOW is used to explicitly modeling previously tacit knowledge on fluid representations of information. We take fluid information very seriously and discuss it in detail (see below), but we do not claim it must become a requirement in all cases.

We model, analyze and improve information flows in software projects. Models are often sketched on whiteboards and redrawn in PowerPoint or other graphical editors. The notation must, therefore, be simple and avoid unnecessary detail.

The syntax shown in Fig. 10.1 was designed to convey the concepts of information flow:

- Stores are depicted by easy-to-draw symbols that are provided in most drawing tools: A document symbol and a human face. Humans are the most important *fluid stores*, while documents are the classical storing device of *solid information*.
- Identifiers refer to individuals or roles, depending on the purpose of a model.
- Multiple document or person symbols refer to one or more stores of the same document type or group of persons. Details are omitted intentionally.
- Flows are represented by arrows. All flows originating from a solid store are solid. All flows originating from a fluid store are fluid.
- Flows originating from an activity can be either solid or fluid: A model builder can express an intention or assumption by using fluid or solid style.
- Tags on arrows can be used to highlight specific types of information flowing. Requirements and derived information are the default type.
- Experience is depicted in a different color or in gray.
- The activity symbol is a box. Flows may be attached to each side. The box indicates decomposition: there are different options to implement an activity.

10.3 Designing Feedback and Information Flows

In this section, problems and feedback during the development large business applications are visualized using the FLOW notation. The visualization will help to understand and compare different flows of feedback. Step by step, a more desirable situation will be designed. In subsequent sections, support for implementing that vision will be presented.

The main challenges for requirements and feedback in large applications have been described above. In short, the aspects were:

Many users:	There are many users of the application Who provides requirements and feedback?
Unclear flows:	How do requirements and feedback reach developers?
Motivation:	He way from a user to the designers is long and takes time There is no immediate advantage to the users reporting feedback How can people be motivated to give feedback?
Speed:	How can one speed up the flow of feedback and reaction?
Errors:	Requirements and feedback may be polluted on the long way from source to developers. How can errors be avoided?
Context:	How to capture the context of feedback effectively?
Effort:	How to reduce the effort for processing feedback?

The above challenges are now considered one by one. A series of FLOW diagrams visualize the argumentation.

10.3.1 Designing Information Flows for Large Business Projects

Many stakeholders and users. There are large groups of stakeholders and several developers in a project. The feedback from stakeholders to developers is specified as a fluid flow because we cannot rely on written feedback. Fluid feedback is more convenient to provide for stakeholders, but it is more challenging for storing and analyzing.

Figure 10.2 makes no further statements about the nature and implementation of this flow. By analyzing the situation, it turns out that all stakeholders may provide requirements, including management, system administrators and users of the application. Users are considered a specific kind of stakeholders. This fact is modeled by a generalization relationship. It is not explicitly part of the FLOW notation, but adopted as an extension.

Both feedback and requirements are types of information flows. We assume that "giving feedback" requires using the application. Only users do that (Fig. 10.3), while other stakeholders (e.g., managers) may provide requirements, but not feedback. In the next step, we want to follow the information flows more closely. At this point, it is not obvious where stakeholders (including users) get the information

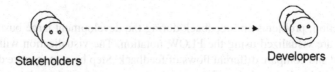

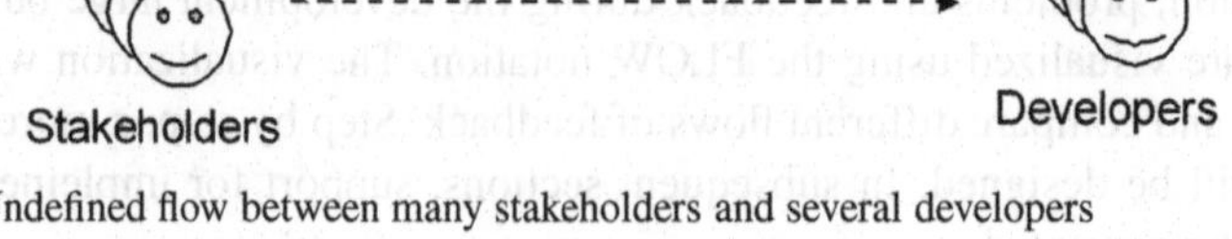

Fig. 10.2 Undefined flow between many stakeholders and several developers

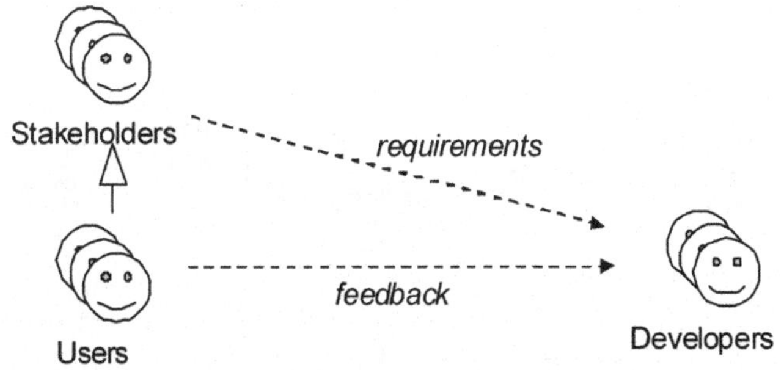

Fig. 10.3 Users as source of feedback in development

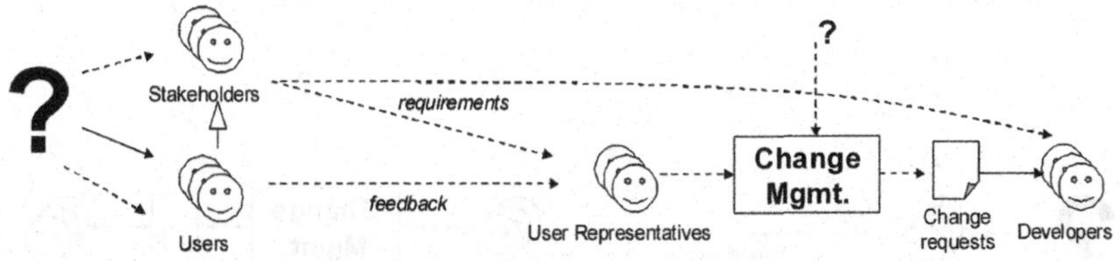

Fig. 10.4 Long flows between stakeholders and developers, with unclear aspects

that enables them to give feedback and formulate requirements. It is not realistic to let users communicate with developers via phone calls or emails (fluid flow). There should be an instance that decides about the feedback that eventually leads to changes. Change management as in Fig. 10.4 is a usual way of organizing this filtering activity. A group of user representatives receive the fluid input of users and take it into change management. As a result, there is a document containing change requests. Those are the definite basis for developers. It is (intentionally) unclear in Fig. 10.4 who makes decisions in change management.

The information flows in Fig. 10.4 and respective *processes are long and tedious*. Why should a user or other stakeholder take the time and effort to provide input? Triggering improvements in an application are the most obvious reason. Developers provide a new release to users. Another information flow that acts as an incentive is an immediate visibility of feedback to peer users. When feedback is available to other users, they can directly respond to problems, maybe even resolve misunderstanding or spurious flaw. Social recognition may encourage more people to contribute feedback and responses. Short-term visibility of feedback can be an important incentive for turning a group of users into a Community of Practice [335].

For clarity, we focus on users and their feedback *only* (Fig. 10.5). The branch of stakeholders and their requirements can be discussed in an analogous way.

Speed. At this point, the process of improving the application is rather long. User representatives, change management with written change requests, and the developers writing a new release are chains of information flows and transformations.

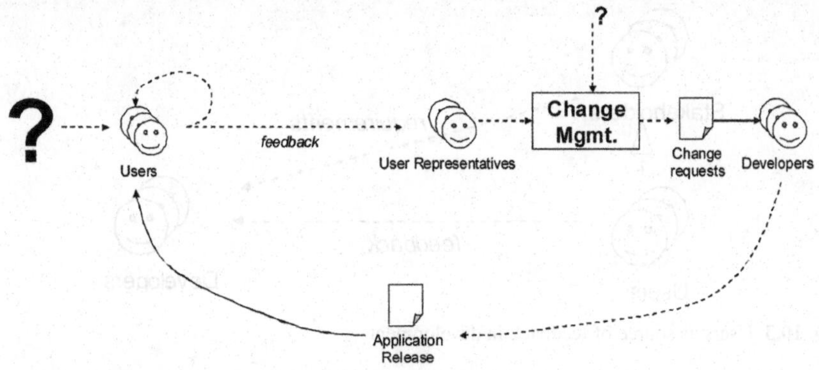

Fig. 10.5 Improved releases and social recognition among peers as incentives for feedback

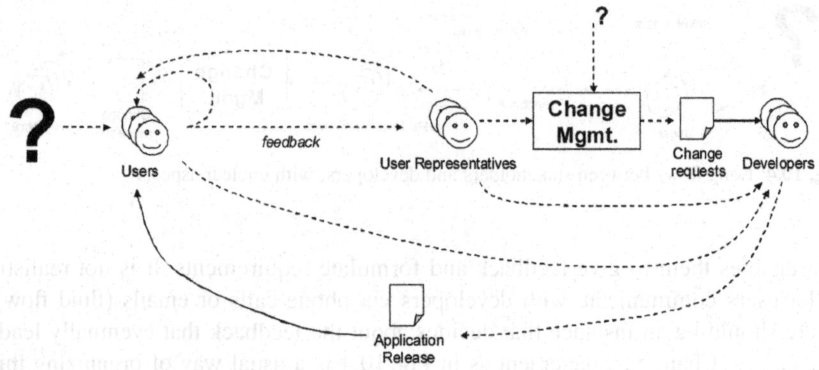

Fig. 10.6 Increasing speed through direct and fluid information flows

It may be faster to allow direct communication links among most participants. Fluid information flows are usually faster than solid ones. This leads to Fig. 10.6.

However, Fig. 10.6 looks very *cluttered and difficult to organize*. There are many different paths of information, and most of them are fluid. The entire model looks very fluid, which generally implies fast flows but high risks for losing information, or polluting it with errors. Therefore, we *design* an activity into the communication model. Obviously, users will use the application at some point. By including that activity into the information flow model, we emphasize its importance. Within the FLOW model, we are only interested in the implications on information flow, but not in any other application details. In Fig. 10.6, the Application Release constitutes information for Users – in an unspecified way. Slightly more precise than Fig. 10.6, we state that the application release is needed as a prerequisite or tool for the "use application" activity (i.e., arrow from bottom). Figure 10.7 also explains where users get the information for their feedback: By using the application, they are stimulated to provide feedback. We want to avoid distracting users from their main task. Therefore, feedback must be collected close to using the application.

We *decide* to let this information flow into the activity of using the application. In addition, we require context to be collected with the feedback. The box representing the activity hides all details. We also decide to provide solid feedback (a document or artifact), which requires some sort of transformation within the use application activity. This document can be read by users. Together with fluid communication from user representatives, the document implements the feedback loop that supports social recognition for users who provide feedback. At a later point, we will have to decide how to implement "use application" with the above-stated properties and information flows.

Avoid errors. Figure 10.7 still contains lengthy flows including several consecutive transformations. This corresponds to an **information flow pattern** that indicates a high risk of errors (see the Chinese Whisper pattern [307]). We *decide* to make better use of the feedback document. In Fig. 10.8, the feedback document will be used in change management directly. User representatives will also use it for making decisions. We assume management will be represented in change management, too.

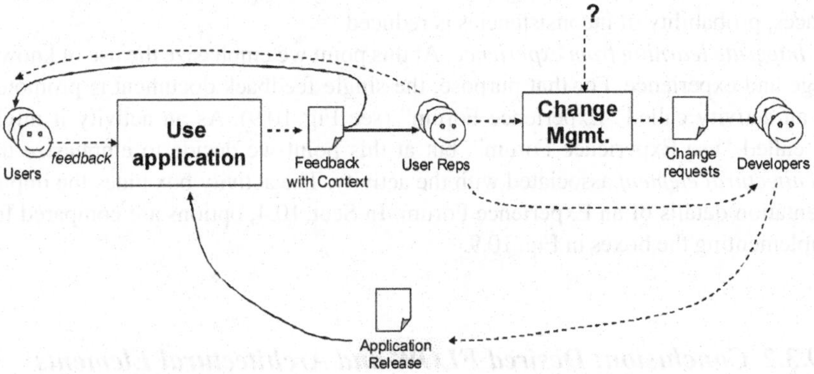

Fig. 10.7 Introducing a black-box activity helps to clarify information flow

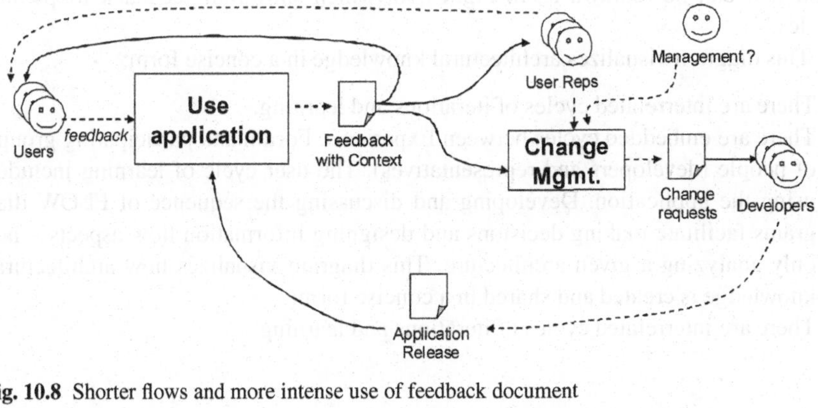

Fig. 10.8 Shorter flows and more intense use of feedback document

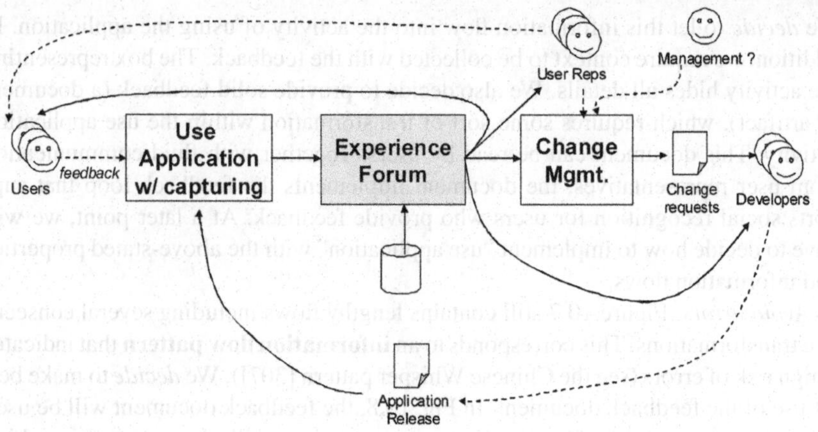

Fig. 10.9 Replacing a simple document by the Experience Forum architectural element

This resolves our last remaining question mark. By using the same document in all places, probability of inconsistencies is reduced.

Integrate learning from experience. At this point we emphasize the use of knowledge and experience. For that purpose, the single feedback document is promoted to an activity called "Experience Forum" (see Fig. 10.9). As an activity it might be called "use Experience Forum", but at this point we decide to emphasize the *architectural element* associated with the activity. The activity box hides the implementation details of an Experience Forum. In Sect. 10.4, options are compared for implementing the boxes in Fig. 10.9.

10.3.2 Conclusion: Desired FLOW and Architectural Elements

The considerations visualized by FLOW diagrams have led to an information flow model. It can be redrawn as in Fig. 10.10, which shows all feedback loops and cycles:

This diagram visualizes architectural knowledge in a concise form:

- There are interrelated cycles of iterations and learning.
- There are embedded cycles between Experience Forum and participating groups of people (developers and representatives). The user cycle of learning includes using the application. Developing and discussing the sequence of FLOW diagrams facilitate making decisions and designing information flow aspects – not only analyzing a given architecture. This diagram visualizes how architectural knowledge is created and shared in a concise form:
- There are interrelated cycles of iterations and learning.

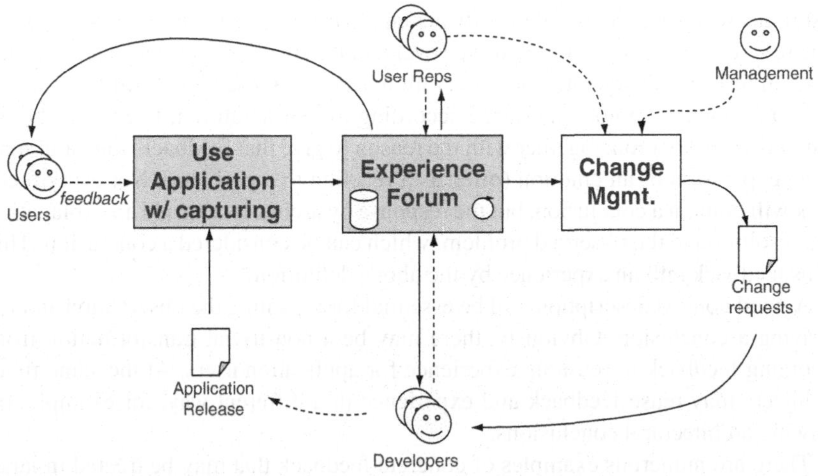

Fig. 10.10 Final flows and activities to be supported. Result of designing information flows

- There are embedded cycles between Experience Forum and participating groups of people (developers and representatives). The learning cycle of users includes using the application in practice.
- There must be interesting stuff in the center box.
- The sequence of FLOW diagrams facilitated making decisions and designing information flow aspects – not just analyzing a given architecture. The diagrams themselves constitute knowledge relevant for software architecture.

In Sect. 10.4, the center box is discussed in detail.

10.4 Designing an Experience Forum

This section outlines the principles and activities involved in a systematic experience exploitation [282]. Architecture knowledge management includes handling of experiences. Architecture is an area that relies on learning by experience, since there are only a few general principles guiding it (such as information hiding, three-tier-architectural pattern, etc.). Experience is regarded a special kind of knowledge.

We use "information" as the general term covering feedback, experience, and other information relevant to a software architect's task. We adopt a pragmatic definition for experience, as consisting of (1) an observation, (2) a related emotion and (3) a conclusion, according to [281].

According to this definition, there needs to be an authentic source (observation), not just a belief or theoretical deduction. An emotional response is the key for remembering what happened. Both good and bad emotions may trigger that effect. In addition, an experience useful in software engineering must include a conclusion: It may refer to the reason for the observed event, or it may refer to its consequences. By generalizing and abstracting, the observation becomes reusable in "similar" cases.

Requirements are not experience according to that definition. Feedback should contain an observation, together with the reason to give that feedback; the latter may be an expression of an emotion (often as a reaction to a problem). Not every feedback will contain a conclusion, but the response by architects can add an explanation or a resolution to the observed problem, which can be considered a conclusion. This turns feedback into an experience by the above definition.

A good context description will be essential for repeating the observation and for deriving a conclusion. Obviously, there may be a non-trivial transformation from incoming feedback to reusable experience for application users. At the same time, architects may reuse feedback and experience in a different way, for example, by drawing architectural conclusions.

There are numerous examples of concrete feedback that may be treated in large projects. Figure 10.11 shows an excerpt from a UML model of relevant feedback. In this example, comments and ratings provide options to describe feedback. Reference to business processes is made, which typically happens in SOA projects very explicitly.

Several types of feedback are distinguished:

- Bug Reports describe a software defect, incorrect functionality.
- Feature Requests refer to missing functionality from the users' point of view.
- Process Shortcomings are directed to flawed business processes rather than poor implementation.
- Process Experience refers to a full triple of (observation, emotion, and conclusion) with respect to a process step or use scenario.
- Software Support Requests are questions rather than observations. Users want to know how to use a feature or achieve a certain result.

There may be other examples of feedback in other environments. We focus on business applications in the following discussions. Other mechanisms will be needed to implement the concepts in other areas.

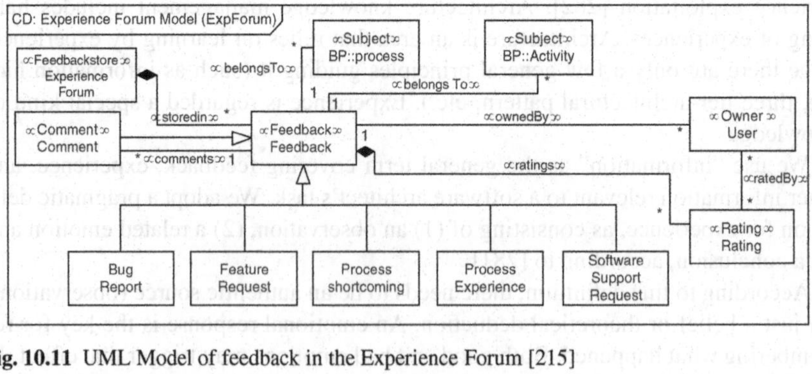

Fig. 10.11 UML Model of feedback in the Experience Forum [215]

10.4.1 Learning Cycles in General and in Software Architecture

Iterative and evolutionary development approaches imply cyclic processes. These processes reflect the cyclic learning models of Kolb [186], improvement cycles like the Quality Improvement Paradigm [31]. Some cycles are shown in Fig. 10.10. Others may occur within the activity labeled "Experience Forum". In this section, we describe typical activities of experience management. An systematic learning from experience requires rich interaction on a platform for sharing with several knowledge workers [102]. It is the main purpose of an Experience Forum to organize and enable those interactions. There is a wide range of possible implementations for an Experience Forum, including help desks, ontologies, and Wikis. We briefly compare some of them and explain why we consider a forum a good compromise.

The following activities are at the core of experiential learning in software engineering:

- *Experience activation*. How stakeholders become aware of a reusable insights.
- *Experience collection*. How experience and its context can be secured.
- *Experience engineering*. How collected material can be compared, validated, and transformed into more reusable pieces of knowledge and experience.
- *Experience dissemination*. How results reach those who need them.

Figure 10.12 shows a typical learning cycle including a computer-based "experience base" [286] that can support it. It is essential to note that the cycle needs to keep turning for effective learning from experience. We use an of several interrelated learning cycles:

- Users learn by using the application with the extended experience mechanisms
- Developers learn by accessing the Experience Forum, and through development iterations
- User representatives learn through interaction with the Experience Forum, and through longer cycles.

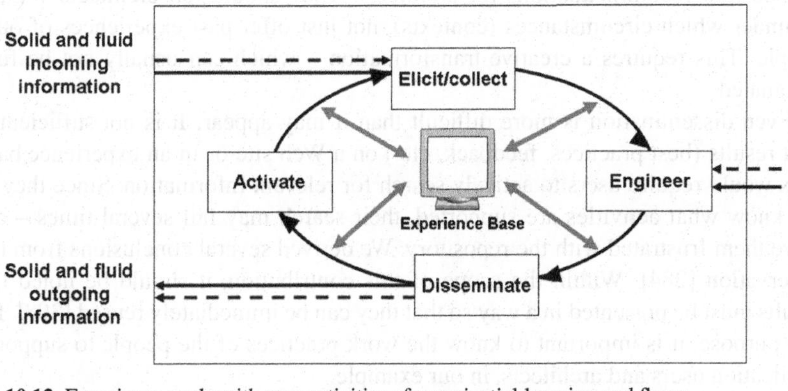

Fig. 10.12 Experience cycle with core activities of experiential learning and flows

Unlike usual representations of the experience cycle, Fig. 10.12 also shows incoming and outgoing flows of information as the "flow interface" [285] of the experience cycle. Depending on its implementation, experience engineering can include external knowledge from other sources (input from the right in Fig. 10.12). Note that the terminology used below slightly differs from traditional terms presented in the introductory chapters of this book. This is due to a different emphasis in the following presentation of experience engineering [282]. For example, activating experience refers to making someone aware of his or her experiences. In this context, it is more adequate to consider activation a first step of "externalization" or "codification".

Experiences need to be activated. It is not sufficient to wait for feedback and experience to pop up [284]. Instead, there should be mechanisms for provoking creative breakdowns [289]. During periods of intense work, such a breakdown is needed to make knowledge workers aware of the experience or insights they just gained. Obviously, the delicate balance must be kept between too little activation and too many interruptions (breakdowns).

Collecting and storing feedback and incoming material is a necessary but not sufficient condition for implementing the full experience cycle. Management and software engineers tend to confuse storing experience with the full learning cycle. Storing and searching require technical support. However, the remaining parts of the experience cycle cannot be skipped or neglected without major drawbacks [30, 286].

Experience engineering includes the tedious tasks of validating, comparing, and transferring incoming material into more reusable elements. Without experience engineering, false feedback and misleading statements of experience will be stored and distributed to others. This puts the credibility of an experience exchange at risk. Sometimes, input sources are inconsistent due to different contexts. Therefore, comparing and analyzing contexts adds a lot of value to the consolidated output.

It is a major misunderstanding to expect altruistic behavior. An expert or user needs reasons to provide input [88]. It is also unrealistic to expect that others will be eager to get and reuse experience [278]. Instead, most knowledge workers, such as architects, consider experience yet another source of support for their main task of designing an application. Therefore, experiences and other input should be transformed into recommendations for architects. They should tell architects what to do under which circumstances (contexts), not just offer past experiences of other people. This requires a creative transformation – which can usually not be fully automated.

Even dissemination is more difficult than it may appear: It is not sufficient to post results (best practices, feedback, etc.) on a Web site or in an experience base. This would require users to actively search for relevant information. Since they do not know what activities are supported, their search may fail several times – and leave them frustrated with the repository. We derived several conclusions from this observation [284]. Within the scope of this contribution, it should be noted that results must be presented in a way so that they can be immediately reused [308]. For this purpose, it is important to know the work practices of the people to support – application users and architects, in our example.

The experience cycle in Fig. 10.12 shows activities and dependencies; information will flow along the dependency arrows, and between activities and the experience base. This informal notation is not completely consistent with the FLOW notation defined above. Therefore, a few comments are in place to clarify the relationship between the two models:

- The Experience Forum requires certain incoming and outgoing flows of information. This is called the "flow interface" of the activity [285].
- The entire experience cycle needs to be covered within Fig. 10.12. The input and output of the experience cycle needs to match the information flow interface of the Experience Forum. Parts of the experience cycle (including some of its activities) may not be visible in Fig. 10.10: they are internal parts of the Experience Forum activity.

10.4.2 Mechanisms for Feedback and Experience

As reports from Ericsson [167] and DaimlerChrysler [149] illustrate, experience cycles can be implemented in different ways. In this section, we briefly present one way of implementing experience cycle of architects and other stakeholders, through what we call a forum:

A forum is an informal opportunity for people to meet and exchange their observations, conclusions, and opinions. Often, problems raised by one person are answered by another person. The public answer is available to all participants. In contrast to a helpdesk, not all participants have a problem when they log in. Some act as recommenders who consider social recognition as an incentive [88]. Communities of practice are voluntary groups of people interested in a common topic [335]. A forum can support communities of practice by offering synchronous and asynchronous options for communication. In contrast to a Wiki, a forum facilitates direct interactions for asking and answering questions, or for discussing issues.

Experience is being activated by questions and discussions, or by a real-world problem that someone describes in the forum. Dissemination occurs during the replies. However, in a forum there might be several replies. Since they are written (solid), others may find the advice later. Dissemination can occur through this channel, too. Collecting is, therefore, supported in a trivial way by keeping old discussions. If there is a moderator sorting and filtering contributions, a first step of engineering is achieved. However, a wide range of further engineering and dissemination mechanisms can be integrated into a forum.

Many mechanisms comply with the flow interface of our Experience Forum activity. We consider a forum a good compromise between effort and result. A forum is open to accommodate different engineering mechanisms. User representatives and architects should support the Community of Users by analyzing input. This will increase their own understanding, and they may be able to provide immediate help. They can use the forum for answers. Therefore, we suggested an "Experience *Forum*" as the default implementation.

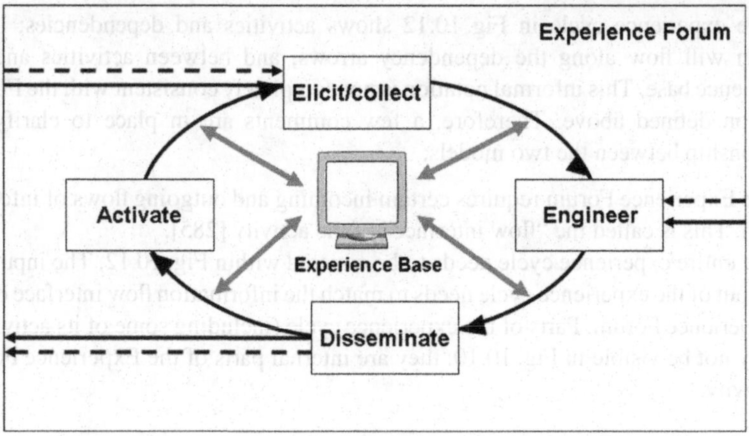

Fig. 10.13 An Experience Forum may contain some or all steps of the experience cycle

The forum needs to be integrated within the information flow depicted in Fig. 10.10. In particular, feedback must be captured while users carry out their main task: using the application. The answers to questions and feedback must be channeled back to reach them in that same context: Context is essential for proper dissemination. We propose to integrate the entire interface of the Experience Forum into the SOA application user interface. The Experience Forum box is shown around the experience cycle in Fig. 10.13.

10.5 Supporting Feedback and Experience in SOA Projects

The feedback and experience support mechanisms proposed above can effectively be implemented. We sketch a solution available to SOA application development as an example.

10.5.1 SOA: Aligning Software Services with Business Processes

The main driver behind SOA is the idea of better aligning the business with its supporting IT infrastructure. Software should be easily maintainable and it should be possible to quickly change it in order to adapt to changing business environments. Different roles need to collaborate for an SOA to work properly. Especially business process designers and software developers need to work together to closely couple business requirements and processes to the software. Only such collaboration guarantees that changes to the business requirements can be anticipated and implemented in the software in a short time-frame.

In general, services do not need to be offered by the same organization that is using them. Services from external partners may also be incorporated into the applications. This way it is possible to technically support business processes that span multiple departments and companies. The *Service Consumer* is the actual user of a service. Typically, this is the company searching IT support for its business processes. *Service Providers* are actually hosting the service and are typically the developers of the service implementation.

The following characteristics of SOA applications are relevant for implementing experience mechanisms as designed above:

- An SOA application consists of services that are either reused or built.
- Services need to be combined or "orchestrated" in order to support business processes.
- The flexibility promised by services requires technical and organizational support. For example, the ability to generate an orchestration from a business process, or an option to integrate application elements or user interfaces with reused services.

The most typical technical choice for implementing the abstract idea of an SOA is Web services. Web services are based on HTTP for transmitting the data that are in turn encoded in XML. Being pushed by marketing organizations, Web services have gained much attention. In consequence, several tools are offered to support Web services. Because Web services are platform-independent they are well-suited in most integration scenarios.

In short, SOA promises integrating the IT with the business in order to support the business. In order to do this, software is divided into services that can be arranged flexibly. All other facets of SOA are connected to this main goal.

10.5.2 SOA as an Example for Large Business Application Projects

SOA is a typical area of architecture highlighting some of its problems in a specific way: For achieving this integration IT architects and business architects need to communicate. Typically, IT architects do not know what is necessary in the current business setting. Vice versa, Business Architects know their business processes, but cannot deal with all the technical details. This gap possibly leads to defects in both the business processes and the software support. Often, business processes are defined only during the project, which causes misunderstandings and affects application quality. The need to remove defects puts more time-pressure on the project, which may cause further defects and mistakes. Determining an appropriate granularity of services is another core issue.

In order to overcome problems like these, explicitly optimizing information flows is an important step. Information and knowledge, in particular knowledge gained from practical experience, is a worthwhile approach. Architects learn from their mistakes and from the experiences users make with the newly developed business processes and software. This includes the development of user interfaces and the granularity of tasks for the users. Information flow models helped to conceive concepts and mechanisms for systematic reuse of feedback and experience. Unlike other large business application projects, SOA offers opportunities for weaving experience management mechanisms into the business application.

10.5.3 Integrating Feedback into SOA Applications

The concept of integrating experiences in a large business project relies on tool support to make it work in practice. The support software has to make the proposed information flows "affordable" in terms of time and effort for all stakeholders involved. Required software components must be non-intrusive and quickly available. Gathering feedback is a common task in all SOA applications. It should not be re-implemented in every application, but the needed functionality should become part of the SOA infrastructure. This way, it is possible for all SOA applications to benefit from the experience mechanisms without adding their own implementation.

Our technical solution is the Experience Forum for SOA applications [217]. An implementation was integrated into the SOA-Me platform [215] that supports service composition and human interaction with the application. Its principles are as follows:

- Business applications consist of services. Service detection is not affected by our approach; we do not further discuss it here.
- Business processes are the backbones of SOA applications. Business processes are modeled in a notation like BPMN [337] or EPC [226].
- Tools like SOA-Me [215] can generate service orchestrations from business process models. They integrate references to services. As a result, an operational SOA application is created.
- There are advanced options for creating basic user interfaces from extensions of business process models. User interfaces can be generated from abstract models. This technique is called model-based user interfaces [216, 249, 324].

These principles are illustrated in Fig. 10.14. Services are combined according to business processes. They are orchestrated (combined) by SOA-Me and can include user interfaces. In principle, the orchestration is extended by generating access to an Experience Forum. Feedback can be entered, and existing feedback relevant for the task at hand is displayed. SOA-Me is a feasibility prototype. It serves as a proof of concept and demonstrates the above-mentioned concepts for "integrating feedback mechanisms into SOA at a very low cost".

The *key concept is the easy access to the application and service context.* Users do not have to specify where they are (in terms of user interface) or what they do (in terms of business process steps). Nevertheless, receivers of feedback like developers, architects, or peer users can benefit of complete context information. It is attached for free.

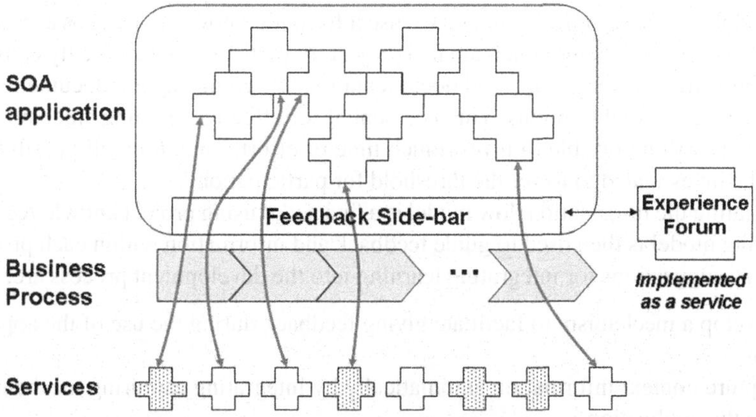

Fig. 10.14 Generator orchestrates SOA application from services and business process

Since an application is generated from services according to business processes (Fig. 10.14), it is easy to use the links for feedback contextualization. Precise links to the services and interface elements can be included with any feedback given. They would be useless without context, though. Therefore, a contextualization feature is added during generation. Since the generator "knows" the business process step and the application screen of each experience entry field, it can take care of attaching that information. A side-bar for the "Use Application w capturing" activity in the flow model of Fig. 10.10 can be integrated into the application interface. It enables users to read and type in short notes. It is active at all times and works asynchronously with the main application. It displays feedback and information that is related to the current *task at hand* and the position of the user within the application. *Experience engineering interfaces* include direct access features to search, filter, and follow context hyperlinks. Feedback is entered into the Experience Forum, which is implemented as a central experience service. It is generated into the SOA application as part of the SOA infrastructure.

10.6 Summary

Building large applications using existing process models and building blocks requires skills and knowledge from several different domains. It reaches from technical details of building those applications and architectural principles to knowledge of the application domain. No architect can cover everything at the beginning of a project. By their very nature, large and long-lived applications will go through an evolution.

We suggest treating that evolution as a technical iteration and a learning process at the same time. Systematic learning from feedback and experience requires a methodology and technical support. We use information flow modeling as a methodology to design the communication in a project. In particular, we explicitly consider fluid information along with solid documentation. By going beyond documents, we consider light-weight options. This is essential for effective learning since no contributor is willing or able to invest much time or effort. Therefore, all possibilities must be investigated to lower the threshold for participation.

Creating the information flow model is a first act of using project knowledge. The resulting model is then used to guide feedback and information within each project. Our key suggestions for integrating learning into the development process are:

- Develop a mechanism to facilitate giving feedback during the use of the application.
- Capture context information automatically by integrating capturing mechanisms into the application.
- Use an Experience Forum for collecting, engineering and enriching, as well as disseminating feedback and full experience.
- Provide short-term reactions in the application context to users and their representatives. Make sure to display information in a matching task context only.
- Enable architects to use feedback for deriving higher-level architectural conclusions. They lead to learning at the architectural level and to mid- or long-term improvements of the application.

The information flow models specified the capturing and Experience Forum activities. From an architectural perspectives, those activities need to be supported as architectural elements. Those elements in association with SOA applications were implemented as an example and a feasibility prototype at Leibniz Universität Hannover. An advanced approach towards generating SOA orchestrations facilitates the seamless integration of experience support mechanisms into the business application itself.

Other types of projects will require different ways of implementing that integration. On a conceptual level, projects and environments may face slightly different situations and challenges. Information flow models can be modified to accommodate different communication needs. Mechanisms and architectural elements will be specified by their interfaces within the model using the FLOW notation. In a separate step, the implementation of each "activity box" can be designed. This step should consider the core principles of experience exploitation, and it should always try to handle context information automatically. On top of those core principles, many decisions can be adapted by architects.

On a conceptual level, we propose to exploit knowledge on information flows explicitly. In addition, we suggest extending Kruchten's popular formula [192] by one more term:

Architectural knowledge =
architectural design + architectural design decision + ***feedback***

Integrating experience exploitation in application development facilitates learning on several levels: Users are encouraged to act as a Community of Practice and learn using the application. Architects learn by getting more feedback and rich context information. Finally, a company learns by improving its information flow and communication infrastructure, using information flow models and building custom-made support for their architects.

Acknowledgements The work on information flow was supported by DFG project *InfoFLOW* (2008–2011). Good comments by the editors helped to improve this chapter.

Chapter 11
AKM in Open Source Communities

Ioannis Stamelos and George Kakarontzas

Abstract Previous chapters in this book have dealt with Architecture Knowledge Management in traditional Closed Source Software (*CSS*) projects. This chapter will attempt to examine the ways that knowledge is shared among participants in Free Libre Open Source Software (*FLOSS*[1]) projects and how architectural knowledge is managed w.r.t. CSS. FLOSS projects are organized and developed in a fundamentally different way than CSS projects. FLOSS projects simply do not develop code as CSS projects do. As a consequence, their knowledge management mechanisms are also based on different concepts and tools.

11.1 Introduction

One should not expect to find in FLOSS the same knowledge management approaches and tools that are in use or considered in CSS. With respect to the architectural knowledge views (Chap. 2) the *dynamism-centered* view requires formalization of architectural knowledge and is probably distant from the "*spirit*" of OSS which is centered on the creation of source code. Also the *requirements-centric* view requires a cohesive team that co-evolves the requirements and the architecture in an iterative fashion, and therefore is more appropriate for closed development environments in which the collaboration is more direct. The *decision-centric* view seems to be very attractive for FLOSS projects, since the explicit documentation of architectural decisions' rationale will enable distant developers to better capture the essential characteristics of FLOSS projects; however to the best of our knowledge

Ioannis Stamelos (✉)
Aristotle University of Thessaloniki, Greece, e-mail: stamelos@csd.auth.gr

George Kakarontzas, Department of Computer Science and Telecommunications, TEI of Larissa, Greece, and Aristotle University of Thessaloniki, Greece, e-mail: gkakaron@teilar.gr

[1] We use the term FLOSS in order to accommodate all three terms: Free, Libre, Open, that are in use to denote open source software

M. Ali Babar et al. (eds.), *Software Architecture Knowledge Management*,
DOI: 10.1007/978-3-642-02374-3_11,

it is not currently used (at least not explicitly with tools specific to this approach) in FLOSS. For several reasons (that we will explain later in this chapter) it seems that the predominant approach to knowledge management is the *pattern-centric* approach.

This chapter attempts to provide answers to such questions, as:

- How do FLOSS processes differ from CSS processes? How are FLOSS projects organized and managed? Which are the incentives and motivations behind participating in a FLOSS project? How is architecture defined, implemented and assessed in FLOSS? Which is the current understanding about the level of quality of FLOSS architectures w.r.t. CSS architectures?
- How is quality pursued and achieved in FLOSS in general? How are decisions made for shaping FLOSS architectures? Is there anything like FLOSS architecture documentation?
- How is knowledge managed in FLOSS in general, who are the knowledge creation and maintenance mechanisms and tools in FLOSS, is FLOSS knowledge personalized, codified or both? How is domain AK matched with application AK? Who are the carriers of AK in FLOSS? How do all these apply to AKM in particular? What is the role of major software companies that support FLOSS on a regular basis?
- What should be expected in the future regarding AKM in FLOSS? Which are the research directions? What are the implications for software architecture education?

Initially, the chapter discusses briefly the fundamental differences between CSS and FLOSS processes providing the context for the analysis that follows. Then it proceeds by briefly discussing software architecture in FLOSS and moves into the core issue, i.e. how software architectural knowledge is generated, captured and managed by FLOSS communities. Sources for the chapter material are academic papers and books, and web resources, such as FLOSS project discussion lists, blogs, wikis, web pages and white papers, combined with authors' personal studies and experience with/on FLOSS, or FLOSS like projects.

11.2 FLOSS Projects in General

FLOSS projects often provide excellent examples of self-organized, successful projects, producing highly effective systems [119]. They are based on open, self organized communities of volunteers, who manage to develop, support and maintain software effectively. This unique kind of virtual communities provides an excellent environment for learning how to communicate with, cooperate with and ultimately learn from other members of the community. Knowledge generation and sharing [302, 301, 303] is implicit in the everyday operations of FLOSS communities.

One interesting variation of FLOSS is the so-called hybrid FLOSS projects. Such projects are initiated and supported by companies that are interested in developing the FLOSS system at hand, but want to collaborate with volunteer or paid developers and users, in order to achieve better results in terms of effort and quality of development. Hybrid FLOSS projects provide a means for developing software with mutual benefit, both for FLOSS communities and software companies. Some of these projects started from companies and were later donated to the FLOSS community for their further evolution and development.

Another variation of FLOSS projects concerns research originated projects. Such projects evolve from the research efforts of academics and other researchers to open source software implementing these efforts. The FLOSS software and the academic research then co-evolve and contribute "iteratively" to one-another with the FLOSS software providing useful feedback for "untested" research ideas, and new research ideas used to point the FLOSS software to initially unanticipated directions.

There are many differences between FLOSS processes and CSS processes. Typically CSS processes are quite formal, with clearly defined, large scope, phases and pose many constraints on software development, attempting to impose discipline and produce high quality software products. CSS processes foresee one or more Architectural phases. As an example the well known waterfall model has two such phases, namely Architectural Design followed by Detailed Design. However [122, 68] FLOSS processes are much less formal, with fewer, lower scope phases, such as fast debugging and releasing. Architecture and design decisions are handled by the initiator or the core group of developers before opening the source code to FLOSS participants and therefore are not subject to open discussion and negotiation [122]. This model of architecture development seems to make certain views to AKM less "natural" for FLOSS. For example the requirements-centric view is based in the co-evolution of the requirements and the architecture. However the bulk of FLOSS developers who are sometimes the source of new and interesting requirements are not part of the core architecting team or associated with this team directly.

Software architecture is requirements and quality driven. Major driver for design decisions in FLOSS is modularity which is necessary in order to divide work among FLOSS participants. Modularity helps newcomers to locate modules of their own interest and focus on them, without bothering about other, irrelevant system architecture modules.

If FLOSS lacks an explicit architecture definition phase and consequently explicit architectural documentation, then how is architecture defined, implemented and assessed in FLOSS? The adoption of FLOSS in many organisations has raised the issue of FLOSS quality evaluation. Due to the nature of FLOSS development where standard practices include open access to the source code, shared software artifact repositories, peer review of committed code, asynchronous global development and lack of formal support, traditional software quality models may not be sufficient.

An array of quality models specifically targeted to FLOSS development can be found in the literature, but most of them are either purpose specific (e.g. they focus on the business or application domain of the FLOSS system) or require significant human intervention [273]. However, little attention has been paid up to now for assessing high level system architecture in FLOSS. There is definitely space here for further investigation and research. Software Architecture Reconstruction (SAR) tools such as those evaluated in [138] can play a significant role in FLOSS projects which are interested in starting an AKM effort.

11.3 Architecture Knowledge Management in FLOSS

In general it is hard to deal with the issue of architecture knowledge management in FLOSS. The reason is that there are hundreds of thousands of FLOSS projects nowadays[2]. They also differ a lot in terms of procedures followed and constraints imposed on their participants. Many FLOSS projects, especially the small ones provide their community with the freedom to work as they wish. However, in large projects there is more discipline and it is there that architectural knowledge may gain a lot of attention and is therefore easier to study. In the following section we present some case studies and we attempt to provide an indicative answer regarding the extent to which architectural knowledge is stored and managed in FLOSS projects.

11.4 How does Architectural Knowledge Appear in FLOSS?

In many FLOSS projects architectural knowledge appears explicitly in terms of project documents describing system architecture and providing relevant information, such as the rationale behind certain architectural decisions. On the other hand, there are FLOSS projects (even large ones) where architecture is not described explicitly and must be inferred from existing documentation or the code itself.

In relation to the different views on architectural knowledge (Chap. 2), we can recognize that FLOSS follows mainly the *pattern-centric* view. The main reason for this is that architectural patterns provide a common vocabulary and frame of reference to ease architectural knowledge sharing among developers. In the case of FLOSS this is profoundly important since developers are at different locations, come from different backgrounds and the communication of architectural knowledge becomes therefore harder. The use of patterns enables conformance of source code developed by different teams of developers at different locations with the core architecture of the project. At the same time it eases understanding since architectural patterns and the rationale for their use are well documented and already known to the developers. Furthermore the extensive literature on architectural patterns (e.g. [64, 277, 180]) partially counterbalances the often observed lack of documentation in FLOSS projects. For all the above reasons the pattern-centric view is used (albeit implicitly) in most FLOSS projects.

[2] SourceForge alone hosts almost 200K projects at the time this chapter is written

Two problems often associated with the use of patterns in general, including architectural patterns are:

1. They are not enforced in the source code and developers can accidentally violate them while developing their systems. However most FLOSS projects provide the core architecture and the independently developed components must plug in this provided framework. In the case of FLOSS, this is not considered a significant limitation on the implementation approach however, but rather essential in the way FLOSS software is developed: the developers must follow precise rules to achieve interoperation of their source code with the rest of the system (e.g. implement specific interfaces) which makes accidental violation of the core architectural patterns more difficult, so this problem is partially solved. At the same time research efforts that statically enforce conformance of object-oriented source code with architectural descriptions such as ArchJava [4], might solve this problem entirely in the future if they become more mainstream and widely used.
2. The second problem with patterns is that their textual description is inherently not appropriate for the automatic application of patterns in the source code. Research efforts such as the formalization of design patterns [311] and the use of Model Driven Software Development (MDSD) methods based on rules [49] aim at solving this problem. However in the case of FLOSS automatic application of patterns may very well be irrelevant since FLOSS developers often prefer developing source code as a creative intellectual exercise, rather than using automated code generation techniques.

Also in terms of AKM we distinguish between the following broad categories of FLOSS projects:

1. *"Pure" FLOSS projects*. In these projects AK exists in many forms: wikis, HTML pages, forums, mailing lists, video casts, podcasts, books etc. (e.g. Apache HTTP server). Therefore in these projects AK is not managed explicitly but rather emerges gradually.
2. *Hybrid FLOSS projects*. In these projects which evolved from a CSS project usually owned by a company and later evolved to a FLOSS project, there is an initial core team of developers which has designed the core architecture and has documented it (e.g. Apache Axis and Jini). The core architecture is usually well thought with an explicit rationale serving the functional and quality requirements of the application, and this contributes in the success that many of these projects enjoy. Usually these projects use design or architectural patterns as a vehicle to both achieve desired quality properties and communicate architectural knowledge.
3. *Research originated OSS projects*. These projects have evolved from the research efforts of a research group or research community. AK for these projects takes the form of research papers and/or books which explain in details the architectural decisions. In many cases such projects have contributed even in the creation of new architecture standards for their domains, such as the Globus toolkit contribution to the standard architecture for grid computing. Effectively academic

papers and/or standardization documents serve as documents describing architectural decisions, which is consistent with the decision-centric view of AKM. However AKM decision-centric specific tools are not used to formally document these decisions and trace the decisions to the systems' architecture.

We see a fruitful ground for application of the decision-centric view of AKM, both for hybrid and research-originated FLOSS projects. Mature tools, especially web-based tools such as the Architecture Design Decision Support System (ADDSS) reported in [67] and Sect. 6.3.3, can be used effectively especially for their advance groupware support, which can of great use to FLOSS projects.

11.4.1 "Pure" FLOSS Projects: Apache HTTP Server

Let's consider the case of an important, unanimously considered as successful, FLOSS project, namely Apache. Such project provides its community of developers and users with a documentation area in the official project Web site maintained by Apache Software Foundation[3], hosting a wealth of Apache projects. Each project provides its own documentation area (e.g. documentation for Apache HTTP Server, considered as an entire subproject[4] and a special wiki is dedicated to documentation[5]). Various architecture related pieces of information are provided through this site, for example the standards implemented by various Apache projects[6]. However, documentation is mainly meant to support users and not all desirable information (architecture documentation, design rationale, etc) can be found about the Server's architecture.

An online report by O.A. Dragoi,[7] reports the conceptual architecture of Apache Web Server. What is interesting is not the architecture itself[8] but the way the report was made: "The conceptual (high level) architecture has been inferred from a number of Apache related documents and from the way source files are grouped and named". Design rationale is also reported, e.g. the rationale "behind having modules defining handlers for more than one phase is that a module might save internally data on the request being processed ...".

In other cases, Apache projects do provide explicitly some useful architectural information. One such example is the Apache Tomcat Server (an implementation of the Java Servlet and JavaServer Pages technologies) which provides interested readers with a textual documentation of the description of the Tomcat Server

---

[3] http://www.apache.org/

[4] http://httpd.apache.org/docs-project/

[5] http://wiki.apache.org/httpd/. For another example of a FLOSS wiki providing architectural information see http://wiki.zmanda.com/index.php/Software_architecture

[6] http://projects.apache.org/docs/standards.html

[7] http://www.grad.math.uwaterloo.ca/~oadragoi/CS746G/a1/apache_conceptual_arch.html

[8] Because of http request handling, Apache architectural style is close to 'implicit invocation'

architecture.[9] In particular, the topics covered are the Architecture Overview, the Server Startup and the Request Process Flow. However, no documentation is provided that explicitly justifies the decisions made. Sometimes, documentation is given in standard diagrammatic form (see for example the UML sequence diagram for server startup[10]).

Architecture related information can also be found in books that are easy to find because the open nature of FLOSS projects provide the opportunity to research, explore, understand and document independently what has happened or is happening in those projects. As an example, [28] provides its reader with a short description of the fundamentals of Apache architecture. Ridruejo [213] is more focused on Apache and gives also an overview of Apache architecture. Kew [178] is even more to the point, providing both an overview and a detailed picture. Bits and pieces can also be found in various Internet freely available resources, such as slides of conference presentations and consultant firms' Internet pages.

Because of the lack of formal documentation that is frequently encountered in pure FLOSS projects, tutorials and other sources of knowledge often appear on an individual basis, trying to alleviate the problem. One such example is the Apache Tutor,[11] constructed by the author of [178] that, quoting from its home page, "aims to be the definitive independent online source of help and information for applications built on the Apache webserver". It is interesting to note that "Both contents and interactivity is important, and the software used provides for multiple authors to contribute to content development, at more than one level" and "All articles are published in an interactive framework, and invite comments (annotations) from readers, as well as online editing." As with FLOSS code development, the development and maintenance of these Internet FLOSS knowledge resources is sought to be made on a voluntary basis.

11.4.2 Hybrid OSS Projects: Apache Axis and Jini

This section discusses two examples of open source software architectures and their rationale. These particular projects were chosen based on their use of architectural means to achieve specific quality requirements that are essential for their provided services. The first such project is Apache Axis which requires flexibility and extensibility and uses a well-known design pattern to satisfy these requirements. The second project we discuss is Jini Starter Kit which is an open source implementation of the Jini specifications. Jini's architecture is specifically designed to addresses the challenges of distributed computing [332]. These two projects are examples of the hybrid OSS project category since they both started from companies and later became open source community projects. Also in terms of the AKM views, both

[9] http://tomcat.apache.org/tomcat-6.0-doc/architecture/index.html

[10] http://tomcat.apache.org/tomcat-6.0-doc/architecture/startup/serverStartup.pdf

[11] http://www.apachetutor.org/

projects are examples of the pattern-centric view since they use design and architecture patterns extensively to achieve specific quality goals and at the same time, as a side-effect (intended or not) to communicate the rationale of these decisions to participating developers.

11.4.2.1 Apache Axis

Apache Axis[12] is a Simple Object Access Protocol (SOAP) engine. It evolved from the Apache SOAP project which started as a contribution from IBM of an early implementation of the SOAP protocol to Apache in 1999.

Essentially Axis processes SOAP messages and can be used in two distinct ways: as a server and as a client. Used as a client Axis can be embedded in applications using the Axis API and prepare messages for requests. Used as a server Axis can processes incoming messages. There is a multitude of transport protocols, web services protocols and services in which Axis must remain open. Therefore the predominant quality requirement for Axis is extensibility and flexibility that enables adaptation in any specific situation. To achieve better extensibility and flexibility Axis adopted the Chain of Responsibility design pattern [130] for its core part which handles the processing of messages. With this design pattern the handlers of a call are arranged in a chain and the call is processed from any handler in the chain which has the required knowledge and knows how to handle a message.

The consequences of the chain of responsibility design pattern are:

1. The inherently low coupling between the collaborating components, since components are not required to know a priori which other components will handle a request.
2. The flexibility in changing the responsibilities or adding more responsibilities even at system runtime, by adding more handlers or replacing existing handlers.
3. The handling of a message is not guaranteed if there is not a handler in the chain that knows how to handle a specific request or if the chain is not configured properly.

The rationale of the architecture design of Axis is explained in detail in the Axis Architecture Guide.[13] As can be seen in Fig. 11.1, a chain of handlers is a handler itself by extending the Handler interface and therefore it can be combined with other chains which contain other handlers recursively.

This allows Axis to contain three chains, global, transport and services, which contain a number of handlers internally. The Transport chain is responsible for processing the transport protocol of a message (e.g. HTTP, SMTP, etc.). Global chains are applied in all messages regardless of the specific service that is requested. Finally service chains are the service handlers of messages and contain the application logic for the processing of a message. In Axis used as a server the sequence of chains

[12] http://ws.apache.org/axis/

[13] http://ws.apache.org/axis/java/architecture-guide.html

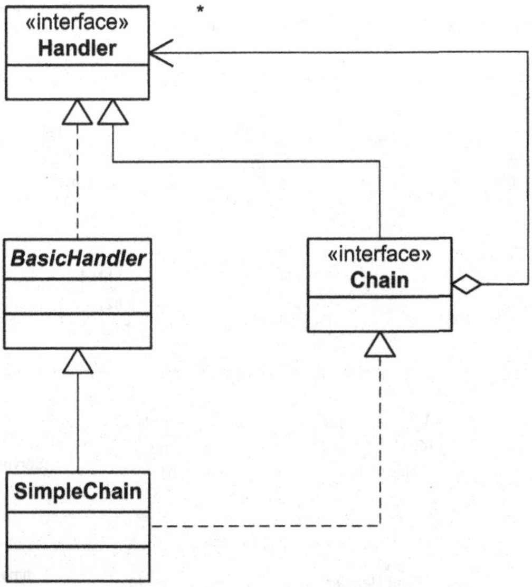

Fig. 11.1 Handlers and chains in Axis

is first the transport chain, then the global chain and finally the service chain and in Axis used as a client this sequence is reversed. A chain is an ordered sequence of handlers. When Axis is used as a server in the service chain the request is serviced by the service implementation and the flow changes direction from request to response. When Axis is used as a client the flow changes direction in the transport chain. The actual handler which changes the direction of the flow by processing a request and producing a response (server), or by sending a request and receiving a response (client) is called the pivot handler. The sequencing of chains, the chain handlers and the pivot handlers in Axis are depicted in Fig. 11.2.

11.4.2.2 Jini Starter Kit

Jini Starter Kit is an implementation of the Jini technology for distributed computing [83]. Jini specification and implementation were initially developed at Sun Microsystems and were later released as open source under the Apache 2.0 license with an announcement from Sun[14]. Jini is now available as an open source project[15].

Jini has a very interesting architecture which addresses many of the issues involved in distributed object computing [332]. Essentially Jini architecture exposes the differences of distributed object computing to the application programmers instead of attempting to hide them so that local and remote objects are treated the

[14] http://www.sun.com/smi/Press/sunflash/2005-10/sunflash.20051019.5.xml

[15] http://www.jini.org

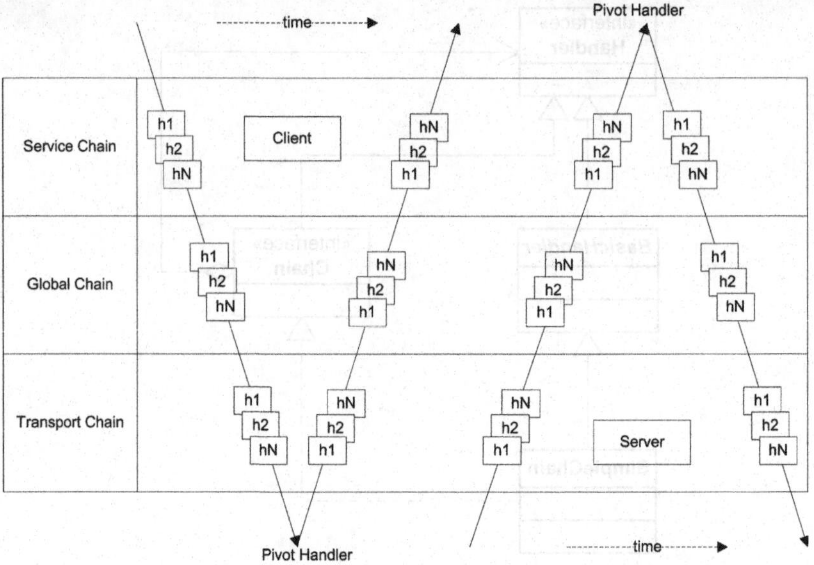

Fig. 11.2 Chains, handlers and pivoting in core Axis message handling

same way. This exposure complicates applications' programming but the additional complication is not unnecessary and can in fact be considered essential for the development of robust and reliable distributed object applications. More specifically the differences of distributed computing in relation to local computing include differences in latency, memory access, partial failure and concurrency [332]. Jini uses the concept of a federation of services which come together to achieve a task on behalf of a user. The dynamic nature of Jini allows services to be added and removed from the system dynamically at any time. A service can be anything, for example a service that prints documents, a service that represents a device, a document management service etc. Jini provides an infrastructure service, called the Lookup Service, an application of the Lookup architectural pattern [180], which allows services to be registered and later discovered by other services. The Lookup Service is therefore the bootstrapping mechanism of a Jini system. A service uses first a discovery protocol to discover the Lookup Service and then a join protocol to join the Lookup Service. As can be seen in Fig. 11.3, a service first emits a multicast message looking for a Lookup Service. The service has a service object with a service interface and is described additionally with service attributes. These attributes will be later used in addition to the service's interface from clients looking for services. The service joins the Jini system by transferring the service object and the service attributes to the Lookup Service.

A client uses a Lookup Service to request a service with a particular interface using also additional attributes that describe the required service. A service object is then downloaded to the client. The client then uses this object to communicate directly with the service provider as depicted in Fig. 11.4.

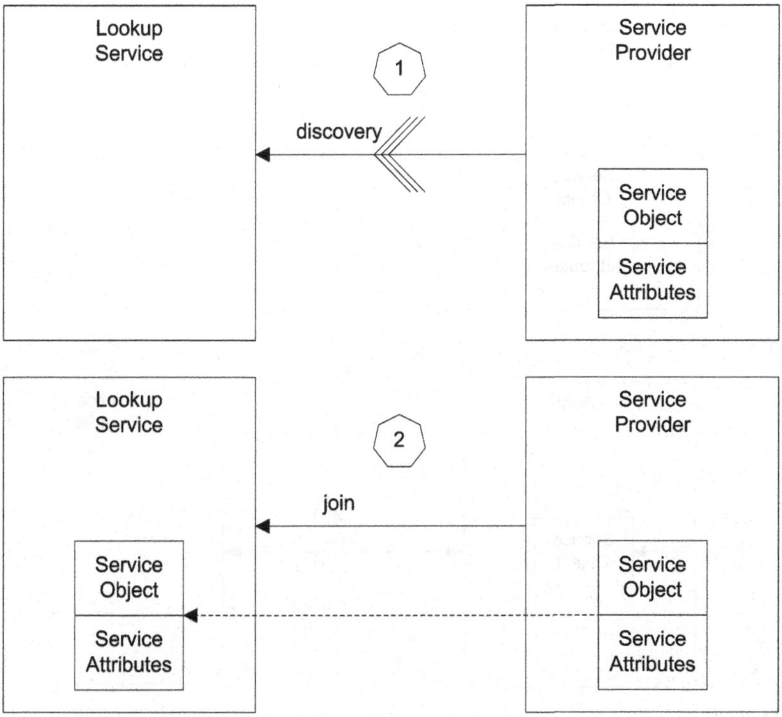

Fig. 11.3 Jini discovery and join protocols

Services in Jini are not assumed to be available for ever since network partitions and other problems may in fact make them unavailable. Jini applies here the Lease architectural pattern [180], and uses leases to ensure that registered services are in fact available. Each registered service is granted a lease and is required to renew this lease periodically. Failure to do so will result in the removal of the service from the Lookup Service registry. Leases are also used in other services (besides the Lookup Service) and can be exclusive, which means that a service can only be used by one user at a time, or non-exclusive.

Jini also supports distributed transactions that span multiple services as well as distributed events for asynchronous communication of services.

11.4.3 Research Originated FLOSS Projects: The Globus Toolkit

Globus Toolkit[16] is a FLOSS project which provides implementation of standard grid computing protocols and services. Globus has contributed largely to these standards.

[16] http://www.globus.org

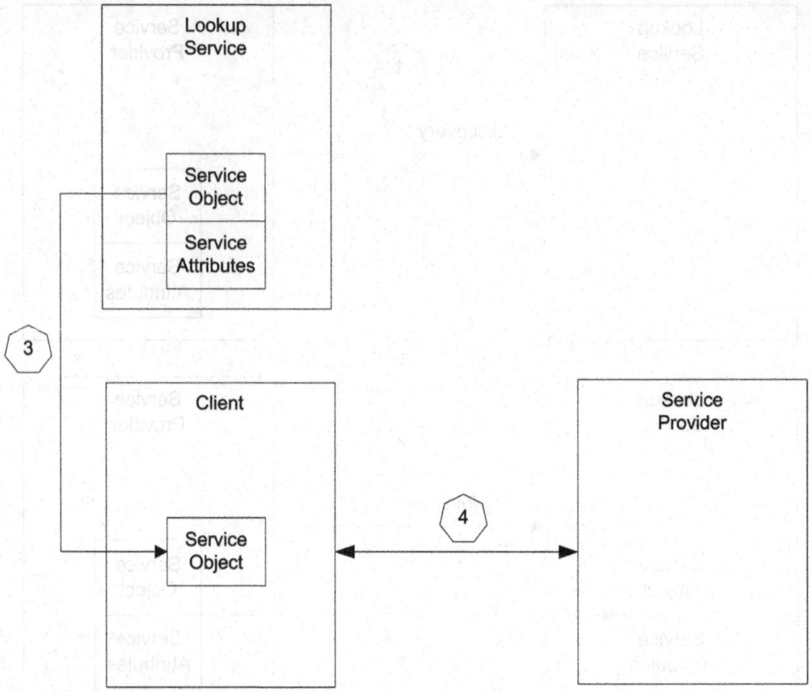

Fig. 11.4 Client service discovery

The architecture of Globus Toolkit follows the hourglass model. In this model there is a core of basic services over which global services and applications are developed. Under the basic services there is an interface layer with local operating and resource clustering systems (e.g. PBS and Condor pools).

Globus services are grid services which follow the Open Grid Service Architecture (OGSA). The main goal of OGSA is the standardization of the basic services for grids so that these services are interoperable. OGSA is a set of principles which describes the way that grid services look and behave, but does not specify the details for the implementation of grid services and grid containers hosting these services. The Open Grid Services Implementation (OSGI) is an additional standard describing all the necessary implementation details.

Globus Toolkit implements the OGSI standard and provides higher level grid services which are based on OGSA. As is mentioned in the project's website: "Since the release of the Globus Toolkit 3.0, the Globus Project offers an open source collection of Grid services that follow OGSA architectural principles. The Globus Toolkit also offers a development environment for producing new Grid services that follow OGSA principles. OGSA is a product of the Grid community at large, and it has a major focal point in the Global Grid Forum (GGF). Members of the Globus Alliance have made significant contributions to the development of OGSA".

Globus toolkit is therefore an example of the co-evolution of research and FLOSS software which also influenced to a large extent the formation of grid standard which were also adopted by other grid offerings both commercial and open source. The extensive research publications around Globus and the related publications on the grid in general which emerged from this work[17] constitute a significant body of knowledge concerning not only the Globus toolkit architecture but also the grid services architecture in general. Another important aspect of this project is its influence in grid standards which also constitute a very important form of architectural knowledge. All these documents constitute an informal type of decision-centric AKM, however as we mentioned earlier there is not a formal binding or tracing, between this knowledge and architectural decisions that are implemented in the Globus toolkit source code.

11.4.4 Architectural Knowledge Resources in FLOSS

We have already seen above that knowledge in FLOSS is mainly stored in communication media, e.g. wikis, mailing lists and forums. However, occasionally FLOSS projects provide themselves more dedicated and organized structures that implicitly support knowledge management in the FLOSS world. One such example is the FLUID[18] project.

FLUID project is "an open, collaborative project to improve the user experience of community source software". In other words, FLUID provides a "living library of sharable user interface components that can be reused across community source projects. These components are built specifically to support flexibility and customization while maintaining a high standard of design quality". The project site does not provide just code: it provides also User Experience,[19] i.e. a repository of design models and other resources, tools, and documentation to assist user interface design and implementation.

Another example of an open community that stores and manages knowledge in the form of patterns is the Open Management Consortium[20]. They propose, define and discuss innovative pattern-based solutions to common problems, such as the "Adaptive Deployment" and "CodeData Split" patterns. Each pattern initiates a discussion thread and patterns are specified in templates that consist of predefined fields. Such fields are *Intention, Motivation, Applicability, Structure, Consequences, Implementation, Known Uses, Related Patterns.*

It is interesting to notice that architectural knowledge is maintained also in the form of Anti-patterns, i.e. patterns that produce a negative effect, theyshould be

[17] http://www.globus.org/alliance/publications/papers.php

[18] http://wiki.fluidproject.org/display/fluid/Open+Source+Design+Pattern+Library

[19] http://fluidproject.org/index.php/user-experience

[20] http://openmanagement.org/community/omc

avoided and whenever they appear, they must be addressed by some counter-measures. One such Anti-pattern is the "Service Monolith" proposed by Alex Honor.[21]

Independent of the activity they generate, these projects are good examples of how FLOSS world of projects can combine agile and open development processes with development tools that go beyond the typical configuration management and bug tracking systems.

11.5 Future Trends and Expectations

What should be expected in the future regarding AKM in FLOSS? FLOSS world is continuously evolving and software architecture will most probably draw more attention than today.

The abundance of hybrid FLOSS projects, sponsored by companies, will probably lead to more organized software development modes. In such a context, architectural decisions are expected to be more transparent and justified, with the rationale behind them better explained. As Fidgerald [122] points out, "analysis and design are expected to be more complex because of the need to address vertical business domains with hard to meet requirements". This suggestion leads to more stringent requirements for software architecture, and therefore renders the need for better software architecture resources more urgent. It is also reasonable to expect that such information will be better organized and stored in specific tools to allow more visibility in the project.

An interesting research direction which is to the best of our knowledge unexplored would be to integrate SAR tools with existing and readily available FLOSS resources such as wikis, mailing lists and so forth. The integration that we envision is using SAR tools to identify potential problems such as potentially fragile classes (e.g. due to large number of dependencies) and then automatically seek information in existing FLOSS resources for these potential problems that may explain their status. For example [138] refers to an example evaluation of a project using the JDepend tool, which uncovered a package being both highly abstracted and relatively unstable. This high abstraction seems to imply that the package is intended for reuse, and therefore its relative instability is particularly problematic. The authors used discussions with the development team to find out why: "In order to explore this measure, we constructed a set of views around this package and presented them to the development team. The package turned out to be undergoing extensive migration from a previous design. In order to accommodate compatibilities with existing packages, the product package had to maintain a high level of dependencies with other packages. When the migration is complete in near future, the package will be refactored into several components to improve its modifiability and reusability" [138]. An example of identifying the "extensive migration" using an existing OSS resource is to consider the number of recent commits of this particular

[21] http://openmanagement.org/community/open_standards/omc_design_patterns

package classes. This information is available from FLOSS tools. Future research can identify such "interesting" pieces of information from existing OSS resources and use SAR integration with these resources in a constructive approach, to produce architectural knowledge.

One should also expect more FLOSS projects related to software architectural knowledge to appear. FLOSS communities have proved to be self-sustainable and continuously evolving. We have already seen a number of FLOSS projects and Web sites that aim to support FLOSS participants in decision making and managing architectural solutions. It is reasonable to expect such projects to flourish in the future. They will not only produce design resources for FLOSS communities, but they will also provide a valuable resource for software engineering learners, who are willing to explore and exploit informal and spontaneous sources of software architecture information.

The latter consideration provides interesting opportunities for software architecture education. As already mentioned, educating novice software architects is one of the hardest tasks a software instructor has to face, partially because of the abstraction needed and the lack of clear understanding of the implications of architectural decisions. A universe of FLOSS projects that will focus in software architecture would provide an additional source of education material that can be combined with formal educational resources, such as course materials and dedicated management learning systems.

Communicating architectural decisions' rationale is a very important aspect in the success of FLOSS projects. It will allow the core architecture team to disseminate architectural knowledge in a more direct and systematic way to developers. It will also allow developers to grasp this knowledge much faster and easier. For these reasons we consider the *decision-centric* view of AKM a particularly relevant approach for FLOSS projects. As we mentioned earlier web-based tools for AKM that support group communication [67] (Sect. 6.3.3) can be tested effectively in FLOSS projects. Therefore the use of such decision-centric tools for AKM in FLOSS can be of mutual benefit for both communities (FLOSS and AKM).

11.6 Summary

We have reviewed the software architecture knowledge landscape in FLOSS. Such endeavor is not easy because of the multitude of FLOSS projects and the many different ways those projects are organized and run. An exhaustive search concerning this issue in FLOSS is simply not possible. However, to the best of our knowledge, we have found out that architectural knowledge is indeed present in FLOSS, but in most cases is not "managed" in the proper meaning of this term, in the sense that tools and methods used or proposed in closed source are not taken into account in FLOSS.

In relation to the different AKM views, the pattern-centric view is used (mainly in hybrid and research-originated FLOSS projects), although its use is implicit.

However we believe that the decision-centric view with Web-based tools may also be very appropriate for the FLOSS community, which has a culture of using web-based tools anyway for many aspects of software development (communication, bug tracking, etc.)

We have reviewed certain cases in FLOSS where architectural knowledge is at least stored in some way, available for consultation by interested FLOSS participants. Typical means for storing information (not only about architecture) in FLOSS are discussion lists and threads, wikis, forums etc. We have also encountered open content Web sites that provide resources (in the form of management and design patterns) for specific application domains, such as user interfaces.

FLOSS belongs clearly to Earl's behavioural school of knowledge management (see Table 1.3). In particular, it belongs to the organisational school, focusing on networks for sharing knowledge, supported by communities, aiming to draw knowledge from a pool of gifted software developers and implicitly redistribute new knowledge to the community of users and developers through FLOSS mechanisms and tools.

Another interesting global issue about knowledge management in FLOSS is the "organisational memory", mentioned in Chap. 1. The FLOSS universe has a good organisational memory, because its members esteem one another, and seeking and finding undocumented knowledge pieces becomes natural and welcomed. While seeking already documented knowledge is considered harmful, because it simply wastes other people time, asking clever questions and trying to answer interesting questions is considered as important as (almost) writing good code. Knowledge providers and mentors receive credits for their support to newcomers and are considered valued members of the community. In addition, migration from one FLOSS project to another is free and frequent, and helps a lot towards disseminating knowledge and ultimately in building the FLOSS organisational knowledge and memory.

Table 11.1 summarizes the Architecture Knowledge Management activities in FLOSS.

Table 11.1 (Architectural) Knowledge Management activities in FLOSS

Architectural Knowledge Management Activity	Creation	Sharing	Distributing	Capturing
Mechanism	Core development team decisions	Participation in project related discussions	Posting of architectural block diagrams and short text descriptions	Inspection of code and other relevant documentation
Tools		Mailing lists, forums, etc	Project Web sites, wikis, blogs	Configuration management tools

Finally we have speculated about the future of AKM in FLOSS, expecting more and better AKM infrastructure and richer AKM resources. We have also identified software architecture education to be greatly facilitated by those increasing resources in the future.

Chapter 12
Architectural Knowledge in an SOA Infrastructure Reference Architecture

Olaf Zimmermann, Petra Kopp, and Stefan Pappe

Abstract In this chapter, we present an industrial case study for the creation and usage of architectural knowledge. We first introduce the business domain, service portfolio, and knowledge management approach of the company involved in the case. Next, we introduce a Service-Oriented Architecture (SOA) infrastructure reference architecture as a primary carrier of architectural knowledge in this company. Moreover, we present how we harvested architectural knowledge from industry projects to create this reference architecture. We also present feedback from early reference architecture users. Finally, we conclude and give an outlook to future work.

12.1 Introduction: Middleware Services and SOA Infrastructure Design in IBM Global Technology Services

This section gives an overview of IBM Global Technology Services and its middleware service product line. It introduces SOA infrastructures as the technology domain the case study is concerned with, as well as supporting assets and the knowledge management strategy employed by IBM Global Technology Services.

In this first section, we briefly review general architectural concepts such as viewpoints, methods, and reference architectures. Not all of these concepts pertain to architectural knowledge explicitly; however, they helped us to create and leverage such knowledge successfully. An understanding of our usage of these concepts helps to appreciate the central role of architectural knowledge in the case. As a reader who is familiar with these concepts and is primarily interested in our usage

Olaf Zimmermann (✉)
IBM Research, Zürich, Switzerland, e-mail: olz@zurich.ibm.com

Petra Kopp and Stefan Pappe
IBM Global Technology Services, Heidelberg, Germany, e-mail: [pkopp,pappe]@de.ibm.com

M. Ali Babar et al. (eds.), *Software Architecture Knowledge Management*,
DOI: 10.1007/978-3-642-02374-3_12, © Springer-Verlag Berlin Heidelberg 2009

of architectural knowledge, as opposed to its context in the case, you may want to skip this first section.

12.1.1 Company Overview: IBM Global Technology Services

IBM Global Services is one of the world's largest business and Information Technology (IT) services providers. It is a rapidly growing part of IBM; at present, over 190,000 professionals serve clients in more than 160 countries. IBM Global Services comprises two major divisions: *IBM Global Business Services* and *IBM Global Technology Services (GTS)* [153]. In this chapter we focus on GTS services which pertain to IT infrastructure elements such as middleware.

GTS is structured into four business areas: *Integrated Technology Services (ITS)*, *Maintenance and Technical Support Services*, *Strategic Outsourcing*, and *Managed Business Process Outsourcing*. These business areas support clients in a number of ways: Some clients decide to develop and integrate applications themselves; for such clients, GTS provisions hardware and/or software and provides maintenance support. Other clients seeks help in the design, implementation, and management of IT solutions; ITS offers a portfolio of related service products. Finally, turnkey solutions and management of applications and infrastructure can be provided to clients through outsourcing and managed services capabilities.

The case study presented in this chapter concerns the ITS business area, which has a project-centric nature. We focus on SOA infrastructure services delivered in IT strategy projects, as well as in the architecture, design, and implementation phases of application development and integration projects.

12.1.2 From Labor-Based to Asset-Based Services: Service Products and Service Product Lines

The ITS strategy builds on an *asset-based business model*. ITS ensures a globally consistent service delivery and a high quality of project results by standardizing its services as *reusable assets* [238]. Following this asset-based business model, the success of a service project is no longer bound to the personal skills and experience of the individual project team members exclusively, but is ensured by the reuse of predefined service assets. This is especially important for emerging geographies and new topic areas in which the skill and experience base has not been fully established yet.

ITS calls its service assets *service products*, acknowledging their standardized nature. This name also conveys the vision of services being developed, packaged, documented, and maintained just like software products. Service products precisely define the nature and structure of the professional services in a globally consistent fashion; they codify a significant part of the intellectual property of ITS. The portfolio of service products spans a wide range of topic areas such as middleware services including SOA infrastructure design and implementation, systems and service management consulting and implementation services, but also storage and server design including capacity planning, health checks and managed services [153]. Service products respond to a shift of client preferences from custom developed and integrated application islands to packaged, integrated, and pretested end-to-end *solutions*.

ITS is organized into *service product lines*. Each service product line owns multiple related service products jointly targeting a certain technology domain. The sum of the service products across all service product lines supports rapid, asset-based project initiation and delivery and enables clients to focus their attention on the core competencies differentiating them from their competitors; related savings can be invested in additional revenue-generating capabilities. The service product lines in ITS complement hardware from the IBM Server and Technology Group and software from IBM Software Group. This portfolio allows GTS to combine services, hardware, software, and knowledge of business processes seamlessly and effectively, which helps to provide the desired end-to-end solutions.

Service products in all service product lines are built through strong investments in research, intellectual property creation and management, acquisitions, and brand discipline – all of which are needed to create a competitive portfolio. In this chapter, we focus on selected *SOA infrastructure services* which are offered by the *middleware service product line*. Two examples of service products in this service product line are “SOA Integration Services – Connectivity and Reuse” and “Design and Implementation for WebSphere ESB”. We will introduce these service products in Sect. 12.1.3.

12.1.3 Middleware Service Product Line: SOA Infrastructure Services

On *Service-Oriented Architecture (SOA)* [187] projects the *architectural views* [188] on a system under construction are synthesized. To do so, numerous functional and non-functional requirements must be analyzed. During this analysis, functional requirements are captured as use cases, stories, and business process models; non-functional requirements concern *software quality attributes* [157] in areas such as performance, scalability, and interoperability. During architectural analysis and synthesis, many *architectural decisions* are identified, made, and enforced [346].

At the early elaboration points, the conceptual architectures of SOA-based systems are straightforward to define: They are variations of logically layered two- or three-tier client-server architectures, which use message passing patterns to let *service consumers* and *service providers* communicate with each other. Workflow patterns are used to *compose* atomic services into business process-centric end-to-end solutions. A *service registry* can serve as design time or runtime directory of service providers available to respond to requests from service consumers [344].

An *SOA infrastructure* defines the physical viewpoint of an SOA. It concerns the design, installation, and configuration of middleware components such as *Enterprise Service Buses (ESBs)* which are responsible for service request routing, adaptation, and mediation (brokerage), *business process orchestration engines* performing service composition, and *service registries and repositories* supporting service provider publishing and lookup. Individual service consumers and providers of various types (e.g., business function services and technical utility services) are designed, developed, and then deployed into such SOA infrastructure, which is supported by an underlying operating system, server and storage hardware, and network.

Several characteristics make SOA infrastructures challenging to design:

- An SOA infrastructure usually hosts *more than one application*. These applications might differ in their non-functional characteristics and might change over time. An SOA infrastructure has to satisfy the requirements of all hosted applications and anticipate future change (scalability).
- If the SOA vision of *service virtualization* is realized (i.e., architectural principles such as provider location, platform, protocol, and format transparency are promoted) [344] and the application logic is refactored into a *service pool*, fixed application boundaries no longer exist, which makes the infrastructure hosting the service pool challenging to design: The number of service consumers and the amount, size, and structure of the service invocation messages are not known upfront; these volume metrics may even vary over time. The same holds true for service providers and response message characteristics, respectively.
- There are rich and subtle *dependencies between the architectural elements*. In an SOA, there are many service consumers which call composite services and atomic service providers with the help of ESBs and business process orchestration engines. These dependency relations often have many-to-many cardinalities. Sometimes the dependency relations cannot even be specified upfront, e.g., when the involved middleware provides dynamic, adaptive service invocation, integration, and composition capabilities.
- SOA infrastructure may have to be able to support modern development and deployment paradigms such as *Web 2.0 mash ups*, *software as a service*, and *Cloud Computing* [310]. Such infrastructures face advanced requirements such as multi tenancy, separation of duties, flexible and measurable Service Level Agreements (SLAs), and the like.

Examples of related service products are "SOA Integration Services – Connectivity and Reuse", "SOA Integration Services – Design and Implementation for WebSphere Message Broker", and "SOA Integration Services – SOA Healthcheck". The first service product concerns service consumer-provider connectivity, the second one a certain implementation platform for the ESB pattern, the third one the analysis of an already existing SOA infrastructure.

Client project examples. To illustrate the technical domain of SOA infrastructure design further, let us briefly introduce two client scenarios now.

An insurance company engaged GTS to construct an SOA and to design and deploy an integrated value chain for its insurance brokers that would improve communication and offer an optimized suite of insurance services. The GTS team architected, deployed, and implemented a robust SOA infrastructure leveraging IBM WebSphere software. The solution included an integration of the client's existing IBM CICS backend running on zSeries nodes, along with implementation of a clustered pair of IBM xSeries servers running the Microsoft Windows XP operating system to host a new ESB and service registry platform. With the new integration solution, the client is able to serve its partners and customers more efficiently and has sharpened its competitive edge. The service product "SOA Integration Services – Connectivity and Reuse" was used to design and implement the outlined solution.

A world-leading manufacturer of welding systems used SOA to cut its file support costs by 95% and improve its return-on-capital-employed ratio by working with GTS to create an integration platform based on IBM WebSphere Message Broker for Multiplatforms and a CISCO Linux driver. This new mission-critical ESB integration platform allows the client to automate its delivery and replenishment processes and to integrate its existing backend system and its new supply chain management software. This implementation leveraged the service product "SOA Integration Services – Design and Implementation for WebSphere Message Broker".

Having introduced the case study domain both from a business and from a technical perspective, let us investigate which role architectural knowledge plays in the case.

12.1.4 Supporting Assets: Methods and Reference Architectures

To support its asset-based business model and the creation and usage of service products, GTS leverages many supporting assets as carriers of architectural knowledge. In this section, we introduce two particularly relevant types of such assets, *methods* and *reference architectures*.

Methods. IBM Global Services has long recognized the importance of using software engineering and architecture design *methods* [146] to provide repeatable means of delivering proven solutions and to achieve project success and, in turn, client satisfaction. A method framework called *IBM Unified Method Framework (UMF)* organizes the work performed by practitioners and enables the design and delivery of end-to-end solutions such as those outlined in the previous section.[1] UMF provides prescriptive guidance on "what" needs to be created by a project team in terms of common work products and "how" to produce these work products in terms of activities, tasks, and roles as defined in [239].

UMF provides a common language among IBM practitioners delivering solutions to clients, thus providing consistency across solutions. This requires a common structure: In response to this need, *Unified Method Architecture (UMA)* defines a metamodel underpinning UMF. UMA was developed as a common metamodel

[1] The predecessor of UMF, the IBM Global Services Method, has been used on client projects since 1998. The method changed its name several times during this period.

for the integration of several IBM methods including the Rational Unified Process (RUP), the IBM Global Services Method, Rational Summit Ascendant, the IBM World Wide Project Management Method (WW/PMM), and others.

UMA defines a *method framework* consisting of *method content* and a *process*. UMA represents a consistent and repeatable approach to accomplishing a set of objectives based on a collection of techniques and practices:

- *Method content* represents the primary reusable building blocks of the method that exist outside of any predefined project lifecycle (process).
- The *process* shows the assembly of method content into a sequence or workflow (represented by a work breakdown structure) used to organize a project and to develop a solution. A *task* is the smallest unit of work in a UMA process; tasks can be aggregated into *activities* and *phases*.

Method content contains the following *work products*, which define the inputs and outputs of tasks as method elements:

- *Artifacts* are tangible inputs and outputs that may come with examples or a predefined template. They serve as basis for reuse. "Use case model" and "software architecture document" are examples of such artifacts.
- *Deliverables* are a grouping of task outputs that represent value to a client or other project stakeholders; typically they are the result of packaging several other work products for sign-off and delivery.
- *Outcomes* are intangible results. They are used to convey the completion of tasks and activities with results that are less tangible than artifacts (e.g., trained practitioners, installed software, configured system).

Reference architectures. GTS leverages *reference architectures* [34] to support the service product development and usage. A reference architecture defines a to-be-model of and blueprint for solutions recurring in a particular domain. It has a well-defined scope, specifies the requirements the solutions satisfy, and captures related architectural decisions. It is the objective of reference architectures to guide practitioners through the architecture design activities and to communicate related best practices (e.g., solution building blocks that worked for other practitioners who encountered similar design problems on already completed projects).

Reference architectures may take different forms depending on their usage scenario and target audience: A reference architecture used by a software vendor to position products during presales differs from one used by a professional services firm to divide labor and to exchange knowledge between projects. We use the term in the latter form, faithful to the vision of *Enterprise Solutions Structure (ESS)* [252]: An ESS reference architecture provides a consistent set of officially approved, method-conformant work products (e.g., design artifacts) for a particular application domain and architectural style (here: enterprise applications and SOA). To build an economy of scale, it is imperative to agree on a particular terminology set and standardize the structure of and the relationships between the work products (e.g., design artifacts). To accomplish these goals, the artifacts in reference architectures must conform to the notation prescribed by the method employed. In our context,

UMF recommends the usage of the *Unified Modeling Language (UML)* [271] for many artifacts.

Reference architectures take a governing role during service product creation, ensuring architectural consistency and quality and avoiding undesired overlap.

12.1.5 Architecture Knowledge Management Strategy and Approach

GTS follows a hybrid knowledge management strategy; both *personalization* and *codification* as defined in Chap. 1 are practiced. Personalization is achieved with the help of *communities of practice* [135] and Web 2.0 collaboration tools such as *application wikis* [291], but also more traditional forms of technical exchange such as education courses and conferences. In this case study, we primarily focus on the codification part of the hybrid strategy. With respect to the architectural knowledge views discussed in Chap. 2, our strategy primarily reflects the *decision-centric* view. Additionally, since the reusable knowledge captured is partly based on existing SOA patterns, our approach also fits the *pattern-centric* view.

As outlined in the earlier sections, the codification part of the hybrid strategy is implemented by service products and reference architectures. Both service products and reference architectures use the work products defined by UMF. The development and lifecycle management of the service products is governed by an asset creation approach called *Integrated Service Offering Development (ISD)*. ISD is both a management system and a process. The ISD management system uses *team-based management* [69] for managing investments, portfolios, products, and projects. The ISD process uses phases and decision checkpoints to drive a project from initiation to completion. Furthermore, ISD leverages project management methods to ensure that projects deliver the specified results and that they complete on time and within budget. During development and lifecycle management, a team of senior architects assures the technical quality and integrity of the service product content.

In addition to the centralized ISD model, a supporting decentralized approach is deployed to be able to leverage the experiences of the entire GTS practitioner population efficiently: The *Community Development Model (CDM)* implements a platform for practitioners from across the company to harvest assets from actual client engagements which are then centrally vetted, hardened, and contributed to the community as service product enhancements. CDM focuses on specific assets identified by service product portfolio managers; contributions are called for regularly. An incentive system is in place. These contributions save effort during service product development and increase the service product quality. Additionally, CDM shifts the minds of practitioners towards an asset and reuse culture.

In the remainder of the chapter, we focus on codification. We present one of the reusable assets we created to implement this part of the hybrid knowledge management strategy in the middleware service product line of GTS.

12.2 An SOA Infrastructure Reference Architecture

SOA Infrastructure Reference Architecture (SOAI RA) is the reference architecture of the middleware service product line of GTS. In this section we present the motivation for SOAI RA and give an overview of its artifacts. We also present an architectural decision model and an operational model as exemplary artifacts.

12.2.1 Objectives and Artifact Overview

SOAI RA is a primary carrier of codified architectural knowledge for the middleware service product line of GTS. It is the premier means of coordinating the creation of the technical content of the service products pertaining to middleware services (e.g., service products dealing with SOA infrastructure design and implementation). Using a well-defined set of UMF artifacts, SOAI RA is understood by all service practitioners (as explained previously, UMF is the method commonly employed on GTS projects). SOAI RA assumes SOA [187, 344] to be the architectural style of choice and a middleware platform implementing the SOA principles and patterns to be available. IBM Software Group provides such a platform [154].

Objectives and usage scenarios. The overall objective of SOAI RA is to accelerate the design and assure the quality of scalable, reliable SOA infrastructures which host one or more SOA applications. SOAI RA steers the SOA design work with consistent architectural principles, patterns, and best practices recommendations.

SOAI RA can be used to *accelerate* the solution outline, macro design, and micro design phases of a SOA project (these phases are defined in UMF) by shortening the time it takes to define and build the various architectural artifacts by reusing (adopting) those already available in SOAI RA.

SOAI RA can also be used to *facilitate technology and product selection activities* as its architecture elements may serve as a link between *enterprise architecture* efforts [241] and concrete SOA implementations on projects.

Reference architectures are particularly important if an asset- rather than a labor-based strategy for service delivery is in place. As already outlined, GTS has such strategy. In this setting, another objective of SOAI RA is to *ensure architectural consistency* and compatibility between the service products: Service products such as "SOA Integration Services – Connectivity and Reuse" and "Design and Implementation for WebSphere ESB" must complement each other.

SOAI RA can also be applied to engagements that do not use any service product, *speeding up project delivery* with templates and examples for important architectural artifacts and *reducing technical risk* through best practices reuse.

Artifact overview. SOAI RA follows a *Model-Driven Development (MDD)* [331] approach, making use of the UML [271] tools IBM Rational Software Modeler and IBM Rational Software Architect [154].

A dual reference architecture consumption strategy is in place: SOAI RA users can work with the models directly. Alternatively, they can study exported and generated reports, which are available in textual form (i.e., HTML and PDF documents). SOAI RA concentrates on models for the following UMF artifacts:

- System context
- Use case model
- Non-functional requirements
- Architectural decisions
- Logical Component Model (CM)
- Physical Operational Model (OM)

The *system context diagram* shows the major relationships to external systems and resources that are leveraged within SOAI RA. When UMF is employed, UML or informal rich pictures are used to create system context diagrams. The *Use Case Model (UCM)* captures how practitioners work with SOAI RA, but also shows how humans users or applications interact with an SOA infrastructure (use case is a UML term). *Non-Functional Requirements (NFRs)* define the quality attributes [157] of the system and the constraints under which the system must be built. Constraints are technical limitations imposed upon a solution by external forces. NFRs are typically captured in free form or in structured text. In SOAI RA, the NFR artifact specifies selected quality attributes to consider on SOA projects, e.g., interoperability.

Logical component modeling per se is the responsibility of an application architect, often based in a professional services firm such as IBM Global Business Services, providing business analysis, design and development services (among others). The SOAI RA component model captures the application and middleware components that are relevant for SOA infrastructure design: When creating a specified OM (see below), infrastructure architects must have an understanding of the logical components hosted by the infrastructure under design. UMF recommends using UML component and/or profiled class diagrams as CM notation.

The *Operational Model (OM)* is a key artifact in SOAI RA. UML or informal rich pictures are commonly used to create OMs. SOAI RA provides a *conceptual OM* and a *specified OM*; it does not go down to a *physical OM* level of elaboration. The two SOAI RA OMs serve as an umbrella for and bridge between the physical OMs which are defined in service products.[2]

Architectural decisions is another key work product in SOAI RA. For SOAI RA we adopted the metamodel and the decisions from the *SOA Decision Modeling (SOAD)* project [347]. Unlike most reference architectures, SOAD captures the decisions to be made during adoption of the reference architecture on a particular project (which we refer to as design *issues*), not those already made during the creation of the reference architecture (decision *outcomes*). This focus shift helps to tailor SOAI RA according to project needs: Not all SOA infrastructure design projects require

[2] The three-level OM hierarchy supports an iterative and incremental refinement approach to infrastructure design, which is in line with the advice given by common architecture design methods [146]. For instance, a technology-neutral design of locations, nodes, and deployment units (conceptual OM) should be established before platform-specific ESB communication protocols and products such as HTTP or Java Massage Service (JMS) are selected (specified OM) and configured in the selected ESB product (physical OM) [80, 342].

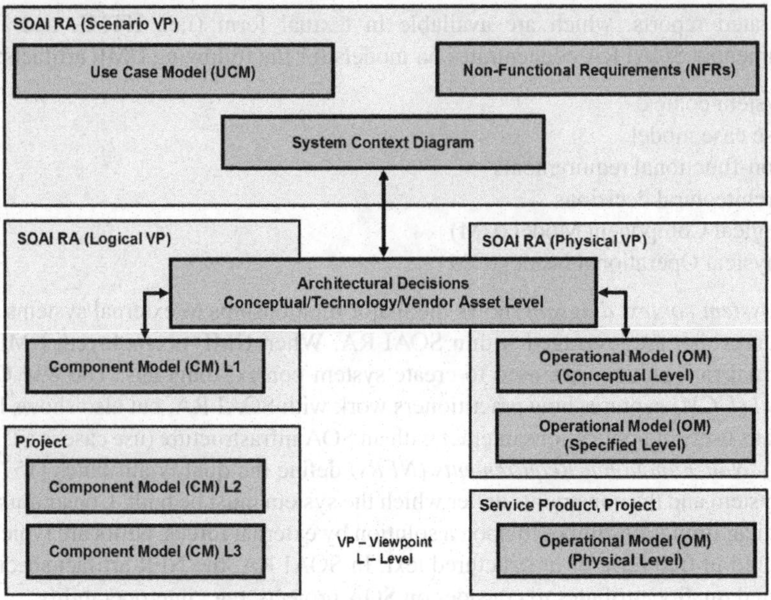

Fig. 12.1 SOA Infrastructure Reference Architecture overview

all SOAD decisions as not all SOA patterns such as ESB, service composition, and service registry are always used. Selecting such patterns and related implementation platforms is part of the decision making.

Figure 12.1 illustrates the artifacts and viewpoints in SOAI RA. For instance, the system context, the use case model, and the NFR artifacts all belong to the *scenario viewpoint* in Kruchten's 4 + 1 view model [188], whereas the CM belongs to the *logical viewpoint* and the OM to the *physical viewpoint.*

The figure also shows that architectural decisions are not only used in their traditional role of capturing design rationale and decisions made, but also to organize the reference architecture. Bidirectional links to and from the level 1 CM and the conceptual OM are maintained. We provide more information about this central role of the decision model and the three levels of architectural decisions (conceptual, technology, and vendor asset level) in Sect. 12.2.2.

12.2.2 Decision Viewpoint: SOA Decision Modeling

SOAI RA adopted the results of the *SOA Decision Modeling (SOAD)* project. SOAD is an industrial research and knowledge engineering project we have been conducting since January 2006. It has three project objectives and types of results:

1. Defining the *concepts* of a decision-centric architecture design *method*, e.g., a knowledge domain *metamodel* optimized for reuse and collaboration. These concepts are introduced in separate publications, e.g., [347].

2. Providing reusable decision *content* (architectural knowledge) for SOA projects taking the form of a *Reusable Architectural Decision Model (RADM) for SOA* which is instantiated from the metamodel. Its content originates from several large-scale SOA projects conducted since 2001. Excerpts from this RADM are featured in other publications, e.g., [347]. The full model became part of SOAI RA.
3. Demonstrating how the decision modeling concepts can be implemented and how the decision content can be managed collaboratively with the help of a *tool*. Architectural Decision Knowledge Wiki [229], made publicly available in March 2007, serves this purpose.

We now review the SOAD concepts, content, and tool contributions that are particularly relevant within the context of our case study and this chapter [347].

Concepts. The knowledge domain metamodel is the SOAD concept most relevant for this case study. It remained stable since September 2006 except for minor revisions such as renaming classes and attributes.

We distinguish decisions made and decisions required to facilitate reuse: An *ADIssue* instance informs the architect that a single architecture design problem has to be solved. *ADAlternative* instances then present possible solutions to this problem. *ADOutcome* instances record an actual decision made to solve the problem including its rationale. Closely related ADIssues are grouped into *ADTopicGroups*, which form a hierarchy. Dependencies between ADIssues are modeled as a *dependsOn* association; in [347], we define more dependency relations. The metamodel is shown in Fig. 12.2.

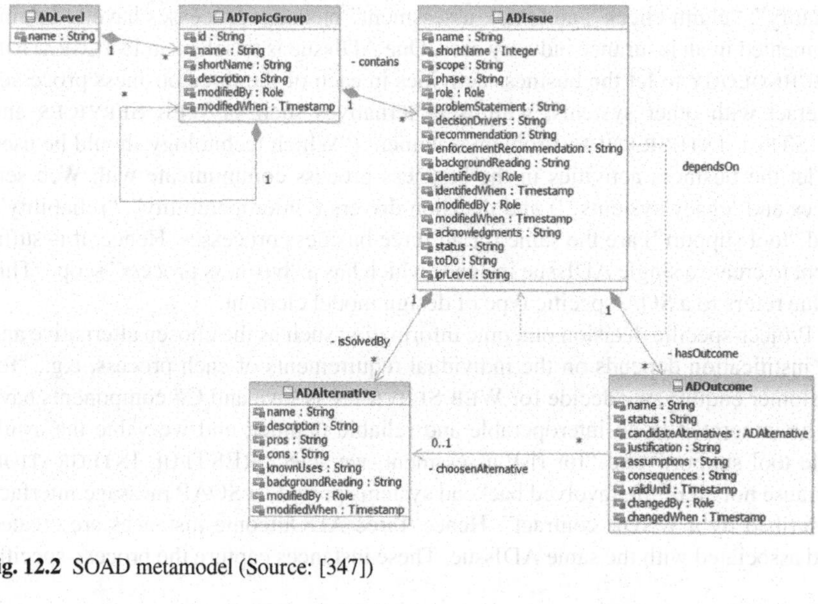

Fig. 12.2 SOAD metamodel (Source: [347])

ADIssue and ADAlternative provide reusable, project-independent background information about decisions required: The *problemStatement* characterizes an ADIssue on an introductory level, while *backgroundReading* and *knownUses* point to further information. The *decisionDrivers* attribute states types of NFRs, including software quality attributes and environmental constraints such as budget and skill availability; the patterns community uses the term *forces* synonymously. The *role* and *phase* attributes serve as a link to methods such as UMF. A *recommendation* attribute conveys subjective information, which may be a simple rule of thumb ("best practice"), a weighted mapping of forces to alternatives, or a pointer to a more complex analysis process to be performed outside the decision model. The recommendation should refer to decision drivers and pros and cons of alternatives. With the *backgroundReading* attribute, supporting material such as primers and tutorials can be referenced.

ADOutcome instances capture project-specific knowledge about decisions made: The *justification* information refers to actual requirements ("sub-second response time in customer interface"), as opposed to the ADIssue-level decision drivers which only list types of requirements ("performance, i.e., response time and throughput"). These two aspects of the knowledge have different reuse characteristics: the ADIssue information has even more reuse potential then the project-specific ADOutcome rationale. A second reason for factoring out ADOutcome as a separate entity is that the same ADIssue might pertain to many elements in a design model, e.g., business processes and service operations in SOA. Therefore, *types* of logical and physical design model elements are referenced via the *scope* attribute in the ADIssue. ADOutcome instances then are created dynamically on projects, and can refer to design model element *instances* via their *name*.

To give an example, a business process model might state that three "customer enquiry", "claim check", and "risk assessment" business processes have to be implemented in an insurance industry case. One ADIssue is to select an INTEGRATION TECHNOLOGY to let the business activities in each of the three business processes interact with other systems, with ADAlternatives such as WEB SERVICES and RESTFUL INTEGRATION. Problem statement ("Which technology should be used to let the business activities in the business process communicate with Web services and legacy systems?") and decision drivers ("interoperability", "reliability", and "tool support") are the same for all three business processes. Hence, it is sufficient to create a single ADIssue instance which has a "business process" scope. This value refers to a SOA-specific type of design model element.

Project-specific decision outcome information such as the chosen alternative and its justification depends on the individual requirements of each process, e.g., "for customer enquiry, we decide for WEB SERVICES as Java and C# components have to be integrated in an interoperable and reliable manner, and we value the available tool support" and "for risk assessment, we select RESTFUL INTEGRATION because not all of the involved backend systems provide a SOAP message interface described by a WSDL contract". Hence, three ADOutcome instances are created and associated with the same ADIssue. These instances capture the process-specific

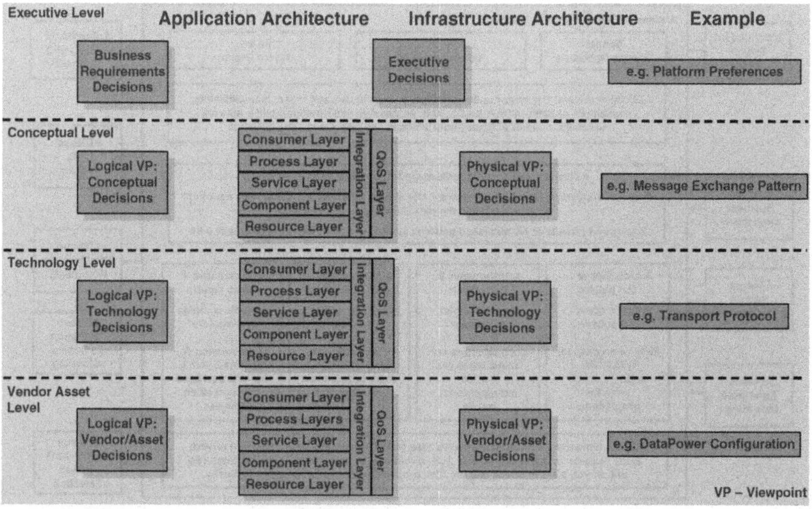

Fig. 12.3 Layers and levels in RADM for SOA (Source: [347])

decisions and their rationale. They refer to the actual business processes in their name attributes ("customer enquiry", "claim check", and "risk assessment").

Content. The RADM for SOA is organized into levels and layers: An overarching *executive level* comprises issues regarding requirements analysis and technical decisions of strategic relevance. A *conceptual level*, a *technology level* and a *vendor asset level* follow [347]. Architectural layers further structure the RADM. Figure 12.3 shows the resulting model structure (each box represents an ADTopicGroup comprising ADIssues dealing with the same topic area on one refinement level).

The same top-level topic groups are defined on the conceptual, the technology, and the vendor asset level. The level and topic group hierarchy serves as a table of decision model content. The hierarchical structure is motivated by our observation that the technical discussions during SOA design often circle around detailed features of certain vendor products, or the pros and cons of specific technologies, whereas many highly important strategic decisions and conceptual concerns tend to be underemphasized. These discussions are related, but should not be merged into one; they reside on different refinement levels. Separating design concerns in such a way is good practice; e.g., RUP recommends a similar incremental approach for UML class diagrams used as design models. We adopted this recommendation for decision models and made the three refinement levels explicit in the RADM for SOA.

There are topic groups for seven *logical SOA layers*, consumer, process, service, component, resource, integration, and QoS layer, which are introduced in [20]. Two topic groups on each level contain issues pertaining to the logical and physical viewpoint that can not be assigned to any layer. The model can be tailored and irrelevant parts removed, e.g., if only issues dealing with processes, but not issues dealing with

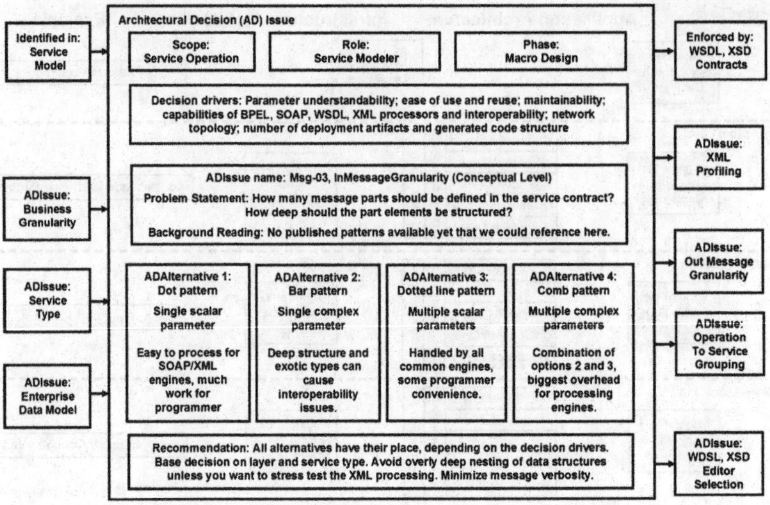

Fig. 12.4 Sample issue and alternatives in SOAI RA

ESB integration are of interest in a particular project context. About a dozen subject area keywords are defined and expressed as *topic tags*, e.g., "session management", "transaction management", "workflow", and "error handling".

Figure 12.4 is an excerpt of an ADIssue description in the RADM for SOA. The issue deals with the InMessageGranularity of a service operation. This issue qualifies as a an architectural decision to be included in the RADM for SOA, as its outcome has a significant impact on the quality attributes of the SOA-based system under construction and the issue recurs for each service operation.

In many cases, the ADAlternatives of an ADIssue in the RADM for SOA refer to an already existing patterns, e.g., those documented by Buschmann et al. [64], by Fowler [126], or by Hohpe and Woolf [148]. In this case, no patterns are available yet; we plan to publish the descriptions of the issue and its pattern alternatives (Dot, Bar, Dotted Line, and Comb) in the future.

At present, the RADM for SOA consists of 86 ADTopicGroups and 389 ADIssues with about 2000 ADAlternatives. The knowledge base is still growing, now at a slower pace than in the beginning of the project. While this growth could continue infinitely, we plan to freeze the knowledge engineering once the 500 most relevant issues have been compiled. The knowledge base will still have to be reviewed periodically to ensure that the contained information remains up to date. Issues and alternatives will become obsolete as technology evolves; new ones will be required. The SOAD level and layer structure helps to organize these activities and reduce the related effort; conceptual knowledge dates at a slower pace than that on the technology and on the vendor asset level.

Tool. Architectural Decision Knowledge Wiki is a Web-based collaboration system and application wiki which implements the SOAD metamodel as well as additional concepts. It supports about 70 use cases. The tool is featured in [291, 347].

12.2.3 Physical Viewpoint: Operational Model

Applications employing SOA as their architectural style require a reliable SOA infrastructure which complies with the corporate-level technology standards and runs inside existing or new operating environments such as datacenters. The IT organizations of enterprises must provide such SOA infrastructures.

SOA infrastructures must be able to support the development, deployment, and management of service consumers and providers, and host SOA middleware such as ESBs, business process orchestration engines, service registries, but also components in application servers which implement service consumers and providers in some programming language (e.g., BPEL, C#, or Java).

The Operational Model (OM) in SOAI RA is positioned to rapidly design such SOA infrastructures, and plan the capacities of the underlying hardware (i.e., server and network resources). Examples of such hardware capacity aspects are CPU speed, main memory size, disk space, and network adapter capacity (throughput).

An OM may be defined for a *particular IT system*, designed to meet specific functional and non-functional requirements. An example is a WebSphere Process Server [154] environment required to support service composition (business process choreography) in a Customer Relationship Management (CRM) solution. In such a case, the specified OM (see Sect. 12.2.1) defines all functional and non-functional characteristics of the model elements, while the physical OM provides a detailed configuration and capacity plan, which serves as a blueprint for the acquisition, installation, and subsequent maintenance of the infrastructure resources (i.e., server hardware, network equipment, and middleware).

In a reference architecture context, an OM can describe a *template of how (parts of) an IT infrastructure may be constructed* in order to satisfy some generalized set of functional and non-functional requirements. In this case, the OM leaves placeholders, requiring tailoring and integration with other partial OMs to satisfy a particular set of concrete requirements. The purpose of such a generalized OM may be to support enterprise-wide standardization of all SOA infrastructure environments (e.g., WebSphere Process Server). Such standardization simplifies procurement, education, and systems management.

SOAI RA adopts the OM notation and terminology defined in the IBM Architecture Description Standard (ADS) [342] and the OM technique defined in IBM UMF [80]. Hence, three perspectives are taken during the design of the OM in SOAI RA, answering the following questions:

- Which *network zones* are given or required (e.g., locations, security zones created by application gateways and transport-level firewalls)?
- Which hardware *nodes* appear in these network zones?
- Which presentation, execution, and data *deployment units* are deployed on these nodes to host application and middleware components?

As motivated in the SOAI RA overview above, SOAI RA contains a conceptual OM and a specified OM; the physical OM has to be developed on each project adopting SOAI RA. Hence, SOAI RA provides zone, node, and deployment unit definitions

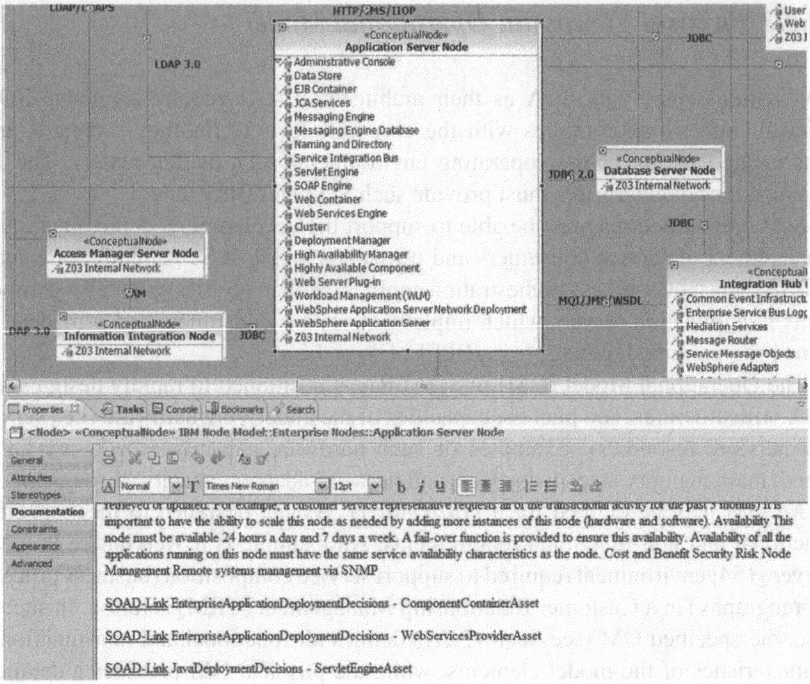

Fig. 12.5 OM to (SO)AD linkage in SOAI RA

at the conceptual level and details those by adding NFR and other information at the specified level. Figure 12.5 is a screen caption of a UML class diagram in IBM Rational Software Modeler. The classes are annotated with a stereotype called ≪`ConceptualNode`≫ which indicates that they represent an OM concept. The nodes host deployment units, which correspond to SOA infrastructure elements. For instance, the “application server node” hosts a “service integration bus” unit.

Figure 12.5 also shows that nodes in the conceptual OM are linked to SOAD issues, which are made available via the Architectural Decision Knowledge Wiki tool (as introduced in the SOAD overview in Sect.12.2.2). In the example, the application server node in the conceptual OM has issues such as Component Container Asset and Web Services Provider Asset attached. This link between OM elements and SOAD issues is a key feature in SOAI RA: It uses the *scope* attribute defined in the SOAD metamodel introduced previously.

We follow the same approach to link logical components and related issues. With this approach, we make architectural knowledge available in the tool the architect works with during design; however, we do not model the rather rich issue descriptions in the same UML model, but couple architecture elements and related issues loosely to ensure flexibility and usability of the two parts of the architectural knowledge, logical CM and physical OM on the one hand (design artifacts) and architectural decision knowledge on the other hand (rationale).

12.2.4 Summary of Approach and Benefits

The UMF artifacts in reference architectures represent the recommended architectural to-be model to begin with (and aim for) when delivering service projects. They codify many lessons learned and best practices from projects around the world. To harvest such lessons learned and best practices, project-specific deliverables get assessed for applicability, are quality assured, sanitized, and hardened into artifacts generally reusable in similar projects. In short, reference architectures are a way to make collective project experiences and knowledge explicit and available to a wide audience, i.e., all GTS practitioners.

Reference architectures pave the way for the consistent development of different service products. SOAI RA is the reference architecture of the GTS middleware service product line; it makes service products combinable. This is important since client projects can become quite large and complex and often deploy more than a single service product. SOAI RA and other reference architectures not only make service products combinable, but also offer an integrative approach across IBM hardware, software, and services products: They simplify the end-to-end solution design by establishing modeling standards (e.g. naming conventions), which are also shared between presales and project delivery functions.

GTS practitioners benefit from SOAI RA in several ways: First and foremost, they learn from experienced peers how to model a solution, how to create the artifacts required by UMF, and how to design an SOA infrastructure properly (*education* use case). In this regard, a reference architecture codifies tribal knowledge.

A reusable asset that meets the wants and needs of practitioners and is easy to adopt can increase *productivity*: In particular, SOAI RA aims to accelerate the early project activities, allowing practitioners to tailor the provided artifacts according to the client-specific requirements and project context they are confronted with. The more of the hard design and modeling problems have already been solved in a reusable, standardized fashion, the more time practitioners can spend with their clients to resolve the particularly relevant, case-specific design issues.

Furthermore, reference architectures have a *quality assurance* effect: Best practices from projects around the world are captured in the reference architecture.

Moreover, SOAI RA improves *collaboration* both within GTS and across IBM lines of business: It facilitates the knowledge exchange between projects and within a community of practice by establishing a common vocabulary.

Finally, the model-driven approach in SOAI RA opens the door to *automation*: Due to the standardization of target architecture, it becomes possible to generate parts of the code and deployment artifacts directly from the models.

Having summarized the motivation, anatomy, and benefits of SOAI RA, let us now present how we harvested its architectural knowledge from projects. We will return to the benefits when presenting user feedback in Sect. 12.4.

12.3 Harvesting SOA Decision Knowledge from Projects

In this section, we give an overview of the architectural knowledge engineering activities we conducted to create the Reusable Architectural Decision Model (RADM) for SOA used in SOAI RA. We also define a four-step process and related guidance to syndicate architectural decision knowledge from projects.

12.3.1 Sources of Architectural Decision Knowledge

The first source of input for the RADM for SOA was personal project experience [345, 348]. As a second step, we factored in selected architectural knowledge from projects technically led by peers, leveraging a company-wide SOA and Web services practitioner community with more than 3500 members. We screened several hundred architectural decisions from more than 30 projects from several geographies and industries. A third type of input was systematic literature screening, e.g., SOA and patterns books, technology introductions, and vendor documentation.

Originally, we had employed an ad hoc approach to incorporating these sources of input. This ad hoc approach to asset harvesting turned out to be more labor intense than originally anticipated: We were tempted to fix quality problems straight away, adding our own expertise prematurely. This approach did not scale and did not produce a satisfying model. Hence, we switched to a systematic approach. It consists of a basic four-step *knowledge harvesting* process and related decision modeling *guidance*.

12.3.2 Architectural Knowledge Harvesting Process

To overcome the limitations of our original ad hoc approach, we followed four knowledge harvesting steps. Figure 12.6 illustrates these four steps, which we call *Review*, *Integrate*, *Harden*, and *Align (RIHA)*:

These steps are characterized as follows:

1. In the review step, raw input from completed projects (decisions made) is screened. This has the objective to assess the relevance and quality of the input. ADIssue and ADAlternative instances for all decisions that are decided to be included in the RADM are created.

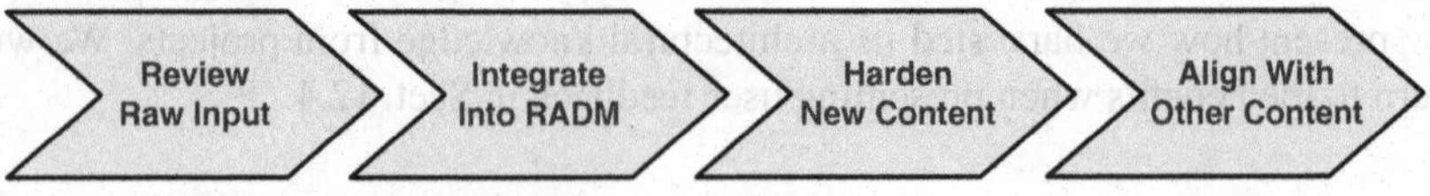

Fig. 12.6 Four-step knowledge harvesting process (RIHA)

2. In the integrate step, existing information in the raw input is copied into appropriate attributes defined in the SOAD metamodel (see later).
3. In the harden step, the issue is decomposed if necessary, e.g., if there is a violation of the level structure because concepts, technology characteristics, and product features are covered in a single ADIssue. Moreover, the issue and alternative information is completed in this step, for example with less obvious alternatives, missing pros and cons, additional decision drivers, and additional decision dependencies. The contributing project might have to be contacted to clarify certain aspects.
4. In the align step, the new model element is reviewed and edited for readability and consistency with already existing parts of the model.

It is worth noting that it is possible to iterate and harvest knowledge incrementally, although Fig. 12.6 seems to suggest a linear process.

12.3.3 Guidance for the Four RIHA Process Steps

Review step. During the review step, two *qualification criteria* are applied to decide whether an issue should be included in a RADM:

1. The first criterion is the *reuse potential*: Is a real architecture design problem described, does the raw input qualify as an architectural decision? Does a candidate issue pertain to one of the principles and patterns defining SOA as an architectural style? Does it present real alternatives? Will it recur, i.e., does it have sustainable, long lasting character or is it a tactical or temporary decision? Does it avoid to reference proprietary features or characteristics?
2. The second criterion is *technical* and *editorial quality*: Is the issue technically sound, particularly the justification for the chosen design? Did the contributing project succeed? Does its description read well? Is established terminology used, e.g., are the referenced design model elements defined in the literature? Can issue and outcome be separated from each other?

A high reuse potential as indicated by the answers to the questions regarding the first criterion is mandatory. If there are doubts about the technical quality of the candidate issue, it is not used; the editorial quality can be improved with reasonable editing effort if there is a strong need for the issue (e.g., high reuse potential). The contributing practitioner may be contacted in such a case to obtain additional information about the circumstances under which the decision was made.

Integrate, harden, and align steps. When integrating and hardening knowledge that qualifies for inclusion in the RADM, the raw input is mapped to the SOAD metamodel as indicated in Table 12.1 (transitioning from decisions made to decisions required).

In [347], we define quality heuristics for architectural decision models, which advise on the number of nesting levels and how to work with the logical and temporal

Table 12.1 ADM to RADM attribute mapping during asset harvesting

Knowledge type	Raw input from project	RADM for SOA content	SOAD attributes and further comments
Problem	Outcome (often has an embedded issue)	ADIssue	Problem statement, background references
Solution	Chosen alternative	ADAlternative	Description, known uses
Rationale	Justification	ADIssue	Recommendation
Rationale	Justification	ADIssue	Decision drivers, pros and cons of alternatives from "because" sentence in justification
Requirements link	Assumptions	ADIssue	Decision drivers
Dependencies	Consequences, related decisions	Related decisions	Dependency types in [347]; often missing in raw input
Scoping	Decision name, design model references	ADIssue	scope attribute
Method linkage	Timestamp, decision maker	ADIssue	phase, role attributes

dependency relations defined in that paper. We now present several additional guidelines. All of these are suggestive rather than normative.

A meaningful name for the issue must be found. The patterns community advises us that finding good names is essential when creating a pattern language, but also hard; the same holds for issue and alternative names. Names should be compact, but expressive. They must be self-explaining, e.g., when appearing in a tool that does not display any other attributes in a particular view. Names should be generic so that they do not to have to be changed often, but also be expressive so that they can serve as identifiers for issues and alternatives in the RADM. The entire description of an issue and its alternatives should adopt the terminology established by the principles and the patterns defining SOA as an architectural style.

All alternatives listed for an issue must solve the same problem. As a consequence, all alternatives must reside on the same refinement level, e.g., conceptual and technology alternatives are assigned to different (but related) issues. The alternatives of an issue should be disjoint and unambiguous to make solutions comparable and support code generation as an additional form of decision enforcement in an MDD context [346]. They should catch all known mainstream solutions as well as a few exceptional ones that have been applied in practice. If a solution is known under several names (e.g., facade and wrapper pattern), the alias names should be listed in the description attribute. By convention, the alternatives are ordered from common and recommended to exceptional; if present, fallback alternatives such as CUSTOM CODING or OTHER LANGUAGE appear last. The same ordering scheme should be applied consistently for all issues. A "good enough" approach is followed; it is not a primary goal to be complete. The accuracy of the knowledge has higher priority than its quantity.

The information about decision drivers should use a consistent vocabulary. An established NFR or quality attribute taxonomy should be used. It may originate from enterprise architecture guidelines [241] or an industry standard such as [157]. The more homogeneous and consistent the vocabulary is, the simpler it becomes to tailor the model and to use it during the decision making. For instance, consistently named decision drivers can easily be searched for in the decision model, and decision support systems and tradeoff analysis methods can be applied seamlessly when resolving one or more of the issues in the decision model. Some examples of valid decision drivers are:

- Functional and nonfunctional requirements, e.g., as described in other artifacts in a reference architecture.
- General quality attributes from software architecture and software engineering literature and forces in pattern books.
- Decisions made earlier, for example prior to project initiation.
- Architectural principles that have been stated for an industry, the company, a line of business (domain), or the current project.
- Non-technical influence factors such as education needs, license cost, available skills, and experience in the project team.

The recommendations attribute in the ADIssue class in the SOAD metamodel should refer to the decision drivers. The same holds for the pros and cons information in the ADAlternative class and, later on when capturing decisions, for the justification attribute in ADOutcome instances.

According to our experience, descriptions of issues and their alternatives should not exceed 1,000–1,200 words or one to three HTML pages in a generated report. Longer descriptions are difficult to display in a user-friendly way and time consuming to study. If more information is required, the issue should summarize the problem and refer to a separate document via the background reading attribute.

Subjective information must be clearly separated from objective information. The SOAD metamodel has been designed to facilitate this separation (e.g., objective decision drivers vs. subjective recommendation). The writing style and editing quality must meet professional standards, e.g., be informative and accurate, but also keep the reader interested. According to our experience, a suggestive tone has higher chances to succeed than an authoritative one: The asset consumer should have the impression that the RADM intends to help and provide orientation in a complex problem and solution space, not to create additional, unnecessary efforts or technical complexities.

Additional decision capturing advice is available in the documentation of Architectural Decision Knowledge Wiki [229].

12.4 Consuming SOA Decision Knowledge

In this section, we discuss our own experience with the SOAD concepts and the RADM for SOA content, as well as feedback from early adopters of SOAI RA.

12.4.1 SOAD Usage during Creation of SOAI RA

Usage of SOAD within the SOAI RA project made evident that architectural decisions recur: Another SOA reference architecture project had already compiled a draft version of an architectural decisions artifact, which we received in January 2007. It captured 50 decisions and 42 of these decisions were already covered by our RADM for SOA which at that time contained about 100 issues.

The model-driven approach of SOAD was seen to be superior to text template-based decision capturing. From a tool perspective, filtered report generation was an important feature (easing reviews and reference architecture customization). Unlike previous reference architectures that only capture *decisions made* during reference architecture development (outcomes), SOAD documents the *decisions required* during adoption of the reference architecture (issues). This distinction caused some misunderstandings because we had named the issue an "AD" initially; after the renaming, the separation of problem and solution was welcomed.

Depth, breadth, and technical quality of the RADM for SOA content were acknowledged and appreciated by the reviewers. One early action point was to explain the level and layer structure in detail; consumers of the SOAI RA can not be assumed to be familiar with these concepts (even if they are standard concepts in MDD and software architecture). To do so, we authored supporting documentation and added the topic group hierarchy to the architectural decision report generation feature in the Architectural Decision Knowledge Wiki tool. To make the position in the hierarchy clear in the issue name, we defined naming conventions.

Early users appreciated the knowledge captured in single issues and alternatives, but struggled to stay orientated when being confronted with several hundred issues, even when being supported by the scope, phase, and role attributes and the decision topic hierarchy in the Architectural Decision Knowledge Wiki tool. As a second step after having added the attributes, we provided additional search, filter, and export capabilities for ease of orientation and consumption. Finally, we added concepts such as entry points and decision status management based on the modeled decision dependencies. These concepts are explained in detail in [347].

12.4.2 User Experience with SOAD and SOAI RA

SOAD has been used on ten industrial SOA projects so far. Architects reviewed up to 200 out of 389 issue descriptions and reused up to 50 issues during their decision making on projects. Acceleration of the design activities and quality improvements were reported on these cases; all practitioners welcomed vision and approach of SOAD. Architectural Decision Knowledge Wiki was downloaded from IBM alphaWorks more than 630 times (the download is free of charge; registration is required); 220 users are registered in an IBM internal hosted instance. The RADM for SOA was transferred to four IBM lines of business.

Experience with SOAD concepts (metamodel). The fundamental hypothesis that *architectural decisions recur* if the same architectural style is employed on multiple projects in an application genre was confirmed numerous times. We interacted with several hundred architects during the project. Only one of them disagreed, which turned out to be a misunderstanding: We do not claim and require that the decision *outcome* always is the same; only the *issue*, expressing the need for a decision and the related background information has to recur to make SOAD work.

The attributes in the SOAD metamodel were rated well. They were seen to be understandable intuitively, conveying useful information, and giving enough information about the aspects of a decision that matter during decision making. A few additional attributes were suggested, for instance the organizational reach of a decision.

While the concept of refinement levels was acknowledged, the four levels in the RADM for SOA were not seen to be the only solution. Other model organization schemes such as architectural viewpoints and panes as defined by The Open Group Architecture Framework (TOGAF) [241] were suggested. Decision dependency management was seen as important differentiator of SOAD.

Experience with SOAD content (RADM for SOA). Model scoping and the level of detail on which individual decisions are represented in the RADM for SOA were appreciated and seen as appropriate (i.e., issues modeled that are not obvious or trivial, captured knowledge relevant on SOA industry projects and documented in an understandable way). Acceleration of decision identification and improved decision making quality were reported. In one case, the effort for the creation of a SOA principles deliverable decreased from eight to five person days because thirteen out of fifteen required decisions were present in the RADM for SOA and could be reused.

Some confusion regarding proactive vs. retrospective decision modeling occurred; one user simply copied the issue descriptions and the recommendation attribute in the RADM to outcome instances in his deliverable. This caused negative feedback from a senior architect in a team-internal quality assurance review. We can conclude that the writing style has a significant impact on the success of a RADM. User expectations must be managed; SOAD is not designed to make architectural thinking obsolete. Project-specific requirements and RADM content must be matched.

A rollout to additional, non-SOA application domains such as archiving solutions and systems management is planned.

Experience with tool (Architectural Decision Knowledge Wiki). The user feedback regarding the value of Architectural Decision Knowledge Wiki was encouraging: users appreciated that all knowledge required during architectural decision making can be conveniently located in a single place and that the system comes with a set of initial content (i.e., samples and decision modeling guidance). The realized use cases were seen to be meeting practitioner wants and needs. The presentation of ADIssues, ADAlternatives, and ADOutcomes on a single HTML page received positive reactions. However, users reported that they found it rather difficult to orient themselves and navigate in large models. In early versions, the static topic group hierarchy was the only order defined; the decision dependency relations were not fully leveraged at that point. Additional visual elements were requested, as well as a closer integration with other tools for architects.

12.5 Summary

In this chapter, we presented SOA Infrastructure Reference Architecture (SOAI RA) as a resuable asset supporting SOA infrastructure design, a basic process for harvesting architectural knowledge from industry projects, related decision modeling guidance, and usage experience with the asset. SOAI RA is a primary carrier of architectural knowledge in the middleware service product line of IBM GTS; it implements the codification part of the hybrid knowledge management strategy of GTS.

Many challenging NFRs and other forces have to be met in SOA infrastructure design. They conflict with each other and keep on changing; many of them remain tacit. In SOA design, architects are confronted with a broad decision tree. The many conceptual, technology, and vendor asset level alternatives vary in their pros and cons with respect to decision drivers such as functional requirements, cost, and quality attributes. There are numerous dependencies between the decisions, which lead to combinations that work and others that do not work. Many tradeoffs must be made, which often requires investigating clusters of related decisions. Moreover, priorities and assessments vary by role, e.g., application architect, integration architect, and infrastructure architect. It is hard to make generic recommendations; a prototype project or studies are often required to resolve a particular design issue. Reference architectures such as SOAI RA can assist practitioners when they tackle complex design issues.

According to our experience, providing a knowledge repository is not sufficient to make a codification strategy for knowledge management successful, no matter how good such tools and their content may be. The available knowledge has to appear in the tools and practices used by practitioners in their daily work. Any lookup step, even if supported by powerful search and filter technologies and notification and recommendation features, means additional efforts which practitioners are often not willing or not able to invest. Further tooling innovations are required to overcome this inhibitor for a successful use of architectural knowledge.

We envision several advanced usage scenarios for the concepts presented in this chapter. Project managers can use architectural decision models for planning purposes. Work breakdown structures and effort estimation reports can be created, as open decisions correspond to required activities. Health checking is another application area: If there are many, frequent changes or many questions are still unresolved in late project phases, the project is likely to be troubled. Product selection decisions define which software licenses are required, and on which hardware nodes the required software has to be installed. Moreover, the outcome of product-specific asset configuration decisions can serve as input to software configuration management. The decision model can also serve enterprise architects; they can maintain a company-specific instance of the decision model, consisting of a subset of issues and alternatives accompanied by company-specific recommendations. Such an approach authorizes solution architects on projects to make decisions ("freedom of choice") without sacrificing architectural integrity ("freedom from choice").

Chapter 13
Successful Architectural Knowledge Sharing: Beware of Emotions

Eltjo R. Poort, Agung Pramono, Michiel Perdeck, Viktor Clerc, and Hans van Vliet

Abstract This chapter presents the analysis and key findings of a survey on architectural knowledge sharing. The responses of 97 architects working in the Dutch IT Industry were analyzed by correlating practices and challenges with project size and success. Impact mechanisms between project size, project success, and architectural knowledge sharing practices and challenges were deduced based on reasoning, experience and literature. We find that architects run into numerous and diverse challenges sharing architectural knowledge, but that the only challenges that have a significant impact are the emotional challenges related to interpersonal relationships. Thus, architects should be careful when dealing with emotions in knowledge sharing.

13.1 Introduction

In recent years, Architectural Knowledge (AK), including architecture design decisions, has become a topic of considerable research interest. Management and sharing of AK are considered to be important practices in good architecting [192, 325, 295]. There has not been, however, much published research into the usage of AK related practices in industry.

In the beginning of 2008, the members of the architecture community of practice in a major Dutch IT services company[1] were surveyed. The main reason for this

Eltjo R. Poort (✉) and Michiel Perdeck
Logica, Amstelveen, The Netherlands e-mail: eltjo.poort@logica.com,michiel.perdeck@logica.com

Agung Pramono, Viktor Clerc, and Hans van Vliet
VU University Amsterdam, The Netherlands e-mail: agungpramono@yahoo.com,viktor@cs.vu.nl,hans@cs.vu.nl

[1] In this paper, this company will be identified as ABC

M. Ali Babar et al. (eds.), *Software Architecture Knowledge Management*,
DOI: 10.1007/978-3-642-02374-3_13,

survey was to establish a baseline of current practice in AK sharing, and to gain insight into the mechanisms around architectural knowledge sharing and related challenges in projects. In terms of the architectural knowledge views discussed in Chap. 2, the questions originated from a *decision centric* mindset. The architects were asked about the content, manner, reasons and timing of the AK sharing they did in their latest project. They were also asked about the challenges they faced. Furthermore, they were asked to identify various properties of their latest project's context, such as project size and success factors.

Even though the architects surveyed all work for the same IT services company, according to the survey 64% of them is doing so mostly at customers' sites. As a consequence, the survey results represent a mix of AK sharing practices in ABC and in ABC's customer base, which includes major Dutch companies and government institutions.

13.2 Survey Description

The invitation to participate in the survey was sent out by e-mail to 360 members of the Netherlands (NL) Architecture Community of Practice (ACoP) of the ABC company. The ACoP consists of experienced professionals practicing architecture at various levels (business, enterprise, IT, software, and systems architecture) in project or consultancy assignments. The survey was closed after 3 weeks. By that time, 142 responses were collected; 97 respondents had answered the majority of the questions (93 had answered all). The other 45 responses were discarded because no questions about AK sharing had been answered. The survey consisted of 37 questions: 20 directly related to AK sharing, and 17 related to the context in which the AK sharing took place.

13.3 Analysis

The analysis of the 97 valid survey responses was performed in three phases: first, the current state of AK practice and challenges was established by comparing the respondents' answers to the 20 AK related questions. The analysis of four of these questions is presented in Sect. 13.3.1: three questions about AK practices and one about challenges in AK sharing. In phase one, we examined the responses by ordering and grouping them.

Second, the relationship between the AK practices and challenges and their context was analyzed by determining significant correlations between the AK-related responses and some of the 17 context-related questions. The two context factors of project success and project size are analyzed systematically in Sect. 13.3.2. The result of phase two is a set of statistically significant correlations between responses to AK related questions, and the size and success of the projects they pertained to.

In the third phase of the analysis, we reasoned and discussed about the results from the first two phases. Two of the authors have been practicing architects in the ABC company for more than a decade. Based on reasoning, literature and their experience we deduced causality and impact mechanisms from the correlations, leading to an observed impact model that is presented in Sect. 13.3.3. Further discussions are presented in Sect. 13.4.

13.3.1 State of AK Sharing Practice

In this section, the responses to four of the AK related questions are analyzed, presenting the results of phase 1 of the analysis.

The four questions are:

- What type of architectural knowledge have you provided to or acquired from ABC in your latest assignment?
- Why did you share architectural knowledge to your colleagues in ABC?
- When did you share architectural knowledge in your latest assignment?
- What challenges in architectural knowledge sharing did you experience in your latest assignment?

Each question was provided with a set of predefined responses, determined in consultation between two experienced architects and two researchers. There was also the possibility for open text for missing answers. Respondents were asked to signify the applicability of those responses on a five-point Likert scale. Table 13.1 lists the predefined responses to the questions, sorted by their average response values, which are listed in the third column. Each question is further analyzed in the following subsections. The two rightmost columns in the table list the Spearman's rho correlations between the responses and the project context factors, which will be analyzed in Sect. 13.3.2. We will start with the analysis of the responses without taking into account their contexts.

Architectural Knowledge Types *What type of architectural knowledge have you provided to or acquired from ABC in your latest assignment?*

The distribution of the response values is visualized in Fig. 13.1.[2] With the exception of reference architectures and legal knowledge, all types of architectural knowledge appear to be shared more or less equally. The least shared type of AK is legal knowledge: over 75% indicate they do not or hardly share it with ABC.

AK Sharing Motivation *Why did you share architectural knowledge to your colleagues in ABC?* The distribution of the response values is visualized in Fig. 13.2. These data tell us that most architects are either impartial to or agree with almost all motivation responses.

[2] The figures in this chapter use the codified response IDs of the **ID** column in Table 13.1.

Table 13.1 AK related responses, average values and correlations

Architectural knowledge types	*ID*	*avg*	*prj succ rho*	*prj size rho*
Standards; principles and guidelines	s_akt_std	2.95	−0.062	0.012
Tools and methods	s_akt_tlsmeth	2.80	−0.096	.234∗
Known and proven practices	s_akt_prctc	2.71	0.135	−0.017
Product and vendor knowledge	s_akt_prodkn	2.71	0.187	−.244∗
Requirements	s_akt_req	2.71	0.178	−0.113
Design Decisions including alternatives; assumptions; rationale	s_akt_dd	2.69	0.1	−0.025
Business knowledge	s_akt_buskn	2.61	0.082	−0.023
Patterns and tactics	s_akt_ptrn	2.46	0.044	0.011
Reference architectures	s_akt_ra	2.28	0.074	−0.014
Legal knowledge	s_akt_legal	1.79	0.097	0.03
AK Sharing Motivation	*ID*	*avg*	*prj succ rho*	*prj size rho*
To build up my professional network	s_akw_bldnetw	3.89	0.116	−0.009
I just like to share my knowledge	s_akw_like	3.84	0.115	−0.107
Personal relation with colleague(s)	s_akw_persrel	3.81	−.230∗	0.037
We all work for the same company	s_akw_samecomp	3.77	0.109	−0.147
To enhance my professional reputation	s_akw_reput	3.59	0.042	0.022
To contribute to the company's business goals	s_akw_compbusgls	3.53	0.054	−0.014
I hope the favour will be returned some day	s_akw_return	3.39	−.204∗	0.147
I will be recognised as a contributor	s_akw_recog	3.32	0.018	−0.107
I have received useful information from him/her	s_akw_reciproc	3.32	−.223∗	−0.019
My management expects me to	s_akw_mgtexpect	3.09	.275∗∗	−0.091
This may work in my favour at my next salary review	s_akw_salary	2.69	0.002	0.037
AK Sharing Timing	*ID*	*avg*	*prj succ rho*	*prj size rho*
Whenever needed to solve problems	s_akh_problems	3.48	0.153	−0.035
At the end of the project	s_akh_prjend	3.41	0.027	0.002
When colleagues ask me to do so	s_akh_collask	3.39	0.048	−0.066
When management ask me to do so	s_akh_mgtask	2.59	0.177	−0.052
Whenever I have time	s_akh_freetime	2.57	−0.025	0.065
In the evening	s_akh_evening	2.53	0.012	−0.008
Continuously during the project	s_akh_prjcnt	2.34	.205∗	−0.133
AK Sharing Challenges	*ID*	*avg*	*prj succ rho*	*prj size rho*
Difficulty to achieve common understanding of requirements	s_chl_requnders	3.82	−0.146	0.055
Difficulty to achieve appropriate participation from relevant stakeholders	s_chl_stkhpart	3.66	−0.165	0.017
Diversity in customer culture and business	s_chl_custdiv	3.61	−0.102	0.051
Poor quality of information	s_chl_infqual	3.42	−0.11	0.071
Lack of information	s_chl_inflack	3.31	−0.086	0.12
Inconsistency in information obtained from different sources	s_chl_infincons	3.26	−0.114	0.088
Lack of time	s_chl_time	3.25	0.06	−0.017
Delays in delivery	s_chl_delays	3.24	−0.167	0.194
Difficulty of obtaining the appropriate skills within the project	s_chl_skills	3.24	−0.115	0.11
Conflicts and differences of opinion	s_chl_conflict	3.19	−.214∗	0.156
Difficulty to organise effective meetings	s_chl_effmeet	3.09	−0.153	0.17
Lack of informal communication	s_chl_lackinformal	3.01	−0.204	.226∗
Inaccessibility of technical facilities	s_chl_tinacc	2.99	−0.183	.272∗∗
Growing and shrinking of project population	s_chl_growshrink	2.82	−0.117	.317∗∗
Lack of trust between the project locations	s_chl_sitetrust	2.77	−.272∗∗	.244∗
Project personnel turnover	s_chl_persto	2.67	−0.116	.270∗∗
No appreciation from (project or competence) management	s_chl_mgtappr	2.60	−0.125	.241∗
No willingness to share knowledge	s_chl_nowill	2.39	−.224∗	.245∗

*Correlation is significant at the 0.05 level (two-tailed).
*Correlation is significant at the 0.01 level (two-tailed).

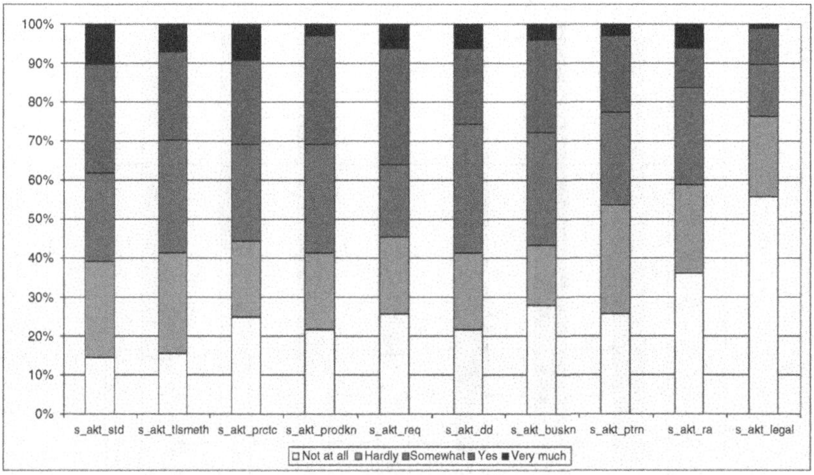

Fig. 13.1 Architectural Knowledge types

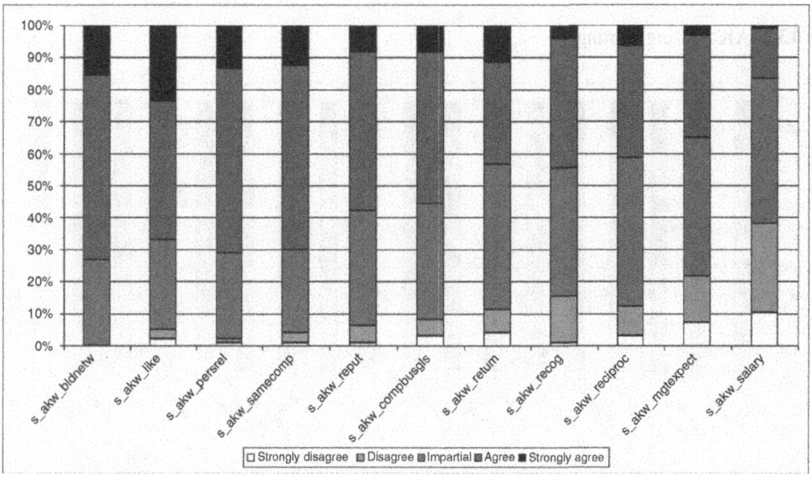

Fig. 13.2 AK Sharing motivation

The only motivation that more architects disagree with (38%) than agree with (17%) is salary. A related finding is the unpopularity of management expectation as a motivator: 65% of respondents are at most impartial to this motivator.

AK Sharing Timing When did you share architectural knowledge in your latest assignment?

The distribution of the response values is visualized in Fig. 13.3. By far the most popular times to share AK are when problems occur, at the end of projects and when asked by colleagues (other than managers); these three timings are all used often or very often by over 50% of the architects. Almost 30% of architects indicate

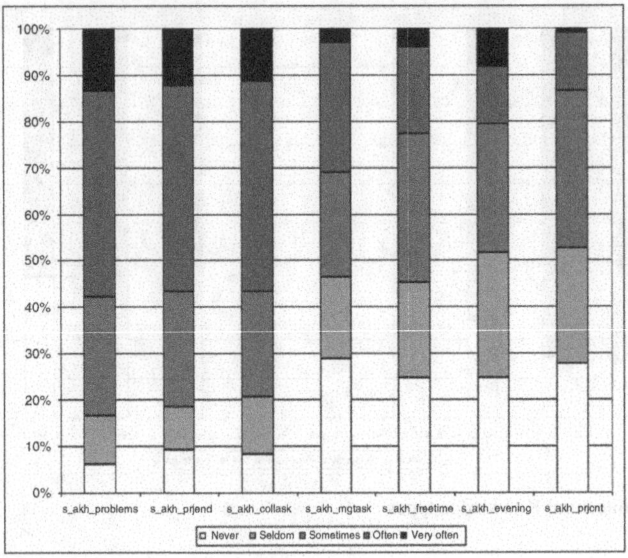

Fig. 13.3 AK Sharing Timing

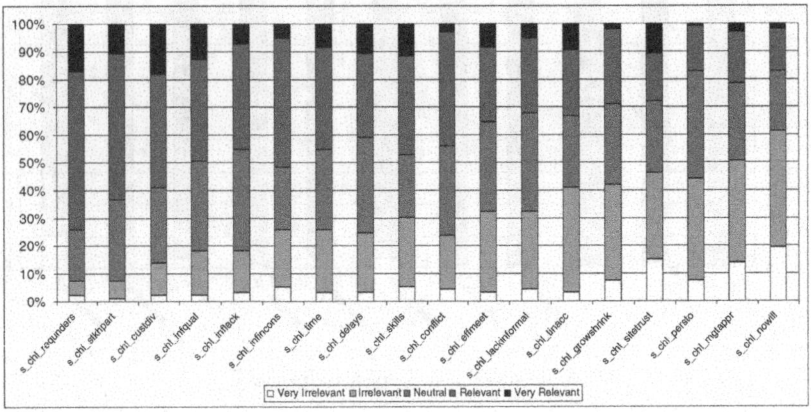

Fig. 13.4 AK Sharing Challenges

they never share AK "when management asks me to do so". We assume this is because in those cases management does not ask – an assumption supported by the observation that there is no lack of willingness to share (see Fig. 13.4). This fortifies our previous observation about management expectation as a motivator.

AK Sharing Challenges *What challenges in architectural knowledge sharing did you experience in your latest assignment?*

The distribution of the response values is visualized in Fig. 13.4. The ordering of the challenges by average response value in Table 13.1 allows an interesting categorization of challenges with descending response values:

s_chl_requnders, s_chl_stkhpart, s_chl_custdiv are all related to communication issues on group level (as opposed to personal level); this is the category of challenges that most architects consider relevant in their latest projects

s_chl_infqual, s_chl_inflack, s_chl_infincons are about issues with quality or absence of codified AK; this is the second most commonly relevant category of challenges

s_chl_time, s_chl_delays are related to planning; this is the third most commonly relevant category of challenges

other challenges all less commonly relevant than the three categories mentioned above, are related to obtaining resources, interpersonal issues, teaming, continuity and management

In discussions about challenges in knowledge sharing, "knowledge is power" [27] is often cited as a reason for professionals not to want to share knowledge. In our survey however, *lack of willingness to share knowledge* emerges as the least relevant challenge, which the majority of architects find irrelevant, and which only 18% find relevant. The next least relevant challenge is *lack of management appreciation*, which only 21% find relevant. The unpopularity of this response suggests that, even though we have seen in Sect. 13.3.1 that both salary and management expectations are at the bottom of the list of reasons to share AK, architects are not actively discouraged by their management's apparent disinterest. Seeing that 65% of respondents are at most impartial to management as a motivator (Fig. 13.2) and almost 80% are at most impartial to management as a challenge (Fig. 13.4), one might conclude that *architects do not see management as an important factor in Architectural Knowledge Sharing*. As we will see later on, they might be wrong about this.

13.3.2 AK Practices in Context

In this section, we analyze the relationship between the AK practices and challenges and their project context, by examining significant correlations between the AK-related responses and some of the context-related questions. The two context factors analyzed here are project success and project size.

The first context factor analyzed is project success, as perceived by the architects. Perceived project success[3] is determined by asking the architects how they rated seven aspects of project success on a five-point Likert scale from Poor to Excellent. The aspects they rated are: Sticking to budget, Delivery in time, Client satisfaction, Management support, Personnel turnover, Solution quality and Team satisfaction. The combined answers of these seven aspects were subsequently averaged to obtain a quantification of overall project success per case. Cronbach's alpha test for internal consistency [84] was used to verify that these seven responses measure the same construct of success ($alpha = 0.82$).

[3] We use the terms "project success" and "perceived project success" interchangeably, always meaning the success as perceived by the architects and reported in the survey

The second context factor analyzed is project size. Projects were assigned an exponential size category between 1 and 5, based on the number of project members: 10 or less became category 1, 11–30 category 2, 31–100 category 3, 101–300 category 4, and over 300 category 5.

Table 13.1 shows the Spearman's rho correlations between project success and the AK practice related responses in column *prj succ rho*. Correlations between project size category and the AK practice related responses are in column *prj size rho*.

Correlations with a positive or negative slope of over 0.2 and a significance level of under .05 (indicated by one or two asterisks) are considered significant and discussed here. In the discussion of the correlations, some speculation is presented as to the underlying mechanisms, based on the experience of the practicing architects among the authors.

Cause and Effect. One of the objectives of this survey was to gain insight into mechanisms around architectural knowledge sharing in projects. In other words, we were looking for ways in which Architectural Knowledge Sharing impacts projects and vice versa – questions of cause and effect.

When analyzing correlations like the ones found in this survey, the question of causality between the correlated measurements deserves careful consideration. The mere presence of a correlation by itself does not imply a causal relationship. In order to determine potential causality, we resorted to three additional means: reasoning, literature and the experience of two of the authors as practicing architects in ABC.

The four categories of measurements we are correlating here are:

AKS Practices. The responses related to the type, motivation and timing of architectural knowledge sharing

AKS Challenges. The responses to the question: *"What challenges in architectural knowledge sharing did you experience in your latest assignment?"*

Project Success. The perceived success of the respondents' latest project

Project Size. The size of the respondents' latest project (category based on number of project members)

There are six possible correlations between these four categories. We are not analyzing correlations between AKS Practices and Challenges. Figure 13.5 visualizes potential causality arrows for the five remaining possible correlations. In this figure and Fig. 13.8, a causality arrow from A to B symbolizes that A has impact on B, implying that making changes to A would cause related changes in B. The arrows are based on the following reasoning:

Project Size ↔ Project Success. Project size is well known to influence project success in many ways, both in literature [54, 168] and experience, so the primary arrow of causality is from Size to Success

Project Size ↔ AKS Practices. Experience indicates that mechanisms determining project size are only marginally impacted by architectural knowledge sharing; on the other hand, project size determines factors like organizational and physical distance between project members, which are obvious factors in AKS. We

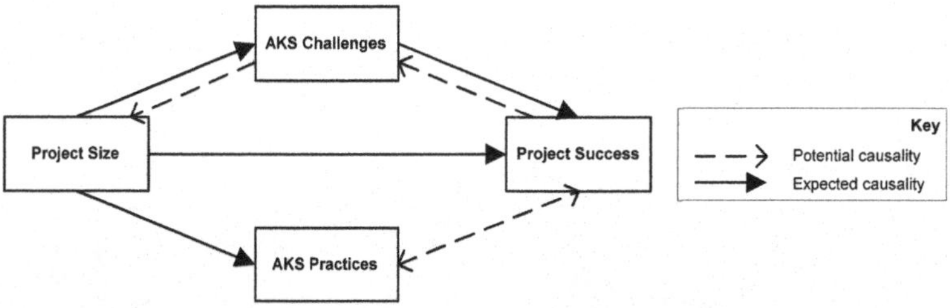

Fig. 13.5 Causality as deduced from reasoning, literature and experience

conclude that any correlation found means that project size impacts AKS, and not the other way around.

Project Size ↔ AKS Challenges. Like with AKS Practices, project size causes AKS challenges. There are some challenges that may in time conversely influence project size: for example, difficulty to obtain the appropriate skills may either lead to a smaller project because there is no staff available, or to a larger project because the lower skill level is compensated by adding more staff. We conclude that there is a primary causal arrow from project size to AKS challenges, and a potential secondary reverse arrow.

Project Success ↔ AKS Practices. Examples of causality in both directions are experienced: e.g., a more successful project may lead to a better atmosphere causing more knowledge to be exchanged, or conversely more knowledge sharing may contribute to a more successful project. We conclude that we cannot a priori attach causality direction to correlations found between project success and AKS practices.

Project Success ↔ AKS Challenges. The word *challenge* is used here as a synonym for *obstacle*, which can be defined as *something that makes achieving one's objectives more difficult*. Since the objective here is a successful project, the primary arrow of causality is by definition from Challenge to Success. There is also a possibility of reverse causality here: challenges may be exacerbated or caused by (lack of) project success, e.g. the atmosphere in an unsuccessful project may lead to lack of trust.

The causality arrows between the four categories of measurements as visualized in Fig. 13.5 will be elaborated at the end of this section, based on correlations measured.

Correlation with project success. We now discuss the correlations between architectural practices and challenges and project success. In column 4 of Table 13.1, we find eight significant correlations. Summarizing, in more successful projects, architects tend to:

- Be less motivated to share AK for interpersonal relationship reasons, but are more motivated by their management's expectations
- Face less challenges related to interpersonal relationships

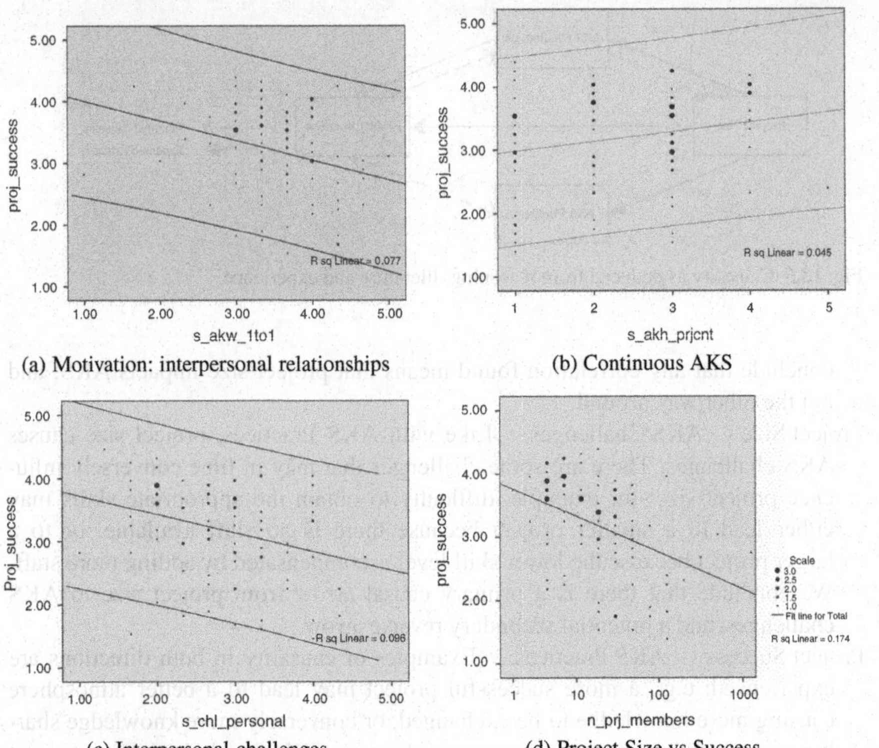

(a) Motivation: interpersonal relationships (b) Continuous AKS

(c) Interpersonal challenges (d) Project Size vs Success

Fig. 13.6 Various AKS parameters plotted against project success

We find no correlation between project success and the type of the Architectural Knowledge shared.

Motivation: s_akw_persrel, s_akw_return, s_akw_reciproc Remarkably, all motivation responses that are related to one-to-one relationships between colleagues show a significant negative correlation with project success. Figure 13.6a visualizes this relationship, showing a clearly downward slanting cluster: the x-axis represents the individual architects' average mark given to these three responses.[4] There are many possible explanations, but in view of our findings about AK sharing challenges a few items further down, the most plausible one appears to be related to trust. Problems in projects tend to reduce trust, which might cause architects to place more value on interpersonal motives.

Motivation: s_akw_mgtexpect Even though management expectations are considered one of the least important motivations for sharing AK by the architects, it is the only motivation that has a positive correlation with project success. The explanation may also be related to trust levels: architects working on successful

[4] The lines in the scatter plots in this section represent linear regression fit lines and their 95% confidence interval.

projects have more confidence in their management, and hence are more inspired or motivated by them.

Timing: s_akh_prjcnt The only AK sharing timing response that has a correlation with project success is continuous AK sharing during the project. However, visual inspection of Fig. 13.6b suggests that this is a spurious effect.

Challenges: s_chl_conflict, s_chl_sitetrust and s_chl_nowill Since there is by definition a causality between AKS challenges and project success, we *expect* to find correlations. Remarkably, only three challenges are significantly correlated with project success. These three challenges, all with a very clear negative correlation, have in common that they are related to interpersonal relationships and emotion: conflicts, trust and willingness to share AK. We have plotted the correlation between project success and the individual architects' average mark given to these three responses related to interpersonal challenges in Fig. 13.6c. As for the other challenges, finding *no* correlation indicates one of two things: either the challenge is so insignificant that the correlation is too small to be measured in a sample this size, or the challenge is somehow neutralized.

From these correlations, we can draw the following conclusion: the only significant AKS challenges that are not neutralized in projects are those related to emotion and interpersonal relationships. In less successful projects, there is less trust and willingness to share AK, and more conflict. This appears not to affect the type of AK shared. It does, however, have a significant effect on architects' motivation to share architectural knowledge: in more successful projects, they are more motivated by management and less by interpersonal relationships between colleagues.

Correlation with project size. We proceed to discuss the correlations between architectural practices and challenges and project size, as documented in column 5 of Table 13.1. We find nine significant correlations. Summarizing, in larger projects, architects tend to:

- Face significantly more challenges of multiple kinds
- Share more knowledge about tools and methods, but less about products and vendors

Project size has no effect on AK sharing motivation or timing.

s_akt_tlsmeth Architects in larger projects share slightly more information related to tools and methods than architects in smaller projects. This is likely due to the fact that there are simply more developers to educate on tools and methods.

s_akt_prodkn Architects in some smaller projects tend to share more knowledge related to products and vendors. We suspect that this is due to the fact that in larger projects, decisions about products and vendors are often made on a higher (management) level, whereas smaller project architects are more likely to be involved in these decisions, and hence have to share more knowledge related to products and vendors.

AKS challenges Table 13.1 shows that out of the 18 types of challenges surveyed, seven are significantly correlated to project size. We have also calculated the aggregated AKS challenge level as the average of each architect's challenge-related

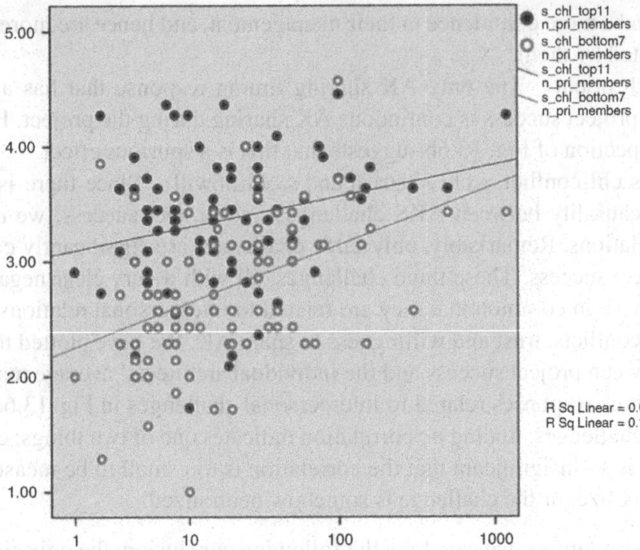

Fig. 13.7 AKS Challenges versus project size

responses. It turns out this aggregated AKS challenge level is correlated to project size with a correlation coefficient of 0.356 at a 0.001 significance level. The seven challenges at the bottom of Table 13.1 are the only ones that are also individually correlated to project size. Apparently, some challenges are universal, and others are considered less relevant in smaller projects, bringing down their average response value. We have illustrated this by plotting the average response values of both the seven least commonly relevant and the 11 most commonly relevant challenges against project size in Fig. 13.7. The figure confirms that there is indeed a clear upward trend, and that it is steeper for the less commonly relevant challenges.

Based on the fact that larger projects are likely to include more distinct departments or locations, and the well-known issue of tension between departments, we would expect larger projects to suffer more from emotion-related challenges. We do indeed find correlations between project size and lack of both willingness (0.245) and trust (0.244), but no significant correlation with the challenge of conflicts and differences of opinion.

13.3.3 Refined Model of Causality

We now use the correlations observed in Sect. 13.3.2 to obtain a more detailed picture of causality. Figure 13.8 shows the causality arrows between the four categories of measurements as visualized in Fig. 13.5, but the AKS category boxes have

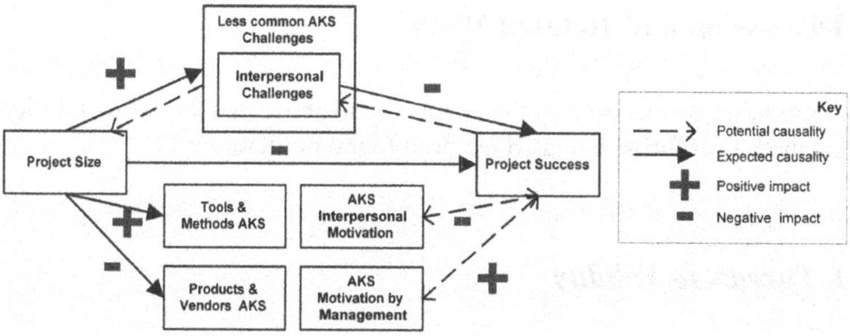

Fig. 13.8 Causality as observed

been replaced with more specific subcategories corresponding to the responses that showed correlations. Additional symbols show whether correlations are positive or negative. Specifically, we have:

- Replaced the generic box *AKS Challenges* with a box *Less common AKS Challenges*, representing the seven least common AKS challenges that have significant positive correlations with project size.
- Created a box *Interpersonal challenges* inside the *Less common AKS Challenges* box, representing the three challenges related to willingness, trust and conflict that are negatively correlated with project success.
- Replaced the generic *AKS Practices* box with four specific boxes representing the practices that we have found to be correlated with either project size or project success.
- Added + and − symbols to the causality arrows representing the sign of the observed correlations.

There is one correlation that we had not discussed yet: that between project size and perceived project success. Figure 13.6d displays a very clear relationship between project size and perceived project success. Perceived project success and the logarithmic project size category described above show a negative Spearman's rho correlation coefficient of −0.449, with a significance of 0.000. This is in line with results found by [168], and conversely provides some additional validation that our input data behave according to known properties of IT projects. Brooks [54] gives a clear explanation of one of the mechanisms that cause this correlation. Surprisingly, a more recent survey [111] does not find this correlation.

Figure 13.8 summarizes in one picture the combined mechanisms in the interplay between AKS and project size and success. We see how project size impacts some challenges, and which challenges impact project success. We also see that project size impacts the type of knowledge shared, and we observe a relationship between AKS motivation and project success, a relationship with an as yet undetermined arrow of causality.

13.4 Discussion and Related Work

In this section, we further discuss the results found above and threats to validity, and we relate them to additional related material found in literature.

13.4.1 Threats to Validity

These results are based on a survey of architects in one IT services company in one country. This limitation is somewhat softened by the fact that 64% of respondents work mostly at customers' sites, but the results are certainly influenced by cultural aspects of both the ABC company and the Netherlands location. It would be very interesting to repeat the survey in other companies and locations.

The ordering of the responses in Table 13.1 and the response value distribution bar charts is based on average response values. The meaning of the average number itself is not clear, since the Likert-scale is not equidistant. An alternative ordering quantity would be the percentile responses of e.g. the two most positive Likert values. This would have the advantage of being able to say exactly what the ordering quantity means, but the disadvantage of ignoring the information inherent in the detailed distribution of responses. Visual inspection of the bar charts shows that, with the exception of Fig. 13.1, the order of the responses would not be that much different, specifically in those cases where we have based reasoning on the response ordering. As an example: the "seven least commonly relevant challenges" in Fig. 13.4 that we have discussed above would also be the seven bottom-most challenges if ordered by percentile of respondents answering "Relevant" or "Very Relevant".

A final threat is caused by our approach of doing multiple statistical tests, and deriving our model from significant statistical results found in those tests. This approach implies a risk of introducing spurious statistical results in the model. We have mitigated this risk by using reasoning, experience and literature, but it would be interesting to further validate the model by using it to predict results in other surveys.

13.4.2 Project Success in Literature

Project success has long been an active research topic. Traditionally, project success is defined in terms of meeting time, cost and quality objectives [251]. These correspond to the first three of the seven project success criteria used in our survey. More recently, it has been observed that projects can be successful in ways that cannot be measured by these traditional criteria. Based on these insights, Baccarini et al. [25] have constructed a conceptual framework for project success. Baccarini's framework distinguishes between *Project Management Success*, which includes the three traditional criteria of time, cost and process quality, and *Product Success*, which adds criteria related to the product in a more strategic way, involving the product's goal and purpose and product satisfaction. In Baccarini's framework, our criteria would all fall in the Project Management Success category, with the exception of Solution Quality. Team Satisfaction in Baccarini's framework can relate to both project and product; in our experience, this is especially true for architects, who derive a large part of their job satisfaction from product quality. This observation is confirmed by research by Linberg et al. [210] and more recently by Procaccino et al. [257], who observe that developers' perception of project success often deviates significantly from the traditional criteria. Developers (including architects) tend to judge success by criteria that extend beyond the project, sometimes even to the extent that even canceled projects can be successful in their eyes.

13.4.3 Motivation and Emotion in Architectural Knowledge Sharing

An interesting finding about motivation in this survey is the observed shift in motivation source from colleagues to management in more successful projects. Could there be an either/or effect, in the sense that the 1-on-1 motivation by colleagues and motivation by management are somehow mutually exclusive? In that case, one would expect a negative correlation between these two motivation sources, which we did not measure (Spearman's rho = 0.107 with a two-tailed significance of 0.295). We conclude that the mechanisms causing these shifts are independent. The finding does, however, cause one to wonder about architects' apparent indifference to management expectations as either a motivator or a challenge. The well-known Chaos Reports [305] already showed empirical evidence for management attention being a key project success factor.

Markus already identified the importance of being aware of one's motivation long before the term *architect* was used in the context of system design: "Self-examination of interests, motives, payoffs, and power bases will lend much to the implementor's ability to understand other people's reactions to the systems the implementor is designing..." [219]. In literature, motivation is reported to have the single largest impact on developer productivity[42, 221]. Moreover, in system development, the architecture represents the system's earliest design decisions with the highest impact on success [34]. Combining these facts, it is only to be expected that the motivation to share Architectural Knowledge is correlated with project success. Our results not only point to the importance of motivation and its source, but also shed some light on the mechanisms through which motivation and emotion impact project success through Architecture Knowledge management.

Finally, some words on the topic of *emotion*, a term that we introduced in Sect. 13.3.2 as the common element between the three only challenges that have a significant negative correlation with project success: *Conflicts and differences of opinion*, *Lack of trust between the project locations* and *No willingness to share knowledge*. During the analysis, we often wondered how it was possible that we did not find any significant correlation between the *other* challenges in AKS and Project Success. Consider, for example, the most commonly encountered challenge: *Difficulty to achieve common understanding of requirements*. How can a project be successful without common understanding of requirements? As stated above, the only plausible explanation is that all of these other challenges are apparently neutralized. With neutralize we mean that if these challenges occur, there are other factors that prevent them from having a significant impact on project success. In the case of our example, these could be compensating activities to promote the common understanding of requirements, such as client meetings. In the end, the only challenges that are not neutralized are those related to lack of trust, willingness, conflicts and differences of opinion: all issues in interpersonal relationships that have a strong negative emotional connotation. Apparently, it is harder for architects to neutralize challenges when such negative emotions are involved. This is a phenomenon that the practicing architects among the authors have often observed in real life, and it should be no surprise, given that architects are human beings. The significant finding here is that these emotional challenges are not neutralized where all other challenges are, and hence they merit extra attention, leading to the warning in our title: *Beware of Emotions*

We conclude:

FOR ARCHITECTS, TO UNDERSTAND THEIR MOTIVATION AND DEAL WITH EMOTIONS ARE CRUCIAL KNOWLEDGE SHARING SKILLS.

13.5 Summary

We set out on this survey with two goals, which were both achieved: to establish the current state of architectural knowledge sharing in the ABC company and its customers, and to gain insight into the mechanisms around architectural knowledge sharing in projects. In order to gain this insight, we looked at architects' responses to four questions about AK sharing, and the correlations between these responses and their latest projects' success and size, and we reasoned about impact mechanisms and causality.

The analysis revealed the following mechanisms:

- Architects face many challenges sharing architectural knowledge in projects
- These challenges are more numerous and diverse in larger projects than in smaller ones.
- The most common of these challenges are related to group level communication issues, the quality of codified knowledge and planning issues.
- However, these common challenges are not correlated with project success, so apparently they are generally neutralized somehow.
- The only challenges that *are* correlated with project success are the ones related to interpersonal relationships: conflicts, trust and willingness to share knowledge.

- Architects' motivation to share knowledge is more personal in less successful projects.
- Architects do not see management as an important factor in Architectural Knowledge Sharing, but those architects that are motivated by management tend to work in more successful projects.

Our final conclusion is that *dealing with emotions* is a crucial factor in how architectural knowledge sharing leads to successful projects. It is very important for architects to understand their motivation, and they should be careful when dealing with emotions when sharing knowledge.

Acknowledgements This research has been partially sponsored by the Dutch Joint Academic and Commercial Quality Research and Development (Jacquard) program on Software Engineering Research via contract 638.001.406 GRIFFIN: a GRId For inFormatIoN about architectural knowledge.

References

1. Ackerman, M.S., Halverson, C.A.: Reexamining organizational memory. Comm. ACM **43**(1), 59–64 (2000)
2. Akerman, A., Tyree, J.: Using ontology to support development of software architecture. IBM Syst. J. **45**(4), 813–825 (2006)
3. Al-Naeem, T., Gorton, I., Babar, M.A., Rabhi, F.A., Benatallah, B.: A quality-driven systematic approach for architecting distributed software applications. In: Proceedings 27th International Conference on Software Engineering (ICSE), pp. 244–253. St. Louis, MO (2005)
4. Aldrich, J.: Using types to enforce architectural structure. In: Seventh Working IEEE/IFIP Conference on Software Architecture (WICSA 2008), pp. 211–220. IEEE (2008)
5. Aleksovski, Z.: Using background knowledge in ontology matching. Ph.D. thesis, VU University Amsterdam (2008)
6. Aleman-Meza, B., Halaschek, C., Budak Arpinar, I.: Collective knowledge composition in a peer-to-peer network: A survey for peer-to-peer applications. In: Rivero, L.C., Doorn, J.H., Ferraggine, V.E. (eds.) Encyclopedia of Database Technologies and Applications, pp. 74–77. Idea Group (2005)
7. Ali-Babar, M., de Boer, R.C., Dingsøyr, T., Farenhorst, R.: Architectural knowledge management strategies: Approaches in research and industry. In: 2nd Workshop on Sharing and Reusing Architectural Knowledge – Architecture, Rationale, and Design Intent (SHARK/ADI '07). ACM, Minneapolis, MN, USA (2007)
8. Ali-Babar, M., Gorton, I.: A tool for managing software architecture knowledge. In: 2nd Workshop on Sharing and Reusing architectural Knowledge – Architecture, Rationale, and Design Intent (SHARK/ADI). ACM, Minneapolis, MN, USA (2007)
9. Ali-Babar, M., Gorton, I., Jeffery, R.: Capturing and using software architecture knowledge for architecture-based software development. In: 5th International Conference on Quality Software. IEEE Computer Press, Melbourne, Australia (2005)
10. Ali-Babar, M., Gorton, I., Kitchenham, B.: A framework for supporting architecture knowledge and rationale management. In: Dutoit, A., McCall, R., Mistrìk, I., Paech, B. (eds.) Rationale Management in Software Engineering, pp. 237–254. Springer, Heidelberg (2006)
11. Ali-Babar, M., Kitchenham, B., Maheshwari, P., Jeffery, R.: Mining patterns for improving architecting activities - a research program and preliminary assessment. In: Proceedings of the 9th International Conference on Empirical Assessment in Software Engineering. Keele, UK (2005)
12. Ali-Babar, M., Northway, A., Gorton, I., Heuer, P., Nguyen, T.: Introducing tool support for managing architectural knowledge: An experience report. In: Proceedings of the 15th IEEE International Conference on Engineering of Computer-Based Systems (ECBS), pp. 105–113. IEEE Computer Society (2008)

13. Ali-Babar, M., Zhu, L., Jeffery, R.: A Framework for classifying and comparing software architecture evaluation methods. In: Proceedings of the 15th Australian Software Engineering Conference, pp. 309–319. Melbourne, Australia, IEEE Computer Society (2004)
14. Allmann, C., Winkler, L., Kölzow, T.: The requirements engineering gap in the OEM-supplier relationship. J. Univers. Knowl. Manag. **1**(2), 103–111 (2006)
15. America, P., Rommes, E., Obbink, H.: Multi-View Variation Modeling for Scenario Analysis. Springer, Heidelberg (2003)
16. Androutsellis-Theotokis, S., Spinellis, D.: A survey of peer-to-peer content distribution technologies. ACM Comput. Surv. **36**(4), 335–371 (2004)
17. Ankolekar, A., Krötzsch, M., Tran, T., Vrandečić, D.: The two cultures: Mashing up web 2.0 and the semantic web. Web Semant. Sci. Serv. Agents World Wide Web **6**(1), 70–75 (2008)
18. Antoniou, G., van Harmelen, F.: A Semantic Web Primer. MIT, Cambridge (2004)
19. Argyris, C., Schön, D.A.: Organizational learning II: Theory, method and practise. Organization Development Series. Addison Wesley, Boston MA (1996)
20. Arsanjani, A.: Service-Oriented Modeling and Architecture. IBM developerWorks (2004)
21. Arumugam, M., Sheth, A., Arpinar, I.B.: Towards peer-to-peer semantic web: A distributed environment for sharing semantic knowledge on the web. In: International World Wide Web Conference (WWW) (2002)
22. Aurum, A., Jeffery, R., Wohlin, C., Handzic, M.: Managing Software Engineering Knowledge. Springer, Berlin (2003)
23. Avgeriou, P., Kruchten, P., Lago, P., Grisham, P., Perry, D.: Architectural knowledge and rationale - Issues, trends, challenges. ACM SIGSOFT Software Eng. Notes **32**, 41–46 (2007)
24. Babu, T.L., Seetha Ramaiah, M., Prabhakar, T.V., Rambabu, D.A.: ArchVoc – Towards an ontology for software architecture. In: Second Workshop on SHAring and Reusing Architectural Knowledge – Architecture, Rationale, and Design Intent (SHARK/ADI). ACM (2007)
25. Baccarini, D.: The logical framework method for defining project success. Proj. Manag. J. **30**, 25–32 (1999)
26. Bachmann, F., Merson, P.: Experience using the web-based tool wiki for architecture documentation. Tech. Rep. SEI-2005-TN-041, Carnegie Mellon University (2005)
27. Bacon, S.F.: Religious Meditations (1597)
28. Bales, D., Greenwald, R., Stackowiak, R.: Oracle Application Server 10g Essentials. O'Reilly, California (2004)
29. Barbacci, M.R., Ellison, R., Lattanze, A.J., Stafford, J.A., Weinstock, C.B., Wood, W.G.: Quality Attribute Workshops (QAWs). Tech. Rep. CMU/SEI-2003-TR-016, SEI, Carnegie Mellon University, USA. (2003)
30. Bartsch-Spörl, B.: Transfer of experience – issues beyond tool building. In: Workshop on Learning Software Organizations, pp. 3–8. Fraunhofer Publica, Kaiserslautern, Germany (1999)
31. Basili, V., Rombach, H.: The TAME project: Towards improvement-oriented software environments. IEEE Trans. Software Eng. **14**(6), 758–773 (1988)
32. Basili, V.R., Caldiera, G.: Improving software quality reusing knowledge and experience. Sloan Manag. Rev. **37**(1), 55–64 (1995)
33. Basili, V.R., Caldiera, G., Rombach, H.D.: The experience factory. In: Marciniak, J.J. (ed.) Encyclopedia of Software Engineering, vol. 1, pp. 469–476. Wiley, New York (1994)
34. Bass, L., Clements, P., Kazman, R.: Software Architecture in Practice, 2nd edn. Addison Wesley, MA (2003)
35. Bass, L., Kazman, R.: Architecture-Based Development. Tech. Rep. CMU/SEI-99-TR-007, Software Engineering Institute (SEI), Carnegie Mellon University, Pittsburgh, USA (1999)
36. Batini, C., Ceri, S., Navathe, S.B., Navathe, S.: Conceptual Database Design: An Entity-Relationship Approach. Addison-Wesley, MA (1991)
37. Bechhofer, S., van Harmelen, F., Hendler, J., Horrocks, I., McGuinness, D., Patel-Schneider, P., Stein, L.: Web ontology language (OWL) reference. W3C Recommendation. http://www.w3.org/TR/2004/REC-owl-ref-20040210/ (2004)

38. Beck, K.: Extreme Programming Explained: Embrace Change. Addison-Wesley, Boston (2000)
39. Bengtsson, P., Lassing, N., Bosch, J., van Vliet, H.: Architecture-level modifiability analysis (ALMA). J. Syst. Software **69**(1–2), 129–147 (2004)
40. Bittner, K., Spence, I.: Use Case Modeling. Addison-Wesley, Boston MA (2002)
41. Bjørnsson, F.O., Dingsøyr, T.: Knowledge management in software engineering: A systematic review of studied concepts and research methods used. Inform. Software Tech. **50**(11), 1055–1168 (2008)
42. Boehm, B.: Software Engineering Economics. Prentice-Hall, Englewood Cliffs NJ (1981)
43. de Boer, R.C., Farenhorst, R.: In search of architectural knowledge. In: 3rd Workshop on Sharing and Reusing architectural Knowledge (SHARK). Leipzig, Germany (2008)
44. de Boer, R.C., Farenhorst, R., Lago, P., van Vliet, H., Clerc, V., Jansen, A.: Architectural knowledge: Getting to the core. In: Proceedings of the 3rd International Conference on the Quality of Software-Architectures (QoSA), pp. 197–214. Springer, Heidelberg, LNCS 4880 (2007)
45. de Boer, R.C., van Vliet, H.: Architecture knowledge discovery with latent semantic analysis: Constructing a reading guide for software product audits. J. Syst. Software **81**(9), 1456–1469 (2008)
46. de Boer, R.C., van Vliet, H.: On the similarity between architecture and requirements. J. Syst. Software **82**(3), 544–550 (2009)
47. Booch, G.: Handbook of Software Architecture. URL http://www.booch.com/architecture/index.jsp
48. Bosch, J.: Software architecture: The next step. In: Oquendo, F., Warboys, B., Morrison, R. (eds.) Software Architecture, First European Workshop (EWSA), pp. 194–199. Springer, Heidelberg, LNCS 3047 (2004)
49. Boussaidi, G.E., Mili, H.: A model-driven framework for representing and applying design patterns. In: 31st Annual International Computer Software and Applications Conference, pp. 97–100. IEEE (2007)
50. Bradbury, J.S., Cordy, J.R., Dingel, J., Wermelinger, M.: A survey of self-management in dynamic software architecture specifications. In: 1st ACM SIGSOFT Workshop on Self-Managed Systems, pp. 28–33. Newport Beach, California (2004)
51. Bratthall, L., Johansson, E., Regnell, B.: Is a design rationale vital when predicting change impact? - A controlled experiment on software architecture evolution. In: 2nd International Conference on Product Focused Software Process Improvement, pp. 126–139. Springer Verlag. Lecture Notes in Computer Science 1840 (2000)
52. van den Brink, P.: Social, Organization, and technological conditions that enable knowledge sharing. Ph.D. thesis, Technische Universiteit Delft (2003)
53. Broekstra, J., Kampman, A., van Harmelen, F.: Sesame: A generic architecture for storing and querying RDF and RDF schema. In: Proceedings of the 1st International Semantic Web Conference (ISWC), pp. 54–68 (2002)
54. Brooks, F.P.: The Mythical Man-Month. Addison-Wesley, Reading, MA (1975)
55. Brown, J.S., Duguid, P.: Organizational learning and communities-of-practise: Toward a unified view of working, learning and innovation. Organizat. Sci. **2**(1), 40–57 (1991)
56. de Bruin, H., van Vliet, H.: Quality-driven software architecture composition. J. Syst. Software **66**(3), 269–284 (2003)
57. de Bruin, H., van Vliet, H., Baida, Z.: documenting and analyzing a context-sensitive design space. In: Bosch, J., Gentleman, M., Hofmeister, C., Kuusela, J. (eds.) Software Architecture: System Design, Development and Maintenance, Proceedings 3rd Working IFIP/IEEE Conference on Software Architecture, pp. 127–141. Kluwer, Dordecht (2002)
58. Buckingham Shum, S., Hammond, N.: Argumentation-based design rationale: What use at what cost? Int. J. Hum. Comput. Stud. **40**(4), 603–652 (1994)
59. Burge, J.: Software engineering using design rationale. Ph.D. thesis, Worcester Polytechnic Institute. URL http://www.wpi.edu/Pubs/ETD/Available/etd-050205-085625/ (2005)
60. Burge, J., Brown, D.: An integrated approach for software design checking using rationale. In: Gero, J. (ed.) Design Computing and Cognition, pp. 557–576. Kluwer, Dordecht (2004)

61. Burge, J., Brown, D.: Rationale-based support for software maintenance. In: Dutoit, A., McCall, R., Mistrìk, I., Paech, B. (eds.) Rationale Management in Software Engineering, pp. 273–296. Springer, Heidelberg (2006)
62. Burge, J., Brown, D.: SEURAT: Integrated rationale management. In: Proceedings of the 30th International Conference on Software Engineering (ICSE), pp. 835–838. ACM (2008)
63. Burge, J., Brown, D.: Software engineering using rationale. J. Syst. Software **81**(3), 395–413 (2008)
64. Buschmann, F., Meunier, R., Rohnert, H., Sommerlad, P.: Pattern-Oriented Software Architecture: A System of Patterns. Wiley, New York (1996)
65. Buxton, J.N., Randell, B.: Software engineering techniques: Report of a Conference sponsored by the NATO Science Committee, Rome, Italy, 27–31 October 1969. NATO, Scientific Affairs Division, Brussels (1970)
66. Capilla, R., Nava, F., Dueñas, J.C.: Modeling and documenting the evolution of architectural design decisions. In: 2nd Workshop on Sharing and Reusing architectural Knowledge – Architecture, rationale, and Design Intent (SHARK/ADI), p. 9. ACM (2007)
67. Capilla, R., Nava, F., Pérez, S., Dueñas, J.C.: A web-based tool for managing architectural design decisions. In: 1st ACM Workshop on Sharing Architectural Knowledge (SHARK). Torino, Italy, ACM (2006)
68. Capiluppi, A., Lago, P., Morisio, M.: Characterizing the oss process. In: 2nd Workshop on Open Source Software engineering (2002)
69. Chowdhury, F.: Practice of team based management. http://www.bdresearchers.org/Article/PracticeofTeamBasedManagement (2008)
70. Clarke, R.: Web 2.0 as syndication. J. Theor. Appl. Electron. Commerce Res. **3**(2), 30–43 (2008)
71. Clements, P., Bachmann, F., Bass, L., Garlan, D., Ivers, J., Little, R., Nord, R., Stafford, J.: Documenting Software Architectures : Views and Beyond, 1st edn. Addison Wesley, Boston MA (2002)
72. Clements, P., Kazman, R., Klein, M.: Evaluating Software Architectures: Methods and Case Studies. Addison-Wesley, MA (2001)
73. Clements, P., Kazman, R., Klein, M., Devesh, D., Reddy, S., Verma, P.: The duties, skills, and knowledge of software architects. In: 6th Working IEEE/IFIP Conference on Software Architecture (WICSA), p. 20. IEEE Computer Society, Mumbai, India (2007)
74. Clements, P., Northrop, L.: Software Product Lines: Practice and Patterns. Addison-Wesley, Boston (2002)
75. Clerc, V.: Towards architectural knowledge management practices for global software development. In: 3rd Workshop on Sharing and Reusing Architectural Knowledge (SHARK), ICSE 2008. ACM (2008)
76. Clerc, V., Lago, P., van Vliet, H.: Assessing a multi-site development organization for architectural compliance. In: Proceedings of the 6th Working IEEE/IFIP Conference on Software Architecture. IEEE Computer Society (2007)
77. Clerc, V., Lago, P., van Vliet, H.: Global software development: Are architectural rules the answer? In: Proceedings of the 2nd IEEE International Conference on Global Software Engineering (ICGSE 2007), pp. 225–234. IEEE Computer Society (2007)
78. Clerc, V., Lago, P., van Vliet, H.: The architect's mindset. In: Proceedings of the 3rd International Conference on the Quality of Software-Architectures (QoSA). Springer, Heidelberg, LNCS 4880 (2007)
79. Conklin, E., Burgess-Yakemovic, K.C.: A process-oriented approach to design rationale. In: Moran, T., Carroll, J. (eds.) Design Rationale: Concepts, Techniques and Use, chap. 14, pp. 393–427. Lawrence Erlbaum Associates (1996)
80. Cook, D. Cripps, P., Spaas, P.: An Introduction to the IBM Views and Viewpoints Framework for IT Systems. IBM developerWorks (2008)
81. Coplien, J.O., Harrison, N.B.: Organizational Patterns of Agile Software Development. Prentice Hall, Englewood Cliffs, NJ (2004)
82. Coplien, J.O., Schmidt, D.C.: Pattern Languages of Program Design. Addison Wesley, Boston MA (1995)

83. Coulouris, G., Dollimore, J., Kindberg, T.: Distributed Systems: Concepts and Design, 4th edn. Addison Wesley, Boston MA (2005)
84. Cronbach, L.J.: Coefficient alpha and the internal structure of tests. Psychometrika **16**(3), 297–334 (1951)
85. Cui, X., Sun, Y., Mei, H.: Towards automated solution synthesis and rationale capture in decision-centric architecture design. In: 7th Working IEEE/IFIP Conference on Software Architecture (WICSA '08), pp. 221–230 (2008)
86. Damian, D.: Stakeholders in global requirements engineering: Lessons learned from practice. IEEE Software **24**(2), 21–27 (2007)
87. Damian, D., Izquierdo, L., Singer, J., Kwan, I.: Awareness in the wild: Why communication breakdowns occur. In: 2nd International Conference on Global Software Engineering, pp. 81–90. IEEE Comput. Soc. (2007)
88. Davenport, T., Probst, G.: Knowledge Management Case Book – Best Practises. Publicis MCD, Germany (2000)
89. Davenport, T.H., Prusak, L.: Working Knowledge: How Organizations Manage What They Know. Harvard Business School Press, Cambridge, MA (1998)
90. Davies, J., Fensel, D., Van Harmelen, F., NetLibrary, I.: Towards the Semantic Web: Ontology-driven Knowledge Management. Wiley, New York (2003)
91. Decker, B., Ras, E., Rech, J., Jaubert, P., Rieth, M.: Wiki-based stakeholder participation in requirements engineering. IEEE Software **24**(2), 28–35 (2007)
92. Desouza, K., Awazu, Y., Baloh, P.: Managing Knowledge in Global Software Development Efforts: Issues and Practices. IEEE Software **23**(5), 30–37 (2006)
93. Desouza, K.C.: Barriers to effective use of knowledge management systems in software engineering. Comm. ACM **46**(1), 99–101 (2003)
94. Desouza, K.C., Evaristo, J.R.: Managing knowledge in distributed projects. Comm. ACM **47**(4), 87–91 (2004)
95. Dierkes, M., Berthoin Antal, A., Child, J., Nonaka, I.: Handbook of Organizational Learning and Knowledge. Oxford University Press, New York (2001)
96. Dingsøyr, T., Conradi, R.: A survey of case studies of the use of knowledge management in software engineering. Int. J. Software Eng. Knowl. Eng. **12**(4), 391–414 (2002)
97. Dingsøyr, T., Lago, P., van Vliet, H.: Assumptions promote Learning about Architectural Knowledge. In: von Wangenheim, C.G., Rocha, A.R. (eds.) 8th International Workshop on Learning Software Organizations, pp. 59–67. Rio de Janeiro, Brazil (2006)
98. Dingsøyr, T., Moe, N.B.: The impact of employee participation on the use of an electronic process guide: A longitudinal case study. IEEE Trans. Software Eng. **34**(2), 212–225 (2008)
99. Dingsøyr, T., Røyrvik, E.: An empirical study of an informal knowledge repository in a medium-sized software consulting company. In: Proceedings of the 25th International Conference on Software Engineering (ICSE25), pp. 84–92. IEEE Computer Society, Portland, Oregon, USA (2003)
100. Dingsøyr, T., Røyrvik, E., Djarraya, H.K.: Practical knowledge management tool use in a software consulting company. Comm. ACM **48**(12), 96–100 (2005)
101. Dobrica, L., Niemela, E.: A survey on software architecture analysis methods. IEEE Trans. Software Eng. **28**(7), 638–653 (2002)
102. Drucker, P.: Post-Capitalist Society. Butterworth Heinemann, Oxford (1993)
103. Dueñas, J.C., Capilla, R.: The decision view of software architecture. In: Morison, R., Oquendo, F. (eds.) 2nd European Workshop on Software Architecture. Pisa, Italy (2005)
104. Dutoit, A.H., Paech, B.: Rationale management in software engineering. In: Chang, S.K. (ed.) Handbook of Software Engineering and Knowledge Engineering, vol. 1. World Scientific Publishing, Singapore (2001)
105. Dybå, T.: Enabling software process improvement: An investigation on the importance of organizational issues. PhD thesis, Norwegian University of Science and Technology (2001)
106. Dybå, T., Dingsøyr, T.: Empirical studies of agile software development: A systematic review. Inform. Software Tech. **50**(9), 833–859 (2008)
107. Earl, M.: Knowledge management strategies: Towards a taxonomy. J. Manag. Inform. Syst. **18**(1) (2001)

108. Easterby-Smith, M., Lyles, M.A.: The Blackwell handbook of organizational learning and knowledge management. Blackwell Publishing, Oxford, UK (2003)
109. Ebert, C., Man, J.D.: Effectively utilizing project, product and process knowledge. Inform. Software Tech. **50**(6), 579–594 (2008)
110. Ehrig, M., Tempich, C., Broekstra, J., van Harmelen, F., Sabou, M., Siebes, R., Staab, S., Stuckenschmidt, H.: SWAP: Ontology-based knowledge management with peer-to-peer technology. In: Workshop on Ontology-based Knowledge Management. Co-located with the German Conference on Knowledge Management, Lecture Notes in Informatics (2003)
111. Emam, K.E., Koru, A.G.: A replicated survey of IT software project failures. IEEE Software **25**(5), 84–89 (2008)
112. Euzenat, J., Shvaiko, P.: Ontology Matching. Springer, New York (2007)
113. Farenhorst, R., Izaks, R., Lago, P., van Vliet, H.: A just-in-time architectural knowledge sharing portal. In: Proceedings of the 7th Working IFIP/IEEE Conference on Software Architecture (WICSA7), pp. 125–134. IEEE Computer Society (2008)
114. Farenhorst, R., Lago, P., van Vliet, H.: EAGLE: Effective tool support for sharing architectural knowledge. Int. J. Cooper. Inform. Syst. **16**(3/4), 413–437 (2007)
115. Farenhorst, R., Lago, P., van Vliet, H.: Prerequisites for successful architectural knowledge sharing. In: Proceedings of the 2007 Australian Software Engineering Conference (ASWEC 2007), pp. 27–36. IEEE Computer Society (2007)
116. Farenhorst, R., van Vliet, H.: Experiences with a wiki to support architectural knowledge sharing. In: Third Workshop on Wikis for Software Engineering (Wiki4SE) (2008)
117. Feigenbaum, L., Herman, I., Hongsermeier, T., Neumann, E., Stephens, S.: The semantic web in action. Scientific American (2007)
118. Feldmann, R.L., Althoff, K.D.: On the status of learning software organisations in the year 2001. In: Althoff, K.D., Feldmann, R.L., Mller, W. (eds.) Learning Software Organizations Workshop, Lecture Notes in Computer Science, vol. 2176, pp. 2–6. Springer, Kaiserslautern, Germany (2001)
119. Feller, J., Fitzgerald, B.: Understanding Open Source Software Development. Addison Wesley, Boston MA (2001)
120. Fensel, D.: Ontology-based knowledge management. IEEE Comput. **35**(11), 56–59 (2002)
121. Fischer, G., Ostwald, J.: Knowledge management: problems, promises, realities, and challenges. IEEE Intell. Syst. **16**(1), 60–70 (2001)
122. Fitzgerald, B.: The transformation of open source software. MIS Q. **30**(3), 587–598 (2006)
123. Folmer, E., van Gurp, J., Bosch, J.: A framework for capturing the relationship between usability and software architecture. Software Process Improv. Pract. **8**(2), 67–87 (2003)
124. Foster, I.: What is the grid?. URL www-fp.mcs.anl.gov/~foster/Articles/WhatIsTheGrid.pdf (2002)
125. Fowler, M.: Analysis Patterns: Reusable Object Models. Addison-Wesley, Boston MA (1997)
126. Fowler, M.: Patterns of Enterprise Application Architecture. Addison-Wesley, Boston MA (2003)
127. Fowler, M.: Who needs an architect. IEEE Software **20**(5), 11–13 (2003)
128. Fowler, M., Rice, D., Foemmel, M., Hieatt, E., Mee, R.: Patterns of Enterprise Application Architecture. Pearson, Boston MA (2002)
129. Galster, M., Eberlein, A., Moussavi, M.: Transition from requirements to architecture: A review and future perspective. In: 7th ACIS International Conference on Software Engineering, Artificial Intelligence, Networking, and Parallel/Distributed Computing (SNPD), pp. 9–16 (2006)
130. Gamma, E., Helm, R., Johnson, R., Vlissides, J.: Design Patterns: Elements of Reusable Object-Oriented Software. Addison-Wesley, Boston MA (1994)
131. Gant, J., Gant, D.: Web portal functionality and state government e-service. In: Proceedings of the 35th Annual Hawaii International Conference on System Sciences (HICSS), pp. 1627–1636. IEEE Computer Society (2002)
132. Georgas, J.C., Taylor, R.N.: Towards a Knowledge-Based Approach to Architectural Adaptation Management. In: 1st ACM SIGSOFT Workshop on Self-managed systems, pp. 59–63. Newport Beach, California (2004)

133. Ghosh, T.: Creating Incentives for Knowledge Sharing. Tech. rep., MIT Open Courseware, Sloan school of management, Cambridge, MA, USA (2004)
134. Girvan, M., Newman, M.: Community structure in social and biological networks. Proc. Natl. Acad. Sci. **99**(12), 7821–7826 (2002)
135. Gongla, P., Rizzuto, C.R.: Evolving communities of practice: IBM global services experience. IBM Syst. J. **40**(4), 842–862 (2001)
136. Gorton, I.: Essential Software Architecture. Springer, Heidelberg (2006)
137. Gorton, I., Haack, J.: Architecting in the Face of Uncertainty: An Experience Report. In: Proceedings of the 26th International Conference on Software Engineering (ICSE 2004). Edinburgh, Scotland (2004)
138. Gorton, I., Zhu, L.: Tool support for just-in-time architecture reconstruction and evaluation: An experience report. In: 27th International Conference on Software Engineering (ICSE'05), pp. 514–523. ACM (2005)
139. Gruber, T.R., Russell, D.M.: Design knowledge and design rationale: A framework for representing, capture, and use. Tech. Rep. KSL 90-45, Knowledge Systems Laboratory, Standford University, California, USA (1991)
140. Haase, P., Siebes, R., van Harmelen, F.: Peer selection in peer-to-peer networks with semantic topologies. In: ICSNW, pp. 108–125 (2004)
141. Hall, H.: Input-friendliness: Motivating knowledge sharing across intranets. J. Inform. Sci. **27**(3), 139–146 (2001)
142. Hall, J., Jackson, M., Laney, R., Nuseibeh, B., Rapanotti, L.: Relating software requirements and architectures using problem frames. In: IEEE Joint International Conference on Requirements Engineering, pp. 137–144 (2002)
143. Hansen, M.T., Nohria, N., Tierney, T.: What is your strategy for managing knowledge? Harv. Bus. Rev. **77**(2), 106–116 (1999)
144. Harrison, N.B., Avgeriou, P., Zdun, U.: Using patterns to capture architectural decisions. IEEE Software **24**(4), 38–45 (2007)
145. Hislop, D.: Mission impossible? communicating and sharing knowledge via information technology. J. Inform. Tech. **17**, 165–177 (2002)
146. Hofmeister, C., Kruchten, P., Nord, R., Obbink, H., Ran, A., America, P.: A general model of software architecture design derived from five industrial approaches. J. Syst. Software **80**(1), 106–126 (2007)
147. Hofmeister, C., Nord, R., Soni, D.: Applied Software Architecture. Addison Wesley, Boston MA (2000)
148. Hohpe, G., Woolf, B.: Enterprise Integration Patterns. Addison-Wesley, MA (2004)
149. Houdek, F., Schneider, K.: Software experience center. The evolution of the experience factory concept. In: International NASA-SEL Workshop (1999)
150. Huysman, M., de Wit, D.: Practices of managing knowledge sharing: Towards a second wave of knowledge management. Knowl. Process Manag. **11**(2), 81–92 (2004)
151. Huysman, M., Wulf, V.: IT to support knowledge sharing in communities, towards a social capital analysis. J. Inform. Tech. **21**, 40–51 (2006)
152. IBM: Rational Unified Process. IBM Rational Software (2007). http://www.ibm.com/software/awdtools/rup/
153. IBM Global Technology Services: Services Overview. http://www.ibm.com/services/us/index.wss
154. IBM Software Group: Product Overview. http://www.ibm.com/software
155. IEEE1471: IEEE Recommended Practice for Architectural Description of Software-Intensive Systems. Tech. rep., IEEE (2000)
156. International Standards Organization (ISO): ISO/IEC 9126-1:2001, Software Quality Attributes, Software engineering – Product quality, Part 1: Quality model (2001)
157. ISO/IEC 9126-1: Software Engineering – Product Quality – Part 1: Quality Model. ISO (2001)
158. ISO/IEC 42010 WD3: Architectural description, working draft 3. ISO, Geneva (2008)
159. Jansen, A.: Architectural design decisions. PhD thesis, University of Groningen (2008)
160. Jansen, A., Avgeriou, P., van der Ven, J.S.: Enriching software architecture documentation. J. Syst. Software, doi: 10.1016/j.jss.2009.04.052 (2009)

161. Jansen, A., Bosch, J.: Software architecture as a set of architectural design decisions. In: Proceedings of the 5th IEEE/IFIP Working Conference on Software Architecture (WICSA), pp. 109–119. IEEE Computer Society (2005)
162. Jansen, A., Bosch, J., Avgeriou, P.: Documenting after the fact: Recovering architectural design decisions. J. Syst. Software **81**(4), 536–557 (2008)
163. Jansen, A., van der Ven, J.S., Avgeriou, P., Hammer, D.K.: Tool support for architectural decisions. In: 6th Working IEEE/IFIP Conference on Software Architecture. Mumbai, India. pp. 44–53. IEEE Computer Society (2007)
164. Jansen, A., de Vries, T., Avgeriou, P., van Veelen, M.: Sharing the architectural knowledge of quantitative analysis. In: Proceedings of the 4th International Conference on the Quality of Software-Architectures (QoSA), pp. 220–234. Springer, Heidelberg, LNCS 5281 (2008)
165. Jarczyk, A.P., Loffler, P., Shipmann, F.M., III.: Design rationale for software engineering: A survey. In: Proceedings of the 25th Hawaii International Conference on System Sciences, vol. 2, pp. 577–586 (1992)
166. Jeffery, R., Basili, V.: Validating the tame resource data model. In: Proceedings of the 10th International Conference on Software Engineering (ICSE 1988). Singapore (1988)
167. Johannson, C., Hall, P., Coquard, M.: Talk to Paula and Peter – They are experienced. In: F.B.G. Ruhe (ed.) International Conference on Software Engineering and Knowledge Engineering (SEKE'99), Workshop on Learning Software Organizations. LNCS, vol. 1756, Springer, Heidelberg (1999)
168. Jones, C.: Software Assessments, Benchmarks, and Best Practices. Addison-Wesley, Boston MA (2000)
169. Kalfoglou, Y., Schorlemmer, M.: Ontology mapping: the state of the art. Knowl. Eng. Rev. **18**(01), 1–31 (2003)
170. Kankanhalli, A., Tan, B.C.Y., Wei, K.K.: Contributing knowledge to electronic knowledge repositories: An empirical investigation. MIS Q. **29**(1), 113–143 (2005)
171. Karsenty, L.: An empirical evaluation of design rationale documents. In: Proceedings of the SIGCHI Conference on Human Factors in Computing Systems: Common Ground, pp. 150–156 (1996)
172. Kazman, R., Abowd, G., Bass, L., Clements, P.: Scenario-based analysis of software architecture. IEEE Software **13**, 47–55 (1996)
173. Kazman, R., Bass, L., Klein, M.: The essential components of software architecture design and analysis. J. Syst. Software **79**, 1207–1216 (2006)
174. Kazman, R., Bass, L., Klein, M., Lattanze, T., Northrop, L.: A basis for analyzing software architecture analysis methods. Software Qual. J. **13**, 329–355 (2005)
175. Kazman, R., Bass, L., Webb, M., Abowd, G.: SAAM: a method for analyzing the properties of software architectures. In: 16th International Conference On Software Engineering (ICSE-16), pp. 81–90. IEEE Computer Society Press, Sorrento, Italy (1994)
176. Kazman, R., Klein, M.H., Barbacci, M., Longstaff, T.A., Lipson, H.F., Carrière, S.J.: The architecture tradeoff analysis method. In: ICECCS, pp. 68–78 (1998)
177. Kazman, R., Kruchten, P., Nord, R., Tomayko, J.: Integrating Software Architecture-Centric Methods into the Rational Unified Process. Tech. rep., Software Engineering Institute, CMU/SEI-2004-TR-011 (2004)
178. Kew, N.: Apache Modules Book: Application Development with Apache. Prentice-Hall, Englewood Cliffs, NJ (2007)
179. King, R.: How cloud computing is changing the world. Business Week Online (August 2008)
180. Kircher, M., Jain, P.: Pattern-Oriented Software Architecture: Patterns for Resource Management, Volume 3. Wiley, New York (2004)
181. Kiryakov, A., Ognyanov, D., Manov, D.: OWLIM - A pragmatic semantic repository for OWL. In: Proceedings of the 6th Web Information Systems Engineering (WISE), pp. 182–192. Springer, Berlin (2005)
182. Kitchenham, B., Hughes, R., Linkman, S.: Modeling software measurement data. IEEE Transactions on Software Engineering **27**(9), 788–804 (2001).

183. Klems, M., Nimis, J., Tai, S.: Do clouds compute? a framework for estimating the value of cloud computing. In: Seventh Workshop on E-Business (WeB2008), Lecture Notes in Business Information Processing (LNBIP). Springer, Berlin (in press)
184. Klyne, G., Carroll, J., McBride, B.: Resource Description Framework (RDF): Concepts and Abstract Syntax. W3C Recommendation (2004). URL http://www.w3.org/TR/rdf-concepts/
185. Kneuper, R.: Supporting Software Processes Using Knowledge Management. In: S.K. Chang (ed.) Handbook of Software Engineering and Knowledge Engineering, pp. 579–606. World Scientific, Singapore (2001)
186. Kolb, D.: Experiential Learning experience as a source of learning and development. Prentice-Hall, Englewood Cliffs, NJ (1984)
187. Krafzig D., Banke K., Slama D.: Enterprise SOA. Prentice-Hall, Englewood Cliffs, NJ (2005)
188. Kruchten, P.: The 4 + 1 View Model of Architecture. IEEE Software **12**(6), 42–50 (1995)
189. Kruchten, P.: The Rational Unified Process, An Introduction, third edn. Addison-Wesley, Reading, MA (2003)
190. Kruchten, P.: An Ontology of Architectural Design Deciions in Software-Intensive Systems. In: 2nd Groningen Workshop on Software Variability Management. Groningen, The Netherlands (2004)
191. Kruchten, P., Capilla, R., Dueñas, J.C.: The Decision's View Role in Software Architecture Practice. IEEE Software **26**(2), 36–42 (2009)
192. Kruchten, P., Lago, P., van Vliet, H.: Building up and Reasoning about Architectural Knowledge. In: C. Hofmeister, I. Crnkovic, R. Reussner (eds.) Quality of Software Architectures, Proceedings 2nd International Conference, LNCS, vol. 4214, pp. 43–58. Springer, Berlin (2006)
193. Kruchten, P., Lago, P., van Vliet, H., Wolf, T.: Building up and exploiting architectural knowledge. In: Proceedings of the 5th IEEE/IFIP Working Conference on Software Architecture (WICSA), pp. 291–292. IEEE Computer Society, USA (2005)
194. Kwan, I., Damian, D., Storey, M.A.: Visualizing a Requirements-centred Social Network to Maintain Awareness Within Development Teams. In: Workshop on Requirements Engineering Visualization (REV). Minneapolis-St. Paul, MN, USA (2006)
195. Lago, P., Avgeriou, P.: First Workshop on Sharing and Reusing Architectural Knowledge. ACM SIGSOFT Software Eng. Notes **31**(5), 32–36 (2006)
196. Lago, P., Farenhorst, R., Avgeriou, P., de Boer, R.C., Clerc, V., Jansen, A., van Vliet, H.: The GRIFFIN collaborative virtual community for architectural knowledge management. In: A. Finkelstein, A. van der Hoek, J. Grundy, I. Mistrìk, J. Whitehead (eds.) Collaborative Software Engineering. Springer, Berlin (in press)
197. Lakoff, G., Johnson, M.: Metaphors we live by. The University of Chicago Press, Chicago (1980)
198. Lampson, B.W.: Hints for computer system design. Oper. Syst. Rev. **15**(5), 33–48 (1983)
199. van Lamsweerde, A.: From system goals to software architecture. In: M. Bernardo, P. Inverardi (eds.) Formal Methods for Software Architectures, LNCS, vol. 2804, pp. 25–43. Springer, Berlin (2003)
200. Lee, J.: Design rationale systems: understanding the issues. IEEE Expert **12**(3), 78–85 (1997)
201. Lee, L., Kruchten, P.: Capturing software architectural design decisions. In: 20th Annual Canadian Conference on Electrical and Computer Engineering (CCECE'07). IEEE, Vancouver (2007)
202. Lee, L., Kruchten, P.: Customizing the capture of software architectural design decisions. In: 21st Annual Canadian Conference on Electrical and Computer Engineering (CCECE'08). IEEE, Niagara Falls, ON (2008)
203. Lee, L., Kruchten, P.: A tool to visualize architectural design decisions. In: S. Becker, F. Plasil, R. Reussner (eds.) 4th International Conference on the Quality of Software Architecture (QoSA). LNCS, vol. 5281, pp. 43–54. Springer, Berlin (2008)
204. Lee, L., Kruchten, P.: Visualizing software architectural design decisions. In: R. Morrison, D. Balasubramaniam, K. Falkner (eds.) European Conference on Software Architecture (ECSA 2008). LNCS vol. 5292, pp. 359–362. Springer, Berlin (2008)

205. Letsche, T., Berry, M.: Large-Scale Information Retrieval with Latent Semantic Indexing. Inform Sci **100**(1–4), 105–137 (1997)
206. Liang, P., Jansen, A., Avgeriou, P.: Selecting a high-quality central model for sharing architectural knowledge. In: Proceedings of 8th International Conference on Quality Software (QSIC 2008), pp. 357–365. IEEE Computer Society Press, USA (2008)
207. Liang, P., Jansen, A., Avgeriou, P.: Sharing architecture knowledge through models: quality and cost. The Knowl. Eng. Rev. **24**(3) (2009)
208. Liang, P., Jansen, A., Avgeriou, P.: Collaborative Software Architecting through Knowledge Sharing. In: A. Finkelstein, A. van der Hoek, J. Grundy, I. Mistrìk, J. Whitehead (eds.) Collaborative Software Engineering. Springer, Berlin (to appear)
209. Lin, K.J.: Building web 2.0. Computer **40**(5), 101–102 (2007)
210. Linberg, K.: Software developer perceptions about software project failure: a case study. J. Syst. Software **49**(2–3), 177–92 (1999)
211. Lindvall, M., Rus, I., Jammalamadaka, R., Thakker, R.: Software tools for knowledge management. Tech. rep., DoD Data Analysis Center for Software (2001)
212. Lohmann, S., Heim, P., Auer, S., Dietzold, S., Riechert, T.: Semantifying requirements engineering - the softWiki approach. In: Proceedings of the 4th International Conference on Semantic Technologies (I-SEMANTICS), pp. 182–185 (2008)
213. Lopez, D.: Sams Teach Yourself Apache 2 in 24 Hours. Sams (2002)
214. Lua, E.K., Crowcroft, J., Pias, M., Sharma, R., Lim, S.: A survey and comparison of peer-to-peer overlay network schemes. Commun. Surveys Tutor., IEEE **7**(2), 72–93 (2005)
215. Lübke, D.: An Integrated Approach for Generation in Service-Oriented Architecture Projects. Phd thesis, Leibniz Universität Hannover (2007)
216. Lübke, D., Lüecke, T., Schneider, K., Gòmez, J.M.: Model-driven development of business applications using event-driven process chains. In: 2006 GITMA International Conference, pp. 95–98. Global Information Technology Management Association, Orlando, USA (2006)
217. Lübke, D., Schneider, K.: Leveraging feedback on processes in SOA Projects. In: I. Richardson, P. Runeson, R. Messnarz (eds.) EuroSPI. LNCS, vol. 4257, pp. 195–206. Springer, Berlin (2006)
218. Lyytinen, K., Robey, D.: Learning failure in information systems development. Inform. Syst. J. **9**, 85–101 (1999)
219. Markus, M.L.: Power, politics, and M.I.S. implementation. Commun. ACM **26**(6), 430–444 (1983)
220. Matinlassi, M., Niemela, E., Dobrica, L.: Quality-driven architecture design and quality analysis method: A revolutionary initiation approach to a product line architecture. Tech. Rep. 456, VTT Technical Research Centre of Finland, Espoo (2002)
221. McConnell, S.: Rapid Development. Microsoft Press (1996)
222. McDermott, R.: Learning Across Teams – How to build communities of practice in team organizations. Knowledge Manage. Rev. **2**(8) (1999)
223. McDermott, R.: Why information technology inspired but cannot deliver knowledge management. Calif. Manage. Rev. **41**(4), 103–117 (1999)
224. Medvidovic, N., Taylor, R.: A classification and comparison framework for software architecture description languages. IEEE Trans. Software Eng. **26**(1), 70–93 (2000)
225. Meier, J., Homer, A., Hill, D., Taylor, J., Bansode, P., Wall, L., Boucher Jr, R., Bogawat, A.: Application Architecture Guide 2.0–Designing applications on the .NET platform. Microsoft, Redmond, WA (2008)
226. Mendling, J., Nüttgens, M.: EPC Markup Language (EPML) – An XML-based interchange format for Event-Driven Process Chains (EPC). Inform. Syst. e-Bus. Manage. (ISeB) **4**(3), 245–263 (2005)
227. Mills, J.A.: A pragmatic view of the system architect. Commun. ACM **28**(7), 708–717 (1985)
228. Moran, T., Carroll, J.: Design Rationale: Concepts, Techniques, and Use. Lawrence Erlbaum Associates, USA (1996)
229. Schuster N., Zimmermann, O.: Architectural Decision Knowledge Wiki. http://www.alphaworks.ibm.com/tech/adkwik

230. Naiburg, E.J., Maksimchuk, R.A.: UML for Database Design. Addison-Wesley, Reading MA (2001)
231. Napster: (2009). URL free.napster.com
232. Networked European Software and Services Initiative (NESSI) – Grid: Grid vision and strategic research agenda (2008). URL www.soi-nwg.org
233. Newman, M., Girvan, M.: Finding and evaluating community structure in networks. Phys. Rev. E **69**(2) (2004)
234. Nonaka, I., Takeuchi, H.: The Knowledge-Creating Company : How Japanese Companies Create the Dynamics of Innovation. Oxford University Press (1995)
235. Nuseibeh, B.: Weaving Together Requirements and Architectures. IEEE Comput. **34**(3), 115–117 (2001)
236. Obbink, H., Kruchten, P., Kozaczynski, W., Hilliard, R., Ran, A., Postema, H., Lutz, D., Kazman, R., Tracz, W., Kahane, E.: Report on Software Architecture Review and Assessment (SARA), Version 1.0. At http://philippe.kruchten.com/architecture/SARAv1.pdf. Tech. rep. (2002)
237. Obbink, H., Mller, J.K., America, P., van Ommering, R., Muller, G., van der Sterren, W., Wijnstra, J.G.: Copa: A component-oriented platform architecting method for families of software-intensive electronic products (tutorial). In: SPLC1, the First Software Product Line Conference. Denver, Colorado (2000)
238. Object Management Group: Reusable Asset Specification, Version 2.2 (2005)
239. Object Management Group: Software & Systems Process Engineering, Metamodel Specification (SPEM) (2008)
240. O'Leary, D.E.: Wikis: From each according to his knowledge. Computer **41**(2), 34–41 (2008)
241. Open Group: The Open Group Architecture Framework, Version 8.1.1. http://www.opengroup.org/togaf
242. O'Reilly, T.: What is Web 2.0 – design patterns and business models for the next generation of software. http://www.oreillynet.com/pub/a/oreilly/tim/news/2005/09/30/what-is-web-20.html
243. Oxford Dictionary and Thesaurus. Oxford (1995)
244. Parnas, D.L.: On the criteria to be used in decomposing systems into modules. Commun. ACM **15**(12), 1053–1058 (1972)
245. Parnas, D.L.: On a 'buzzword': hierarchical sructure. In: J.L. Rosenfeld (ed.) IFIP Congress 74, pp. 336–339. North-Holland, Stockholm, Sweden (1974)
246. Parnas, D.L.: On the design and development of program families. IEEE Trans. Software Eng. **2**(1), 1–9 (1976)
247. Parnas, D.L., Clements, P., Weiss, D.M.: The modular structure of complex systems. IEEE Trans. Software Eng. **11**(3), 259–266 (1985)
248. Passant, A., Mulvany, I., Mika, P., Maisonneauve, N., Lser, A., Cattuto, C., Bizer, C., Bauckhage, C., Alani, H.: Mining for Social Serendipity. In: H. Alani, S. Staab, G. Stumme (eds.) Social Web Communities, no. 08391 in Dagstuhl Seminar Proceedings, pp. 21–26. Schloss Dagstuhl, Schloss Dagstuhl – Leibniz-Zentrum fuer Informatik, Germany (2008)
249. Paternó, F., Santoro, C.: One Model, Many Interfaces. In: C. Kolski, J. Vanderdonckt (eds.) Fourth International Conference on Computer-Aided Design of User Interfaces, pp. 143–154. Kluwer, Dordrecth (2002)
250. Perry, D., Wolf, A.: Foundations for the Study of Software Architecture. ACM Software Eng. Notes **17**(4), 40–52 (1992)
251. Pinto, J., Slevin, D.: Project success: definitions and measurement techniques. Project Manage. J. **19**, 67–72 (1988)
252. Plachy, E.C., Hausler, P.A.: Enterprise solutions structure. IBM Syst. J. **38**(1), 4–11 (1999)
253. Pohl, K., Sikora, E.: COSMOD-RE: Supporting the Co-Design of Requirements and Architectural Artifacts. In: E. Sikora (ed.) 15th International Requirements Engineering Conference, pp. 258–261. IEEE Computer Society, USA (2007)
254. Pohl, K., Sikora, E.: Structuring the Co-design of Requirements and Architecture. In: P. Sawyer, B. Paech, P. Heymans (eds.) 13th Working Conference on Requirements Engineering: Foundation for Software Quality (REFSQ), LNCS, vol. 4542, pp. 48–62. Springer, Trondheim, Norway (2007)

255. Polanyi, M.: The Tacit Dimension, *Anchor Books*, vol. 540. Doubleday, Garden City, New York (1967)
256. Probst, G.J.B.: Practical Knowledge Management: A Model That Works. Prism, Arthur D. Little (1998). URL http://know.unige.ch/publications/Prismartikel.PDF
257. Procaccino, J.D., Verner, J., Shelfer, K., Gefen, D.: What do software practitioners really think about project success: an exploratory study. J. Syst. Software **78**(2), 194–203 (2005)
258. Prudhommeaux, E., Seaborne, A.: SPARQL Query Language for RDF. W3C Working Draft (2006). URL http://www.w3.org/TR/rdf-sparql-query/
259. Ramesh, B., Jarke, M.: Towards Reference Models for Requirements Traceability. IEEE Trans. Software Eng. **27**(1), 58–93 (2001)
260. Ramil, J.F., Lehman, M.M., Kahen, G.: The FEAST Approach to Quantitative Process Modelling of Software Evolution Processes. In: F. Bomarius, M. Oivo (eds.) Profes, LNCS, vol. 1840, pp. 311–325. Springer, Oulu, Finland (2000)
261. Ran, A., Kuusela, J.: Design Decision Trees. In: 8th International Workshop on Software Specification and Design, pp. 172–175 (1996)
262. Rapanotti, L., Hall, J.G., Jackson, M., Nuseibeh, B.: Architecture-driven Problem Decomposition. In: 12th IEEE International Requirements Engineering Conference (RE), pp. 80–89 (2004)
263. Rechtin, E.: Systems Architecting: creating and building complex systems. Prentice-Hall, Englewood Cliffs, NJ (1991)
264. Regli, W., Hu, X., Atwood, M., Sun, W.: A Survey of Design Rationale Systems: Approaches, Representation, Capture and Retrieval. Eng. Comput. **16**(3–4), 209–235 (2000)
265. Risson, J., Moors, T.: Survey of research towards robust peer-to-peer networks: search methods. Comput. Networks **50**(17), 3485–3521 (2006)
266. Rittel, H., Webber, M.: Planning Problems are Wicked Problems. In: N. Cross (ed.) Developments in Design Methodology, pp. 135–144. Wiley, New York (1984)
267. Robbins, J.E., Hilbert, D.M., Redmiles, D.F.: Using critics to analyze evolving architectures. In: Joint proceedings of the second international software architecture workshop (ISAW-2) and international workshop on multiple perspectives in software development (Viewpoints '96) on SIGSOFT '96 workshops. ACM, San Francisco, CA, USA (1996)
268. Robillard, P.N.: The role of knowledge in software development. Commun. ACM **42**(1), 87–92 (1999)
269. Royce, W.E., Royce, W.: Software architecture: Integrating process and technology. TRW Quest **14**(1), 2–15 (1991)
270. Rozanski, N., Woods, E.: Software Systems Architecture: Working With Stakeholders Using Viewpoints and Perspectives. Addison-Wesley, Boston (2005)
271. Rumbaugh, J., Jacobson, I., Booch, G.: The Unified Modeling Language Reference Manual, The (2nd Edition). Pearson Higher Education (2004)
272. Rus, I., Lindvall, M.: Knowledge management in software engineering. IEEE Software **19**(3), 26–38 (2002)
273. Samoladas, I., Gousios, G., Spinellis, D., Stamelos, I.: The sqo-oss quality model: Measurement based open source software evaluation. In: IFIP 4th International Conference on Open Source Systems (OSS 2008), pp. 237–248. Springer, Berlin (2008)
274. Schaffert, S., Bry, F., Baumeister, J., Kiesel, M.: Semantic wikis. IEEE Software **25**(4), 8–11 (2008)
275. Schmidt, D.C., Buschmann, F.: Patterns, frameworks, and middleware: their synergistic relationships. In: Proceedings of the 25th International Conference on Software Engineering. IEEE Computer Society, Portland, Oregon (2003)
276. Schmidt, D.C., Fayad, M., Johnson, R.E.: Software patterns. Commun. ACM **39**(10), 37–39 (1996)
277. Schmidt, D.C., Stal, M., Rohnert, H., Buschmann, F.: Pattern-Oriented Software Architecture: Patterns for Concurrent and Networked Objects, vol. 2. Wiley, New York (2000)
278. Schneider, K.: Realistic and Unrealistic Expectations about Experience Exploitation. In: Conquest 2001, pp. 171–182. ASQF Erlangen (2001)

279. Schneider, K.: Experience Based Process Improvement. In: J. Kontio, R. Conradi (eds.) Proceedings European Conference on Software Quality (ECSQ 2002), LNCS, vol. 2349, pp. 114–123. Springer, Berlin (2002)
280. Schneider, K.: What to Expect from Software Experience Exploitation. J. Universal Comput. Sci., www.jucs.org, **8**(6), 44–54 (2002)
281. Schneider, K.: Generating Fast Feedback in Requirements Elicitation. In: P. Sawyer, B. Paech, P. Heymans (eds.) Requirements Engineering: Foundation for Software Quality (REFSQ 2007), LNCS, vol. 4542, pp. 160–74. Springer, Berlin (2007)
282. Schneider, K.: Experience and Knowledge Management in Software Engineering. Springer, Berlin (2009)
283. Schneider, K., Basili, V.R., von Hunnius, J.: Experience in Implementing a Learning Software Organization. IEEE Software **19**(3), 46–49 (2002)
284. Schneider, K., Hunnius, J.v.: Effective experience repositories for software engineering. In: Proceedings International Conference on Software Engineering, pp. 534–539. IEEE Computer Society, Portland, Oregon (2003)
285. Schneider, K., Lübke, D.: Systematic tailoring of quality techniques. In: B. Hindel (ed.) World Congress of Software Quality 2005, vol. III – Online Complement, pp. 121–130. iSQI, Munich, Germany (2005)
286. Schneider, K., Schwinn, T.: Maturing experience base concepts at daimlerChrysler. Software Process Improve. Pract. **6**, 85–96 (2001)
287. Schneider, K., Stapel, K.: Informationsflussanalyse für angemessene Dokumentation und verbesserte Kommunikation. In: H. Züllighoven (ed.) Software Engineering 2007, pp. 263–264. Köllen, Hamburg, Germany (2007)
288. Schneider, K., Stapel, K., Knauss, E.: Beyond Documents: Visualizing Informal Communication. In: B. Berenbach, O. Gottel (eds.) Third International Workshop on Requirements Engineering Visualization (REV 08), pp. 31–40. IEEE Computer Society, Barcelona, Spain (2008)
289. Schön, D.A.: The Reflective Practitioner: How Professionals Think in Action. Basic Books, New York (1983)
290. Schultze, U., Leidner, D.E.: Studying knowledge management in information systems research: Discourses and theoretical assumptions. MIS Quart. **26**(3), 213–242 (2002)
291. Schuster, N., Zimmermann, O., Pautasso, C.: ADkwik: Web 2.0 collaboration system for architectural decision engineering. In: Proceedings of the 19th International Conference on Software Engineering & Knowledge Engineering (SEKE), pp. 255–260 (2007)
292. Schwaber, K., Beedle, M.: Agile Software Development with Scrum. Prentice-Hall, Englewood Cliffs, NJ (2002)
293. Schwartz, D.G.: Encyclopedia of Knowledge Management. Idea Group Reference, Hershey, USA (2006)
294. Senge, P.M.: The Fifth Discipline: The Art & Practise of The Learning Organisation. Century Business (1990)
295. Shaw, M., Clements, P.: The Golden Age of Software Architecture. IEEE Software **23**(2), 31–39 (2006)
296. Shaw, M., DeLine, R., Klein, D., Ross, T., Young, D., Zelesnik, G.: Abstractions for software architecture and tools to support them. IEEE Trans. Software Eng. **21**(4), 314–335 (1995)
297. Shaw, M., Garlan, D.: Software Architecture: Perspectives on an Emerging Discipline. Prentice-Hall, Upper Saddle River, NJ (1996)
298. Shipman III, F., McCall, R.: Integrating different perspectives on design rationale: Supporting the emergence of design rationale from design communication. Artif. Intell. Eng. Des., Anal. Manuf. **11**(2), 141–154 (1997)
299. Siebes, R.M.: Semantic routing in peer-to-peer systems. Ph.D. thesis, VU University Amsterdam (2006)
300. Soni, D., Nord, R., Hofmeister, C.: Software architecture in industrial applications. In: 17th International Conference on Software Engineering (ICSE-17), pp. 196–207. ACM (1995)
301. Sowe, S., Stamelos, I., Angelis, L.: Identifying knowledge brokers that yield software engineering knowledge in OSS projects. Inform. Software Technol. **48**(11), 1025–1033 (2006)

302. Sowe, S.K., Karoulis, A., Stamelos, I.: A constructivist view on knowledge management in open source virtual communities. In: A.D.D. Figueiredo, A.P. Afonso (eds.) Managing Learning in Virtual Settings: The Role of Context, pp. 290–308. IGI Global (2005)
303. Sowe, S.K., Stamelos, I., Angelis, L.: Understanding knowledge sharing activities in free/open source software projects: An empirical study. J. Syst. Software **81**(3), 431–446 (2008)
304. Stachoviak, H.: Allgemeine Modelltheorie. Springer, Wien, New York (1973)
305. Standish Group: Chaos Report (1994)
306. Stapel, K., Knauss, E., Allmann, C.: Lightweight process documentation: just enough structure in automotive pre-development. In: R. O'Connor, N. Baddoo, K. Smolander, R. Messnarz (eds.) EuroSPI, Communictions in Computer and Information Science 16, pp. 142–151. Springer, Dublin, Ireland (2008)
307. Stapel, K., Schneider, K., Lübke, D., Flohr, T.: Improving an industrial reference process by information flow analysis: A Case Study. In: J. Münch, P. Abrhamsson (eds.) PROFES 2007, LNCS vol. 4589, pp. 147–159. Springer, (2007)
308. Stolze, M.: Visual critiquing in domain oriented design environments: Showing the right thing at the right place. In: J.S. Gero, F. Sudweeks (eds.) Artificial Intelligence in Design'94, pp. 467–482. Kluwer, Dordretch (1994)
309. Swan, J., Scarbrough, H., Preston, J.: Knowledge management – the next fad to forget people? In: J. Pries-Heje, C. Ciborra, K. Kautz, J. Valor, E. Christiaanse, D. Avison, C. Heje (eds.) 7th European Conference on Information Systems, vol. 2, pp. 668–678. Copenhagen, Denmark (1999)
310. Tai, S.: Software Service Engineering. Presentation at Schloss Dagstuhl seminar. http://www.dagstuhl.de/de/programm/kalender/semhp/?semnr=09021 (2009)
311. Taibi, T. (ed.): Design Pattern Formalization Techniques. IGI Publishing (2007)
312. Tanenbaum, A.S., van Steen, M.: Distributed systems: principles and paradigms, second edn. Addison-Wesley, Reading MA (2007)
313. Tang, A., Avgeriou, P., Jansen, A., Capilla, R., Ali-Babar, M.: A comparative study of architecture knowledge management tools. J. Syst. Software (in press)
314. Tang, A., Babar, A.M., Gorton, I., Han, J.: A Survey of the Use and Documentation of Architecture Design Rationale. In: Proceedings 5th Working IEEE/IFIP Conference on Software Architecture (WICSA5), pp. 89–98. IEEE Computer Society (2005)
315. Tang, A., Han, J.: Architecture Rationalization: A Methodology for Architecture Verifiability, Traceability and Completeness. In: Proceedings 12th Annual IEEE International Conference and Workshop on the Engineering of Computer Based Systems (ECBS '05), pp. 135–144. IEEE, USA (2005)
316. Tang, A., Jin, Y., Han, J.: A Rationale-Based Architecture Model for Design Traceability and Reasoning. J. Syst. Software **80**(6), 918–934 (2007)
317. Tang, A., Nicholson, A., Jin, Y., Han, J.: Using Bayesian belief networks for change impact analysis in architecture design. J. Syst. Software **80**(1), 127–148 (2007)
318. Tang, A., Tran, M.H., Han, J., van Vliet, H.: Design reasoning improves software design quality. In: S. Becker, F. Plasil, R. Reussner (eds.) 4th International Conference on the Quality of Software-Architectures (QoSA), LNCS, vol. 5281, pp. 28–42. Springer, Berlin (2008)
319. Telang, R., Mukhopadhyay, T.: Drivers of Web portal use. Electron. Commerce Res. Applic. **4**, 49–65 (2005)
320. Terveen, L.G., Selfridge, P.G., Long, M.D.: Living design memory: framework, implementation, lessons learned. Hum.-Comput. Interact. **10**(1), 1–37 (1995)
321. Thomas, D.M., Bostrom, R.P., Gouge, M.: Making knowledge work in virtual teams. Commun. ACM **50**(11), 85–90 (2007)
322. Tiwana, A.: The Knowledge Management Toolkit: Orchestrating IT, Strategy, and Knowledge Platforms. Prentice-Hall, Englewood Cliffs, NJ (2002)
323. Toulmin, S.: The Uses of Argument, 2 edn. Cambridge University Press (2003)
324. Traetteberg, H., Molina, P.J., Nunes, N.J.: Making model-based UI design practical: usable and open methods and tools. In: N. Nunes, C. Rich (eds.) 9th International Conference on Intelligent User Interface, pp. 376–377. ACM, Funchal, Madeira, Portugal (2004)
325. Tyree, J., Akerman, A.: Architecture Decisions: Demystifying Architecture. IEEE Software **22**(2), 19–27 (2005)

326. van der Ven, J., Jansen, A., Avgeriou, P., Hammer, D.: Using architectural decisions. In: Proceedings of the 2nd International Conference on the Quality of Software-Architectures (QoSA), LNCS, vol. 4214, pp. 1–10. Springer, Berlin (2006)
327. Vincenti, W.: What Engineers Know and How They Know It. John Hopkins University Press (1990)
328. van Vliet, H.: Software architecture knowledge management. In: Proceedings 19th Australian Software Engineering Conference (ASEC 2008), pp. 24–31. IEEE Computer Society (2008)
329. W3C: Semantic Web (2009). URL www.w3.org/2001/sw
330. W3C: Web Ontology Language (OWL) (2009). URL www.w3.org/2004/OWL
331. Wahler, M.: Using Patterns to develop consistent design constraints. PhD thesis, Swiss Federal Institute of Technology Zurich (2008)
332. Waldo, J., Wyant, G., Wollrath, A., Kendall, S.: A note on distributed computing. Tech. Rep. SMLI TR-94-29, Sun Microsystems (1994)
333. Wang, X., Zhang, D., Gu, T., Pung, H.: Ontology based context modeling and reasoning using OWL. In: Proceedings of the 2nd IEEE Annual Conference on Pervasive Computing and Communications Workshops (PerCom), pp. 18–22. IEEE Computer Society (2004)
334. Weaver, B.N., Bishop, W.L.: The Corporate Memory : a profitable and practical approach to information management and retention systems. John Wiley, New York (1974)
335. Wenger, E.: Communities of practice : learning, meaning and identity. Cambridge University Press, Cambridge, UK (1998)
336. Wenger, E.C., McDermott, R., Snyder, W.M.: Cultivating Communities of Practice. Harvard Business School Press, Boston (2002)
337. White, S.A.: Business Process Modeling Notation Specification. Tech. rep., Object Management Group Standard (2006)
338. Williams, L.G., Smith, C.U.: PASA: An architectural approach to fixing software performance problems. In: Proceedings of the International Conference of the Computer Measurement Group. Reno, USA (2002)
339. Winkler, S.: Information flow between requirement artifacts. In: P. Sawyer, B. Paech, P. Heymans (eds.) International Working Conference on Requirements Engineering: Foundation for Software Quality (REFSQ 2007), LNCS, vol. 4542, pp. 232–246. Springer, Trondheim, Norway (2007)
340. Yakovlev, I.V.: Web 2.0: Is it evolutionary or revolutionary? IT Profession. **9**(6), 43–45 (2007)
341. Ye, Y., Fischer, G.: Context-Aware Browsing of Large Component Repositories. In: 16th International Conference on Automated Software Engineering, pp. 99–106. Coronado Island, CA, USA (2001)
342. Youngs, R., Redmond-Pyle, D., Spaas, P., Kahan, E.: A standard for architecture description. IBM Syst. J. **38**(1), 32–50 (1999)
343. Zhuge, H.: The Knowledge Grid. World Scientific, Singapore (2004)
344. Zimmermann, O.: An Architectural Decision Modeling Framework for Service-Oriented Architecture Design. PhD Dissertation, Universität Stuttgart, Germany. Dissertation.de - Verlag im Internet (2009)
345. Zimmermann, O., Doubrovski, V., Grundler, J., Hogg, K.: Service-Oriented Architecture and Business Process Choreography in an Order Management Scenario. In: OOPSLA Conference Companion. San Diego, CA, USA (2005)
346. Zimmermann, O., Gschwind, T., Kuester, J., Leymann, F., Schuster, N.: Reusable Architectural Decision Models for Enterprise Application Development. In: S. Overhage, C. Szyperski (eds.) Proceedings 3rd International Conference on the Quality of Software-Architectures (QoSA), LNCS, vol. 4880 pp. 15–32. Springer, Berlin (2007)
347. Zimmermann O., Koehler J., Leymann F., Polley R., Schuster N.: Managing Architectural Decision Models with Dependency Relations, Integrity Constraints, and Production Rules. J. Syst. Software (2009), doi:10.1016/j.jss.2009.01.039
348. Zimmermann, O., Milinski, M., Craes, M., Oellermann, F.: Second Generation Web services-oriented architecture in production in the finance industry. In: OOPSLA Conference Companion (2004)

Index